"A troubling history of good intentions gone awry."

"It's an interesting story, and the hard truths are the right and *disturbing* questions..."
—Eliot Fremont-Smith, *The Village Voice*

"The final and culminating volume of the remarkable Making of the President series... an account of the 1980 presidential campaign that is *lucid, knowledgeable, and at times savagely witty*...a remarkably acute analysis of the passing of several of the nation's most powerful political machines...a fine...discussion of the revolutionary impact of television on the conduct of national politics. It is difficult to read this book, as it is difficult to read anything White has written, without being seduced by his rare literary grace, his matchless knowledge of the political system, and his constant searching for deeper and deeper meaning in the phenomena he examines....We will have no clearer or more eloquent statement of the slow, painful souring of a generation's golden and, ultimately, unattainable dream."
—*Harper's*

"A book that will be welcomed, read, and debated by almost everyone with more than a casual interest in American politics. It is a book that stimulates, aggravates, and, in many more important ways, rewards....[The] long-term analysis, which occupies more than half the book...will give this work its lasting reputation....[White] has brought the men and women, the sights and sounds, the scenes and the controversies of this age of upheaval in American politics into vivid life as has no other writer. It is *an achievement any of us could envy*—and all of us can savor and enjoy."
—David S. Broder, *Saturday Review*

"*Fascinating*...required, if controversial, reading"
—*Cosmopolitan*

"The most thoughtful reporter of our time...White has become, almost like the presidency itself, an institution.... Beneath all the violent political shifts of the crowded years, beneath the chicanery, the media trickery, the demagoguery, the crude macho grasp for power—beneath all this White perceives something about the country which, let us hope, is both *profound and true*."
—Clifton Fadiman, *Book-of-the-Month Club News*

"*Outstanding...perceptive*...White shows where the country has been and asks where it might be going."
—*ALA Booklist*

"*Insightful and absorbing*...White offers an intelligent, stimulating, and controversial assessment of our electoral institutions—the parties, the primaries, and the conventions...a *timely and lasting* historical assessment of a most important political era—an essential resource for scholars and the informed public."
—*Library Journal*

"[White's] Presidential post-mortems have long since established his *political acuity, objectivity and reliability...rich* in *revealing* recollections of past campaigns.... Of all White's 'Presidential' books this is the wisest and most far-seeing.... In his pages you will learn how we got here from there, and in the process discover how brilliantly, if sometimes painfully, White has restored your perspective." —*John Barkham Reviews*

"*Superb*"
—*Indianapolis Star*

"*Disquieting and provocative*... the issues [White] raises need confronting, and his book, a major statement from a respected journalist, will be intensely debated."
—*Publishers Weekly*

"Just as fascinating as [White's] previous books and adds the dimension of reflection"
—*Richmond* (Virginia) *News Leader*

Books by Theodore H. White

THEODORE H. WHITE

AMERICA
IN SEARCH
OF ITSELF

THE MAKING OF THE PRESIDENT
1956–1980

A Cornelia and Michael Bessie Book

WARNER BOOKS

A Warner Communications Company

Warner Books Edition
Copyright © 1982 by Theodore H. White
All rights reserved.
This Warner Books edition is published by arrangement with
Harper & Row, Publishers, Inc., 10 East 53rd Street, New York, N.Y. 10022
Warner Books, Inc., 666 Fifth Avenue, New York, N.Y. 10103

W A Warner Communications Company

Printed in the United States of America
First Warner printing: June 1983
10 9 8 7 6 5 4 3 2

Library of Congress Cataloging in Publication Data

White, Theodore Harold, 1915–
   America in search of itself.

   Reprint. Originally published: 1st ed. New York,
N.Y.: Harper & Row, c1982.
   "A Cornelia and Michael Bessie book."
   Includes index.
   1. Presidents—United States—Election.   I. Title.
E839.5.W48 1983   973.92   82-17423
ISBN 0-446-37098-3 (U.S.A.)
ISBN 0-446-37560-8 (Can.)

For
John King Fairbank

CONTENTS

PART III: *The Election of 1980*

AMERICA IN SEARCH OF ITSELF

OF ITSELF

———

The Making of the President
1956–1980

DIALOGUE WITH THE READER
BY WAY OF A PREFACE

There is always that first question in telling any story—where to begin?

This time it was particularly important to me to pick the proper beginning. The campaign of 1980 would be the last, I promised myself, in a series of stories about American politics that I had begun in 1960. The plan, back then, was to follow every four years with another book about the Making of the President until 1980. At the end there would be an account of twenty-four years of passage of power in American politics, telling how we got from there to here. This time I wanted to add it up. But where was there?

Elections are important; they give Americans not only their chief sense of participating in their government but, more importantly, a sense of control. Control is what politics are all about. But this time, in the campaign of 1980, there was a questioning not only of control but of national purpose itself. Somehow, public affairs had gone off the track, almost as if the country had lost its way into the future. There was no sense of coherence in government; it did not respond; it could not manage. Nor was it the fault of the Carter administration alone, or the Nixon administration, or the Johnson administration. It went much farther back than any of the seven national campaigns I had covered.

I had reported such campaigns for a quarter of a century and had seen what was, in retrospect, one of the great periods of change in American history. Historians are scholars who tell us later what it all means, after time has burned off passing detail, and left the ridges of change bare; their job is to make us aware of man in his time and place, by dividing the past into periods, or epochs, or eras. We reporters are the servants of history, offering up our daily or passing tales for them to sort out. I could not present myself as a historian. But what I had been reporting in 1980 was so much more than a campaign that it simply had to be seen as a climactic episode in a much longer period of time than I had attempted to write of before.

Thus, insistently: where to begin?

Personalities are always a staple of both reporting and history, and so I could, if I wished, begin with that rich array of characters who have marched across the stage since the war:

• Truman, a man of such endearing candor and courage. No one since has had his gift of plain speaking. Once I wrote him a note congratulating him on his China policy. He answered with a curt "thank you," and said he had cut off aid to Chiang's regime because he found "our money was being poured down a rat-hole. They were a bunch of crooks."

• Eisenhower, rubicund, cheerful, charming, the most gifted among the storytellers at the White House until Reagan. Only years after he passed from the scene did I realize how cold, efficient, and calculating was his mind.

• Kennedy, so lithe and graceful. I remember him saying a few hours after his paper-thin victory in 1960: "The margin is thin, but the responsibility is clear."

• Lyndon Johnson, who tried so hard and failed so greatly. I remember my last meeting with him, as he jingled coins in his pocket, while scratching his groin. He presented me with a monologue, a lecture, telling me exactly how I was to present him to history, what his major accomplishments were—and then abruptly dismissed me.

• Richard Nixon, a quintessentially insecure man, so solid on the large decisions of state, so squalid in detail. He was uncomfortable with people. Once I asked him how he could bear campaigning, shaking hands all day, smiling, and he finished the thought for me: ". . . and all the while you're smiling you want to kick them in the shins."

I could run through the parade of candidate personalities, including the losers, all so intriguing: the jolly Humphrey, the thoughtful Stevenson, the innocent McGovern, the indignant Goldwater, the magisterial Rockefeller.

But if I had now learned anything after the years of reporting at home and abroad, it was that most personalities rise above the flow of events only when thrust up by forces under the surface. A rare personality—a Roosevelt, a Churchill, a Mao, a Monnet—might alter the direction of the forces, and make his own life a legend, a starting point of future departures. But I had met only one President who might qualify as a genuine hero in that range, John F. Kennedy. He had changed things.

Thus in 1980 I had to consider Ronald Reagan and Jimmy Carter. Neither seemed to me to carry in his personality the vitality that moves history. It seemed rather that they were both men who were carried up or borne down by forces outside themselves.

Carter had come to power on the tide of disgust following Nixon ("I want to see us once again have a nation that's as good and honest and decent and truthful and competent and compassionate and as filled with love as the American people"). And Reagan: He had been running for President for twelve years. Twice his own party had rejected him. Now, in 1980, it was not he that had changed but the American people. They were ready to listen to him describe the erring ways of their government.

So, then, there was the old reportorial way of beginning, with the classic engagement of ambitions, actions, and events. But since the forces that shaped the election of 1980 were so much more important than the personalities, that old-fashioned beginning would not do.

For a proper historian of our times there was only one overtowering beginning—the Year of Victory, 1945.

All things flowed from that victory, and for the historians, 1980 would close off what they would probably call the "Postwar Period."

The intoxication of that victory had lasted for a generation. First, the sense of power which had convinced a peaceful nation that its armed force, mobilized almost overnight, could and should forever police and reorder the world. Second, the seductive belief that in any contest between good and evil, good always triumphs. We, our soldiers, had proved that Right makes Might. The imperative legacy of Virtue also descended from the war. As Eisenhower's divisions tore open the Nazi concentration camps, Americans realized for the first time how deep human depravity could go. They accepted in their politics the moral mandate not to let such evil happen again. With this came an assumption of responsibility for the entire world—to nurse it, feed it, encourage it, at whatever cost to the American people.

The spin-offs of the great victory were equally important. American learning had contributed so largely to the victory that it was impossible to ignore the role of scholars in American life. In the First World War, a deputation of American chemists visited Secretary of War Newton Baker and offered their services. Baker, according to James B. Conant's account, had thanked them, then added, "But the army already has a chemist." In World War II, mathematicians made American cryptography the finest among the warring nations, electronics wizards perfected radar, physicists made the bomb. Not only the physical scientists but the social scientists contributed: economists had surgically dissected the industries of Germany and Japan, psychiatrists had screened air force personnel. Modern management began with the war. Computer pioneers introduced the army to data processing, digital judgments of cost-effectiveness. They had begun data analysis by calculating the trajectories of artillery, by developing proximity fuses; and had gone on to operational analysis to master antisubmarine warfare. Without such people, the war might not have been won; and such thinkers, largely from the groves of academe, would go on to achieve in American life the status of a mandarinate until, like the Chinese mandarins, they lost touch with reality.

One last spin-off must be mentioned only because it is so scantily recognized in the transformation of American politics. To reward its war veterans, Congress passed an act almost as creative as the Homestead Act of 1862—the G.I. Bill of Rights, the first of the modern entitlements. In prewar America, to go to college was to pass from hoi polloi to the elite. In 1938, when I graduated from college, only one and a quarter million students attended all American universities. But the G.I. Bill of Rights invited all among the sixteen million veterans who had served in the armed forces to go to school on government grants. Almost half—7.8 million—took advantage of the invitation! They were to change American life, culture, and politics. By 1960, such veterans staffed the political corps of both John F. Kennedy and Richard M. Nixon, ousting the old professionals who had until then made politics their calling. Scores of these veterans would soon be senators, hundreds congressmen. By the campaign of 1980, as they, in turn, were passing from the stage, they were leaving behind a different kind of nation, a nation of open politics. Reagan would probably be the last United States President to have worn a uniform in World War II—unless his Vice-President, George Bush, succeeded him, in which case, Bush, a genuine war hero, might very well be remembered as the last national leader ever to have served in actual combat.

This book will have to come back again and again, in telling the story of 1980, to the legacy of the victory. But the victory of 1945 was as far away from 1980 as Theodore Roosevelt's presidency had been from Appomattox. To start this book with the legacy of victory would be to flavor the campaign of 1980 with grandfather tales. And the story of 1980 did not unroll in a victorious nation. It unrolled in a humiliated nation with a sense of victory squandered, searching itself and its way, questioning its own beliefs because the old ideas did not stretch to cover present reality.

Where would one begin a book about a nation that questioned its own beliefs?

That kind of book would, certainly, have to begin in the storm decade of the sixties, which opened an age of experiment, an age of hope.

Whether the final Reagan victory of 1980 would be seen as a restoration or a counterrevolution would have to depend on how you read the 1960s, a decade that began with a sense of total and unlimited power to do the nation's will both at home and abroad.

Perhaps the passage from the sixties to the seventies could be called a passage of paradox.

The sixties had begun with the great purpose of John Kennedy to make American life, American politics, and American opportunity open to all. But the seventies had ended with an attempt to peg citizens into categories by race, sex, and ethnic heritage. By the end of the seventies, America was, officially, in many jurisdictions a racist society. In trying to eradicate racism, the politics of the sixties and seventies had institutionalized it. Race and sex might now define who was entitled to what promotion and what job opportunity. The passage of paradox had begun by trying to eliminate the forced busing of little children to specified schools because of their race and color. It ended by insisting on it. Race and heritage defined, at least in the Democratic party, the precise proportions of delegates to political conventions.

The effort to save America's cities offered another paradox. More brains than ever before focused on the decay of America's cities. At the end, with all the attention and programs, big cities were on their way to tragedy: they had become warehouses for the very poor or enclaves of the very rich, while common civility had become a memory.

Another paradox: The sixties had begun with a Kennedy Commission to examine the mechanics and financing of American elections. Reform had followed reform as men of good intention tried to purge the money changers from the temple. Such reforms had finally caught and trapped the Nixon campaign of 1972, and unzipped the Watergate scandals. But the reforms had incubated the political action committees of 1980, which poured unprecedented sums of money into politics. These committees, the vicious as well as the virtuous, made loose money more important in the purchase of political influence, in leverage on Congress and President, than at any time in living memory. Access was now openly for sale.

The passage from the sixties to the seventies is a blurred one, for Americans tend to think in terms of decades like the thirties, the forties, the fifties, the sixties, as if history turned a new chapter in each year beginning with a zero and closed ten years later with another zero year. But the underswells of politics do not work that way. The storm decade of the sixties, for example, ran from the death of John Kennedy in 1963 to the departure of Richard Nixon in 1974, a period of eleven years minus three months.

At the heart of the upheaval was the liberal idea, and guiding it was liberal dominance, in Congress, in academia, in the press, on television, in the great foundations and "think tanks." Under Republican Presidents, as under Democratic Presidents, the liberal idea prevailed—that the duty of government was to conceive programs and fund them so that whatever was accepted as right and just, at home or abroad, would come to pass, whatever the cost, whatever the contradiction between good intentions and prevailing reality. Nowhere was a warning more clearly voiced than by one of the dominant liberals of the time, John Gardner, then Secretary of Health-Education-Welfare, who warned his friends: "There are some people who have what I think of as a vending machine concept of social change. You put in a coin and out comes a piece of candy. If you have a social problem you pass a law and out comes the solution."

The trouble with this liberal idea was that liberals, looking back, could not distinguish between their genuine triumphs and their failures. Their peril in the eighties would be that the good they had done might be washed away with their blunders.

All in all, when I reflected on my reporting of the upheaval of the sixties and its consequences in the seventies, I realized I had ignored the ferment of ideas within politics. But it was now too late to go back to analyze the ideas that had changed America, and brought about the election of Ronald Reagan, the most resolute ideologue in the modern presidency.

A story beginning with ideas was no proper starting place for a writer who had begun as an outdoors reporter.

In a book which was both a summing up and a story, I would have to start with a theme as well as a date. And neither the theme nor the date could be entirely novel.

The theme had to be, as all historians would probably accept, that the election of 1980 marked the end of an era. But what, exactly, was coming to an end? An end to the power of America around the world? An end to a system of politics that had outlived its time? An end to the good intentions of the sixties, which had tried to unleash goodwill and only imprisoned it in a codex of regulations beyond anyone's comprehension? An end to the politics of hope?

What had come to issue, it seemed to me, in 1980 was the nature of the federal government's power. The campaign was about the consequences and reach of government, about the murky limits that separate the public interest from individual right. It was about America's pride, and America's role in the turbulent outer world.

It was best, then, to choose as a beginning a specific arbitrary date, close enough to the events of 1980 to tell my last story of an election—yet significant enough to invite the reader to rove back and forth from that date to the forces shaping the candidates.

That date, November 4, 1979, with which this book now begins, is the most plausible date for the beginning of the action of 1980. If it happened to be exactly one year in advance of the voting day of November 4, 1980, that was accident. But November of 1979 could not be ignored. In the three months following that Sunday in 1979, all the forces that made the election of 1980 a watershed in American politics would surface sharply enough to become distinct.

November 4, 1979, was the day when a handful of wild people in faraway Iran seized the American Embassy in Teheran, held our emissaries as hostages, and humiliated the proudest nation on earth.

PART I
WHERE WE STARTED

CHAPTER ONE

THE CLUTCH OF
CIRCUMSTANCE: 1980

It was still dark in Washington, not quite three o'clock on Sunday morning, November 4, 1979. Most of the capital slept, except for the watch officers of the Pentagon, the White House, and the State Department, when the Operations Center on the seventh floor of State came alert. A message was coming through from Teheran, where the clock already read eleven. A mob of demonstrators, said the message from Iran, had cut the chains that barred the iron gates of the U.S. Embassy in the Iranian capital; they were surging across its twenty-seven-acre compound and had begun an attack on the U.S. chancery.

The alert was immediate. By four o'clock, Secretary of State Cyrus Vance had arrived at the Operations Center; from there he awakened President Carter, weekending at Camp David. By five o'clock, the key members of the department's Iranian task force were gathered to monitor the information. And slowly in the Operations Center they could feel the sources of information shriveling. The Islamic revolution had already choked off understanding; it was now clipping off talk.

By early dawn in Washington, only four telephone connections to Teheran remained open, three of which led to the so-called Iranian Ministry of Foreign Affairs. There, three American diplomats, led by L. Bruce Laingen, chargé d'affaires, had come to pay a visit to Ibrahim Yazdi, the momentary foreign minister of Iran. When news of the terrorist coup reached them, Laingen held open a telephone line to Washington from the foreign minister's suite, and his two deputies, in the basement, held two other telephones off the hook. They had come as diplomatic visitors but were now, in effect, refugees, soon to become hostages. From their fragmentary reports, those in Washington gathered that the American Embassy had been penetrated by perhaps some 450 terrorists who described themselves as students responding to the call of Ayatollah Ruhollah Khomeini to commemorate his exile fifteen years before and to honor the "martyrs" of the previous year's revolution.

Laingen reported to Washington the reassurance of Foreign Minister Yazdi that the government would have the terrorists cleared from the embassy compound within twenty-four hours, just as it had done in a similar seizure on February 14. Yazdi's reassurance was coupled with that of Prime Minister Mehdi Bazargan, who reported that the Ayatollah's son, Seyyed Ahmed Khomeini, would arrive the following day with holy authority to disperse the rioters. Veteran diplomats in Washington could imagine the conversations— the shrug of shoulders, the smile of reassurance, the phrases American diplomats have heard all across the Third World: So sorry. You must understand our people. Their pride. Their past humiliation. The emotions of the young. . . . But all will be put right, no need to worry.

Yet there was indeed much to worry about. When Seyyed Ahmed Khomeini arrived the next day, rather than dispersing the terrorists, he assured them his father applauded their action. Forthwith, the Iranian prime minister, Bazargan, resigned. Four days later, the foreign minister, Yazdi, also resigned. Yazdi was replaced in a few days by a new name, Abolhassan Bani Sadr, who in a few weeks was also removed, and in little more than a year was an exile in Paris. For the rest of the year, one strange Iranian name succeeded another as, slowly, the United States government realized that there was in this far-off land no responsible government at all with which it could deal. An era of diplomacy was ending; the world America had dominated for thirty years was, finally, coming apart. Short of all-out war, America was powerless to deal with a world where civilization as we had known it was ending. The first issue of the campaign of 1980 had rung its alarm—the shaming of American pride.

It would have been difficult to explain this problem of statecraft to the American people at any time—but it was particularly difficult that week of November 4, 1979, for American politics were coming to a boil. The practice of American politics has brought about a ritual ballet, in which presidential candidates mincingly tiptoe through a new set of laws every four years. In order to get federal matching funds for a presidential campaign, it is wisest that they formally announce their candidacies close to the end of the preceding year. But once they announce, they are cut off by other laws and regulations from appearing on the national television networks except as news figures. The networks are bound by the Federal Communications Commission to give no special exposure to one candidate without offering equal time to all his rivals in the field.

The week of initial crisis in Iran was thus, accidentally, the week when most of the major candidates were preoccupied with the minuet of public announcement, to the exclusion of grand world affairs abroad. The most important of the announcements of candidacy scheduled—to no one's surprise—was that of the crown prince of Camelot, Senator Edward Moore Kennedy of Massachusetts. As luck would have it, on the very evening of the crisis day, November 4, 1979, Kennedy was scheduled to appear in a talk with Roger Mudd, then of CBS. The talk had been pretaped because Kennedy was calendared to reveal the open secret of his candidacy three days later. Thereafter, CBS would be forbidden to offer such time to Kennedy without offering equal time to all. The interview amounted to a small disaster. The senator had thought of Mudd as a personal friend; Mudd thought of himself as a journalist. Surgically Mudd dissected Kennedy on the tube and left him shredded, as a man without any real purpose in his pursuit of the presidency. Few people saw the Kennedy-Mudd interview, because the preponderant majority of American viewers watched instead a television showing of *Jaws,* an audience-grabbing movie, full of clean horror and clean thrills. The Mudd-Kennedy interview was one of those television episodes destined to be more important in recall than on the day of its screening.

If the most important candidacy to be announced that week was Edward M. Kennedy's, there were others at least as important historically. Three days earlier, on Thursday, the first of November, Howard Baker, senator from Tennessee and Republican minority leader, had already announced his candidacy. Then, like a string of popping firecrackers, other announcements followed for the next fortnight. Kennedy would announce formally on November 7. The next day, the eighth, Governor Edmund G. Brown, Jr., of California would proclaim his candidacy. And five days following that, on the thirteenth, yet another governor of California, Ronald Reagan, would announce his candidacy, holding out as the centerpiece of his future foreign policy a North American community of Canada, Mexico, and the United States, a proposal never again to be mentioned in his campaign. Reagan spoke from behind a desk in his usual eloquent fashion, and the American flag behind him announced that here was a patriot. It is noteworthy that he said not a word about the crisis of terror in Iran or the American captives. Reagan was riding forces larger than most observers guessed, and the Iranian crisis would strengthen those forces all through the year.

Reagan's chief rival for the presidency, James Earl Carter, was back in the White House by then, considering options on Iran. But on the fateful Sunday of November 4, he had been at his aerie in Camp David. We can only wonder how much of his attention that evening was divided between the personal challenge of Ted Kennedy—whose "ass" he had promised to "whip"—and the far more important challenge to the power of the American President, whose diplomats Iranian terrorists had kidnapped. Carter would helicopter back from Camp David to Washington, after watching the Mudd-cutting of Kennedy.

Meanwhile, his advisers were consulting.

The first gathering of Carter's advisers met at seven on the morning of Monday, November 5. They met without the President, in the barred, windowless, map-walled underground cell called the White House Situation Room, to consider the options to lay before the President when he arrived from Camp David. The group—called the Crisis Management Team—was to meet every morning at seven until the end of the year so as to have ready for the President each day when he came to work a full report on the malice of the previous day. On this morning, the National Security Council chief, Zbigniew Brzezinski, presided. As eyes and ears of the President, he sat at the head of the table, flanked, on his left, by Secretary of State Vance; on the other side, by Vice-President Walter Mondale. Present also were the chief of the CIA, the chairman of the Joint Chiefs of Staff, the Attorney General, the Secretary of Defense, the Secretary of the Treasury. The demands of the outlaws in Teheran were, by now, clear: The United States must physically expel the onetime Shah of Iran, dying in a New York hospital, and hand him over to the merciless Islamic justice of the Ayatollah. The street situation in Teheran was, however, obscure—would immediate military action result in immediate death to the hostages? And if there was to be military action—where, how, with what forces? Or if America was to negotiate—how, through whom, with whom?

These were the options put to the President the next day, Tuesday, November 6, when he met with the National Security Council in the majestic Cabinet Room of the White House. Carter opened the meeting with a phrase already familiar, which would become more so. This, he said, was the gravest crisis he had faced in office. He had used a similar phrase to describe the gasoline shortage in August; was to use it again to describe the Russian invasion of Afghanistan the next month. He continued: The essential thing was to free the hostages, to get them out alive. He did not want a single American shot —*not one.* Get the hostages out first; then we could punish "them," them being the Iranians.

At this, the first meeting of the National Security Council on the Teheran crisis, negotiation seemed the wisest course. The President would send former attorney general Ramsey Clark directly to Iran, to seek an opening of reason with Clark's friends in the Iranian revolutionary leadership; the United Nations would be asked to intercede. But also, the small American task force in the Indian Ocean, moving to an allied rendezvous off Mombasa, East Africa, would be diverted to circle in a show of force off Iran.

The lead in the effort to free the hostages was given, as tradition required, to the Secretary of State, Cyrus Vance, and for the next several months he held that lead, slowly organizing economic pressure and world condemnation of the terrorist regime in Iran. But two misconceptions obstructed the negotiating path. One was that the United Nations could serve as a useful forum of discussion; the second was that reason might reach the shifting sanhedrin of mullahs, imams, and holy men who governed Persia in the name of Islam and Ayatollah Khomeini.

Of the negotiating effort, the most biting summary was that later made by Captain Gary Sick of U.S. Naval Intelligence. "Nobody knew what kind of person Khomeini was," said Sick, a lean, shrewd man, part executive, but more scholar, the National Security Council's resident expert on Iran. "In every day of this early crisis," he said, "and right through until this day, there's been this American inability to understand the true fanaticism of this man, not moved by any sense of compassion, by any concern for law, by any understanding of international tradition. We'd been dealing with people like Kim Il-sung, Mao Tse-tung, and other dictators. So it was difficult for us to grasp the total, unyielding, unwillingness of this man to consider any other factor outside his own limited view of the world. Khomeini was beyond the experience, if not the imagination, of anyone in the United States government. We made that mistake repeatedly—of trying to deal with Khomeini as if he were a government."

It is impossible in the rhetoric of liberal American politics, of which Carter was a true expression, to disdain or denounce people of other traditions as inherently evil, genetically inferior, or culturally vicious. It would have been most accurate to put upon Khomeini the epithet first applied to his people two thousand years ago, when the free Greeks of antiquity faced the repeated savagery of the Persians and dubbed the Persian/Iranians "barbarians." But the thrust of American diplomacy in this century has always been characterized by its desire to separate enemy governments from the support of their supposedly "friendly" people. To call all Iranians "barbarians" would have subjected Carter, at home and abroad, to a charge of racism. Yet, by his early refusal to deal with barbarians as barbarians, Carter gave legitimacy to the holding of American hostages, bound and blindfolded, as if the terrorists were indeed negotiating a legitimate political cause.

Long afterward, sentiment would swing against Carter, holding that he had been weak and should have struck immediately. But at the beginning, the first sentiment that surfaced, both in the polls and in public opinion, was that the President, in his restraint and self-control, reflected a proud American seeking of peace. In New Hampshire, where the first open primary contest with Kennedy would take place, the President had been running among his own Democrats at the short end of a 53/18 split with Kennedy. By the first week in January, his conduct of the Iran crisis had reversed that margin completely; he stood for the flag and his polls showed him running ahead of Kennedy, 35 to 31. By the day of the primary itself, February 26, that lead would have increased to 61/39. Indeed, Kennedy, who was bold enough to criticize the Shah (and, inferentially, Carter) in December, was scolded from one end of the country to the other for undermining the President.

By the beginning of 1980, the drama of the hostages had become the drama of the season. Their plight led every news show. Each night, CBS's Walter Cronkite signed off with ". . . the fortieth [sixtieth . . . ninetieth . . . one hundred twentieth] day of captivity." Soon, each evening at eleven-thirty, ABC would devote an entire half hour to the crisis, all in full color, with a villainous cast of characters—Black-Hood Mary, pouty Ghotbzadeh (ultimately himself to be jailed), the grille gates of the embassy as background, the mobs chanting and waving their fists into the camera's eye. For that majority of voting Americans who get their chief news from television, Teheran was the inescapable public dilemma of winter and spring. And always: Should we choose war, and hit? Or can we talk it out?

The perplexity was overriding. How should American power be used? Were the lives of the hostages worth the national humiliation that the student terrorists demanded? If one yielded up the body of the Shah for release of fifty-three American captives, would that expose fewer or more American diplomats to Third World kidnappers in the future?

America was now living in a world of new states led significantly by madmen and resentful puppets of bizarre historical background. Mohammed Riza Pahlevi, the self-proclaimed Shahanshah, seeking refuge in our country, was the son of a six-foot-six mountaineer who had been illiterate until reaching command. First a Russian mercenary in the Teheran Cossack Guard, the founding father had been lured away from the Russians by British Intelligence and installed in Teheran, where, forthwith, he proclaimed himself of imperial descent. His son, our ward, had been driven out after World War II by a Russian-inspired coup led by a Moslem hysteric named Mossadegh, who in turn had been chopped off in 1953 by a CIA coup, which reinstalled the son on the throne. Whereupon an inflation of grandeur caused Mohammed Riza Pahlevi to see himself as the heir of Cyrus and Darius. Elsewhere, too, America had acquired the assets of the decaying British Empire: in Saudi Arabia, we dealt with a royal family created by Lawrence of Arabia from the offspring of a bandit desert chieftain; in Jordan, we recognized as king the grandson of another bandit chieftain. The Shah was the most difficult of all such illegitimate rulers. He had been a cruel tyrant to his people, far more cruel than Chiang K'ai-shek, whom we had abandoned for much less reason. But he had been a staunch American ally. Should we hand over this exiled monarch, now dying in an American hospital, to the merciless Islamic revolution? Conscience revolted at that thought, and the President's answer had to be: No.

The President's public response to the kidnappings had brought approval as near widespread as public opinion in a crisis can be. But within the President's councils no such unanimity prevailed; a generations-old contradiction of council was secretly beginning to surface again. From Woodrow Wilson's Colonel Edward House to Franklin Roosevelt's Harry Hopkins, one man has acted, in every international crisis, as the President's personal eyes-and-ears on the world. By 1961, John F. Kennedy had institutionalized this function in a Special Assistant to the President for National Security Affairs, McGeorge Bundy, who would monitor the work and reporting of the chief barons of the cabinet—Dean Rusk at State and Robert McNamara at Defense. For a dozen years, national security advisers grew in importance, to the consternation of secretaries of state, until finally, in 1973, the National Security Adviser Henry Kissinger won the title as well as the function of Secretary of State and became chief of all American foreign policy, civil and military. Now, in this Iranian crisis, relations between the Secretary of State, Vance, and the Security Adviser, Brzezinski, were troubled, not only with the old built-in institutional rivalry but with sharply variant personality differences.

The old rivalry had broken out within days of the kidnapping. Following Vance's lead, the President had immediately come down hard for exploration of every negotiating way out of the crisis. But by Friday of the first week, he had told Brzezinski he was also prepared to use force if necessary; and agreed that nonmilitary members should be excluded from the Crisis Management Team's deliberations. Thus, then, while Brzezinski that second weekend spent a Sunday at the Pentagon exploring force options, of which Vance was unaware, Vance was exploring peaceful negotiations, from which Brzezinski was excluded.

From the third week on, with but one slight wavering in January after the Russian invasion of Afghanistan, the National Security Adviser's choice of options was to strike. Strike fast, strike hard, not only for the lives of the hostages and the national honor, exhorted Brzezinski, but for the national interest. The choice of the Secretary of State remained otherwise: to negotiate, continue to negotiate, negotiate, until economic pressure and reason would wear the Iranians down.

Brzezinski later explained that there was a generation gap between himself (then fifty-one) and Vance (sixty-three). People of Vance's generation—so thought Brzezinski—who had served at command level in the Vietnam War had been traumatized by that disaster. Vance had been Deputy Secretary of Defense in an earlier National Security Council, which met in the same familiar Cabinet Room on the evening of February 6, 1965, fifteen years earlier. Vance had supported the hot-blooded American aerial retaliation for the surprise Vietcong attack on our men at Pleiku in Vietnam. This had led to full-scale American involvement in the Vietnam tragedy.

Such senior statesmen as Vance, thought Brzezinski, still lived with the memory of that disaster and feared the use of force. He himself feared more the show of weakness.

Carter, fundamentally a good-willed man, had weighed in for weeks, then months, on the side of Vance—to seek peace through the agencies of the United Nations. Not until the end of February did the more recent truths of the United Nations begin to sink in. The United Nations is a fictional body where several forums are wrapped together in a glass-walled monolith. Occasionally the UN serves as a place for superpower negotiations; occasionally it invites and groups great and small powers in scientific and goodwill missions; but chiefly it exists as a forum where the Third World denounces and demands concessions from the First World. By spring it had failed in its intercession for mercy and justice from the Iranians of the Third World; and, thus, the President's councillors slowly swung round from negotiation to force.

Of the use of force it may be said that it should be wielded by the brave but governed by the wise. Here Mr. Carter blundered. With the failure of the last of his peace-seeking efforts, Vance, exhausted, had flown down to Florida on April 10 for a four-day weekend in the sun, his first rest since the crisis broke. In Vance's absence, Carter called a National Security Council meeting in which it was decided that the U.S. would mount a helicopter raid from the Persian Gulf into Teheran to free the hostages by force. A helicopter raid is a very tricky business; landing in a hostile big city, prepared to kill, is even trickier.

When Vance returned to Washington on Sunday evening, the thirteenth, he learned to his astonishment that this decision of war had already been made without him—without the Secretary of State! He called the President immediately that evening. Carter received him the next morning privately, promised to reconvene the National Security Council so that Vance could plead to reverse the decision. Vance was heard out at the Council, bootlessly. The decision would *not* be reversed. He spoke with the President again on Thursday. But the President was firm—he had swung from talk to force. The Secretary of State responded that in that case he must resign; his letter of resignation, of protest and principle, followed on Monday, April 21, to be released only after the helicopter mission was history—whether it won or lost.

It was not, Vance later explained, that he shrank from the use of force; sometimes force is necessary. But "I was the only man on that council," he said, later in 1980, of his experience, "who knew the problems in moving troops. I'd been around too long. I was Secretary of the Army and I'd seen how complicated it was to move one company of infantry from Oxford, Mississippi, to the campus of Old Miss during the crisis there." Vance recalled not only the University of Mississippi troubles, as well as the Vietnam experience, but also the extraordinary practical difficulties of directing combat battalions, unprepared for riot or street fighting, *within* the United States. He had been the official responsible for deployment of U.S. troops within the country during the black riots of the 1960s in the big cities. Now, in 1980, here was the National Security Council preparing to move substantially less than a battalion into a fanatic nation of thirty million, some six thousand miles from home. It would not work. And even if the raid did work, Vance had insisted to the Council, some of the hostages would be hurt or killed; if they were rescued, other Americans would surely be picked up; many Iranians would be killed. This could explode into a holy war between Islam and the West. "An aircraft carrier can do anything," Vance had said, "but occupy land." He had long since learned that American power had its limits.

The realization of these limits on their power as a nation would come to the American people only on the morning of April 26, when, opening their newspapers or tuning in on their TV, they learned that a helicopter mission the day before to rescue the American hostages had failed. Behind that failure lay weeks, months, of planning. The original second-level ships of the Indian Ocean task force had gradually been lifted to a formidable strike force—four aircraft carriers (one more than had faced the Japanese at the Battle of Midway), four hundred aircraft, thirty-three support vessels, a marine landing force of 1,800, plus 32,000 other airmen and seamen, a force larger than any other power could maintain so far from home. Yet it was not enough. From the beginning of the secret discussion of retaliation, all military thinking had been tethered to the mileage range of American helicopters. They would have to strike from the aircraft carrier U.S.S. *Nimitz,* in the Arabian Sea, no less than 800 miles into Iran, to reach Teheran; but their round-trip range, without refueling, was published as 686 miles. They would therefore have to set down in the dark somewhere in hostile desert over 500 miles from the carrier, rendezvous with other American planes, refuel, then swoop on Teheran in a raid that could succeed only by maximum surprise, maximum efficiency, maximum luck. None of these wishful premises was to hold.

By the morning of the raid, maximum disaster had struck. Eight Americans had died; the raid had been aborted; nothing had been won but shame. The morning papers and television shows, then the follow-up stories, told Americans as much of the truth as could be told them. First, in the emotional synopsis of a crazy venture in a crazy world, came the revolutionary realization: there was no way Americans could punish their Iranian tormentors. For the more critical, the details that followed were appalling—a minimum force used where only all possible maximum would have warranted such a gamble; the tip of the shaft of the huge American arms effort reduced to only eight helicopters; these so badly maintained and prepared for the critical excursion that no less than three failed. Behind it all, a wild political fancy that a handful of men sent to kill so far from home, in so bloodthirsty an environment, would snatch away at least fifty-three live bodies and return safely.

Carter loyalists insisted, to the end, that it was Iran and the impact of the crisis that undid the authority of their President. "The President's chances for reelection," Hamilton Jordan, Carter's chief political strategist, said much later, "probably died on the desert of Iran with the eight brave soldiers who gave their lives trying to free the American hostages."

If the first of the dominant conditions of the campaign of 1980 —the National Humiliation—was now clear by April, it had already been overtaken by the second of the dominant conditions. That condition was the Great American Inflation, which unsettled the country with the most corrosive folk fear since the Great Depression.

Unlike the Humiliation, the Great Inflation offered no precise date for its breakthrough in the campaign of 1980. It had been growing at increasing speed since the Iranian crisis had choked down world oil in the summer of 1979. But the ultimate jolt, if any date could be used to prick out a condition with an episode, came on February 22, 1980. On that date, inflation burst into a new area of consciousness as the statisticians recorded the Consumer Price Index jumping to reach an annual inflation rate of 18 percent—a rate which, if it persisted, would alter American life forever.

February 22, a Friday, was one of those campaign days when issues, ambitions, and personalities can all be squeezed to intersect in one place, in a jumble of concerns. It was the weekend before the New Hampshire primary, and the range of candidates and causes under consideration by the 324,000 registered voters of New Hampshire that day was enormous. Far away, a five-member United Nations mission was en route to Iran to negotiate the release of the hostages in Teheran; a few days later they were to be humiliated. Special-interest groups, from the right-to-life movement to the National Rifle Association, were muddying local politics. Nine presidential candidates (or their wives) were crisscrossing the little state, three Democrats and six Republicans holding forth on issues from big government to the price of heating oil (which had doubled in New Hampshire in the previous twelve months). All seriously believed they might, in this snow-mantled circus, strike the spark that would kindle their candidacies nationally.

Of the candidates exercising in this, the nation's first primary, I chose, out of nostalgia and affection, to follow Edward M. Kennedy. His journey that day across southern New Hampshire pinpoints my memory of inflation's intrusion into the year's politics.

Only a man of unflagging will would have put himself through the exertion of inflation day in New Hampshire, which was to begin, for Kennedy, with a visit to the Carpenter Center in Manchester. Years ago the building had been the Carpenter Hotel, a dingy mousetrap for traveling salesmen and the favorite rendezvous for New Hampshire's then insignificant Democratic politicians. Now it had been made into a senior citizens' center, an expression of government's growing concern for the aging.

As we wait for Senator Kennedy, who is quite late, the old people grow restless. It is well after noon when the senator arrives.

His tactics for this day have been planned to link to the strategy of the next month. That strategy recognizes that to remain a serious rival of Jimmy Carter, Kennedy must, in this Tuesday's New Hampshire primary, finish close enough behind Carter to make a strong showing in Massachusetts the following Tuesday. If he cannot dominate his home state primary, he is through. Up to now, Kennedy, in his two and a half months of campaigning, has made every mistake a veteran politician could. But the mistakes are less important than the invisible burden he bears: the charge that eleven years ago he abandoned a woman in distress, leaving her to drown in the car he was driving; then lied about it. Moreover, he is accused by gossip of being a womanizer, and his estranged wife, Joan, has been living apart from him in Boston. So, to run well in New Hampshire and remain "viable" for Massachusetts, Pennsylvania, and New York down the road, Kennedy must polish his image as a good family man while attacking the special-interest groups that are so mercilessly twisting his record.

Today, February 22, is his forty-eighth birthday, so birthday parties are strung across his route of rallies through southern New Hampshire.

These are the tactics; but a far greater event has overtaken his planning, and this has made Kennedy late. What has happened is a new report on the Consumer Price Index. The CPI, issued by the Bureau of Labor Statistics at the end of each month, is supposed to be an accurate measure of the cost of living. Businessmen and investors have been reacting to its monthly measures for years; but more and more, ordinary people are learning to take their pulse of well-being from its numbers. And this morning, Friday, February 22, the CPI has shown a 1.4 percent jump over the previous month, indicating an annual inflation rate of 18.2 percent, the highest in modern history. Annual inflation at such a rate will cut every pension or fixed salary to half its value in five years! Kennedy has lingered in Boston for the call from his senatorial staff in Washington with the new figures, to be released at nine in the morning. Then, setting out late, ruminating on this news, he has run into a snowstorm, and so now, as he enters the Carpenter Center, he is almost an hour behind schedule.

He troops in as a family man, according to plan, followed by the golden youngsters of the Kennedy clan, a full covey of handsome nieces, nephews, and children, all radiating the Kennedy charisma, having been trained to politics from adolescence. His sister Jean Kennedy Smith arrives too, escorting their mother, Rose Kennedy, now ninety years old but, as the New England phrase has it, "still sharp as a tack." It is a marvelous family gathering, warming the hearts of these forlorn old people who so seldom see their own grandchildren. Here is the Grandmother herself, urging them to vote for Teddy Kennedy, family man. (It should be noted that the Carter campaign, aware of the Kennedy plan, has offered a rival family scenario for the television cameras across town—they have imported both Good Wife Rosalynn Carter and Good Mother Lillian Carter to offer an alternative photo opportunity on this "family day.")

Mother Rose does her dainty, yet elegant, recommendation to the old folks of her son for the presidency. Then the senator does his quips, his jokes, his little stories; he makes his standard tribute to age, to the men and women "who have made this country great," as well as his standard denunciation of the extortionate cost of medicine as old people approach the point of "catastrophic illness." Then he announces the morning news, the 18 percent inflation rate. Now the old folks stir, a perceptible rustle at each one of these festooned birthday tables. Old people love to be recognized for their importance—they vote. But even more, they like to share their lonely worries; and they worry most about prices. What will happen to them? This news that Kennedy brings of the 18 percent inflation rate is frightening; you can feel their silent worry; it is as if they had lost one more battle in a losing war. What politicians promise by day, inflation sneaks away in the night. But this politician shows he cares.

The caravan moves on according to the original tactical planning. Kennedy has shown himself as family man for the cameras; now he is off to another Manchester appearance at West High School in an ethnic ward (French Canadian), where he is scheduled to hit back hard at the new single-interest groups who are undermining his campaign. He attacks the rifle fanatics ("If Kennedy wins, you lose," say the National Rifle Association bumper stickers), and the antiabortion fanatics. It is his best speech of the day, but then he ad libs that which has not been preprogrammed—a few remarks on the morning's inflationary figures, and the peril of prices. Kennedy is fighting at this high school for local votes, for a decent showing in the coming Tuesday primary. But the TV networks will lift these remarks on inflation out of his day's activities because the country is slowly growing hysterical about rising prices, and Kennedy's remarks will sharpen the drama and the issue. Both CBS and NBC, the senior news networks of the nation, will lead that night with the story of inflation, highlighting Kennedy's attack on the peril and the government's inability to control the world of prices and values.

But that breakthrough on consciousness will come only on the evening news, and as I go on following the Kennedy caravan in early afternoon, we listen to the all-news radio stations. For the next two hours, as we drive through southern New Hampshire, the van I am riding tunes its radio loud; and through the radio spurts the reaction of the nation's financial community to the morning's CPI. The reaction is one of near-panic, heightened at each turn of the radio's news cycle, as the big nets report what is happening to the prime rate. Not one American in a thousand understands the prime rate, or has met one face to face; but when the prime rate goes up, people know it is bad. In New York, says the radio at one o'clock, four major banks have jumped from a 15¾ percent prime to 16¼ percent; from Chicago the radio reports that Continental Illinois has followed. The next cycle brings news that Morgan Guaranty in New York has lifted the rate further, to 16½ percent; then Bank of America, Chase Manhattan, and Bankers Trust match Morgan; in Detroit, another huge bank matches the New York banks. By three o'clock this cascade of incomprehensible bits and pieces is capped from Washington: Robert Russell, of the President's Council on Wage and Price Stability, has just blurted that he feels "The underlying rate of inflation has started to explode." There comes a time when, if one must choose between truth and silence, silence is the only responsible course. But Mr. Russell of the Carter administration has chosen to speak the truth, which at that moment is disastrous.

The Kennedy campaign cavalcade pulls into a small town called Hampton in southern New Hampshire, retires to a suite in Lamie's Tavern, considers all the latest news, decides to tape, immediately, a new one-minute commercial, and then, after an hour and a half of consideration, the candidate comes downstairs to make a few remarks to a gathering of union (UAW) leaders of New England. Kennedy has reoriented since the morning. No more Mr. Family Man. He wants to bang it home.

"Do you know what 18 percent inflation means?" he asks. "It means the greatest economic crisis since the Depression . . . no policy or program that Carter proposes will get us out of it." Edward Kennedy has now abandoned the Mama and the Rose Garden jokes and is reaching for Carter's jugular. "It means," he goes on, "young workers can't buy a home, working people can't afford to educate their children. Working people are paying for this energy policy. To those in this room who make over $200,000 a year, I have nothing to say," he continues as the union men and women laugh; he begins to talk about what inflation means to ordinary people, feeling for those themes which would reach their peak of ferocity against Carter later, in the Pennsylvania primary, and which Reagan would make the unshakable foundation of his fall campaign.

For the rest of the year, the campaigns would weave in and out of the theme of inflation. No free democracy has ever solved the problem of inflation; those that have tried have been overturned. But that was in other countries, in other times. Not in America. Now it *was* happening here. And stab, stab, stab, the candidates and television would tell the people that nothing they saved was, really, any longer safe. Like an obbligato now, the morning radio news would begin to report the price of gold. When Carter was elected in 1976, gold had sold for $103 an ounce. In 1979, the flight of the Shah had terrified other sheikhs and royal families of the Middle East to grab for gold, their only safety, and gold had risen from $226 to $500 an ounce. Now, as we drove through New Hampshire, the cost of gold was fluctuating wildly between $700 and $800 an ounce. The price system had been shuddering for a long time; this week it was being shaken by something close to panic.

I rarely listen to the news on radio except when I shave or am driving alone, and by late afternoon I had become bored with the inflation and price reports, and so dozed in the caravan as it drove on through the snow toward the dusk. Every now and then we would interrupt the journey for a Kennedy rally, and thus slowly my attention was diverted from Iran and the inflation to what I was reporting —the Kennedy campaign.

By dark, the Kennedy caravan had begun to shed the correspondents and television crews. They had had their "bite" of Kennedy for the networks, and after all, how much could the nets use of any one of the many candidates in New Hampshire that day: a minute? two minutes? And so, as Kennedy kept rolling and as the snow and wind increased, we found ourselves in an old-fashioned New England blizzard, and in the blizzard, I was back in other times, other campaigns in New England. It was for me as if we were passing from one period back to an earlier one. As a boy, hitchhiking through New Hampshire, I stopped at boardinghouses which advertised: "Dinner! All you can eat for fifty cents!" It was here, a quarter century before, that I had begun to watch presidential campaigns. And now, in the snow, I felt myself slipping away from the campaign of 1980 and going back, back in time; the memories and contrasts unsettled me.

There was, for example, this Kennedy of 1980 whom I was following. He was, to be sure, quite old-fashioned in the planning of his campaign. But he was incorrigibly gallant. There was absolutely nothing to be gained for Edward Kennedy by stopping at *five more* birthday parties that afternoon in the blizzard. In the age of television politics, the campaign day was over. But he had promised to attend those parties, so he would; he was doing what his brother John had done with his afternoon teas for the ladies of Massachusetts when he beat Henry Cabot Lodge in 1952. It was retail vote-getting, not modern candidate marketing; no television crews followed as he went from parlor to parlor, cutting his birthday cake once more, yum-yumming over the blue and white icing; and no soundman was around to snatch on tape the deepening melancholy of his remarks.

The blizzard grew worse as the night wore on, and the caravan crept over the last few miles of sleet and ice until it came to the last stop of the day, a Ramada Inn, where at eleven o'clock the campaign party met the candidate's wife. By this time everyone had forgotten that the day had been planned originally as one to scotch the "character issue," presenting Ted Kennedy as a family man, beginning with his mother in the morning and ending with his wife here in Dover, New Hampshire, at night. Joan Kennedy was radiant, golden, and charming; the candidate himself was as kindly and attentive to her as I have ever seen him be in public—perhaps because there was no TV there to disturb the moment. But very few people had dared the blizzard to greet the Kennedys. Those who had come were old-line faithful, mostly Boston Irish who had moved north to New Hampshire; jovial with their familiar home sounds ("How are ya? Good to see ya!"); several were job-hunting pests; one or two were very serious citizens.

Of the serious citizens, I remember Jack Sanders and his wife, Mary Jo, because it was Sanders who pushed this journey further into the past. Jack Sanders, New Hampshire chairman of the Kennedy campaign, sat there in a corner of the dining room with his wife and two friends, waiting for the candidate. I was reporting that night with an old companion of the road, Mary McGrory, then of the Washington *Star*, a Bostonian by birth, as am I. We had reported the campaign of 1960 together and here we were again, in a motel dining room with a blizzard outside and no room at the inn—nor could we get any car to drive us back to Manchester. Mary McGrory had a nasty cold and, after a strenuous day, was running a fever. It was important to find her shelter. Mr. and Mrs. Sanders, with old-fashioned kindness, offered to put us both up in their home, promising to drive us back the next morning to Manchester, the center of all political happenings in New Hampshire. There the nation's press corps was assembling to report the climactic event of this last weekend before Tuesday's voting: the crucial debate between Ronald Reagan and George Bush, which would determine the Republican nomination. We gratefully accepted. Mrs. Sanders put Miss McGrory to bed immediately, leaving me with her husband to talk before their wood stove.

Sanders was at once part of our time yet also a throwback in his politics. We mused about how New Hampshire and the Democratic party had changed. He talked about these "strange young Democrats" who appeared every four years, drifting through the primaries: people without professions; people discontented with their jobs; people who simply loved the excitement of a national campaign and rolled on every four years to a new candidate, to savor again the excitement. These were the new professionals.

As for him? He was Kennedy chairman because he thought a New England President would be good for the area, would get New England its fair share of the federal handout, as John Kennedy had done twenty years ago, and Lyndon Johnson had done for Texas. This, to me, was a satisfying reason for loyalty, uncluttered by the higher moralities of world peace and compassion, and Sanders escorted me upstairs to bed—a good, old-fashioned bedroom which, obviously, his son had vacated for the visitor of the night. It was just as home used to be many years ago—except that his son's bedside reading was a paperback on how to use computers. I could not understand it—we used to read Tom Swift before going to bed—so I fell asleep.

By morning, the blizzard had gone its way. Snow lay over New Hampshire and the white pines poked out, just as they must have done when the King's navy had found them to be the finest mast timber in the world, thus provoking the first riot of the American Revolution by cutting them down.

The snow carpet made New Hampshire look exactly as it had when I first reported it in a presidential campaign. But I had now been here several times preparing for this primary. And through the dazzling snowscape of this morning's drive, my reflections poked many other observations beyond the beauty of the pines. So much had changed in the old Granite State:

• There were changes in trivia—like the highway signs as one entered the state from Massachusetts. In 1956, "Canucks," French Canadians, had been New Hampshire's underclass. Now, in the ethnic revolution, French Canadians insisted that the state recognize *two* languages. The official road signs read: "Welcome to New Hampshire—Bienvenue à New Hampshire."

• There were the structural changes, like the face of Manchester. Manchester had been, in 1956, a dead city, a dreary contender for the title of the ugliest city of New England. But in the years since, it had changed. The hollow, miles-long stretch of the fossil Amoskeag mills, once the largest cotton mills in the world, had been transformed, their bricks repointed, their sills fresh-painted; they no longer spun and wove raw cotton but produced everything from electronics to high-fashion sweaters. The old trolleys had disappeared from downtown Main Street; a new shopping center had been built with federal funding; some shops even pretended to be boutiques. Manchester was still very far from being one of the beauty spots of New England; but it was no longer the industrial graveyard of the Merrimack valley. It lived again.

• There were changes even more fundamental; like women. I had long dealt with famous national spokespersons of the feminist cause, unrelenting and remorseless women. I did not like such women lobbyists any more than I liked lobbyists who pushed any cause too hard—railway lobbyists, oil lobbyists, black lobbyists, foreign lobbyists, gay lobbyists, or moral lobbyists. But here in New Hampshire the facts invited a different assessment. More than onefourth of the state's legislature were women; half the Governor's Council were women; every major campaign was staffed by women, all the way to the top—not women as stamp-lickers, mail-stuffers, telephone-bank voices, but women as policymakers and leaders. If New Hampshire was a well-managed state, as it was in 1980, women had had a major role in making it so. They did not rant about women's rights; they simply exercised them.

But none of the changes were more important than television, as I recognized when I returned this Saturday morning to Manchester after a cold night out in the yesterday.

The media had made their camp at the Wayfarer Inn just outside Manchester—and "the media" meant, overwhelmingly, television.

A pleasant hostelry, the Wayfarer had not only replaced the old Carpenter Hotel as the political gathering place; it was now, also, the media camp. Anyone who has tuned in to a recent New Hampshire primary is familiar with the Wayfarer Inn, and the toy waterfall against which national broadcasters do their act. Here, at the Wayfarer, NBC occupied one entire wing. CBS, with equal personnel, plus its own studio, occupied another. ABC had taken over a nearby hotel. The Washington *Post,* the Washington *Star,* the Boston *Globe,* bedded down their signature correspondents here. The New York *Times,* too proud to join the horde, had six correspondents and a primary bureau just up the road. In addition, hotels as far north as Concord, as far south as Boston, were full of what has become the gadfly cloud that bedevils presidential reporting. The British Broadcasting Corporation, the Tokyo Broadcasting System, France's Radiodiffusion, the German television net, as well as the Danes, the Swedes, and the Dutch, were scattered about the area. The Harvard *Crimson* had sent up its usual team of student reporters to sharpen their teeth on a national event; the Columbia School of Journalism had outdone the *Crimson* by perhaps ten to one; the young people crawled and swarmed over the Wayfarer Inn, seeking not candidates but communicators; the young people knew that the media were the message.

Twenty-four years ago, in 1956, there had been just seven of us reporters in New Hampshire on the final weekend, footsloggers all. CBS and NBC had both that year sent in a television crew for a quick "news bite," but they had soon left. Now, in 1980, both CBS and NBC had 150 men and technicians here, and ABC probably an equal number. In 1956, only one candidate, Estes Kefauver, had been present in the flesh. This weekend there were nine, or their wives. The old seven-man expeditionary press corps had consisted of an AP man; a UP man; a Boston *Globe* man; reporters of the Concord and Manchester papers, locals; a single magazine reporter, myself; and on the final weekend, the New York *Times* had sent its Boston bureau chief, John Fenton, to Manchester to grace the event with the full majesty of the nation's leading newspaper. This year the *Times* at one point had nine correspondents in the little state at the same time. The handful that had followed Kefauver through the slush and snow of 1956 had grown to a horde of 450 correspondents and, by my own estimate, including the media personnel, perhaps 1,000. And all of these would come to focus this Saturday evening on the event for which I had hurried back from Dover—the debate between George Bush and Ronald Reagan, head-to-head, which, now in retrospect, is a paradigm of what is called a media event.

The debate would take place in the gymnasium of the Nashua High School, a stark architectural cube of beige brick and anodized aluminum panels. With its twisted oaks and surrounding student parking lots outside, with its workshops and meeting places indoors, it was a model of the "comprehensive high school" which great educators had pressed on the nation. This Saturday evening the hall was packed as if all the social studies teachers had urged their students to come see how a President is chosen. The students had been well worked over and were yelling "Reagan, Reagan, Reagan" or "Bush, Bush, Bush," as if for rival basketball teams.

This real live audience, however, was only scenery. Actuality lay to the right and foreground of the hall, where some fifteen or twenty camera crews of all networks and many nations were deployed to catch a visual bite of Americana. No television station was about to carry this debate live; only one radio station was to air it. But the media pen in right foreground excited the youngsters and their parents, as cameras excite all demonstrators. The hall roared with adolescent partisans chanting for their candidates.

Off camera, in the back rooms, another drama was unfolding. There, Reagan's campaign managers had mousetrapped George Bush. They were paying for the hall; they had invited Bush to come; Bush had accepted the invitation put forth in the name of the local newspaper, the Nashua *Telegraph,* and had punctiliously agreed to abide by the newspaper's conditions—one-on-one, man-to-man. But the other Republican candidates had protested, jostling for a share of the camera's attention. And Reagan's men had outwitted Bush's men: they had decided to invite *all* candidates to join them in the hall, without Bush's knowledge.

All this is going on behind scenes. But on camera, the edges of personality are stark. Bush marches to the platform alone, and sits there—and sits there, Yankee stiff, Yankee taut, not knowing what is happening. Then up strides Ronald Reagan—and following him sheepishly, like little boys following their scout leader, come four of the more eminent congressmen of the United States, Messrs. Anderson, Baker, Crane, Dole. To the left sits Ronald Reagan, gracious; to the right sits George Bush, grim. Between them sits Jon Breen, executive editor of the Nashua *Telegraph,* nominal host. Behind, swaying uncomfortably, unseated, are the four others who hope to be President of the United States. The cameras begin to roll; the audience, enjoying this unexpected turn of events, begins to cheer, whistle, hoot.

Then follows what could not have been more than ninety seconds of drama. Ronald Reagan reaches for the microphone to explain the tableau. Mr. Breen snaps aloud to the technicians: "Turn Mr. Reagan's microphone off." Then Reagan jackknifes up from his chair, grabs the microphone in a single swoop, his temper flaring, and yells, "I paid for this show. I'm paying for this microphone, Mr. Green [*sic*]."

The swoop, the grace, the perfect flow of the dramatic gesture, could not have been better if rehearsed a dozen times. Here was an indignant citizen defending his rights; the outraged motorist taking no lip from the motorcycle cop; the workingman talking back to management. The audience of working-class youngsters cheers. Order is restored, as Breen backs down, promising that after the debate each of the restless standing candidates will be given two minutes to present his case. The audience yells: "Give them chairs, let them sit, let them talk." From one of the upper tiers, a buxom young lady with the voice of a torch singer keeps chanting, "Unfair. Unfair. Unfair."

The rest of the debate was a closet drama of no great significance. Very few local voters outside the hall were to hear it. But the cameras had had their snatch of reality: Ronald Reagan's outburst of vivid yet controlled emotion. The debate came late on a Saturday of little news. The next day, Sunday, and on into Monday evening, New England and national television were to fill the news void with the ninety seconds of Reagan's insurrection against the authorities. If any of the major news organs of the nation reported the actual substance of the debate, I am unaware of it.

I returned, like most of the correspondents, to the Wayfarer Inn and its bar, where politicians and candidates courted us as fervently as we, twenty-four years earlier, had courted them. Not until forty-eight hours later, watching television, did I realize that Ronald Reagan had won the Republican nomination, hands down, right there in the Nashua High School, as he offered the cameras an irresistible ninety-second dramatic vignette.

This was a world unimaginable twenty-four years earlier. I *knew* now how the primary voting was going to come out. In 1956, I had sat in the city room of the Manchester *Union-Leader* with several other correspondents and we had sweated out the Kefauver-Stevenson race as the *Union-Leader*'s staff had chalked up on a blackboard the returns, one by one, from the New Hampshire towns. On this primary night of 1980, I would be with NBC—and far away in New Jersey, their computers would be spitting out projections of early returns and exit polls in the major JURGS of New Hampshire. Any fresh college graduate who could press the computer buttons of a major network could understand as quickly as I what the primary results foretold.

But what lay underneath it all?

It was quite clear from the first setting of the stage in 1980 that three great new forces would underlie the election's outcome: The loss of American power abroad first, to be sure. Then, the ravaging inflation. But then would come the new perception mechanisms: the media's growing power not only to shape but to disturb events as they crossed the retina of public attention. These developments had been swelling gradually for a quarter century since I had first come to New Hampshire in 1956; and I could not escape that earlier year if I was to make the campaign of 1980 clear. Few years in modern history had seen America stronger or more hopeful than 1956. And no man stated the comparison of past and present better than the classic historian Edward Gibbon. His rolling phrases suddenly seemed worth recall:

> In the second century of the Christian era [so declaimed Gibbon as he began *The Decline and Fall of the Roman Empire*], the Empire of Rome comprehended the fairest part of the earth, and the most civilized portion of mankind. The frontiers of that extensive monarchy were guarded by ancient renown and disciplined valor. The gentle but powerful influence of laws and manners had gradually cemented the union of the provinces. Their peaceful inhabitants enjoyed and abused the advantages of wealth and luxury. The image of a free constitution was preserved with decent reverence. . . . During a happy period (A.D. 98–180) of more than four score years, the public administration was conducted by the virtue and abilities of Nerva, Trajan, Hadrian, and the two Antonines. It is the design of this, and of the two succeeding chapters, to describe the prosperous condition of their empire; and afterwards, from the death of Marcus Antoninus, to deduce the most important circumstances of its decline and fall; a revolution which will ever be remembered, and is still felt by the nations of the earth.
>
> The principal conquests of the Romans were achieved under the republic; and the emperors, for the most part, were satisfied with preserving those dominions which had been acquired by the policy of the senate, the active emulation of the consuls, and the martial enthusiasm of the people. . . .

Gibbon wrote, of course, looking back in marvel at a long-ago Europe, unified by the Roman legions, whose roads were so finely graded by engineers that a man could post from the Channel to what was then Byzantium in little more than a week—as against the journey of Gibbon's own time, which took months. Gibbon went on to ascribe the general decline to the subtle undermining influence of Christianity—a penetration of goodwill which hardened, institutionally, to cruelty.

An appropriate account of the state of the American nation in the 1950s, and the events that led to the politics of 1980, would have to echo Gibbon. It would go something like this:

As the second half of the twentieth century began, never had the American Republic seemed more at peace or safer from challenge outside its borders. Under the benign leadership of a veteran troop commander and conqueror, Dwight D. Eisenhower, the country prospered. What seemed to be the last of the barbarian assaults in Asia had been repelled in Korea; and the borders of the country at home were deemed secure against all those who tried to enter without permission. The country flourished, not least because millions of the conqueror's veterans had come home safely from the wars, most to be educated in higher learning at the government's largesse. Such men were about to supply the country with vigorous new leadership, in politics as in industry, in science as in protest. The conqueror's Supreme Court was about to recognize the unrest of the blacks in the South, free them from legal degradation and set them on a road to equality. All Americans were now supposedly equal, both in the law and in the marketplace; the cities discharged their citizens to the green of the suburbs. Never had the sun shone fairer across a great nation and its prospects than it did in the age of Eisenhower, when by the whisk of his command a few battalions could bring peace to the Middle East, and by the wise counsel of his economists, the scourge of inflation seemed forever stayed.

It is the design of the two succeeding chapters of this work to describe the prosperous condition and the workings of the republic before the thinking and the resolution of that republic began to change. . . .

That republic was the republic of yesterday. Dwight D. Eisenhower had campaigned in no primaries for his party's leadership. He had been chosen by a cabal of party bosses; only then had he been rammed through a party convention to be offered as the party's choice to the nation's citizens. The practices of that "Old Country" in choosing its leaders would, by the standards of 1980, seem venal, prejudiced, closed to the commoners. Those practices were to become morally intolerable to the Americans of the 1970s and 1980s.

But we must go back to examine that Old Country and its ways as we look for the roots of the campaign of 1980.

CHAPTER TWO

THE OLD COUNTRY

The politics of the Old Country are now, in the 1980s, long ago and far away.

But for Americans fresh from the victory of the second Great War, politics in the decade of the 1950s seemed part of the natural order of things—unshakable and enduring.

American voters still came in packages, and these packages were the building blocks of American politics. Most packages were deliverable by someone who, if he was friendly, was known as the "leader," or if he was hostile, as "boss" of the "machine." These packages were not neat, watertight containers, but lumpy, leaky, string-tied bundles of voters wrapped in various sizes called precincts ("boxes" down South), wards, or congressional districts; these packages accumulated into the blocs deliverable by a major power broker at a national convention, where Presidents were nominated. Blocs were not limited to geographic cutouts; auto workers, mine workers, carpenters, cotton farmers, corn farmers, peanut farmers, dairymen, business-men—all were deliverable packages. But of all the voting packages, the most tightly controlled, and so the most easily delivered, were the ethnic blocs of the Northern industrial cities, the Irish, Jewish, Polish, Italian, black, Hispanic wards of Chicago, New York, Detroit, Philadelphia, Cleveland. These were Democratic votes. Such people wanted something from government, whether a fix for a parking ticket, forgiveness for a lost library book, or a word in the ear of the judge if their boy was caught stealing a banana—and more, much more: above all, jobs for the workingman, contracts for the rich.

The politics of the Eisenhower years seemed placid, changing if at all only under the old roof of the great oral tradition of American politics. Television and education were soon to rupture this tradition, but the way the national system worked then seemed simple, though coarse. An aristocracy of old-stock Protestant heritage conducted national affairs as always. At this high level they and they alone debated war and peace, the management of the national economy, industrial and scientific policy, and, if the Democrats were in power, the welfare of the lower classes. The lower classes were connected to this system only by their voting power and the men who delivered their votes. Since the great Northeastern industrial states had dominated American politics from the Civil War to the years of Truman, the ethnic vote in the big cities of the Northeast was critical in planning the strategy of any campaign, either Republican or Democratic. But such ethnic planning and balancing was always done behind curtains; a mothering hypocrisy was still thought necessary to lubricate the grinding of the gears down below. Theodore Roosevelt, Republican, and Woodrow Wilson, Democrat, had both frowned on the hyphenated American. Americans were Americans. Period. And such moral disapproval buttressed by the emotions of two wars had all but wiped out the community identity of the second-largest ethnic stock in America, the German-Americans.

The Depression had changed much of American folklore and stimulated a revival of self-examination. But still, down into the 1950s, only local political mechanics talked publicly of ethnics in the vernacular of the ordinary American in American life. To talk of such divisions publicly was equivalent to talking openly in the parlor about sex. The elite that governed America recognized that there *were* such ethnic communities, just as they knew of the existence of sex. They were, of course, by the 1950s far more tolerant than their parents of the 1920s, who had thought of Jews as tailors, storekeepers, and sometimes pushy; Italians, their parents had thought, dug ditches, sold fruit, and sometimes became gangsters; Irish had been thought of as politicians, foremen, cops, and heavy drinkers. Blacks in the 1920s had not existed except in the South. Slavs had existed nowhere in the governing calculation of the 1920s, not even in the belt of cities around the rim of the Great Lakes, from Buffalo to Milwaukee. In most small towns, ethnics had been "the foreign element" and blacks "the colored people" or "darkies." The war had forced a revision of this kind of thinking, which had already begun to suffer from the provocation of reality. The strangers in the gates had somehow been delivered by their leadership to nominate and elect people like Franklin Roosevelt, then Harry Truman. They had also offered their sons for the wars, which they had fought as manfully and bravely as any other kinds of Americans. There was an O'Hare Field in Chicago to commemorate that; and an atomic bomb to testify that Roosevelt's acceptance of refugee Jewish scientists had not been entirely whimsy.

But now in the 1950s, under Eisenhower, it appeared that matters had stabilized themselves once more. It was a more humane, open, liberal society than the one that had preceded it in the 1920s, but a society with the right people still in charge of politics. The word "ghetto" had not yet been applied to the black quarters of America's apparently thriving cities. "Ethnics" was a term used in colleges; "minorities" had not yet been legally codified to their entitlements. Detroit's Poles, Chicago's Germans, Boston's Irish, New York's Jews, Newark's blacks, had not yet been analyzed by the demographers who would transfer the techniques of television marketing to the management of political campaigns. "Inner city" meant an inner city; if anyone had spoken then of the "inner city child," he would have meant the children of the Silk Stocking District of New York, Rittenhouse Square in Philadelphia, Back Bay in Boston—who had to be sent to camp each summer to learn sailing or horseback riding.

Nor did the ethnic, or peripheral, neighborhoods feel underprivileged simply because their children would never make the best clubs. What they wanted were jobs—good times, bad times, they felt deprived because the best jobs were closed; and their own jobs swung up or down with fortune's whim. Within the general contentment, however, they lived in communities where people spoke with the same accent, ate the same food, sang the same songs, celebrated the same holidays, and worshiped in the same churches. Living together allowed them to preserve their cultural heritage, yet still shelter as equal citizens under the great roof of the American nation. If not content themselves, all hoped their children would do better than they. When they were in personal trouble, the first step in appeal was through the local machine, which was in contact, somehow, with the remorseless government above. And when they sensed deep national trouble, it was up to the pyramid of bosses to reach out and choose a President, like Franklin Roosevelt, who would get the country out of trouble.

The political system of the Old Country had brought America through the Depression, and on to victory in Europe and Asia. And it worked at home, which was more important. The short Korean War had briefly interrupted the contentment, but it could be, and was, blamed on the Communists—an indiscriminate epithet that covered murderers and innocents alike. By 1954, however, that war had been put away; the world seemed at peace; jobs were plentiful, gasoline was cheap; energy spurted from raw land, abundance from the plowed fields.

I had never covered American politics except for a violent veterans' takeover in the town of Athens, Tennessee, just after the war, when, in 1954, I was assigned to report a senatorial campaign in Illinois. It was all changing, of course, as politics always do, and always will, but at any given moment, to any young political reporter, what he *observes* seems to be what *is,* and what *is* seems permanent. In the next two years, before the campaign of 1956 brought me to the adventures of presidential reporting, I was to see a good deal of the country. And four of the state systems I reported stick particularly in my memory. My notes reflect both my amusement and my entrancement with this strange Old Country as, unnoticeably, it changed.

I began with the politics of Illinois, a state about which I then knew very little, and now know little more.

Each state has its own mysteries and its own history, and within each state the two parties have grown from their peculiar histories, each party with its own internal discords. Only the statehouse correspondents understand their own states. But all states, and all state politicians, revolve in orbit within a larger universe of unknown political forces. An outsider, therefore, can sometimes persuade himself that he sees better how a state fits into the larger politics of the Union than do the students and observers who make their calling the reporting of politics within the state. Illinois is a particularly difficult state to understand, and what the outsider sees, therefore, rests largely on eyewitness fragments.

Thus, for me, the Old Country begins with the Illinois State Fair in the summer of 1954. Most state fairs have since fallen on evil days, scorched by television and the sophistication of a generation that finds it as easy to fly to Paris as to motor down to Salem, Springfield, or Somerville. The Illinois State Fair was once among the greatest in the country, and in 1954, in Springfield, Illinois, this folk festival was at its prime—far more exciting to me than Oberammergau in Bavaria.

I enjoy state fairs: the displays of prize fruits, prize honey, prize corn, prize sunflowers, above all the prize bulls, their scrota slung full of what look like grapefruits. It is always hot in the fair tents where twenty or thirty varieties of prize fowl squawk and cackle. It is smelly, but invitingly so, in the display of the state's native wild animals—raccoons, deer, sometimes bear, occasionally wolves. Mothers sit on the grass feeding and changing their chubby babies while woodchoppers and sheep shearers perform and 4-H Club youngsters carefully groom their calves and lambs. The snack bars, in the old days before the fast-food purveyors wiped them out, offered local fried chicken, hot dogs, barbecue, corn dripping with butter. Everything was for sale, from mammoth yellow farm machines to screwdrivers and trinket jewelry. For the kids there were Ferris wheels, and for the old folks, bingo.

How many such fairs are left in the country, I do not know, but the Illinois State Fair used to be in Class One. And its high point in an election year were the two days—Democrats' Day and Republicans' Day—when the rival parties displayed their local and statewide candidates, as the farmers displayed their prize livestock. It was a show not to be missed and so I went.

Democrats' Day came first. Seven canary-yellow sedans, their sirens wailing, their red lights flashing, roared onto the fairground racetrack and pulled up to disgorge at the platform of honor Democratic dignitaries past and present—Adlai Stevenson, Paul Douglas, Scott Lucas, others. A trumpeter blasted out "The Star-Spangled Banner." All then sat down to watch the parade that opened the proceedings. The Cook County Democrats had rented a special train to bring party loyalists down to Springfield for a day of speeches, sunshine, frolic, and betting on the horses. Led by Richard Daley, not yet mayor, or *capo di capi,* of Chicago, but already one of the senior bosses of the Cook County machine, the Chicago Democrats strutted onto the track, ward by ward. Some carried simple hand-printed signs announcing their ward, others black and gold banners of identification. They enjoyed being part of the Cook County machine. Daley, already growing portly and pushing his stomach before him, was followed by: Ward Four, all-black, then in turn a Jewish ward, a Czech ward, the Polish, German, Irish wards, a Swedish ward. Then came the suburban dominions of Cook County, mostly white-middle-class middle Americans, in shirtsleeves, suspenders, and straw hats, jackets slung over shoulders. Each ward was led by its political leader, and the contrast of faces, postures, skin colors, displayed the

American urban machine in full chromatic exuberance. All marched past, then took their places across from the speakers' platform.

The Democrats' display piece, their prize livestock, was Senator Paul Douglas, running for reelection to the United States Senate. He was preceded by Adlai Stevenson, who quipped and joked. Stevenson was followed by Scott Lucas, a former majority leader of the United States Senate, who made a strident anti-Communist speech, probably to prove that Democrats were just as anti-Communist as Senator Joseph McCarthy, then the nation's foremost red-baiting demagogue. Cook County leader Daley followed, mumbling nonsense. Then came Paul Douglas, the candidate. Douglas was the last and worst of the speakers, rambling on professorially, quoting from Prescott's *History of the Conquest of Mexico*, from Madison, and even from *Piers Plowman*. It was hot, and the Cook County Democrats were sweating in the grandstand, bored, growing impatient for the horse races to begin—so they booed their own candidate to get him off the stand.

New to American political rallies, I feared this meant Douglas would lose, good man and distinguished senator though he was. But of course Douglas was not going to lose. The foundation of his victory was there before him, booing in the grandstands—the machine-tooled wards of Chicago and Cook County, deliverable in their ethnic packages. But the men who controlled those victory blocs—Jake Arvey, about to become boss emeritus, and Dick Daley, soon to become supreme boss—knew that they alone could not carry the state. To carry Illinois they needed a touch of class, men of stature and trans-ethnic appeal, to swing over the downstate Protestants and farmers. Their strategy had worked superbly in 1948, when they had lifted Adlai Stevenson and Paul Douglas from obscurity to prominence. Stevenson was Illinois bred, though he had schooled at Princeton. His grandfather had been Grover Cleveland's Vice-President during Cleveland's second term; he himself had served as Assistant Secretary of the Navy. Paul Douglas was an old-stock patriot too. Though a full-tenured professor of economics at the University of Chicago, he had volunteered for the Marines in 1942 at the age of fifty; as a combat hero he had been wounded in the Pacific, won the Bronze Star, and still carried his crippled right arm in a permanent crook. He was a man of temper, of impossible virtue, a dull speaker, and a good senator. The Arvey/Daley combine of bosses had put up the team of Stevenson (for governor) and Douglas (for senator) in 1948, when Truman's cause seemed hopeless in Illinois. Between them, Stevenson (with 572,067 majority) and Douglas (with 407,000 majority) had managed to pull Truman to a narrow victory in Illinois by 33,612 votes. It would always be a matter of debate among professional politicians in Chicago whether it was the blacks (who went for Truman by majorities up to 9 to 1 over Dewey) or the presence of Stevenson and Douglas on the ticket that pulled Truman through to the narrow win.

Republicans' Day came next, and carrying the banner of the Grand Old Party here in the Land of Lincoln was a man named Joseph T. Meek, the challenger of the sitting senator we had just heard from the day before.

Meek was personally as unremarkable as his name suggested, but as a candidate he is to be remembered—carved out of fundamentalist Republican bedrock, a prime specimen of politics in the Old Country. His candidacy had been imposed on his party by Colonel Robert McCormick, publisher of the Chicago *Tribune,* as autocratic a boss as any the Democrats had produced, though he operated from a totally different base. McCormick, one of the *Tribune* reporters told me, wanted a completely "anonymous senator from Illinois."

He had found his candidate. Meek even looked anonymous. A man of the suburbs, he rode to work on the commuter train, neatly dressed, smooth-shaven, bespectacled, balding, forgettable. Before the state fair opened, I had gone to hear him speak to the Chicago Food Brokers Association—his natural audience, as he immediately told them. I quote from his remarks because he spoke the vintage Republican rhetoric of the middle fifties.

"Gosh," he began, "this sort of thing gives me a kick. I'm talking to folks in my own trade and I don't have to use none of this malarkey. I'm a fellow who grew up in the retail business and knows something about it."

As, indeed, he did. He made his living as the lobbyist for the Federation of Retail Associations of Illinois, the small shopkeepers who, like the men in the audience, were being squeezed by giant supermarket chains on the one hand and rising labor costs and taxes on the other. He hated big mail-order houses, like Sears, Roebuck, with the fervor of a Hubert Humphrey.

"My daddy ran a dry-goods store," Meek went on, "my daddy-in-law ran a grocery. I remember the day a lady came in, laid a catalogue down, and said to my daddy, 'Charlie, can you meet this price?' . . . For two decades I've lobbied for the retailer and the little people.

What's good for the merchant is good for the customer. . . . I'd rather be a lobbyist for the little guy than for the CIO, as my opponent is. . . ."

The issue of the day was the Illinois sales tax, just being raised from 2 percent to 3 percent (it is now 6 percent). Meek shared the outrage of his audience against the ever-growing power of bigness— bigness of business, of labor unions, above all that of government imposing this tax on the state's mom-and-pop stores. He ladled answers to questions from a soup of clichés that was wholesome if not nourishing: His opponent, Douglas? "He's for more buriocracy [sic]." Big business? "I've tried for twenty years to get silk-stocking businessmen out of their chairs and into politics." Then a shrug of the shoulders to his helpless fellows.

No one in the audience raised the trickiest immediate problem of Meek's campaign, which was the bloodletting fight going on between Senator McCarthy of Wisconsin and President Eisenhower. I went up to him afterward and asked which side of the quarrel he was on. Well, said Meek, he was of two minds: his advisers told him McCarthy's endorsement might help him here in Illinois, but Ike was the President and headline-maker, so on balance, Meek hoped for Ike's support.

And there, so many years ago, one could hear in his simple perplexity the enduring schizophrenia that now still rives the Republican party. Foreign aid was a giveaway: "much more useful to use that three billion to cut taxes." Ike's health bill was "socialized medicine." And he wouldn't send a soldier out of this hemisphere to shoot a gun without an act of Congress, "so let them call Joe Meek a nineteenth-century isolationist." As for Joe McCarthy, Meek stuck to the accepted cliché: "his objectives are fine, but sometimes his methods are anathema."

All in all, Meek wanted Dwight D. Eisenhower to join him at Republicans' Day at the fair—and Meek was right.

On Republicans' Day, about a quarter-million people flooded the state fairgrounds because Ike's coming had been broadcast. By ten in the morning every seat in the racetrack grandstand was taken. Bands played while politicians sauntered across a speakers' platform draped with flags and garlanded with roses. When the President at last appeared, the crowd clapped, screamed, whistled, rang cowbells, and the cars jamming the roadways outside honked their horns. Eisenhower, tanned and smiling, reached across the platform to shake hands with Joe Meek, and the photographers got that classic picture of candidate and President together, which was Meek's objective of the day.

But Ike did more than that: When he rose to speak he urged Meek on the audience as "one of those young, virile men who is giving his life to his country." That political chore done, he turned to more agreeable themes. In his fine, booming voice, he said: "I was born and raised in this great Mississippi basin. I feel more at home here than any other place I have been. . . ." (Applause, loud and prolonged.) "Abraham Lincoln would have been proud of the delegation his party has sent to Washington the past two years." (More applause.) Then, still friendly but more presidential, discussing the Korean truce: "A year ago we were still bleeding. This peace is not satisfactory, but it's better than continuing a long, dreary strife without hope of victory. Now we have a chance to draw a line in Indochina. The problems in Iran have been settled. Suez has been settled. The Communist menace has been driven from Guatemala."

A President talking about foreign affairs to a live audience of fellow Americans can almost always hold their hushed attention. And if what he tells them is what they want to hear—as it was in that brief season of the fifties—they become almost worshipful.

Then Ike spoke of domestic affairs, and now he was the head of the Republican party, voicing the party theme that has endured for fifty years. "I've lifted the stifling controls; the American people have shown that their economy can work without war, without Washington bureaucrats. . . . We are taking America back from the bureaucrats and giving it back to the Americans." Then in conclusion, grinning, he told the audience he hoped they would not consider this a political speech. And they cheered him wildly as he left the stand.

It was, of course, the classic Republican speech, as well-formed on the lips of Senator Samuel Hoar of Massachusetts as on the tongue of Richard Nixon or Ronald Reagan. The bureaucracy as enemy is the rhetorical glue that holds the party together. But in the years between 1954 and 1976, when Republicans managed the White House for fourteen years as against the Democrats' eight, federal, state, and local bureaucrats grew in number from 7,432,000 to 15,406,000. The bureaucracy's reach now regulates American life from local sewer specifications to smoking in planes or trains.

At the end of Republicans' Day there came a grace note which today seems unbelievable. As Eisenhower left, I—heeding the oldest rule of the reporter's trade, which is to stick to the heels of the principal—followed right along after him. When the President stepped into the lead car of his motorcade, I hopped into the car following. Four men jumped in after me, and away we zoomed. I assumed the others were also newsmen, and introduced myself— Teddy White of *The Reporter* magazine—and asked who they were. They froze, then sputtered. What the hell was I doing in the Secret Service car? No one had tried to stop me, of course, but I had made a mistake and I apologized. We were speeding now, and there was nothing at the moment that could be done, so they relaxed. After all, no one had shot and killed a President for more than fifty years.

As we drove, they explained President-watching to me. Look, one said, pointing behind—and what I saw was people smiling. The way to judge how a crowd felt about a President was to see what happened after his car had passed. People always smiled and cheered when a President approached, but the moment he passed, they usually stopped. If, however, they kept on smiling, even after he was out of sight, that meant they loved him. They were still smiling long after Eisenhower had passed.

The Eisenhower trip ended at the campus of Northwestern University, and since I felt I already understood the grand politics of Eisenhower, I drove into Chicago to examine the roots of the mythic Cook County machine.

The Cook County machine, in those days, did not talk to the press except for the regulars of Chicago's dailies, with whom they played a game akin to cops and robbers. The machine stole the city blind, but no one was thought guilty unless the reporters caught them red-handed. The one or two insiders who would speak to a foreign (meaning a non-Chicago) reporter would give only the vaguest description of how the city worked. But it did not take much conversation with them or the sociologists at the University of Chicago to grasp that here was the perfect model of the ethnic coalitions that governed all American cities in the North Central quadrangle.

Jake Arvey, the old boss, was aging; his heir apparent was Richard Daley. Daley ran the machine with a tribal justice akin to that of the forest Gauls: all lesser chieftains were equal but the one who was the last to come running when he called muster was destroyed. Each lesser chieftain received his proper share of the spoils for each of the victories. The largest single ethnic bloc in the city was black. Long suppressed, the blacks had finally, under Congressman William Dawson, won their first primitive demand—to control the police on the South Side, their own turf, where white cops used to hunt down blacks on Saturday night to make up their quota of tickets and pinches. The next-largest bloc in Chicago was the Polish-Americans —in those days, Chicago published *two* Polish-American dailies, one of 110,000 circulation, the other of 50,000 to 60,000. The Polish community maintained its own parochial schools, its own burial societies. A police lieutenant of scholarly bent once gave me a guess that it took two thousand families clustered in one neighborhood to maintain a church with a Polish-speaking priest, a parochial school, and a good Polish delicatessen. If you broke up the community, you abolished the base of all three, and thus broke up a culture. Next in size came the German-Americans, who were steadily being absorbed into the larger community or dissolving into suburbia. Their great traditional daily, the *Staats-zeitung,* was now gone; their remaining daily, the *Abendpost,* was falling in circulation. Then came all the others—the Italians, Scandinavians, Slavs, Jews, and last in numbers (surprisingly, to a Boston-born reporter), the Irish. Holding all these ethnic blocs together in the precinct and ward enclaves was the machine, with its neatly calculated distribution of jobs and favors. And the machine was about to elect Richard Daley mayor and supreme autocrat.

Under Daley, ethnic municipal politics were to reach their classic triumph as an art form, as distinctively American as baseball. No Lord Mayor of London, no *Oberbürgermeister* of Berlin, no *Préfet* of Paris, would have understood these politics. All of them could keep their streets cleaner, their subway systems more punctual than the mayors of big American cities could. But none could have kept the communities that once shared American cities from bursting into passions that would have had them at each other's throats. Only one other mayor of the last half century left so great a mark on his city as did Daley—Fiorello La Guardia of New York.

Daley's political machine dealt with the established leadership of Chicago, the leadership of its ethnic communities, industry, culture, and the underworld. His machine offered the city as a platform for each group to do its own thing: the university to advance scholarship, industry to expand production, unions to protect workers, racketeers to rip off the vulnerable. It was a rough machine, and Daley was no stand-in for Sir Galahad. The machine thugs beat up citizens, and occasionally even bloodied hostile reporters; countless functionaries were on the take, as venal as loose laws let. But the Cook County machine's importance was national: in every national election the Chicago machine delivered the most solid Democratic majority of any big city, except for Boston, in the country. For twenty years any Democratic candidate for the presidency had to court Daley—not for the great torchlight parade he would stage, the last of the torchlight parades that had lit American political history since the time of Martin Van Buren, but because Daley could deliver a power package.

Daley's loyalties were always political, not principled. From the beginning, he was one of the earliest underground opponents of the Vietnam War. If the whim had moved him, he could have delivered Chicago's convention delegation to vote for Ho Chi Minh, but he was loyal to the Big Boss in Washington—in convention as in Congress, in the Vietnam War as elsewhere. At the height of his power, Daley owned ten Chicago congressmen in Washington—splendidly arrayed with one black, four Poles, three Irishmen, one Jew, one Italian. They were free, to a certain extent, to vote their consciences and ethnic heritages. But when a Democratic White House needed all ten of those votes for sure—Daley cracked the whip and they wheeled. Only where the White House crowded him on his own ground would Daley resist. He would not, for example, give Lyndon Johnson's poverticians and well-meaning social thinkers a free hand with federal money to undermine his own control of Chicago's political structure.

In the twenty-first year of his mayoralty, 1976, Daley died, on his way to lunch, of a sudden heart attack. Surly, hard-knuckled, brutal, but devoted to his town, he left a prosperous city. Once a stagnant industrial slum, Chicago now had a skyline sharp with towers, turrets, and skyscrapers whose splendor almost rivaled that of New York; and its ethnic communities seemed at peace with one another.

Daley had also left behind a tradition once universal in American politics, but which at his death survived nowhere else but in his own city: that was the tradition of boss control of the nominating process. As Chicago wisdom had it, "If you can't get your name on the ballot, you can't get elected." Daley put names on the ballot, or erased them; so, then, did other bosses, Republican and Democrat, across the country. The revolution of the next twenty-five years would wrench this control from the vagabond professionals of the Old Country and turn it over to two competing, yet interacting, groups—the image-makers and the cause people. In the next twenty-five years an entirely new system of American politics would evolve to replace the old. Victory would go sometimes to those who, by the passion of their causes, could assemble that cast of thousands in demonstration assembled whom television would display; or to the image-makers who, if money could be raised to pay for their services, would practice their art of political portrait painting on the flickering tube.

Chicago's system of politics seemed changeless, a Yellowstone National Park of political curiosities. But New York—New York of yesterday, that city of dreams and dreamers for all the world!—was something else. There, in all its high noon splendor and brilliance, the old system of ethnic politics that underlay its magnificence was in full decay; the change had begun.

As a stranger to Chicago, I could stand at a distance great enough to see the outline of its power structure. But I lived in New York, and closeness made understanding slower and more difficult.

To understand New York in its days of perihelion, one could approach reality only through the legends. And of these legends, two dominated New York politics. The first was Fiorello La Guardia, then less than ten years dead but already recognized as a municipal saint. And the second was the legend of Tammany, not yet dead, but dying.

The legend of La Guardia was the most important. It takes only one such commanding personality per generation to change a city, a state, or a nation. Just as all California politics even today descend from Hiram Johnson, and all contemporary national politics descend from Franklin Roosevelt, all New York City politics in the mid-fifties, and still today, descend from the great mayor.

Fiorello La Guardia was an original, a maverick, a man of temper, wrath, honor, and vision: he was a Republican in a city overwhelmingly Democratic, was elected mayor three times, governed for twelve years, and changed New York forever. His father had been an Italian Catholic, his mother a Venetian Jew. He was born in a New York tenement but brought up in army posts in the American West and in Europe, following his father, a cornetist in army bands. He could speak half a dozen languages, loved the Sunday comics, and loathed Tammany.

His prodigious energy changed not only the thinking of the city but its shape. As a young man, he had seen and admired Vienna's Ringstrasse; as mayor, he duplicated that great circumferential boulevard with waterfront highways and parkways, and ordered built the great new bridges which gave New York such grandeur. He was as tyrannical and dictatorial as Daley; but he dealt with honest men, abhorred crooks, and had different visions. He loved music—and so

New York received its municipal City Center, and incubated the superb New York City Ballet. His gusto extended to food, and he would stalk into hospitals and prisons through kitchen back doors, demanding they "dish out" to him the food they served their clients. He brought blacks into municipal jobs—lowly mop-and-bucket jobs, to be sure, but steady jobs on the city's payroll. He gingered the fire department by riding to their fires clutching the brass rail, wearing a fireman's hat. Had color television been invented then, producers would have become arsonists just to catch the Little Flower in full color at a blaze. He made New York a world air traffic center, simply by buying a ticket from Washington, destination New York, and when the plane alighted in Newark across the Hudson, then the city's air terminal, refusing to get off, insisting he had paid for a ride to New York and must be landed at the airstrip in Queens that now bears his name. No tribute to La Guardia I ever heard is more moving than one from a cabdriver a few days after New York's 1958 gubernatorial election. The driver was Irish, and a Democrat, but he told me he had voted against Harriman, the Democrat, for Rockefeller, the Republican. I said that was odd for a good Democrat. "Naw," he said, "they're all crooks. I give them all one term and vote them out the second time." Did that mean, I asked, that he had voted against La Guardia the second and third times around? He braked the cab, pulled over, turned to me, and said, "Mister, La Guardia was different. He had the city in his heart."

That was true; New York never had a better mayor. But what La Guardia despised most was what had kept the city together for a century—the Tammany machine. La Guardia despised bosses, large and small, the tinhorns, gamblers, and grafters who had mobilized the immigrant voters and mulcted them for so long. ("I could beat those bums on a laundry ticket," he once boasted.) Probably, in his own mind, his greatest achievement was to wreck, forever and irreparably, the prototype of all American ethnic urban machines, celebrated by social observers from Lord Bryce and Lincoln Steffens to Murray Kempton and Maurice Werner.

Which brings us to the second of the legends that still lingered in New York City in the mid-fifties: the legend of Tammany Hall. Now that it is dead, it is permissible to give it cautious praise, or think of it romantically. But in its prime it was rotten from top to bottom, brutal, corrupt, above all cynical. And yet its claim on the historic record makes it the original taproot of the Democratic party of the United States, which is the world's oldest continuous living party, older by far than any Tory, Labor, Liberal, Communist, or Socialist party in the world.

Tammany had begun honorably enough in Manhattan, only two weeks after the final adoption of the U.S. Constitution, when an upholsterer and paperhanger named William Mooney brought together a group of ragtag Revolutionary War veterans—enlisted men who had slogged through mud and snow with Washington. His purpose was to challenge for control of New York City the former officers of the Revolutionary Army who called themselves the Sons of Cincinnati and thought that they, the leaders of the revolution, were the natural rulers of the town and meant to keep its government in their own proper hands. Mooney called his league of ne'er-do-wells the Society of Saint Tammany and he fought the leaders of the upper class with flair, flavor, and fun.

Tammany's clients, under Mooney's leadership, were organized in local clubs, all with Indian names, whose chief activity, ostensibly, was the manning of volunteer fire-fighting companies. Each club had a sachem. Above them all was a senior conclave, nicknamed the Wigwam, ruled by a grand sachem, known very shortly as the Boss. However sweaty and hairy they seemed to the gentry, these men knew how to get out the votes, and soon they had formed an alliance with the rural South that eventually came to be known as the Democratic party. Tammany passed from grand sachem to grand sachem, all of them rogues, from Aaron Burr (who, in 1800, delivered the city's vote to Thomas Jefferson, then threatened to double-cross Jefferson in the electoral college) to William Marcy Tweed, the infamous Boss Tweed of the Gilded Age, who died in 1878 in New York's Ludlow Street jail.

Tweed was the last white Protestant grand sachem of Tammany. Immigration had been changing New York's ethnic mix for over thirty years, and the immigrants fit comfortably into Tammany's club system, finding there friends, picnics, clambakes, along with jobs and, in some cases, minor dignities and considerable power. After Tweed, the Irish took over Tammany, and seventy years of Irish-American bosses followed, no less corrupt than he and just as colorful, trafficking in favors that ran from prostitution to subway contracts. But Tammany could still deliver the vote. When in 1918 Alfred Smith first ran (and won) for governor of New York, Boss Murphy's machine turned out 387 votes for Smith out of 389 cast in one East Side district. When incumbent Governor Whitman protested that he had at least eight paid and "boughten" votes in that district, a recount was held. The count was correct; the Republicans had simply scuttled Whitman. But Murphy did not rest until he had hunted down the two errant votes. One claimed he had voted for Whitman by mistake; the other was a disgruntled office-seeker.

Waves of reform and disgust would sweep the city from time to time, but Tammany remained sovereign until a final wave of disgust brought La Guardia to power in 1933. And La Guardia wrecked Tammany.

For twelve years, Tammany was deprived of the patronage in favors and jobs that flowed from City Hall. For an overlapping twelve years, Franklin Roosevelt and the New Deal deprived Tammany of the federal jobs and favors that should have been its due under a Democratic administration. Control by Tammany over the machines of the city's outer boroughs vanished; it was reduced to its official title, the Democratic County Committee of New York, meaning Manhattan alone. Into some of the clubhouses, still sporting their Indian names, crept strange, sometimes sinister forces. Racketeers, like Frank Costello, found that the underworld could control a clubhouse by putting up one hundred or two hundred dollars a week to meet the rent or light bill. Such clubhouses could still control court clerkships and judicial nominations. But year by year, Tammany withered to a name in the history books until finally, in the fifties, it lost its own smoke-filled office in the old Wigwam downtown and was reduced to a suite of rooms in the Commodore Hotel. No reporter of politics in New York ever seriously had to consider Tammany after the war; and by the sixties its priceless files and archives were crammed into clothes closets at the Commodore, whence they disappeared. A generous eye could now read those records and find in them a saga—how Protestant Tammany had given the incoming Irish the ground for Saint Patrick's cathedral; how Irish Tammany had given the incoming Jews free bathhouses; how Tammany had distributed Thanksgiving turkeys and Christmas baskets to the deserving poor generations before the deserving poor learned that the federal government was taking over the "safety net." Tammany had also provided first-class public schools to teach the immigrant children; even before the Civil War it had created the first *free* municipal college, a superb institution urging the adolescents of the lower classes to higher learning and distinction; it also created a system of no less than seventeen municipal hospitals, as against one municipal hospital for all of Chicago and one for all of Boston.

But these accepted benefactions were all of the past; and for twelve full years Tammany was an institution of scorn—powerless except for its control of the courts, which it abused. And in the anarchy of powerlessness roved new forces quite unlike those of Chicago, where the Cook County machine still enforced discipline.

The most conspicuously important forces moving in New York politics were ethnic, and among the ethnic forces the chief contenders for power were the Irish, the Italians, and the Jews. Watching the struggle from aloft, holding their noses, were the Protestant elite of the executive class; watching sullenly from below was the growing population of blacks and Puerto Ricans. Far, far below the level of anyone's attention were the Orientals (almost entirely Chinese), who were thought of only as curiosities.

Within the ethnic groups, erratic patterns of aspiration developed. Manhattan Jews were making a lateral entry into national politics, sending their most brilliant and ambitious to Roosevelt's New Deal; Brooklyn and Bronx Jews were still fighting for local recognition at Borough Hall. For Jews, postwar America, before quotas set in, was literally the promised land, and so any bright Jewish youngster could disdain the paving-stone politics of New York while he aspired to direct the Marshall Plan, make bigger and better cyclotrons and bombs, explore medicine or outer space, or adorn a seat of learning as a professor. Paving-stone politics degenerated thus into a struggle between the Irish and the Italians, a guerrilla war that still awaits its own storyteller.

The Italians would have won eventually, anyway. Sheer numbers and a differential birth rate were pushing them to potential power, as the children of the *mezzogiorno* instinctively pulled the voting lever at the name ending with a vowel. Behind them lay years of sadness: Italians held the roughest jobs in the construction trades, in the ditches, on the wharves; Italians had big families and many were hungry; Italians were excluded from the senior dignities of the Catholic Church, as they were from the better jobs of politics, or the higher judgeships; the Irish tossed "Tony" only what was left over. But Italian-Americans increasingly voted, and the time of breakthrough came when Tammany could no longer control them because La Guardia and Roosevelt had wrecked the machine. Yet it took leadership to channel Italian votes into power and two men are significant in this tooth-and-fang war of Italians and Irish for control of Tammany—Albert Marinelli and Carmine De Sapio.

Marinelli was the first—the first New Yorker of Italian origin ever to win a district leadership and sit on Tammany's executive committee, a minor sachem in a cold and shrinking Wigwam. In 1930, in an East Side waterfront district, where Italian longshoremen and their families worked and voted, Marinelli took on the Irish and, aided by a band of strong-arm men from gangster Lucky Luciano's troopers, won his local district leadership. There followed a succession of Italian names that climaxed in Carmine De Sapio. De Sapio had won his battle for leadership against his local Irish (a family named Finn) in 1943 in Greenwich Village, that district of New York where Italian-Americans still live a community life. By 1949, he had parlayed that victory, with the help of reformers and friendly Italian-Americans, into leadership of the New York County Democratic Committee. He was Grand Sachem of Tammany, a lineal descendant of Aaron Burr, Boss Tweed, Boss Charles Murphy. De Sapio, a surly, curt politician, had a hunger for respectability; hitching his star to such eminently respectable characters as Mayor Robert Wagner and Governor W. Averell Harriman, he was invited to the best parties, soon acquiring the reputation of a paving-stone liberal, a man of the people, like La Guardia.

Unfortunately, for all his tight-lipped, secretive behavior, De Sapio's great secret was that he was stupid. He had no sense of the shape or future of New York as it decayed, nor any sense of a larger world beyond. He tried to oppose the Kennedy family in 1960—believing he controlled the New York delegation. Only when he arrived at the Democratic convention in Los Angeles did he realize he had been castrated: New York's delegation had been whittled out from under him by John Bailey, boss of Connecticut, a surrogate of John F. and Joseph P. Kennedy. By 1962, De Sapio had lost his district leadership to an insurgency—and thus his leadership of what remained of Tammany. He went on from blunder to blunder. In 1967, a cabdriver discovered that a passenger had left $11,200 in greenbacks in his cab. The passenger's description fitted De Sapio perfectly, but De Sapio denied any connection with the lost money. Boss Tweed would never have let that much money slip through his fingers—he would have stuffed it in his back pocket. Finally, in 1969, like Boss Tweed, Boss De Sapio was indicted—for conspiring to bribe an official—found guilty, and sent to jail. Over the years, he was succeeded as "boss" of Tammany by a reformer, a black, a woman, and finally another black.

By the time De Sapio was gone, New York politics were in chaos. What remained of the Marinelli–De Sapio legacy was, however, something far more important than local ethnic wars of the fifties. It was the presence of Italian-Americans in American politics as equal partners in the entire Northeast crescent of the United States. From Massachusetts, through Rhode Island, through Connecticut, on through New York, New Jersey, and Pennsylvania, the Italian-Americans had replaced the Irish-Americans as local power brokers.

I tend to stress such ethnic wars in New York because, in retrospect, they seem less sordid and more important than they did at the time. Yet, in retrospect, equally important developments were burgeoning in the New York of the fifties. For example:

• The renascent intrusion of religion into politics. There was the Chancery in New York, which undertook to speak for the entire Roman Catholic Church, and its spokesman, Francis Cardinal Spellman, appointed himself custodian of morals, manners, and patriotism. Cardinal Spellman's residence on Madison Avenue behind Saint Patrick's Cathedral was called the "Power House" by politicians. All candidates—mayoral, gubernatorial, presidential—paid the cardinal court. No one dared cross him on any issue of behavior, family life, or virtue except, occasionally, Eleanor Roosevelt, who thought him at best a shortsighted conservative, at worst a sinister reactionary. Eleanor Roosevelt was afraid of no one; she influenced voters; but Spellman controlled more. A new generation of divines —young and old, Protestant, Catholic, and Jewish—would follow him into politics.

• There was the bureaucracy. For the long years of Tammany ascendancy, the city's bureaucrats had been the prey of Tammany politicians. They had been freed by La Guardia from the yoke of patronage, and a rough system of merit appointment and promotion had made them, by the city's golden age, the most brilliant and capable municipal bureaucracy in the country. With the passage of La Guardia, the bureaucracies began to flex their muscles. First firemen, then policemen, then subway workers, ultimately even schoolteachers, began to pump their unions' money into politics. In years to come, bureaucracies across the country would come to imitate what New York's civil servants were first learning to practice. Their entry into power politics would change local governments everywhere.

• Then—the reformers. New York's educational system was broadening the horizons of the children of the immigrants. Education was working its way into New York's management skills, into its cultural centers, into the news system of which the city was the nation's capital—and even into its politics. The New York reformers —largely Jewish and Protestant, with a seasoning of young college-educated Irish- and Italian-Americans—were small in number. Their initial objectives were limited: to support Adlai Stevenson in his quest for peace, and locally to reform the courts, which La Guardia had been unable to purge. But the reformers represented something larger—the forces of civic goodwill, the idea of a citizens' city seeking the greater welfare of all. The rise of the reformers, along with the rise of the Italian-Americans and the later demands of the blacks and Hispanics, was to transform all New York politics and affect every other city in America, as well as alter the structure of the national Democratic party and, eventually, that of the Republicans.

Of all the forces operating within New York in the age of Eisenhower, none were more significant for the future of national politics than those reformers. They shared with the city's financial leadership, with the creative figures of early television, with the international entrepreneurs, the sense of unlimited American power. They thought they lived in an enchanted city with magic walls protecting them from the ravages of history. From this citadel, once they had cleansed its courts and given voice to the forces of peace, they hoped their ideas might change the nation.

The politics of goodwill were born, thus, in New York; imperial fancies that never crossed the minds of civic Bostonians, Philadelphians, Chicagoans, Los Angelenos, bedazzled the brave reformers who battled Tammany there in the streets. New Yorkers had more than their share of feuds, prejudices, hatreds—but reform politics massaged the American dream. If the color of virtue could be tinted on any proposal, no matter how far from reality, then any simpleton or scoundrel could be elected if only he embraced that virtue. New York itself could be looted and mismanaged; its budget manipulated by ignorant accountants and scheming bankers alike; its taxes wasted by housing builders, subway builders, bridge builders, school reformers, and advocates of a thousand causes. But New York in the 1950s, under the benign Mayor Robert Wagner, became in fact as well as in dream the world capital of goodwill, rivaled only by London. No one in a position of responsibility, neither the toughest banker, nor the most eloquent politician, nor the best union leader, entertained any foreboding that this city, which had shaped urban civilization in America, would later lead the way in that civilization's decay and decline.

One unspoken conviction bound all New York's leadership

groups together: that the foundations of New York were as solid as the rock on which its skyscrapers rested. For a full century, New York was the most important political state in the union, sharing with Washington, D.C., the management of the nation's affairs. New York controlled the nation's finances, provided its finest music and drama, published and reviewed its literature, dominated its culture, thinking, and medicine; and in the future lay control of television time.

New York did even more than that—it moneyed the politics of the nation. Its banks controlled credit in regional banks; and through such banks it controlled delegates to the national conventions. New York's bankers and publishers imposed first Wendell Willkie, then Thomas Dewey, then Dwight Eisenhower on the Republican party. Its rich Democrats, as well as its rich Republicans, played host to mendicant politicians from Montana to Maine. In every election year a seasonal entertainment in New York was the parade of visiting politicians from the outland seeking contributions. "You see," explained a famous East Side hostess, "it takes less money to get a senator elected from Idaho or Montana to the United States Senate than to get a local assemblyman elected from Brooklyn to Albany."

There were thus, in New York, two systems of politics—a local ethnic system where the warring factions vied for spoils; and a national or an imperial system, whose leaders decided on the national candidates, the makeup of cabinets, and the financing of a hundred or more candidacies to the federal Congress.

I shall have to come back to the financing of American elections. But the first sense of the tilt in national leadership from Northeast to Southwest can probably be dated sometime between 1952 and 1954, when imperial New York sensed a serious financial trespass on its domain. The trespass came from Texas. There, a handful of uncouth oilmen had begun to invest in congressional candidacies across the nation. It is now accepted that Vice-President Bush, who comes from Texas, is a civilized gentleman fathered by a Wall Street banker who himself was a senator from Connecticut. In those days, however, the Texas intrusion, at least in New York, seemed outrageous.

Since Texas was apparently the prime new political challenger to New York, I had to visit it. And soon discovered that Texas, like New York, was an outreach state with two entirely different political systems, which could be styled the Texas National Democratic Party and the Texas State Democratic Party.

The Texas National Democratic Party had been a dominant

force in Washington since the days of Speaker John Nance Garner and Senator Tom Connally. But in the 1950s, it probably was the most powerful state delegation in the nation's capital. Sam Rayburn was Speaker of the House. Lyndon Johnson was Senate majority leader. Wright Patman was chairman of the House Banking Committee. W. R. Poage was chairman of the House Agriculture Committee. These men were not, in any sense, bosses. They were largely Southern populists by tradition and understood that the federal government was the power center. In Washington they worked the levers of power, the levers that set cotton, wheat, and rice prices, distributed defense funds, made irrigation grants—and controlled the structure of oil and energy. Country boys all, they worked the national government for all they could squeeze out of it for Texas and smashed away at New York banks and Wall Street. They had no New York counterparts. New York gave to the national government; Texas took. New York's congressmen were hicks compared to the Texans—but the leaders of the Texas National Democratic Party were Americans first, Texans second.

In Texas itself, politics ran otherwise. There the Texas State Democratic Party embraced a rambling anarchy. The large Texans in Washington despised the scrambling politicians back home. Lyndon Johnson, with his gift of description, characterized Texas state politics as "chicken-shit politics." The big oil-rich Texans beginning to disturb national politics were disdained by men like Sam Rayburn. "Selfish, mean old men," he called them, "who got rich under the New Deal and now they're rich, they discover they have to pay income tax." Rayburn added, "They were standing there blowing the bass tuba the day it rained gold."

The Texas State Democratic Party was entirely baffling to an outsider. The voters came in packages, of course, but not in ethnic packages, and it was difficult to identify a boss system. A brutalitarian rural boss like George Parr, the "Duke of Duval County," might deliver the Chicanos of the Rio Grande; but he was a detail in the vast state. If a reporter began, as I did, trying to find the man to see in Texas in the early fifties, there was no one—not a local Daley, nor a Green or a Lawrence (Pennsylvania) or a John Bailey (Connecticut). The political puzzle came not so much from Texas's regional geography or political mechanism as from a historical disjunction. The Texas National Democratic Party defended Texas interests in Washington in the rhetoric of the New Deal; Texas local politics mixed the populist jargon of the 1880s with the businessman's jargon of the

1950s, both forms of discourse overlaid with paranoid anti-Communist rhetoric.

Texas state politics began with oil. A Marxist analysis might have simplified the power of Texas oil, but even that kind of analysis could only vaguely describe the intertwining of the dominant industry with control of the political system.

What had alarmed the liberals of the North, and the national press, was the way Texas oilmen were beginning to buy their way into national politics everywhere. Four such oilmen were particular targets of the Eastern press, vulgar and colorful all, inviting good copy. First was Hugh Roy Cullen, then seventy-two, white-haired, florid, weepy, testy. He was a wildcatter whose drillers had tapped a half-billion barrels of reserves. He gave millions to the University of Houston, to the Houston Symphony (when he attended, the orchestra would play his favorite song, "Old Black Joe," in gratitude), to a dozen other charities. He claimed to have discovered Eisenhower: "a swell fellow," whom he had personally "groomed for the presidency." When Ike displeased Cullen, Cullen would fire off peremptory telegrams of disapproval; even ultraconservative Jesse Jones, of Houston, was suspect to Cullen. Jones, he thought, was trying to run Houston "with . . . a bunch of New York Jews." Cullen invested in congressional races as if they were drilling prospects. Clint Murchison was, perhaps, not quite as rich as Cullen, but his money had helped finance the defeat of such eminent senators as William Benton of Connecticut and Millard Tydings of Maryland. H. L. Hunt, who reputedly grossed a million dollars a day from his wells, was most feared by the New York establishment because they knew that control of the media was the key to power. Hunt was not only buying into politics, but trying to buy into media through such radio and television programs as *Facts Forum;* and into New York publishing. Last among the big four was Sid Richardson, a lonely old man who lived at the Fort Worth Club in an apartment hung with Remingtons. A friend said, "Sid has no more civic responsibility than a coyote, but he's a nice guy." Richardson loved money with a monastic purity; he dabbled less in politics than the others, but when he did, did so more shrewdly. His favorites were Lyndon Johnson and a man named John Connally, who would later bridge the gap between Texas national and Texas state politics.

Among them in 1952, these four men had invaded the politics of no less than thirty other states, had pumped money into well over a hundred congressional races, and were beginning to act as if they could buy up national politics as they bought horses and oil leases. American politics had become used to the reach of New York money across the country, accustomed to the control of Ohio politics or Michigan politics by local unions or money men. But Texans were new and the appetite of these Texans seemed both sinister and unlimited, provoking a counterprotest in the North. Their adventures and crude indiscretions sounded the alarm that over the next thirty years led to attempts to monitor the use of money in politics. From such efforts at monitoring would come the laws that entrapped the Nixon campaign of 1972 and led to the unraveling of Watergate; and from the regulations designed to cripple such private enterprise in national politics would ultimately boomerang back the more sinister political action committees, which by 1980 bedeviled all national politics.

A few weeks of reporting in Texas could make such men seem more colorful than they really were. But if one followed the thread of such reporting, one discovered that Texas politics, at least on the surface, could better be described in the Leninist metaphor: The state was a committee of the ruling class—and the ruling class was Big Oil. Hunt, Murchison, Richardson, Cullen, and a covey of lesser independent clowns and wildcatters were rich beyond dreams. But when such independents hit oil, their oil flowed to the great companies, the majors, whose headquarters were in New York and whose interests were global. Oil flowed from the wells through the pipelines of the majors, at their prices, to their refineries, and from there to worldwide markets which only they controlled. Standard Oil of New Jersey owned Humble Oil of Texas; Socony owned Magnolia; other majors had similar subsidiaries—and to them Texas, richer at that time than Saudi Arabia, whose fields were just beginning to flow, was the most important oil province in the world.

But the quantity of oil that men could pump from Texas's oil fields was controlled by the Texas Railroad Commission, which set the drilling "allowables." This set the Texas price; and the price set in Texas set the price for the world. The pricing of petroleum globally was calculated at Gulf plus cost of transportation—which meant in those sunlit days the Gulf of Mexico, not the Persian Gulf, at that time just another fiefdom of the great oil majors, as was Texas. Texas was a problem for the oil majors. In Texas for generations had run a current of restless populism, with that natural urge common people have to share the wealth. In Texas, with its rural background, the big oil companies were natural targets. And so, just as the Southern

Pacific Railroad had once attempted to control the high ground of California politics, the big oil companies controlled the heights of Texas politics. Their operating chamber was the Texas Senate, then, as now, a body of thirty-one undistinguished men, as important to the oil companies in those days as the forty thieves of the Saudi Arabian royal family are today. Control was accomplished not by coarse bribery but by legal retainers. In every oil-bearing county of Texas, Big Oil needed real estate lawyers, corporate lawyers, above all casualty lawyers. Oil drilling is a dangerous business and men fall from icy rigs in winter, are maimed by falling pipe, slip on oil-slick platforms. The lawyers that Humble, Magnolia, et al. kept on retainer for self-protection made a web of statewide influence, capped in Austin, the state capital, by a lobby called the Mid-Continent Oil and Gas Association, which, when it chose, swung critical control of the Texas State Senate. There was little sinister about the majors' operations in Texas; they wanted the Texas State Railroad Commission kept honest in its allocation of "allowables," which generally it was.

Politics in Texas in the fifties thus seemed as stable as in Cook County. So long as Big Oil and its satellite independents went unsqueezed by government, all the local interests were allowed free play—wheat farmers of the Panhandle, cotton farmers of East Texas, ranchers of the grange, and the gentry who controlled the growing cities. What now, in retrospect, is so intriguing is that neither the majors, the flamboyant big rich, nor the legislators of the state assembly recognized what was happening to the communities of Texas at the time.

What was happening is what later came to be called the Anguish of Modernization, which—as in Iran, or Communist China, or Stalinist Russia—is the wrenching of a people from its past. If ever a state had produced a genuine American yeomanry, Texas had done so. But now new farm machinery and the recurrent drought of the 1950s were pushing people from farms and villages to small towns and growing cities. New industries, especially oil-based industries and the technologies that flowed from them, clustered in the enclave of Houston-Dallas-Beaumont, and were offering city jobs. In 1920, the United States Census had described Texas as a rural state—by 70/30, its people were country people, not city people. By the early 1950s, the count had switched to 40/60, rural/urban. By 1970, Texas was 80 percent urban, only 20 percent rural. On my first visit, Texas was the sixth-largest state in the Union by population, and New York the first. Texas is now the third-largest state, New York only second. And

Texas, once a state of dirt farmers and howling blizzards, has doubled its population in my thirty years of American reporting, from 7,711,000 in 1950 to 14,200,000 as I now write.

What I was seeing then was part of the shift that American politics would recognize later—the shift of gravity from the Frostbelt to the Sunbelt, from northeast to southwest. The early skyscrapers and office towers I saw as I first drove into Houston seemed all fresh and new, standing out like spikes from the cotton fields through which I approached the city. The waves of Northerners and Mid-westerners who were to crowd into such cities were to alter the culture and politics of Texas more remarkably than in any other state in the Union.

As in any state or country where the anguish of modernization disturbs the present with memory of a simpler past, the rhetoric of the past dominated Texas state politics, giving it so primitive a tone that I should reproduce at least one passage. One night I visited a local political rally in Dallas and the candidate was declaiming: "the powah-hungry bosses of the North . . . throwing our Southern segre-gation laws out the window . . . the ruthless interference of Northern bureaucrats . . . the Commonists controlling this union [electricians], the reddest and most vicious labor union of the United States . . . [don't let them] make the Commonistic radicals your lords and mas-ters . . . the revolting spectacle of the rape of our traditional Southern rights . . . Commonists and CIO leaders making strides . . . *Are you going to vote for our traditional way of life?!*"

I was appalled by such rhetoric, for I then took it seriously; I could not see, nor could anyone see, that it was an effort to hold together a community of people calling on their past to resist the threat of a distant Washington government, distant Northern liber-als, and invading ideas. If they were concerned at all by an ethnic undertow in Texas life, Texas politicians did not show it. In East Texas, Texans shared Southerners' contempt for the blacks; in South and Central Texas, they shared the general contempt for Americans of Mexican descent: Hispanics simply did not count.

I was comforted only by a conversation with Maury Maverick, a onetime congressman, a grass-roots rebel, whose family name had been given to describe unbranded cows on the open range. Maverick bore a vintage name, as authentically hallowed as that of a Travis, a Bowie, or a Houston. In his home in San Antonio I visited him, a loquacious old man, out of power but shrewd in understanding.

He laughed at my Northern neurosis about new Texas money in

politics. "When a Texan puts money into politics," said Maverick, "he doesn't give a certified check, like a stupid, degenerate, rich old man's grandson from New York. We give cash. In Texas the law holds that a man running for the legislature can't spend more than $600. But in some campaigns it runs up to $75,000. No one tries to indict anyone else, because they all exceed the limit."

Money, of course, greased Texas politics, said Maverick. But at least 40 percent of Texans could not be bought, or swindled, by the big money boys. He spoke for that 40 percent. Right there in San Antonio, continued Maverick, "my grandfather was for the Union, this town voted for the Union. We've never had a lynching in this town." He was aware of the foaming primitives elsewhere in Texas politics, the dynamiting of a black man's home in Dallas a few weeks earlier, the Houston madness that jailed a man and his wife just recently for saying we ought to recognize Red China. He was appalled at my Northern fear of the oil bogeys. "H. R. Cullen?" he said. "That ignorant son of a bitch? Always fighting with his family. You know his daughter married an Italian? . . . Murchison bragging about his sons? . . . These one-man fortunes are going to break up. These men in the oil business will be finished in ten years—their children have no culture, the whiskey-drinking old bastards." He saw Texas changing more clearly than anyone else I spoke with. "The AFL-CIO are beginning to be good practical organizers . . . we've got some foreigners . . . and this town, this state, are slowly going to accept Negroes."

Maverick's view of Texas's future was correct. It was not to change within the ten years of his prediction. But it was to be transformed so profoundly in the following twenty-five years that today it is more unrecognizable in its culture than Chicago, which insists on remaining the same, or New York, which insists on trying to change.

No one in the early 1950s could foresee what change would bring to the state whose favorite songs were then "Home on the Range" and "The Yellow Rose of Texas." Texas was so rich in resources and striving people that industry would find a new natural base in the state. It would develop in its Gulf complex a dominion of chemical industries comparable to those of New Jersey or the Ruhr. Natural gas, sulfur, alkali (from the offshore oyster beds), salt, and oil would create a complex that now produces 40 percent of all basic petrochemicals in the country. From such industries would develop pioneers in microprocessing and computers whose skills now rival those of the technological frontiersmen of Massachusetts and California. In the early 1950s, only three institutions of higher learning (the University of Texas, Rice, and Southern Methodist) even approached the level of inquiry and research that a score of New England universities boasted. It was impossible to think of Texas as a cultural center, whose state university would someday possess the finest collection of Hispanic-American historical documents this side of Seville; the manuscripts of William Butler Yeats and those of Robert and Elizabeth Browning; along with manuscripts of Virginia Woolf and a vast collection on London's Bloomsbury set; as well as the archives of the Protestant Episcopal Church of America, going back to its New England roots. Impossible, again, to think of live theater flourishing in Texas with two world-famous playhouses, one in Houston, one in Dallas. Impossible again to think that Houston would become one of the four great medical centers of the United States, ranking with Los Angeles, Boston, and New York.

Texas politics and life, in short, were largely devoid of those elements that made New York's politics so romantic and significant. In Texas, politics did not masquerade as virtue. You got what you grabbed, using politics for power without hypocrisy. Texas politicians grabbed for what they could get, from the expansion of Fort Hood to the coming space center in Houston.

Texas politics proclaimed the state as the last frontier of free American enterprise. That thought brought each year ever-increasing numbers of Midwesterners and Northerners to live in the new cities, where they could start all over again. Such people, of course, were to transform Texas, eventually, into a state whose national allegiance went more often to Republicans than to Democrats, a state whose local politics were split between several kinds of Democrats. Far, far away in the future were the dynamics of ethnic politics. Texas was absorbing Mexicans, legal and illegal, from over the border. Its cities were clotting, as were Northern cities, with blacks, who were still unrecognized and would be for another two decades. Eventually, Maury Maverick's San Antonio would be reclaimed by Mexican-Americans, who elected their own mayor and congressman, both loyal more to their origins than to either party. And Houston would, ultimately, elect a black to Congress, a woman, one of the most eloquent members of the House.

All that lay in the future. In the 1950s, Texas's contribution to the nation's thinking was close to zero; it was its naked orientation to power, and its growing meddling in the politics of other states, that disturbed the old Eastern power centers.

Yet just as New York was feeling its financial hegemony in national politics challenged by Texas, it was even more acutely feeling its control of the nation's thinking challenged by another state, soon to replace it as the nation's largest. It was not just that television acknowledged California, as much as New York, as its birthplace and residence, and that television would soon dominate the national mood. It was that California had invented a new kind of politics, far more adaptable to the restless reshuffling of American people.

California, more than New York, even in Boss Tweed's day, was a place of strangers. In 1956, for example, the census estimated that 84 percent of New York State's population was New York–born. That same year, only 40 percent of Californians were California–born, most of them children of recent arrivals. Unlike Texans, whose voters could be called back to honor some common memory like the Alamo, California voters lacked a binding memory. Most of the new voters had come to California in search of something new—opportunity, a new state, a new identity—and the only past they shared was the idea of the United States. Yet ideas native to California also moved California politics, as such ideas had once moved Wisconsin, as much as they still moved New York, California's great East Coast rival.

I was only vaguely aware of the importance of ideas in California politics, because on my first visit, in 1955, I had come seeking a specific story, and only rarely tuned in to other political sounds. I had come because Dwight D. Eisenhower had recently suffered a heart attack, and all four leading Republican candidates to succeed him were Californians. Whoever won the home state would control seventy delegates to the Republican convention, and thus almost certainly the nomination of Eisenhower's successor.

Of the four, Richard Nixon, the Vice-President, was particularly promising; but the other three were equally intriguing—Chief Justice Earl Warren, former governor of the state; William F. Knowland, its senior senator; Goodwin Knight, its incumbent governor. All three had won their original nominations running on both the Republican *and* the Democratic tickets. Even Nixon, at one point (his second nomination to Congress), had been on the tickets of both parties. In short, the party system, as I had known it in the East, simply did not exist.

That odd condition required some tracing back. And tracing back, one came across a curious history of ideas that changed politics. Only superficially did California resemble New York. In New York, the dominant theme would have been Equality, or Opportunity.

California would call its theme Liberation. The harmonics were very
sensibly different. New York voted in ethnic blocs and by tradition;
California voted otherwise, by political practices unimagined in the
East.

The themes and the practices, as I came to see them, rose from
history, for California lay at the sunset rim of the westering impulse,
where Americans came to set themselves free from whatever past
bothered them back East. To be free meant not simply political
freedom. California had always stood for that—indeed, the very first
Republican national candidate, in 1856, had been a Californian, John
C. Frémont, demanding Free Soil. Liberation in California in more
recent times meant the freeing of behavior from custom, of the
individual from the family, of men from neckties, of women from
aprons. It meant a freedom of life styles which would, eventually,
sweep east to undermine older American life styles—a freedom of
sex from marriage, of mating from social conventions, of voters from
party affiliations, of blacks from the white power structure, and later,
for Third World emigrants, a liberation from awe at the world of the
white man. The piston push behind California's rise to national eminence was, as in Texas, demographic, for California was exploding
with incoming strangers. In Texas, however, those who swept into its
new cities came seeking older values; in California, those who came
from afar were divorcing themselves from old values.

Thus, then, in this world of strangers, new kinds of politics were
developing, and American politics in the thirty years I have been
reporting them reflect far more of the California experience than the
older political practices of the East. Loneliness is the curse of people
in strange lands; loneliness was the condition of newcomers to California; loneliness in today's America, adrift in time, is a disease almost
as perilous as inflation. It is the lonely who are particularly vulnerable
to television, to its personalities, its fragments of reality. Exploring
California politics, one had always to remember this underlying condition.

But then one came to the formal politics of the state; and no crisp
classic model for California politics would serve then or now. Lincoln
Steffens's model would not do; nor would Karl Marx's. A straightforward Marxist analysis would, for example, have to start with water.
Water is even more important to California life than oil was to Texas
politics. Flying in from the East for the first time, one noticed the
unforgettable panorama of irrigation—the western slopes of the Sier-
ras speckled with half-moon lakes formed by dammed rivers; then

the Imperial Valley, perhaps the richest farmland in the world, green with irrigation provided by the federal government; then the basin of Los Angeles, a sprawling, palm-fringed garden in the American desert, drawing its water from hundreds of miles away. (It was, and still is, accepted that New York alone pays for its stupendous aqueducts; but most California farmers get their irrigation subsidized by the federal government.)

Management of its water resources has been one of California's great triumphs, as notable an achievement as the management of the floods of the Nile, or the watering of Chengtu. But water, though a continuing matter of controversy, was above politics, too important a matter for partisanship. So, too, was California's superb university system. That system, also, has always been a matter of controversy —but not of politics. The state by the 1950s had created one of the three best public systems of higher education in the Union; it did not mean to yield on its scholastic excellences, however much the behavior of its students or faculty excited mischief-makers of left or right.

With management of water and higher learning removed from current politics, one was forced back on the past as a thread-through to the present of politics. And the past, as in New York, offered a guardian ghost as guide. New York's guardian ghost was La Guardia; in California, it was Hiram Johnson, then ten years dead.

Hiram Johnson had torn California politics apart in the first decade of the twentieth century. A stocky, testy man, born in California in 1866, he entered politics and challenged control of the state by the Southern Pacific Railroad. Such systems of control were quite normal in turn-of-the-century days—the Pennsylvania Railroad controlled Pennsylvania, the Illinois Central controlled Wisconsin, and so on across the country. But such big-money control angered Hiram Johnson, a genuine progressive, and thus, first as a special prosecutor in San Francisco, then as governor, he campaigned against corporate bossism. He wrecked the party system through which the Southern Pacific controlled the state, just as La Guardia thirty years later destroyed New York bossism. Out went patronage, out went party nominating conventions, out went every device by which the serious players control innocent people in politics; out went the labeling of candidates on a primary ballot. Any man could run in either party's primary—or in both! In place of the old system, Johnson left a powerful governorship; a strong civil service; a loose and shifting assembly (the only fingerhold of old-fashioned lobby politics)—and a few major political inventions of his sponsorship. Chief among these were the "initiative" and the "referendum" mechanisms by which voters could, directly, add or subtract laws from California's codex. "Initiative" and "referendum" seemed virtuous in those days, freeing the people to do their will without control by party or bosses. As television and psephology have increasingly learned to array the votes, Hiram Johnson's purpose has been increasingly undermined, while the filter of representative government has slowly been eliminated between emotion and its electoral results. The first twenty-three referenda carried to California's voters in 1911 included a constitutional amendment entitling women to vote in the state—eight years before the nation followed California's lead. From those first referenda, down to Proposition 13 in 1978 (ordering local property taxes to be cut), California's popular initiatives have been one of the truest indexes of what people think or want; and, thus, disturbing.

The politics in the California I visited in the mid-fifties were still framed by Johnson's hopeful progressive ideas of 1910, for ideas last longer than iron. But those ideas held no anticipation of what a new breed of politicians could do with them in the California of the 1950s.

Johnson had wiped out party control of the political system. But the state had no alternative political pattern to offer the torrent of postwar newcomers. The state was, simply, a large province, with a balmy climate and much sunshine which promised liberation from storm, slush, snowshoes, and heating bills. It seemed like a good place to live; and it exploded in a population burst that elsewhere would have been a subject of wonder. In 1930, before the Okies and Arkies rolled west, California had been the sixth-largest state in the Union, with 5,677,000 people. By 1940, the number had grown to 6,907,000 and the state's rank to fifth. By 1950, swollen with Easterners, Midwesterners, Catholics, Jews, blacks, scientists, engineers, teachers, doctors—so many of whom had passed through the state en route to the war in the Pacific and returned, wanting to make their home in the sunshine—California had risen to third-largest state, with 10,586,000 people. The fifties were a decade of torrential inrush; by the time I visited in 1955, it had added 2,330,000 people—of whom 1,500,000 were migrants from out of state! By 1960, it would rise to second state, with 15,717,000 people; by 1970, to first, with 20,-000,000. By 1980, with a population of 22,300,000, it was preeminently the nation's political leader, providing both its President and its political style. Such an inrush of people to a political community has happened nowhere else in the world in so short a period of time. Had Britain grown at such a rate, its population would have exploded from the 46,000,000 of 1930 to 180,000,000 instead of the actual 56,000,000 of today. The wonder is not only that California has preserved the values of democracy which Americans and Britons cherish alike, but that its most recent surge of growth comes from Asian and Spanish-speaking peoples, totally alien to such values, yet absorbed and trying to accept them.

For California politicians during this immense adventure of the fifties, the problem had been to reach out every two to four years to touch lonesome strangers who could not tell name from name, issue from issue, purpose from purpose. Hiram Johnson's reforms had destroyed conventional party means of getting out the vote; outside San Francisco, no such thing as precinct organization existed, and no precinct walkers. The trick was to connect the strangers to candidates by arousing their emotions. Such emotions could not be hung on the open-range nostalgia that moved Texans, or the perfervid patriotism that was standard rhetoric there. In California, every idea-peddler received open hearing. Kooks, Klanners, Kommunists; Environmentalists, Evangelists, Ectoplasmics—all had an open shot at voters' emotions. From Aimee Semple McPherson and Upton Sinclair to Reverend Jim Jones of Jonestown, California politicians have always been aware of the unpredictable in their state.

By the middle 1950s, an entirely new kind of political type, unknown in the East, had thus emerged—the professional image-makers.

The image-makers were paid professionals of a new trade. They were campaign managers who provided a complete valet service for candidates or causes—speech writers, strategists, money-raising specialists, media buyers. Of these, the reverend elders were a mom-and-pop team named Whitaker and Baxter, who had invented the profession in the 1930s, gone national in the late 1940s, and by the time I first met them, in 1955, become to California what the Cook County machine was to Illinois politics. The Cook County machine had to run uphill in Illinois against what was fundamentally a Republican state; the Whitaker and Baxter team ran uphill, like most of their Republican successors since in California, against a demographically Democratic electorate. Clem Whitaker and Leone Baxter had taught their clients—candidates and cause groups alike—how to find their way through the corridors of Hiram Johnson's political architecture. In their time it cost only twenty-five cents a signature to get whatever number of signatures were needed to put a proposition on the ballot. That done, Whitaker and Baxter could—for the appropriate and very large fees required—apply the necessary money, with skill and brains, to the media to persuade the voters to make the proposition into law. Hiram Johnson had believed in direct democracy, do-it-yourself government. Whitaker and Baxter saw that the whole Johnsonian vision depended on persuasion—and they were artists at persuasion, highly paid artists, but not, as in the East, favor mongers or patronage brokers.

I met Clem Whitaker at his office and found him one of those men who talk politics plainly. Politicians, pollsters, advisers usually wriggle in embarrassment when you mention money and ask what they pay or get paid. Not Whitaker. He had spent, he told me, twenty-five million dollars of Charlie Blythe's money on twenty-five campaigns over the past ten years and won every one of them; Blythe was head of Blythe and Company, then San Francisco's leading investment bank. Whitaker explained where the money went. It then cost eight cents to post a letter, so that a mailing to reach a majority of California's 4,500,000 voters cost over $350,000. Then there were second mailings, ads in newspapers and on radio, posters, billboards —the costs mounted quickly. And television was coming in, which would cost even more.

Whitaker and Baxter began to go national in the 1940s. There had been a proposal for compulsory health insurance in California in the mid-forties. The state's doctors retained Whitaker and Baxter, and were able to defeat the proposal. When a similar plan came before Congress in 1949, the team was retained by the American Medical Association. They mailed country-wide, for display in doctors' offices, a color reproduction of *The Doctor*, Sir Samuel Luke Fildes's famous painting of a family physician beside the bed of a sick child. The painting was captioned: "Keep Politics Out of This Picture." Once again, their persuasion techniques were successful, this time nationwide.

Whitaker enjoyed his trade, and so did his wife. "We think running a campaign is a business like any other business," Baxter told me. "We've run seventy-five campaigns in twenty-five years . . . for Warren, for Knowland, for Knight. We believe political parties are through. They'll make deals. They won't stay put. Why should you have campaigns run by defeated politicians? We've put together an organization that *works*. We organize a campaign as an independent business. And we start a new business every two years, with a new organization, new people, a new board of directors. We find it more efficient that way. We have experts. Our writers are good writers; our TV script people are good; we decide on strategy and tactics ourselves. We pick out three or four issues in each campaign and by the time we're done, the people know those issues, know the answers to them. We make the other guys run on our issues; we never run on theirs."

In their Marin County parlor, looking out through a picture window over a canyon with a waterfall, Whitaker and Baxter were the Lunts, the stars, of California politics. He was white-haired, dressed in flamboyant California shirt and shorts. She was younger, her face unlined, her hair still red and her eyes green. They shared a love of politics, but it was a professional love, as if they were surgeons in a clinic; the only rise in emotion I could detect in their talk was when they spoke of capital punishment. They were against it, and I assumed that came from religious roots which I did not probe. They could easily be dismissed, or styled, as mercenaries—but not free-lance mercenaries. They were *Republican* professionals, specialists in aggravating and inflaming *Republican* emotions. Political managers fall into two obvious categories—Republicans and Democrats, as specialized in the states of mind they prepare for operations as surgeons of differing disciplines. Such men as F. Clifton White, Stuart Spencer, John Deardourff, Robert Teeter, Douglas Bailey, as well as the two master professionals of the Reagan campaign, Richard Wirthlin and Lyn Nofziger, are by nature and instinct Republican; they would be as ill-at-ease, and fumbling, in handling a Democratic campaign as their counterparts on the Democratic side, men like David Garth, or the Caddell-Rafshoon team, would be in handling a Republican campaign. Most are masters of a craft which is continuously changing, and so they rise and fall in reputation as public moods change; but the craft itself—professional management of voting emotions—for all its changes since, began there in California, over a generation ago.

Clem Whitaker and Leone Baxter are now gone. But their kind of politics—professional image-making—has not only persisted but thrived; and, in thriving, swept East, where a politics industry has grown up—a gathering of professionals who merchandise control of voter reactions. Image politics, sweeping out from California, would grow to dominate presidential elections, then presidential administrations, then international politics, as foreign statesmen and hoodlum terrorists alike would jockey for time on American television.

Taking it all in all—the politics of California with those of Texas; the politics of oil with the politics of milk; the politics of Minnesota and Oklahoma, of Illinois and Massachusetts, of New York and Pennsylvania—the system in the Old Country seemed, if not trouble-free, at least responsive to need and popular control. Each state conducted its own politics, alternately denouncing yet demanding from Washington's power center those benefits that only the federal power center could grant. Both political parties in all forty-eight states knew what the prize of the big game was: it was control of this federal power center. The first step lay in planning to put together enough of the proper packages to make a majority at the national conventions; the second step was to mobilize, behind the two candidates who emerged, the mass of voters necessary to give a majority in the electoral college. And then—then!—they could share in the greatest power in the world, and the share-out of jobs, privileges, honors, and fame that went with it. The country, at the high plateau of world power, seemed in a phase of happy stability. Only in retrospect do I now recognize how much was changing within the traditional harmonics.

In the Old Country, it was easy to report the plays in the game of politics. It was like reporting the game on a baseball field, with fixed bases and numbered players. Many of the best political reporters, at the time of my entry into the press box, had actually graduated from reporting sports to reporting the game of politics. What made reporting so easy was the sense that though the players or the management might change, the rules would probably stay the same into the future.

What was about to happen, however, was that the rules of American politics were to change—in both their technology and their substance—and to change so dramatically, although peacefully, as to amount to a revolution. There once prevailed a historical theory —now questioned—that revolutions burst on the crest of rising standards of living and expectations. That theory would explain what was going to happen in America in the storm decade of the 1960s. So much energy was building up in the placid 1950s, so many students going to college, so many people taking their first vacations in the sun, so much culture being pumped into the rich system, so many blacks refusing to play "Yassuh, Boss," that something was bound to give.

The changes in technology would be the easiest to describe—for the master technological innovation was the advent of television. All other technologies of vote manipulation—spectrum analysis, focus analysis, regression of questioning, coarse and refined polling, precinct modeling, direct mail, telephone banks—are now subordinate to the spell of the tube. What the masters of the tube did, however, was dissolve the connections of local loyalties to leaders of the old voting blocs and groups. Loyalties to ethnic leaders, machine captains, county packagers, would be able to persist only locally, beneath the attention of the tube. In a national election, however, Americans would vote as the producers of television unveiled reality for them.

The changes in the substance of politics would be far more difficult to describe than the technological changes in the revolution to come. Substance meant, for example, the blacks. What should America do about their demands? Blacks refused to be objects of charity or bullying; they insisted on full equality, but stubbornly refused, as did their friends and their enemies, to define what equality meant. Substance meant other demands of conscience. What should America do about the handicapped, the aged, polluters, women? We were a country so rich and so powerful—if we could reach the moon, why could we not have safe streets? Substance meant reviewing the world, which, in 1945, we had dominated; in which we had become the largest force for the liberation of Africa and Asia; but in which our power was slipping, so that our men would be destroyed in the fields of Vietnam abroad, or cast out of work on the assembly lines of Detroit at home.

But the most difficult part of the revolution to describe is the change in the idea. Everywhere else in the world, politics dominate culture. Not so in America. Americans are not a people like the French, Germans, or Japanese, whose genes have been mixing with kindred genes for thousands of years. Americans are held together only by ideas, the clashing ideas of opportunity and equality—as it were, by a culture of hope. From the mid-fifties to 1980, these ideas and their derivative culture were to push American politics from hope and goodwill to promise and performance so bizarre as, finally, to collapse. In this collapse, by 1980, Ronald Reagan emerged as the national leader. It was not so much that the Reagan team knew how to use the new technology; the Carter people performed better at the technical level. The Reagan leaders held the accusing finger on ideas whose time had apparently come and gone.

It is, therefore, proper to recall the last of the elections in the associations of the Old Country, before it was destabilized. And the election of 1956 began with new departures in politics at home, and new realities in politics abroad.

CHAPTER THREE

CAMPAIGN 1956:
HAIL AND FAREWELL

All presidential campaigns offer both farewells and beginnings. But the campaign of 1956, when I began presidential reporting, was particularly rich in both.

I have often thought that a very engaging chronicle could be written about the unrecognized "lasts" of history—which are often much more disturbing than the conventionally hailed "firsts." "Firsts," whether true or imaginary, are the recognized staples of chronicle: Martin Luther posting his ninety-five theses on the door of All Saints Church in Wittenberg; Robert Fulton launching the *Clermont,* America's first steamboat, on the Hudson River; Michael Faraday watching his magnetized needle slowly turn in its field of force; Conant, Bush, Fermi, Teller, and Oppenheimer watching dawn rise as the bomb mushroomed over Alamogordo. "Lasts" are more elusive. Who can identify the last time or place anyone took a gold eagle or sovereign from his purse and slapped it on the table to pay for dinner? Who can identify the last company of archers sent into battle by a captain who still believed a well-drawn flight of arrows could overmatch a volley of bullets? Who can identify the last time a two-dollar bill was folded into a matchbox and passed to buy a vote?

To distinguish between "firsts" and "lasts" is a cardinal problem shared by both reporters and historians; and farewells and beginnings crisscrossed the campaign of 1956 from its opening in New Hampshire to its ending with the Suez crisis.

At the time, of course, I thought it a thoroughly boring campaign

—devoid of surprises, from the choice of its nominees at convention to the final smashing Eisenhower landslide in November. Only in retrospect did it become interesting—when it became clear that the farewells of 1956 were so much more important than its beginnings. It would be the last time, for example, that the old patrician elite of American life would be in control. It would be the last time, too, that the Democratic and Republican parties would offer two such thoroughly qualified men as Adlai E. Stevenson and Dwight D. Eisenhower to run as rivals in the same year. It was also, possibly, the last time that an American President would be reelected to serve out a full second term of four years.

It would also, unknowingly, bid farewell to the grand alliance that had won World War II. Ironically, it would be General Eisenhower, the commander of that alliance, who would now, as President Eisenhower, a candidate for reelection, undo that alliance. His onetime allies, Britain and France, had blundered into a stupidly timed and worse-managed venture to hold control over Europe's lifeline to the oil of the Middle East. Middle Eastern oil was then marginal for American daily life—thus the Anglo-French grab for access to that oil could be seen as old-fashioned imperialism, or simply immoral. Under the pressure of his campaign, Eisenhower responded to that grab morally, and bade farewell to the reach of the old alliance. No farewell of that campaign of 1956 was of greater significance or longer-lasting impact on American life. It was to echo and reecho in world affairs until its results, a quarter century later, dominated politics. In the long run, the consequences of Eisenhower's blunder at Suez could be seen as history's revenge in the campaign of 1980.

And since the campaign of 1956 is overburdened with its many farewells, large and small, it is only proper to start this chapter with what *did* begin in that campaign—the institutionalization of the presidential primary gauntlet, which was to make conventions almost obsolete as nominating gatherings, and reshape all national politics.

Estes Kefauver should be recorded as the godfather of the American presidential primary system.

Kefauver was himself a personal embodiment of "firsts." He was the first American projected to national political attention by television—in 1951, by the Kefauver hearings on organized crime. He was the first Southern candidate to venture north of the Mason-Dixon line since the Civil War, claim his due share of national attention, and earn the right to challenge for the presidency despite his Southern origin. He was also the first man to recognize how, in the dawning age of television and quickening social conscience, a "down-home boy" could use the primaries to appeal to ordinary people over the heads of their anonymous "bosses."

Primaries had, to be sure, been part of the furnishings of American politics since at least 1905, the legacy of the irrepressible progressives who had struggled to keep the bubble of dissent from being frozen in the lava of corporate America. But primaries had been almost entirely ornamental from their first invention until Kefauver knocked at the gates in 1952, and broke through in 1956. True, Wendell Willkie had been wiped out in a 1944 Wisconsin primary; true, Thomas Dewey had, in 1948, marked the Oregon primary as an ambuscade in his contest with Harold Stassen; and true, Eisenhower's managers in 1952 had used two primaries (New Hampshire and Minnesota) to make their hero far away in Paris seem a more likely winner to the Republican party bosses than sober-sided Robert Taft of Ohio. But Estes Kefauver in 1956 was the first man to see primaries as the corridor to power. Hitherto for half a century, the primaries had been a series of guerrilla sorties, in which insurrectionaries attempted to harass the main forces that power brokers had already fielded for their candidates. Kefauver, however, had no friends among the power brokers; primaries were his only road to the Democratic nomination; he yearned for that nomination; and thus his run against Stevenson in the primaries of 1956 was of a different order than his experiment with primaries four years earlier. It was a warning of things to come, a challenge to the old party system, an appeal directly to the people, coast to coast. For the first time since 1933, no Democratic President sat in the White House and, through presidential authority or party connections, could elevate or dismiss a candidate from public attention. The voters, in their blocs and packages, and thus their bosses, were unstrung from the national leadership. The field was open—or so Kefauver perceived it to be.

Kefauver was a tall, rangy Tennessean of shambling gait, with hands like huge paws, who looked at the world with cold and penetrating eyes; his face, melancholy in repose, could light up with a half-moon grin when he chose to press his smile button. He affected the Southern populist style of primitive or "hick"; his campaign emblem was a coonskin hat which tied him back to Davy Crockett, then a folk hero of a hit song. But underneath the coonskin was a hard, educated mind. He could speak legalese as tightly as any Yale Law

School graduate (which he was). When lubricated with bourbon, he could reach genuine eloquence. And by reputation he was one of the great womanizers of the campaign trail, his prowess admired by bumpkins and men of the world alike. Beyond that he was sagacious and conscientious, a scholarly student of government who co-authored *A Twentieth Century Congress,* a book on congressional reform. Of the score of would-be Presidents I have met on seven campaign trails, he, along with Nelson Rockefeller, Hubert Humphrey, and Adlai Stevenson, seemed most qualified for the leadership denied him.

Kefauver was also an independent thinker. He conducted some of the most important congressional investigations of his time—on drugs and medicines, on monopolies, on the connection between organized crime and politics. A genuine profile of courage rose from his voting record in Congress; he had been on the short end of so many unpopular votes on the Hill. One among many such votes can illustrate: It was a vote on Communism, cast on the Senate floor on August 17, 1954. That summer was the high noon of Senator Joseph McCarthy, the paranoid scourge of anything that could be called Communist. McCarthy had so goaded the Democrats in the Senate with the charge of being soft on Communism that one hot night, led by Hubert Humphrey, they offered a resolution making membership in the Communist Party, ipso facto, a crime. Crazily stampeded, the Senate voted anti-Communist by 81 to 1. The one dissenting vote was that of Kefauver, who was just then facing a hard-rock primitive rival named Pat Sutton in a Tennessee primary for his renomination. Kefauver's solitary vote could only have sprung from conscience since it could only hurt him politically. I asked him later why he had done so. "Well," replied Kefauver, "Ah figured the way that resolution was worded, you could put a man in jail just for what he was thinking in his haid." The language of the resolution was later blunted in conference committee, but Kefauver had shown a kind of stubborn courage most rare in any system of politics. Along with this, however, went a personal coldness, and a scarcely concealed calculation of how he might use other people to push his purpose, which was to prove his undoing.

The Kefauver exertion in 1956 was based on the calculation that now in the age of television the primaries were perhaps the best way to zap the attention of both people and politicians. To go the whole way meant he must start a three-month ordeal. And the place to begin, then, as now, was New Hampshire.

The New Hampshire primary was not originally planned as the overture to the national political opera. It came about because in 1949, a young man named Richard Upton (today still hale and hearty), then speaker of the New Hampshire House of Representatives, wanted his state to spice up its old-fashioned primary with a call for a "presidential preference" line on the ballot of 1952. What gave the new law its unexpected force was its date—the second Tuesday in March, which made it the first primary of the nation. Climate and history had set that date. Ever since 1803, New Hampshire's town meetings had convened at that particular date—because March was "mud season," the best time for politicking in old New England. In winter it was too cold to politick; by April people would be too busy plowing. Thus, at Mr. Upton's suggestion, the century-old town meeting date between the snows and planting time became the first testing of names of men who wanted to be President of the United States.

I came to report in 1956, and it is still amusing to recall the quality of Estes Kefauver's exercise in New Hampshire that year. The primary has since become a set piece in the ceremonial opening of presidential campaigns, like the touching of épées and the duelists' cry "En garde." Despite newer rivals for national attention as the opening engagement of the campaign, its tradition makes it still the most important. That tradition underlines the fact that every single President elected since 1952 has had first to win his party's primary in New Hampshire. That holds true from Eisenhower through Kennedy, Johnson, Nixon, Carter, down to Ronald Reagan in 1980. This record has called together a throng of observers now so large as to smother and crush the efforts of the candidates who fling themselves into the pit. But back then, a quarter century ago, editors considered the New Hampshire primary a "wire story," meaning it was left to the news agencies to cover until the last weekend. New Hampshire had only eight votes of the total of 1,372 at the 1956 Democratic convention. Kefauver alone realized that those eight delegates were the first genuine raw stuff fed to commentators' and columnists' appetites for significance; those eight delegates meant newspaper clippings; the contest for those eight delegates was television bait. But Kefauver's trailing press corps of seven reporters in the final weekend seems now, in retrospect, like a sheriff's posse.

Kefauver had no private chartered plane, no attendant staff. He traveled with no speech writers. Accompanied occasionally by a young briefcase carrier from Washington, he was entirely dependent on local volunteers to get him to and from meetings and airports. His opponent in this primary, the absentee Adlai Stevenson, saw no need to come to fight for just eight delegates—Stevenson was supported by New Hampshire's Democratic party establishment. So Kefauver, who had been visiting the state for three months, was free to play his boss-killer role. Through the slush and snow he slogged, through each little town, buying a pair of galoshes here, a comb there, pausing to talk with the local newspaper editor at another town. He handshook his way through a state in which only 25,000 Democrats voted in the primary, rewiring loyalties as he went, pleading, "Ah'm Estes Kefauver. Ah'm up here to ask for your he'p." And his message was the simple classic over-and-over-repeated theme of all primaries: "Don't let them put one over on you." Down with the bosses. Kefauver was running against Stevenson, of Illinois, of Chicago, of the Cook County machine. Everyone knew that. But Kefauver made it simple: "Don't let those Chicago gangsters take our party away from us."

Kefauver won, of course—with 84 percent of the vote! With that, the dominance of American attention by the New Hampshire primary began. By 1980, New Hampshire was to become as great a ritual as an Aleut potlatch ceremony.

The primaries of 1956 sped swiftly on their simple track.

Stevenson, stung by his defeat in New Hampshire, moved personally to present himself at the next contest, in Minnesota, where he was supported by Minnesota's Senator Hubert Humphrey and Governor Orville Freeman. This could be considered the Minnesota establishment, which permitted Kefauver great form in his folksy way. He stood in the snows of Minnesota as he had in New Hampshire and denounced Humphrey and Freeman as bosses, as he had denounced the Chicago gangsters bossing Stevenson. He joked, for example, about old Granddad. There was this storm, said Kefauver, back there in Tennessee, and the family was sitting on the porch when they noticed old Granddad's hat bobbing back and forth across the flooded meadow. What's that? asked one of the family. Why, that's old Granddad, said a daughter. He said he was gonna plow that field today come hell or high water, and it's sure high water now. Well, said Kefauver, I said I'd come and speak my piece to the people of Minnesota no matter who was against me, come hell or high water, and it's high water now. Then he would go ahead and speak his piece, always both folksy and sensible, rallying the people against the bosses, until stunningly, on Tuesday night, against all prediction, he was sweeping Minnesota by 56 to 43 percent against its Democratic-

Farm-Labor leadership, the most decent, best-organized party west of the Mississippi. The national and television press had not yet been alerted to the high drama in primaries, and I recall sitting in Senator Kefauver's uncrowded hotel room, each of us on a bed, with a bottle of bourbon between us, our only communication relay to the outside world the local radio. Kefauver, not an emotional man, was carried away by the first reports of his upset victory and promised, "When Ah get to the White House, you just come up to the gate, ring that bell, give your name, and Ah'm gonna let you in myself."

The story of the 1956 primaries can be briefly told. Kefauver was up against no inconsiderable rival in Adlai Stevenson, a doughty warrior as well as a highborn gentleman. Stevenson had come to prominence as a patrician, had emerged in politics first as a decoration, then as a substantial governor of Illinois. If now he had to fight for the Democratic nomination, he would. Stevenson carried his first open contest by a write-in vote in Oregon two months later; then carried the fight to Florida the week following, stabbing at Kefauver's Southern base. There he campaigned as hard and effectively, hand-shaking and baby-kissing, as Kefauver had done in New Hampshire, and carried the Southern Democrats of Florida by 230,-285 votes to Kefauver's 216,549. The contest then moved to California, where Stevenson knew how to raise money better than Kefauver; in California, a media state, money buys media. Moreover, Stevenson had won the loyalties of California's reformers four years earlier. In California, Stevenson won by a crushing 62 percent of the vote (carrying all sixty-eight of California's Democratic delegates), which effectively torpedoed Kefauver's challenge.

The exercise of 1956 had thus marked, though none of us knew it, a historic beginning—the beginning of the quadrennial coast-to-coast marathon. The primary campaign trail still opens officially in New Hampshire in winter, and closes four months later, officially, in California. Over the years, this primary system has become a sense-defying sequence of tourneys. By 1972, it had grown to count twenty-one primaries. By 1980, to thirty-six, mocking the gravity that should surround the choice of national leaders. By 1980, the primary season, its excitements and adventures, had incubated a horde of volunteers and activists, Democrats and Republicans, who moved like birds of passage from state to state, each carrying in his knapsack a kit bag of dreams of high office which, perhaps, his candidate might make real in Washington. It had also fostered a corps of highly paid new professionals who knew the time buys, the zones of dominant influence, the polling distortions, the ethnic cross-hatchings, of each state—all the expertise that a national campaign had to command, state by state, across the mountains and the broad Mississippi from the Granite to the Golden state.

In all other respects but the beginning of the primary marathon, the campaign of 1956 was a farewell to an American political system approaching its obsolescence.

The most confused, though most enjoyable, crossing point of hail and farewell in that year of 1956 was the Democratic convention in Chicago.

No less than twenty national conventions had been held in Chicago since the first, in 1860, when Abraham Lincoln had been nominated there. Such American conventions had always been places of carnival as well as contention, but the Democratic convention of 1956, in what was then America's favorite convention city, was the one that said farewell to the carnival.

Chicago is a marvelous convention city because the compression of its downtown spaces within the Loop-encircled blocks squeezes action out into the lovely green lakefront and parade ground, which form a natural amphitheater and stage. Television had discovered its own political power indoors four years earlier when, encircled by the Chicago stockyards, it had helped elevate Eisenhower over Taft as its party's candidate. This time television unfurled its power outdoors as well, and a giant five-story movable TV tower sited in the hotel complex on Michigan Avenue invited participants onto the national stage.

It was learning time for everyone. New magazines waved their formats before the camera eye; the miniwar between Coca-Cola and Pepsi-Cola vied for attention, and the rivalries of the candidates competed with commerce. Girls, pretty girls, were, then as ever, the best natural eye-catchers, and both hucksters and candidates offered them to the eye of the camera. The hucksters paraded their beauties half bare, in bathing suits, or riding astraddle cream-colored mares. But the candidates, whose beauties were drawn from volunteers, outdid the hucksters. The Stevenson girls, wearing Stevenson blue hats and Stevenson aprons, handed out Stevenson buttons, while the Harriman models, a bit older and thus more handsome than the Stevenson girls, wore a deeper shade of blue and longer skirts. The Johnson girls, looking even more chaste, sported red silk ribbons across their bosoms, proclaiming LYNDON. "Happy" Chandler, then

governor of Kentucky and a candidate for the vice-presidency, contributed to the festivities with a band that tooted up and down Michigan Avenue, its front rank of white-skirted drum majorettes pranc-
ing as they marched. No candidate in today's America of equal rights
would any longer dare use woman flesh as camera bait at a convention—but the girls were pretty to watch and this was their last public
appearance as objects rather than subjects of politics.

The entire turf was patrolled by the Cook County machine,
which meant Dick Daley, elected mayor just the year before. This
meant that the streets were controlled for Daley's candidate, Stevenson. Occasionally a sound truck would penetrate the hotel complex,
blaring its Republican message, "We Like Ike"; but overall, the noise
and the setting were, for days, dominated by happy Stevenson
sounds. Daley, as master of the turf, meant to display for television
his man's candidacy in public. As the convention gathered on Sunday
afternoon, white-coated Swedish choristers marched down Michigan
Avenue singing for Adlai. The next day a German-American glee
club sang for Stevenson; one afternoon a band of "School Children
for Stevenson" marched down the avenue, blowing their brasses
horribly out of tune—and the eye of television gobbled them all up.
Every ethnic group in Chicago was being turned out by the Cook
County machine to decorate the scene, except the blacks, either
because their votes were sure, or because they might have had a
negative effect on the camera.

The entire scene was of a gaiety now no longer to be recaptured.
Great publishers and pompous politicians dominated the scene. Both
offered parties where the booze flowed unstoppered. Publishers then
expected front-row boxes at conventions, and fat cats then still paid
for the parties of their political favorites. Through these parties and
the lobbies of the hotels wandered such portly ancients as James
Farley, who still took for granted the dignities and deferences once
accorded to Franklin Roosevelt's coachman; as well as the slim young
John F. Kennedy, lithe in his stride, looking more like a messenger
boy than the herald of a political message. And since this convention
had no important business to transact, parties were its business, their
sights and sounds of more importance to a social than to a political
historian. There they were as always: the bewildered faces of men
dignified in their home places but lost in this sea of other important
men; the taut faces of middle-aged, handsome, but faded women
whose husbands had finally made it—wondering whether they were
at the right party at this hour, or whether there was a party of more

prestige and glamour elsewhere. Politics connect people to power; a convention hums with their buzzing to find the connections. This holds true for both Republican and Democratic conventions. In 1956, I asked at one Chicago nightclub whether there was any difference between a Republican and a Democratic convention. Indeed there was, came the answer. "Democrats pour by the bottle, Republicans pour by the jigger."

By 1960, only four years later, most of the carnival frolic of American conventions had passed. The rich and powerful still held parties, though less drunken, where important people met, gossiped, whispered indoors. But outdoors—the streets—had become the terrain where cause people delivered messages to America by means of the television camera—a terrain too important to be left any longer to freaks, Coca-Cola, *Tiger* magazine, or long-legged beauties. Causes dominated the streets at conventions. By 1960, the first of the great causes, civil rights, was in attendance at Los Angeles to present arms in demonstration for the cameras. By 1968, in Chicago, the turbulence of the streets, invited by television, turned the destiny of presidential choice. And by 1980, in New York, most of the pretty girls were in the hall as delegates themselves, while outdoors, the competition for the TV cameras lay between the demonstrations of the homosexuals and those of the anti-abortionists.

But between 1956 and 1980 much had happened, and much of what had happened can be traced back to the crossing of hail and farewell at the 1956 Chicago Democratic convention.

The Democratic convention of that year was to see the last spirited contest between gentlemen of heritage for the nomination in either party. Kefauver, an outsider, had been eliminated in the primaries; and now Adlai Stevenson of Princeton and Averell Harriman of Yale, thoroughbreds both, were playing politics as their class and fathers had taught them, much as Franklin Roosevelt had played politics in New York and Washington. Gentlemen in politics were supposed to think about the world, the nation, and the people; they enlisted bosses to do their dirty work and make the deals. In their competition, Harriman was hopelessly outgunned by Stevenson; Harriman relied on Carmine De Sapio, while Stevenson had enlisted the old-fashioned Irish-American Boss Mafia headed by Dick Daley. Harriman's Tammany leaders were provincials; they knew the grips but not the national clamps. "You know," said one of Harriman's ablest lieutenants, a gentleman of the upper class, "I hear you can buy all the delegates from the Canal Zone, Puerto Rico, and the Virgin Islands in one package—all twelve of them. But you've got to deal with a fellow named Benitez." Off he rushed to find Benitez for Harriman. But Daley had preceded him. And the Caribbean package of twelve turned up solid on the first ballot for Stevenson. Harriman had relied further on the beginning thrust of civil rights. He hoped to rally liberals by bringing in a minority report on black rights several degrees sharper than the majority report. But Sam Rayburn, presiding over the convention, wanted no uproar over this crescent issue. He permitted no speeches, no debate, no reading of the minority report. Briskly he called for ayes and nays and then, over the noises, thwack, with a stroke of his gavel, he announced the nays had it. So much for civil rights in the politics of the old country. Harriman had relied finally on the authority of former President Truman to turn the tide in his favor. But he found that Truman's authority had evaporated with his presidency.

The balloting on Thursday night was concluded quickly—Stevenson over Harriman by 905½ to 210—and the party that followed it on the third floor of the Blackstone Hotel, which enlisted the social friends of both candidates, might have been drawn from the membership of the Council on Foreign Relations and their spouses, with a touch of Cook County roughnecks thrown in for fiber. Nominations in the future would be fought for by coarser men. Stevenson's bodyguards that night were three handsome young college graduates— one a future ambassador to the Philippines, another a future ambassador to Kenya, the third, Kennedy's future choice to chair the FCC.

It was the afternoon after Stevenson's victory that produced the most memorable vignette of hail and farewell, as well as the last nomination in any convention when a contest went beyond the first ballot. That contest revolved about the choice of a Vice-President, which Stevenson had decided to convert to open drama. Within minutes after he himself had been chosen as presidential nominee, Stevenson strode to the rostrum and announced that the nomination of his running mate the next day would be thrown open to the free choice of the delegates. Consternation. Turmoil. At least three men —all senators—wanted that nomination: Estes Kefauver of Tennessee, who had run the gauntlet of the primaries; Hubert Humphrey of Minnesota, who loved Stevenson; and John Kennedy, then thirty-nine years old, the junior senator from Massachusetts. Kennedy was a new name. Kennedy was handsome, eloquent, Harvard-polished, a war hero—but a Catholic. He had placed Stevenson's name in nomination, but that had earned him no favors from Stevenson, a fact he was ever after to resent. Kennedy, Humphrey, and Kefauver were all good men, but all three had now, overnight, to mount a floor fight for which in other times they might have taken months to prepare.

What followed then, the following afternoon, was one of those glorious, unpredictable scenes that American conventions occasionally provide.

On the rostrum stood Sam Rayburn of Texas, Speaker of the House, in all his glistening bald dignity, skillfully chairing a convention that had come out of control. Rayburn had, personally, been infuriated by Stevenson's insistence on leaving so important a decision as choice of Vice-President to the will of the floor. And the floor roared, as he had anticipated. There in a ready-made cast of thousands, which neither cinema nor television could have afforded to bring together, was the scenery of old American politics—delegates locked in floor blocs, yelling, brawling, their pylons and banners waving, horns blowing. It was clear from the outset of the balloting that Humphrey would end up nowhere, that the floor fight lay between Kefauver and Kennedy. A total of 687 votes was needed for a majority. The first ballot showed: Kefauver 483½; Kennedy 304; Humphrey 134½.

Then came a brief pause; minutes later, the relentless gavel of Sam Rayburn whacked open the call for the second ballot, and there on the floor, American politics were coming apart. It had been axiomatic ever since the defeat of Al Smith in 1928 that the Protestant South would never vote for a Catholic Northerner. But as the balloting now proceeded, one could see the Southern delegates breaking not to another Protestant candidate but to Kennedy! Arkansas, 26 for Senator Gore, Tennessee's favorite son, on the first ballot—26 for Kennedy on the second! Florida, meaningless on first ballot, moving one more to Kennedy on the second! So on down the line, until one came to Texas, then a Baptist state, which had cast 56 votes for Albert Gore on the first ballot—now calling its vote in the yet unfamiliar voice of Lyndon Johnson: "Texas proudly casts its 56 votes for the fighting sailor who wears the scars of battle. . . ."

The balloting now came to its first calculus before switches, and the floor rose as delegations jumped from their seats trying to signal their switches, a drama to be seen for the last time in American politics, screaming men grappling for standards and microphones, open fights bursting out as politics jabbed emotions. Kennedy had ended the first roll call on the second ballot ahead with 618 votes, over Kefauver's 551½. But Rayburn permitted no pause in the floor action. The standards of the state delegations swayed back and forth to catch his recognition for their switches. The yelling ("Mr. Chairman! Mr. Chairman!"), the hooting, the whistling, made the floor seethe, as if racked by waves. The overnight platoons of the major vice-presidential contenders choked the aisles with runners, arm-twisters, pleaders, messengers, con men with badges. Switches followed one on the other, so fast that the then nascent television control of conventions could not keep up.

Midway through the switching, it was obvious that Sam Rayburn had it in his hand to determine the choice of Vice-President—but only if instinct would tell him which of the clamoring delegations to recognize to start a stampede to his choice. Controversy still surrounds Rayburn's critical call. One story holds that Rayburn was persuaded that Tennessee's Gore would switch his state's 32 votes to Kennedy, who was only 38½ votes shy; another version insists Rayburn knew that Tennessee, if called, would switch from one favorite son, Gore, to its other favorite son, Kefauver. Whatever the motive, all one could see was that Rayburn was yielding the next switch to Tennessee—which went from Gore to Kefauver! Oklahoma similarly shifted. Rayburn called Minnesota next—which switched from Humphrey to Kefauver! The stampede to Kefauver was on and grew in noise and intensity as Kefauver's total went up to 755½ and victory, while Kennedy's dropped to 589. Down through the mob on the floor now appeared the procession that surrounds leaders, as the young senator from Massachusetts wove his way to the rostrum, mounted, and most gracefully moved that the nomination be made unanimous. Kennedy had opened the convention, narrating its keynote film; had placed Stevenson's name in nomination; he closed the drama with this graceful concession. The Kennedy mystique, which would hold for a quarter century, began that night.

If there was a beginning to the beginnings of 1960, it began that night. Having been denied a role as Stevenson's Catholic running mate, Kennedy could nonetheless reflect on the astonishing number of convention votes that had surfaced for him, without coaxing, from Protestant states. Had he won that night and gone down to defeat as Stevenson's Catholic running mate, he would have been eliminated forever. Having lost, he could think about the future. In 1956, he played his game for sport, as an overnight caprice between Thursday and Friday. But he had learned that the game might be played in the future for keeps: he would not be excluded from American leadership by his religion. Estes Kefauver had won out over him that night, fairly and squarely, by showing his muscle to power brokers in primaries from coast to coast. Apparently, what impressed bosses was the ability to pull support from ordinary voters in primaries that could coerce headlines and television attention.

What ended that night is now clear: the rationale of the American convention as the great flexible coupling in the American system of politics—a system where states, sovereignties, interests, pressure groups, machine blocs, unions, ethnics, all regarded the national convention as the ultimate bargaining place where wheeler-dealers, cause people, and vested interests traded claims. That old system had given America leaders as ridiculous as Warren G. Harding; but over the stretch of a long century it had also given America a Lincoln, two Roosevelts, a Wilson, and an Eisenhower. After 1956, conventions would no longer choose the nominee; he would emerge as the survivor of the primary trail. And the excitement of the convention would be largely synthetic, packaged for projection outward in the contest between the two parties to grab, dominate, or control public attention.

Thus, the convention of 1956 was a major farewell in American political history, only to be overshadowed very soon by another, far grander, and more ominous farewell, one which echoes through the entire world down to the present—and that was the failure, for the first time, of American nerve to recognize or protect its interests.

The final round of the campaign of 1956 was dreary—Eisenhower against Stevenson for a second time. And perhaps because the final months of the campaign were so uneventful, I found time to practice my old trade as diplomatic reporter at another scene of action, only a taxi ride away from my New York office. There in the hall of the United Nations General Assembly, and in the carpeted diplomatic lobby outside, events were approaching larger drama: the Suez crisis was on its way. My notes of the converging stories, the election and the Suez crisis, remain jumbled in the same notebooks, interlocking to reflect the confusion with which contemporary events so often overwhelm the judgment of those encircled by them.

The world was aquiver with large happenings in the fall of 1956. But all these events, as they approached, had to be debated by two American candidates seeking votes from a people which has always demanded of its government peace and victory at once. Again and again since that year, in 1964, in 1968, in 1972, in 1980, we have watched foreign powers, large and small, make their moves in an election year, hoping that America's politics will cramp its ability to respond abroad—a calculation never more dismally fulfilled than when a madman named Khomeini acted on that hope.

What rises now from my notes and recollections of 1956 is indigestible: I am forced to realize that American politics were then, as they are all too often, moved more by moralities than by realities. In the fall of 1956, the outside world was to test the rhetoric of both presidential candidates; and both, opting for morality over national interest, were to yield a world to win an election.

The world forces in the collisions that coincided with the American election were immensely complicated. So I must simplify. Two grand series of events were happening: in Eastern Europe, the growing resistance of its people to the Soviet empire; in the Middle East, the passionate but aimless revolution of the Arab peoples against targets of opportunity. About Eastern Europe we could do little without accepting war with Russia, and ever since the Berlin uprising of 1953, Eisenhower had decided to let the Russians rule Eastern Europe as they would. But in the Middle East, Eisenhower had given his Secretary of State, John Foster Dulles, free run and Dulles had bumbled.

John Foster Dulles was one of the most counterproductive Secretaries of State in American history. No man ever trained for that post more carefully, sought it more persistently, was, on paper, better qualified—or left behind a greater heritage of disaster. He was a decent, intelligent man—but pious without being principled, and tough without being practical. He had made his way to eminence as a Wall Street lawyer (Sullivan and Cromwell), a profession which requires one to be tough about abstractions, quiddities, quoddities, and the sanctity of signed contracts and treaties.

As Secretary of State, Dulles had conducted himself as a topflight corporate lawyer does for his client—he got it all in writing, each detail spelled out. His paper contracts, called treaties, were of excellent draftsmanship, particularly CENTO and SEATO. Both were supposed to be the Dulles-Eisenhower counterparts of NATO, the creation of Dean Acheson, a much wiser lawyer than Dulles. But the North Atlantic Treaty Organization had reflected reality. The Central Treaty Organization was a paper signed by Middle Eastern dictators with no strength, either popular or military, to back up the signatures. SEATO—the Southeast Asia Treaty Organization—was even worse; its paper signatures represented nothing, but the contract called for us to honor in blood a commitment to common defense of such fictitious countries as South Vietnam. We were to honor that Dulles contract at the cost of 57,692 American lives.

Nowhere had Dulles miscalculated the relation of forces more seriously than in the Middle East. He had been negotiating all through the spring and summer of 1956 with Gamal Abdel Nasser, dictator of Egypt, who had the instincts of a camel merchant and nothing but contempt for lawyers and their laws. The previous winter, Dulles had dangled an American promise of $55 million to start building Nasser's dream—the Aswan High Dam on the Nile; this would be followed by $400 million, half from the World Bank and half from the United States and Great Britain. Nasser entertained Dulles's offer, yet wanted more. He had already made a parallel deal with the Soviet bloc, swapping Egyptian cotton for Czechoslovakian arms. As a neutralist of what came to be called the Third World, Nasser felt that the way to show neutrality was to take money from both sides. In May 1956, however, Nasser made a mistake. He recognized Communist China—an action that outraged Dulles, who saw that stupendous revolution as totally illegal. It chilled Dulles, and as Chester L. Cooper says in his book *The Lion's Last Roar,* "a chilly Dulles was a dangerous Dulles." Not waiting until the American political conventions were over, Dulles decided that he must chastise Nasser; on July 19, with no word of forewarning, the Secretary of State publicly announced that he was canceling America's promise to help build the Aswan Dam. Dulles's arrogance was public humiliation for the equally arrogant Nasser. One week later, Nasser retaliated—on July 26 he seized the Suez Canal!

This raised a problem. The Suez Canal belonged to the English and the French. They had engineered, financed, and dug this world thoroughfare through one hundred miles of desert sands a century earlier. In the years since the Great War, it had become their lifeline to the oil and energy of the deserts. In World War II, the British Suez Canal Base, the equivalent of America's Clark Field in the Philippines, had been the turntable, pivot, and anchor of Allied strength and counterstroke. But for two years, under continuing American pressure that they shed this relic of colonialism, the British had been liquidating their huge and irreplaceable military asset. The final withdrawal of the last British troops came in June of 1956, leaving their interest in Suez defenseless. Now, as Nasser worked out his pique against Dulles by seizing the canal, Europe's oil lifeline was in the grasp of hostiles. And the authority of Western strength had begun to crumble in all the lawless lands. It seemed no threat to the United States at the moment—only in the campaign of 1980 would this loss of authority come to haunt America itself. For the moment, in the 1956 campaign, Suez was a problem for the British and the French.

The case of the British and French was strong in history. They had cleared this canal when the Ottoman Turks held legal title to the sands, and had granted legal passage to the builders. In the real world of now, the Franco-British case was even stronger. Eighty percent of the oil that then fueled the economies of Western Europe came from the Middle East through the Suez Canal. Anthony Eden, then British Prime Minister, reports in his memoirs of his warning to Bulganin and Khrushchev that same spring of 1956. He had told the Russian duumvirate, on their visit to London, that "the uninterrupted supply of oil was literally vital to our economy. . . . I said I thought I must be absolutely blunt about the oil, because we would fight for it." And now Nasser, a hysteric of whom the Third World would later provide many avatars, had his fingers around the British and French jugular. England, in Eden's opinion, had in storage only six weeks' oil.

There was little the British and French could do legally—except invoke the half-forgotten Tripartite Declaration of 1950. That declaration, at the end of the Israeli war of independence, proclaimed that the three great powers of the Western Alliance, Great Britain, France, and the United States, would guarantee peace in the Middle East by intervening to defend any victim against the aggressor. When Nasser seized the canal, an immediate secret consultation between the British and the French military made clear that neither power had ready an immediate strike force to retaliate and recapture it. A military action was planned called Operation Musketeer; but that would take weeks to mount; by then the immediate pretext would have vanished. And Dulles, America's Secretary of State, who had been preaching lectures in anticolonialism at both powers for months, would certainly oppose any naked illegal attack to keep open their oil lifeline. Thus Guy Mollet, the French Premier, came up with an ingenious scheme: Perhaps the Israelis might be invited to counterattack against Arab terrorists in the Gaza Strip—creating the pretext which would let the British and French invoke the 1950 Tripartite Declaration.

It is always unwise for great powers to let themselves be triggered into action by minor nations. This was a lesson to be relearned once more as the Israelis found themselves secretly allied with the

British and French, urged to retaliate against the murdering bands of fedayeen that Nasser was sending across their borders. The trigger finger was to be Israeli; the British and French would then intervene to restore order and reopen the Suez Canal to the commerce of all nations. The Israelis were told, simply, that the closer to the American election they acted, the smaller was the chance of arousing Dulles against them. It was a clumsily conceived plan.

Anthony Eden was key man in all this. But the British Prime Minister was ailing, so thoroughly dependent on medication that his appearance alarmed the British cabinet. Eden disliked both the Israelis and Dulles; he could not talk man-to-man with Dulles, and would not talk to the Israelis. The French thus became the link in this strange conspiracy, dealing with the Israelis, coordinating plans, dates, timings, with the British. The quality of planning was poor. Much had been lost of the precise excellence of Western military men in the eleven short years since their victory in 1945. Suez was to be a surprise strike—but one British armored division was scheduled to come from Southampton, ten days distant; other troops from Malta; the French troops were to come from Algiers, seven days away. Yet they hoped to keep this Mediterranean surprise a secret from the American intelligence agencies. It was best that Dulles and, thus, Eisenhower not be informed in advance. They had an election to face.

All this tangle now closed to snare Dwight D. Eisenhower, who was the President, yet also a candidate. No one can predict the mood of a candidate in an American election as he approaches its last week; by then his personality has been scraped bare. Eisenhower had grown itchy, as candidates always do, and Stevenson had rubbed that itch raw. He had made the axis of his final thrust the fact that Eisenhower (then sixty-six) was too old to be a good President; that he lacked the vigor to master foreign affairs.

Nothing upsets an aging man so much as to be described publicly as old, and Stevenson's gut-punching upset Eisenhower. Everyone knew the President would be reelected—Southern Democrats, Tammany hacks, Cook County district captains, every commentator, all knew. Nonetheless, Stevenson's drilling had begun to affect voters, and by October 26, the Gallup Poll had shown Eisenhower falling to his low of the campaign: 51 for Ike, 41 for Stevenson, 8 Undecided.

What began to happen, in the last ten days of the campaign, was soon to snarl itself in events so complicated that no one was certain of what was going on. The best way to untangle the genuine confusion is to try to separate its elements into three or four theaters of action: the American campaign for the presidency, the Soviet campaign for crushing Hungarian independence, the Anglo-French campaign for recapture of their canal; as well as the first showing of muscle by the Third World at the United Nations, where, lo, for the first time they might pass judgment on white people in a world forum.

This last fortnight of the campaign of 1956, Candidate Eisenhower lay in Walter Reed Hospital. He had gone there not because he was ill; he had undergone a major ileitis operation in June and now had to be certified in good health. This was required politically to refute the image of the feeble President against whom Stevenson claimed he was running. The CIA had, shockingly late, reported to the President there that trouble was stirring in the Middle East. On Sunday, October 28, it reported that the Israelis were, apparently, mobilizing to strike across the Sinai desert. More important, it also reported that the British and French were "into it." Ike's response to this news was, according to an earwitness, sad and nostalgic; he said he had never really trusted the French, they would do anything. But the British? His wartime allies? The British would not do such a thing without telling him first!

Ike, from his hospital room in Washington, cabled an appeal to David Ben-Gurion, Israel's Prime Minister, pleading that no attack be launched. But the old Eisenhower in Washington had no idea that the old Ben-Gurion in Jerusalem was seriously ill with the flu, and a fever that had risen to 103 degrees. Ben-Gurion's commitments had been given; his strike platoons poised; his pledge made to the British Prime Minister, Eden, suffering from a liver ailment and heavily medicated. And the sickest of all was Secretary of State John Foster Dulles, on whom cancer had already begun to work its terminal evil.

Eisenhower's preference was to remain in Washington and deal with the world crisis presidentially. But he was a candidate. To cancel his campaign trip to the South the following day would let the Democrats and Stevenson proclaim once more that the old man was too feeble to exert himself. It was campaign pressure against presidential responsibility.

On Monday, October 29, thus, Eisenhower took off, as scheduled, for a swing to stiffen his Southern votes—to Miami and Jacksonville, then to Richmond, Virginia, then back to Washington. But on that day Ben-Gurion let loose the Israeli army to strike against the

Egyptians who had been shelling his villages. On that day also, Hungarian mobs, in full revolt since October 23, seized their own capital, Budapest, and presented the Russians with the choice of withdrawal or massacre in East Europe. Eisenhower had learned the first news of the Israeli strike at about three-thirty that Monday afternoon, as he left Jacksonville en route to Richmond. And the situation in Hungary was getting bloodier.

By the next day, October 30, one week from the election, events were even more confused. Eisenhower hoped to restrain the Russians by praising their momentary concessions to the Hungarian rebels. But, simultaneously, he had to face the fact that his wartime allies England and France had now delivered a twelve-hour ultimatum to Egypt—that France and England must reoccupy the Suez area to safeguard the canal from the Israelis. Before dark on October 31, the British and French air forces began round-the-clock bombing of Egyptian military targets along both sides of the canal; that same morning, in Europe, the Hungarian rebels seemed to have triumphed, since most of the Soviet troops had pulled out. And Americans, in the last week of a presidential campaign, saw the world coming apart.

In any crisis during an American presidential campaign, it is always best for the candidate to invoke morality (this is called "taking the high road"). Now it was up to Eisenhower as both leader and candidate to address the nation.

By Wednesday afternoon, October 31, Dulles had drafted a speech for Eisenhower, which the President read and immediately cast away. "It read," said Emmet Hughes, the wisest of Eisenhower's advisers, "as if he had caught someone cheating at cards; Dulles was breathing fire and brimstone like an outraged virgin."

The explanation of America's posture was now handed over by Eisenhower to Hughes, a veteran foreign correspondent, far more aware of the real world abroad than was the Secretary of State. Hughes writes best when he writes fast; by six-fifteen, with less than one hour to go to air time, Eisenhower was in his bedroom at the White House in B.V.D.s, reading a Hughes draft in which the compelling and operational statement was: "There can be no peace without law. And there can be no law if we were to invoke one code of international conduct for those who oppose us and another for our friends." It was good campaign rhetoric. Eisenhower loved the phrase and it became for the next week the major premise of American foreign policy; it harmonized with the American idea of equality.

A pox on both your houses, said Eisenhower, denouncing the massacres in Hungary with the same vehemence he directed at the violence in the Middle East. Eisenhower had preempted the moral high ground from Stevenson.

There was, thus, a terrain of military action at Suez and Sinai; a second terrain of Russian massacre in Hungary; a third terrain in the American presidential campaign, and most dramatic of all, in the Assembly Hall of the United Nations, where one could see, as if in caricature, a profile of an old world giving way to the new.

At the United Nations, the Eisenhower-Dulles championing of new moralities had had an electrifying effect, for the UN had in the years since its founding been changing. It now gathered in Manhattan, where its General Assembly met in a handsome hall, whose sloping tiers of seats urged everyone to attend to what the speaker was saying from the green marble rostrum. As Americans formally denounced their onetime allies, in this last week of their presidential contest, a new audience responded, an intoxicating, emotional Third World audience.

From the new rostrum, the once-outnumbered spokesmen of new nations had always denounced the imperialism of the white empires. They had been politely applauded, because the "guilty" white delegates controlled the majority of United Nations votes so securely that they could indulge the rhetoric of the lesser peoples of the Third World. But now in 1956, of the UN's seventy-six constituents, one-third were already members of what was styled the "Triple A bloc"—a code phrase for Arabs, Africans, Asians, all warped by history to hate the white men who had frog-jumped them into the modern world.

That fall of 1956 was a moment of transition in international discourse. The massacre of Hungarians by the Russians had not engaged the emotions of the Triple A bloc—that was white against white. But the strike of the English and French to repossess control of the Suez Canal had thoroughly disturbed them—that was white against colored. The Foreign Minister of Sudan—a coal-black, gold-rim-bespectacled gentleman—speaking in the pure accent of a British public school boy, ripped the rhetoric of the British and French imperialists as "a bluff, a trick, a big lie." The United Nations, not yet as racist as it is now, rang with applause. In this environment moved the American delegation to the United Nations, instructed by Dulles to denounce with all force the actions of its allies the British, the French, the Israelis. As the United States demanded immediate cease-fires in both Suez and Hungary, delegates of the Triple A bloc came up to wring the hands of American delegates.

All the rest of the last week of the campaign of 1956 was dominated not by what the American candidates said but by the bloodshed reported from the outside world. The Russians closed efficiently on Budapest, using artillery and tanks to crush the insurrection. The British and French moved sluggishly and blunderingly to occupy the Suez Canal zone with their paratroopers and slow troop transports. Not until dawn on Monday, November 5, did French and British paratroopers begin to drop. Only on November 6, which was election day in America, did the British and French commandos begin actual landings to back up the paratroopers. All that week, American diplomats had been publicly denouncing this stumbling aggression—all the while wistfully, confidentially, wishing that their onetime allies would strike harder, quicker. The American Sixth Fleet was caught in the combat zone melee, confused by its sympathies with the British fleet and the public report of its country's diplomacy. Admiral Brown of the Sixth Fleet wired back to Washington: "Who's the enemy?" No one could answer. Dulles, exhausted by a week of moralities, judgments, and hypocrisies, had just been carried off to the hospital for an emergency probe of his cancer. A few weeks later, when visited by British Foreign Secretary Selwyn Lloyd, he asked, privately, "Why did you stop?" of the English statesman whom he had tried so hard to stop publicly.

A few days after the election, I spoke with another English diplomat, whom I had come to know and admire in postwar Europe, Sir Pierson Dixon. Pierson Dixon was of the World War II generation and cherished the Anglo-American alliance that had saved the world. Now he was thoroughly disillusioned with America. So was his Prime Minister, Eden, who had long ago watched the sequence of aggressions before World War II—Japan in Manchuria, Italy in Ethiopia, Germany in Sudetenland. "That couldn't be forgotten by him," said Dixon. Nasser of Egypt was on the move now, bribing officers of the Iraqi army, trying to overthrow or assassinate King Idris in Libya, using his fanatic Moslem muezzins to call, over the radio, for assassination of Faisal in Saudi Arabia, of Nuri in Iraq.

Pierson Dixon was the British spokesman at the United Nations, where the United States had just put Britain down. "This is a crisis in Anglo-American relations," he continued. "Ever since World War II, the United Kingdom has followed the United States. We went along with the United States on Guatemala. We went along on Korea.

We went along on Red China, despite our trouble in Parliament. We went along on all United States problems of vital concern—but where our vital concerns were involved, we were judged in terms of morality."

Dixon ruefully continued, "We had come to the conclusion that an outbreak of fighting was bound to come [in the Middle East]. We didn't ask the United States first, because at the end of a presidential campaign it would have put an intolerable burden on American politics."

So the British moved by themselves to recapture the Suez, with the French in support. "Our calculation was," said Dixon, "we could expect from the United States either a hostile neutrality, a benevolent neutrality, or simple neutrality. We never believed that the United States would galvanize the United Nations against us. What stopped us was the fact that the United States had galvanized the UN into considerable action; and that the United States might cooperate with the UN against us in economic sanctions."

How much Eisenhower's last-minute posture influenced the outcome of the election of 1956 can never be known. He was ahead in the polls at all times. Dulles's policy and Eisenhower's acquiescence had opened him, however, to an attack from Adlai Stevenson. Campaigning in Cincinnati as the British were preparing to strike, and the Russians were taking advantage of the situation both in Hungary and in the Middle East, Stevenson proclaimed: "I cannot remember any other series of diplomatic strokes so erratic, naive, and clumsy as the events of the past few years through which Russia gained welcome to the Near and Middle East." But once Eisenhower had taken the moral line, Stevenson was trapped. On November 1, on nationwide radio and television, Stevenson, too, took the moral line: "We now have an opportunity to use our great moral authority, our own statesmanship, the weight of our economic power, to bring about solutions to the complex problems confronting the Free World in the Middle East." Such campaign talk does not stir hearts. Stevenson, in common talk, was a good guy; but Ike was also a good guy; and a soldier; and his imposing record commanded respect. On November 5, the day before the election, the Gallup Poll showed Eisenhower so far ahead of Stevenson as to be unreachable—enough American voters apparently had swung to him in the last ten days to suggest a victory margin of 59 percent to 40 percent.

On Tuesday, November 6, 1956, the voters went to the polls, as radio brought news that added up to chaos. Belatedly, the French and British had landed their troops in Egypt even as the United Nations, backed by America, demanded their withdrawal; the British now controlled the entrance to the canal. In Hungary, the Russians now shelled Budapest at point-blank range, and seized the Hungarian Premier, Imre Nagy, whom they would, in their ungentle way, deport. By dusk, however, the British and French had bowed to American pressure and ceased operations along the Suez Canal. The Russians now had nailed down Eastern Europe. But we had forced our allies out of the Middle East. And the Americans that day by 57.4 percent chose Eisenhower (with 35.6 million votes) over Stevenson, with 42 percent of the vote (26 million). At his victory celebration at Washington's Sheraton Park Hotel, at almost two in the morning, the victorious President modestly summed it up: "Such a vote . . . cannot be merely for an individual. It is for principles and ideals for which that individual and his associates have stood and have tried to exemplify."

The voters apparently liked Eisenhower's message. The country was at peace, and the memory of old victories still lingered. At home, the country settled down quickly after the election, for it had disturbed America less than any election since 1924. Although the last two weeks had brought excitement enough abroad, the Old Country could not sense that both its old familiar and its promising new ways would have to change in the near future because the world of American power was buckling under the surge of restless peoples overseas.

Not until 1968 would the restless outer world become central again to an American presidential campaign. By then, the same bedeviling morality that triumphed over reality in the Suez climax to the campaign of 1956 would have led us on into Vietnam. There, to save Vietnam from Communism, we destroyed, with the best intentions of conscience, an estimated half-million Vietnamese and sacrificed almost 58,000 American lives. And by 1980's election, the Middle East would have become our problem, not that of the British or the French. At home, Eisenhower's monumental highway building program had invited Americans out to suburbia, with its green lawns and shopping malls, and intoxicated them with the cheap gasoline sucked away by tanker from the Middle East. By the election of 1980, twenty-four years after the 1956 election, the Middle East sheikhdoms and desert warlords had raised the price of oil from its 1956 cost of ten cents a barrel to thirty-two dollars a barrel. The

Great Inflation was under way, swollen as much by the cost of oil as by the cost of good intentions at home. Inflation was largely a recognition that the age of plenty was over; printing more money could not paper over the distress.

In retrospect, the coincidence of the Suez crisis with the election of 1956 had befuddled America's ability to discriminate between its moralities and its interests. Election campaigns have, over and over again, sharpened issues for the American people—from the forecast of the Monroe Doctrine in the campaign of 1820, to Ronald Reagan's forecast of the New Economics in the campaign of 1980. The campaign of 1956 had, however, perpetuated an illusion—that American power was unlimited. We could, indeed, undermine the will of our allies; undermining the will of our adversaries would be more difficult. And just over the horizon of history, new enemies were about to join the old and recognized enemies. We had given such enemies the opening to choke off the flow of oil and energy on which the new American way of life depended. That was the largest lesson history would read into the campaign of 1956.

Between the campaign in the Old Country of 1956 and the campaign of 1980 would intervene the storms, alarms, raids, and upheavals of the storm decade, when the best of American thinking continued in the illusion that the national power was as unlimited at home as abroad.

In that passage of politics, too, goodwill and good intentions would prevail over the realities; and with the help of television, change them.

PART II
THE TRANSFORMATION
OF AMERICAN POLITICS:
1960-1979

INTERPASSAGE

IDEAS IN MOTION

There is an underlying rhythm that sweeps through American politics which is usually traced by episodes and wars, styles and movements. But it is almost hopeless to make patterns of these swings by such conventional terms as "liberal years" or "conservative years," and wholly useless to apply the European grids of left versus right.

Such terms are completely inadequate to explain American history, or the political tides that washed out the contours of the Old Country, then gave way to the crests of the sixties and seventies, and then shaped the election of 1980.

America is, above all, about ideas and dreams—far more so than interests. A returning observer, coming home as I did in the early fifties from years of reporting in Asia and Europe, could see how different American politics were from all other political systems—so very different that most Americans scarcely recognized the nature of their history. It was a succession of ideas, molding, changing, kneading together for common purpose migrants from all the world. It was not a fanciful set of ideas, like those of Marx or Cicero; it had no dogmas. But the underlying idea of brotherhood and opportunity was so compelling that, when it was invoked, all other considerations had to yield, all politicians bow.

Yet ideas change and take on new interpretations. And it is impossible to understand Ronald Reagan's victory in 1980 without trying to trace the ideas that had burst in events which, for twenty years before him, changed American life and the use of its power.

A metaphor once occurred to me: that of the "cloud chamber." In the early years of the American apprenticeship in the use of the atom's power, I, like all American reporters, had tried to learn quickly a few basic facts about nuclear matters; and I had come across one of the simpler tools in the early exploration of the atom, the so-called cloud chamber. Into this apparatus—a small chamber supercharged with vapor—an experimenter could inject an invisible nuclear particle. Such an invisible particle might collide with another infinitesimal nuclear particle. If it did, the collision would leave a wake of droplets—as invisible chips broke off, changed direction, ionized their path through the vapor—and become not only visible, but photographable. Physicists could not see the nuclear particles, but they could trace their path by the tiny droplets spurting from the invisible, mothering thrusts, leaving events behind to be recognized.

Thus, in real life, invisible ideas mark their way by the events that result from the collisions they leave behind in men's minds. In America, it was quite clear that so many ideas had crossed the cloud chambers of the American mind in the twenty years between 1960 and 1980 that the country had experienced something tantamount to a revolution. Indeed, it *was* a revolution, except that it was a revolution American style—relatively bloodless but bannered with the slogans of hope and liberty. The revolution had affected life styles, sex relations, race relations, manners, morals, and the uses of science. But most of all, the revolution affected politics. Whether Reagan's victory in 1980 was simply a reformation, or a counterrevolution, remains yet to be seen. But his victory, and all the following chapters of this book, are incomprehensible unless one traces the course of those ideas through American politics in the years that preceded him.

Three fundamental ideas must necessarily be grasped before we can go on to relate in the next three chapters the episodes that clustered about them.

The first of these ideas was as old as the original American revolution: the idea of equality and liberty before the law. It was to be translated, in the two decades before Reagan, into the key slogans of the Democrats: Participation and Entry. All groups were to be included in the public process, the public welfare, and the public service. All groups, lost in the corridors of the Old Country, were to be brought first to light, then to education, then to benefits or entitlements. This idea was to change all political realities, for it led to the definition of groups, by age and sex, by color and race, and each group spawned other groups, splintering the country instead of opening it.

There was a second idea, accepted by all at the beginning of the 1960s, though generally unvoiced: the idea of limitless abundance flowing from unquestioned American power. American abundance could install, as an act of generosity, the first strip steel mills in postwar Europe and Japan; it could urge the Japanese and the Europeans not only to share in the American marketplace but also, more important, in the technology and resources of America and of the world that America dominated. At home, American abundance could promise rewards and entitlements to every group that could be defined as having a moral claim—from the blacks and Hispanics, to the Asians and Indians, from those whose cause was the environment, to those whose cause was education, and those whose cause was the price of sugar, milk, or tobacco. As the abundance was leached away, the promises became more and more burdensome and the result was the Great Inflation and a total change in common thinking. It is as impossible to write of the election of 1980 without examining the curse of inflation as it is to write of the election of 1932 without pondering the Depression.

The third of the great ideas to undergo change was as old as the Constitution—the nature of the federal Union which united the several states. But the Union existed only in a climate of opinion. The Civil War had been as much a fight about the Union as about the extension of slavery; yet it might never have come to pass had not the country been split by the doctrines and opinion-makers of its separate regions and sections. From the Civil War on, technology slowly undermined the states as centers of opinion. The telegraph, telephone, and railways urged the process on; the coming of the national magazines hastened it; by the 1920s, radio and advertising had made the marketplace one, as national brands and chain stores spread; and the films of Hollywood made dreaming national. Then came television, the most unsettling event in Western society since the invention of printing. Arthur Schlesinger, Jr., has said: "Karl Marx held that history is shaped by control of the means of production; in our times history is shaped by control of the means of communication." Television nationalized public opinion, fused the federal Union into an audience. The forum of politics at once broadened with instant reach from coast to coast, yet was squeezed down to access to the handful of network studios. Television weighed in on the side of centralization, remaking the map into ADIs, Areas of Dominant Influence, slicing it into demographic layers. National politics without television would today be inconceivable. So would the victory of Ronald Reagan.

In the next three chapters, I want to look at how these three ideas changed, and in changing, changed the nation.

CHAPTER FOUR

THE GREAT SOCIETY

It was the explosive renascence of the idea of equality that transformed American politics between 1960 and 1980.

There was no real date for the insurgency that idea brought forth. But one could watch it take shape in the streets, in riots and bloodshed, with horrors broadcast into every home. It began with events that I, or any other reporter, could observe or even join. And then one could see it move off the streets into the thinking of the nation, toppling old walls; and as the occupiers moved in, the occupation spread larger than anyone could understand.

Old phrases only dimly recall the transformation of the times: "Liberation," "Participation," "Affirmative Action," "Outreach," "Goals and Timetables." And all of them added up to a paradox: What began as a quest to expand the definition of freedom was to end in the centralization of federal controls on a scale never envisioned by those who dreamed the dreams of the early sixties and still remembered John F. Kennedy calling, "I say this country must move again." New words like "quotas," "entitlements," and the officialese "protected classes" replaced older words, changing the nature of the American government.

In all this, the original and most powerful motor drive was the revolt of the blacks.

It was they who, for years, had been testing the oldest of American ideas, the idea of equality before the law, to see whether that idea, and the laws supporting it, could stand the test of reality. The Black Revolt had been coming for a long time; the battle had been fought in the courts and in Congress, and now in the sixties it would burst into the streets and violence. The blacks were those Americans most deprived of their rights ever since the Constitution first tried to define what the Declaration of Independence meant by defining the nature of the federal Union—and excluding blacks.

Memory flecks the drive of the idea with episode; and it is from 1964, and the succeeding presidential years, that my own memory recalls a handful of episodes most vividly:

• It is spring 1964, the mood of the time still unsettled by the first assassination, and the visions John F. Kennedy had left behind. The Civil Rights Act, which Kennedy had brought before Congress in 1963, is now moving through Congress. If it passes, it will change American society, and the debate has already stretched on through the winter and spring months. But as the debate boils on Capitol Hill, the action is elsewhere, so as a political reporter, I am off to Mississippi, where the Student Nonviolent Coordinating Committee (SNCC) is mobilizing for the bloody adventure that would be remembered as the Mississippi Summer.

I have not been in Mississippi for eighteen years, and now, driving into Jackson, its capital, I am reluctant to ask directions from local whites, who regard all Northerners with squint-eyed suspicion. In the next few months, three young white people from the North will be murdered by them. So with the aid of a Jackson street map, I try to find my destination. I pass through the black district, so different from black ghettos in the North. Grassless lawns, littered with trash; shack houses with peeling paint, boards cracked and broken; raggedy children sitting on porches, peering out on nothing. I pass a black cemetery, pillars of the gates leaning toward each other, the scraggly grass already very high in springtime, but unmowed and unkempt, sad, Faulknerian. It does its own mourning. And there next to the Streamline Bar is 1017 Lynch Street, SNCC storefront headquarters. It is unmarked but instantly recognizable—two students, one black and one white, are standing outside playing catch in friendship; and in the windows are those black and green stickers that say: ONE MAN —ONE VOTE.

The dominant presence here is Bob Moses, the field marshal of the adventure drawing hundreds of students from all over the country. He talks in the accent that New York schoolteachers have indeli-

bly pressed on Harlem children for a generation; but he is a Harvard
M.A. Blinking, soft-spoken, gentle, Moses has been here in Mississippi
for three years, trying to rouse his black people to their rights. They
must be taught to vote; they must be taught to do things for themselves; they must be taught to be unafraid. He is sweet and stubborn
and strong, the stuff of martyrs; he will not kill but will not hesitate
to die. Five blacks here in Mississippi have been killed by unknown
men since the first of the year; Moses has spent seventeen days in
solitary confinement in jail; his people are organizing the Mississippi
Freedom Democratic Party to challenge for the right to vote. A few
whites and most blacks are joined together in this. The white newcomers from the North are being taught that it is just barely possible
for a white boy and a black boy to ride together; but a black boy and
a white girl in the same car, "that's risking your life in Mississippi,"
says Moses. And there is no one in authority to whom Moses can talk,
no contact. No white official in Mississippi dares have contact with
the blacks.

That evening I meet with the governor of Mississippi, Paul B.
Johnson. He is both firm and frightened. If all "they" do is meet and
picket peacefully, there'll be no trouble with the police, he says. But
what if they rouse the Klan? and the Negroes counterdemonstrate?
He has only 250 state highway patrolmen at his command to keep
order. He says he has no room to maneuver, he can't give an inch.

• A few weeks later, in New York, the evening before the opening of the 1964 World's Fair. The papers and television have been
churning out the story of impending disaster. The blacks are threatening to drive in and stall their cars on all the highways feeding to
the fair, blocking all traffic. I drive out to the storefront headquarters
of the "stall-in" organizers, deep in the Bedford-Stuyvesant ghetto,
at 319 Nostrand Avenue, Brooklyn. It lies between a Chinese hand
laundry and a meat market; its broken glass windows are boarded
over. Inside, the blacks glower at the coming of a white stranger, not
at all like the black smiles at SNCC in Jackson, Mississippi. On the
wall a sign: NO STATEMENT WILL BE GIVEN WITHOUT PERMISSION OF
THE CHAIRMAN. Another: NO OUTGOING CALLS AFTER TEN AM MON-
DAY BY ORDER OF ISIAH. A man approaches and says to me, "No
reporters are allowed in here if they talk to *anybody.*"

Isiah finally arrives and consents to talk. He is Isiah Brunson, all
of twenty-two years old, two years out of South Carolina, a carpenter's son. He is soft-spoken, slow, with a fine, thoroughly black face,

hair close-cropped; innocent. But his conversation makes no sense, he is incoherent. I drive back with a black reporter of a New York newspaper, who explains in rage that the whites have broken the social contract; he is deprived of his freedom. He hopes that Isiah's putsch tomorrow will succeed. "You just don't understand," he says. "If a thousand innocent people have to be killed . . . if that's the way it has to be, well, that's the way it has to be."

It seems preposterous that this handful of black youngsters in a boarded-up storefront in Brooklyn can, the next day, paralyze New York City's celebration. Yet their statements have caught the attention of television and the press—that is their leverage. The entire New York police force will be mobilized the next morning; but the dignitaries of the nation, from President Johnson on down, will leapfrog the demonstration and come to the opening of the fair by helicopter. All except Senator Jacob Javits, born in a New York slum himself and now approaching his great authority as senator; he will go by subway, and walk into the fair on foot, black picket lines notwithstanding. I accompany the senator on the subway, no television crowding us in those days. And when we get off the subway expecting to brave the chaos of demonstrations—there is nothing, nothing at all. Isiah's threat had been a nightmare mirage; there are no stalled crowds, no marching pickets, no banners demanding whatever it was that Isiah demanded of New York City.

Isiah Brunson and Bob Moses were both, shortly, to disappear from public attention, perhaps forever. Isiah meant nothing, for he expressed only incoherent rage. Moses was reality, for he spoke from conscience and ideas, and his ideas would triumph.

Across the nation the black revolt had been growing with increasing tempo—in Oxford, in Birmingham, in Tallahassee, in Chicago—for years and years, stretching back to Nat Turner's rebellion in 1831. And now it was coming to the politics, not of Congress, but of the nation; it was coming to the convention of the Democrats in Atlantic City.

The conventions, for all their sham and pageantry, despite all the changes in their functions and their erosion by the primaries, are still theaters of political passion. The conventions are where new groups first beat for entry into the power circle. And now, at Atlantic City, the black demand is to burst with a howl.

The howl comes in a closed and steaming room of committee hearings on credentials, to determine the legitimacy of delegates. Outside, a thin line of pickets, black and white together, ring the convention hall, chanting "We Shall Overcome." They have come from all over the nation and include the young veterans of the Mississippi Summer. They insist that the Mississippi Freedom Democratic Party has a legitimate right to be seated in the national convention because Mississippi blacks have been excluded from the right to vote. Upstairs, in the hearing room, a black woman, Fannie Lou Hamer, is voicing the demand with a wail that torments everyone in the chamber, as she tells what happened in Mississippi when she tried to register to vote. She had been arrested, and she went on:

"It wasn't too long before three white men came to my cell. . . . I was carried out of the cell into another cell where they had two Negro prisoners. The state highway patrolmen ordered the first Negro to take the blackjack. . . . I laid on my face. The first Negro began to beat, and I was beat until he was exhausted. . . . The second Negro began to beat and I began to work my feet. . . . I began to scream, and one white man got up and began to beat me on my head and tell me to 'hush.' One white man—my dress had worked up high —he walked over and pulled my dress down and he pulled my dress back, back up. . . . All of this is on account we want to register, to become first-class citizens, and if the Freedom Democratic Party is not seated now, I question America."

Three days later, the blacks of the Freedom Democratic Party had invaded the convention hall and occupied the seats of the all-white regular Mississippi Democratic delegation. The Mississippi blacks were clearly illegal, the Mississippi whites clearly immoral. But Lyndon Johnson held the Democratic party in his hand; his chief surrogate was the young Democratic attorney general of Minnesota, Walter Mondale, who negotiated with black and white, with Johnson's whip to back him up. All together they worked out a compromise: The blacks of the Mississippi Freedom Democratic Party would be given two voting seats at this convention. But—*far more important*—beginning with the next convention, in 1968, no delegation would be seated from any state where the party process deprived citizens of their right to vote because of race or color.

The Mississippi compromise lay midway between two of the most significant acts of legislation which the Congress of the United States passed in the last twenty years—midway between the Civil Rights Act of 1964 and the Voting Rights Act of 1965. And since the underlying faith of the country in equality had been called to account before the bar of conscience not only by the Democratic party in its convention but by the entire nation, the authority of government required what conscience required: full equality of all citizens before the law. The definition of full equality had just been redefined for the nation by the Civil Rights Act signed by Lyndon Johnson on July 2, 1964, seven weeks before the Democratic convention.

One should linger over the Civil Rights Act of 1964, for it is a watershed in both politics and history. All previous acts of regulation by the federal government had been regulations of things and standards—of railroads and wavelengths, of foods and drugs, of weights and measures. The Civil Rights Act was a new departure: it undertook to regulate behavior. Its purpose was to change the customs and manners of the American people.*

The Civil Rights Act of 1964 guaranteed blacks access to all public accommodations across the nation: not just schools, restaurants, and theaters, but hotels and motels (excluding only the hypothetical "Mrs. Murphy's boardinghouse," if it had five or less rooms). The new law instructed the Justice Department to sue if necessary to enforce desegregation of all such facilities. The Civil Rights Commission was instructed to gather civil rights information and investigate any denial of the right to vote.

It went further: A five-man Equal Employment Opportunities Commission (EEOC) was set up. All of American industry was to fall under its police power; any industry or union ("affecting commerce") which employed more than twenty-five workers was to be summoned to account if it was suspect of discriminating against individuals "because of such individual's color, religion, sex, or national origin." At one stroke now, women and ethnics were also to fall under the protection of government.

All the powers of government, prodigious already, were to be invoked to enforce the new measures. Any program, any activity, any institution, any contractor, benefiting in any way, small or large, from federal funds would find those funds cut off if discrimination against anyone could be proved. Universities and hospitals, hotels and theaters, airlines and mail-order houses, unions and manufacturers, cities and states, could now be summoned to account for their behavior. As a final touch, the act instructed the Census of 1970 to gather statistics by race in order to measure whether denial of voting rights had taken place because of race. Officially, then, the United States was seeking to define race distinctions among its citizens.

One large cautionary note is worth recalling in the watershed

*For a fuller discussion of the background of the Civil Rights Act, see *The Making of the President—1964*. Also, Carl M. Brauer, *John F. Kennedy and The Second Reconstruction* (New York: Columbia University Press, 1977). Also, Howell Raines, *My Soul Is Rested* (New York: G. P. Putnam's Sons, 1977).

Civil Rights Act. Its purpose was to ensure equality; the phrase "protected classes" had not yet entered government jargon. And the act warns that nothing in its text "shall be interpreted to require any employer . . . to grant preferential treatment to any individual or to any group on account of an imbalance which may exist with respect to the total number or percentage of persons of any race, color, religion, sex, or national origin employed by any employer."

That provision was, slowly but inexorably, to be reversed as the culture of liberation overtook the old idea of equality.

No better example of the movement of an idea through the mind of a man can be found than by tracing the idea of civil rights through the politics of Lyndon B. Johnson.

Running for the United States Senate from Texas in 1948, Johnson declared at a rally in Austin: "This civil rights program, about which you have heard so much, is a farce and a sham—an effort to set up a police state in the guise of liberty. I am opposed to that program. I fought it in Congress. It is the province of the state to run its own elections. I am opposed to the anti-lynching bill because the federal government has no more business enacting a law against one kind of murder than another. I am against the FEPC [Fair Employment Practices Commission] because if a man can tell you whom you must hire, he can tell you whom you cannot employ. I have met this head-on."

Thus Lyndon Johnson, congressman and candidate for the Senate in 1948. But Lyndon Johnson as President seventeen years later had been responsible for the passage of the great Civil Rights Act in 1964, and was moving on to drive Congress to pass its substantive partner, the Voting Rights Act, in 1965.

"That bill," said Johnson, in impassioned advocacy of the Voting Rights Act at Howard University on June 4, 1965, would be "not the end . . . not even the beginning of the end. But it is perhaps the end of the beginning. . . . That beginning is freedom; and the barriers to that freedom are tumbling down. . . . We seek not just legal equity but human ability, not just equality as a right and a theory but equality as *a fact and equality as a result.*"

A subtle change had transformed equality of opportunity to equality in result, but Johnson went on to explain:

". . . there are differences—deep, corrosive, obstinate differences. . . . These differences are not racial differences. They are solely and simply the consequence of ancient brutality, past injustice and present prejudice. . . . For the Negro they are a constant reminder of oppression. For the white they are a constant reminder of guilt."

What differences existed, therefore, were now, in Johnson's mind, subject to remedial action, and those deprived of rights were entitled to remedies.

The Great Society programs that accompanied and followed the Voting Rights Act of 1965 were designed largely to remedy past injustice. And at this point, most Americans would have considered, and I certainly so, that Lyndon Johnson was among the great Presidents of all American history.

What followed, however, were events too large to compress in a short sketch on the transformation of politics. Within five days of the signing into law of the Voting Rights bill (August 6, 1965), there followed the first of the historic black riots of the sixties—in the Watts section of Los Angeles. Then followed the other black riots of the sixties, from Newark to Detroit to Boston, all of which were, in essence, revolts against authority, provoked usually by real or imaginary police abuse of authority. With black riots flaming the summer skies from 1966 to 1968, white conscience was tormented, but white fears rose. The cleavage between the races, in the streets and the suburbs, mocked the high eloquence of those who still pursued the hope of harmony and a national community. At the executive and television level of American life, the ablest of the blacks would be increasingly accepted; at the grass-roots level where the rub came, whites would begin to flee from anticipated violence. The cleavage in the streets would be amplified to the cleavage in the black community—between those accepted and moving forward, and those despised and ever more resentful.

But political participation for blacks had been won. There had been only two black congressmen in 1960. By 1980, along with Ronald Reagan, were elected seventeen black congressmen; and their caucus was among the most formidable in the House. Where there had been only 103 elected black officials in the United States in 1964, there were, by 1980, some 4,900. And where the black revolt had once demanded that all school districts be desegregated so that black children would nowhere be clustered as a segregated majority, it now demanded that congressional districts be arbitrarily segregated so that black voters would be clustered together to elect their own black representatives to Congress.

Countless other groups were to follow through the sixties into the seventies, claiming their rights, asserting morality. Clergymen had, for the first time since Prohibition, reentered the forum of politics to mobilize support for the Civil Rights Act of 1964. The handicapped entered the arena; the old people too. So did the gays. So did those whose cause was environment, as well as those whose cause was to protect the nation from any and all fallout from the nuclear world. There, in the arena of public pressure, they joined the older cause people of labor, of big business, and of the farm.

The parochial memory of this reporter is, however, caught most by presidential campaigns and the major new entrants into old politics. Thus, my memory of political movement through the transformation is caught next by the youth revolt, and hangs on the Democratic convention of 1968 in Chicago, the most dramatic convention of modern times.

Youth had never been seen as a separate problem group in American history. "Youth" was a family matter, left to parents; left also to schools, which bred patriotism, and to the old loyalties, which furnished "soldier boys" in time of war. Youth was accepted as a glandular episode in the stages of life, which would, without doubt, be cured by the simple passage of time, when "youth" became parents and taxpayers in their turn.

But by 1967, "student youth" had become a force in American politics, as it had long been a force in countries overseas.

There were first of all the numbers. In 1939, as America prepared for war, only 1.3 million students attended the nation's colleges and universities. By 1968, this number had exploded to 6.9 million. (By 1980, to be sure, their number would have grown further to 11.4 million.) College had in the old days been the entryway for those aspiring to join the elite. By the late 1960s, and more so in the 1970s, college was to become the avenue to any career beyond that of blue-collar worker or supermarket clerk. College youth had reached mass size. In 1968, so much had the country changed that college youth outnumbered farmers by three to one, railway workers by nine to one, coal miners by fifty to one. They had become not only a campus proletariat, but as politically important in carrying states like Wisconsin or Massachusetts as coal miners in West Virginia or automobile workers in Michigan. They had become, in short, a critical mass—ready to let go at the spark of ignition.

The spark of ignition was, by 1967, already there: the war in Vietnam, the most mismanaged war in American history. The war was, in the eyes of educated youth, illegal: no Congress had voted either a declaration of war or a national emergency; yet they were being drafted by executive command for a cause no one properly explained, and their lives were at stake. For a brief period in American politics, new names of passing influence floated to the surface—one remembers Lowenstein, Gans, Hayden, Hersh, Hoffman, Hart, and countless others, all disgusted with the war, all convinced that by demonstration and action they could bring it to a halt.

I remember best a young man named Sam Brown, then twenty-four, a divinity student; he was certain he could organize youth platoons to support Eugene McCarthy in New Hampshire against warmaker Lyndon Johnson. Brown-eyed, curly-haired, slim, and pale-cheeked, he had left Harvard's Divinity School convinced that government must be driven to do what his conscience told him must be done. By early 1968, he had organized the first student mobilization to overturn Johnson, and from a storefront headquarters in Manchester, New Hampshire, he had organized that student movement which was to give substance to Eugene McCarthy's challenge, and force the withdrawal of a President. Brown would go on, later, to be elected state treasurer of Colorado and then, under Carter, would become chief of ACTION, the federal agency directing VISTA and the Peace Corps. But in 1968, a single cause moved him. "Study in universities is irrelevant," he said. "The war is on our minds. The rhetoric of the government is outmoded—the problem is how you affect government."

Episodes of youth in revolt stud the record: the march on the Pentagon in October 1967; the sweep of the early 1968 primaries by McCarthy students, challenged shortly by students who counterorganized for Robert Kennedy. Ivy League and state university students alike were learning to organize transcontinentally, learning to canvass, count votes, computerize projections. One recalls the riots at Columbia University in the spring of 1968; the riots at Harvard in 1969, with its overseers meeting off campus at the medical school across the river, to avoid the demonstrators; then the climactic and tragic confrontation in 1970 at Ohio's Kent State University.

But what remains fixed most sharply in memory is the student intrusion at the 1968 Democratic convention in Chicago. They had come with a spearhead and a shaft. The spearhead was a small group of young men and women, trained in scholarship and research; their documents and analyses of how a convention was organized and how delegates were chosen in the obscene customs of the Old Country pierced every intelligence and prodded change. But their shaft lay in the streets, where their rioting and demonstrating caught the cameras and national attention.

I watched their climax demonstration in Chicago—an almost all-white group of innocents and crazies all jumbled together, controlled by squawk boxes of the National Mobilization Committee to End the War in Vietnam.*

Down Michigan Avenue they march, chanting and yelling: "Peace now, peace now," "Stop the war, stop the war," "Fuck you, LBJ, fuck you, LBJ." Police in triple ranks stand at the corner of Balbo Drive and Michigan Avenue, behind yellow barricades; cellophane sacks of toilet waste are being thrown at the police, bundled packets of leaflets are being hurled from hotel windows, trash cans tossed. In the swaying mass of demonstrators, momentarily halted, fly red flags of the revolution, black flags of anarchists; Omega banners; and Vietcong flags of the enemy.

And then, slam, like a coiled response, the police reserves from Balbo Drive are thrown in. Like a punch, they jolt. The police move, like a wedge, into the packed mob and split it; youngsters are hustled off by the elbows, their heels dragging on the ground; a woman is dragged along the pavement, her head bumping the concrete. The police club; tear gas bursts over the crowd. The squawk boxes of the mobilization call out: "Cool it now, lots of people are getting hurt. . . . Cool it, cool it. . . . Please don't throw things, don't throw things."

I was watching the scene from the third-floor window of the Blackstone Hotel; and my emotions repeated those that had swept me four years before at Atlantic City. My sympathies lay there in the street with the youngsters, as they had rested with the blacks of Mississippi who had, illegally, invaded and occupied the seats on the convention floor. But while abhorring the brutality below, my reason told me that the police were doing what was required—though with too joyful zest; there could be no other recourse, except to force, to defend convention headquarters and the law itself. One hundred yards more and the demonstrators would have overrun the Conrad Hilton Hotel, where both candidates—Hubert Humphrey and Eugene McCarthy—and the headquarters of the Democratic party were established. To permit rioters to overwhelm that most sensitive of all points in the politics of the convention would have been to let violence prevail over process. Thus, the response was necessary—not with the brutality and cruelties of the Chicago police, but necessary nonetheless.

---

*For a full description of the battle of Balbo and Michigan, see *The Making of the President—1968* (New York: Atheneum, 1969), pp. 295–9.

The scene refuses to fade. Lyndon Johnson, as Patrick Moynihan later said, had already been "toppled by a mob of . . . flower children and Radcliffe girls"; they would, in due course during the fall season, undermine and destroy the candidacy of Hubert Humphrey, the most committed liberal of the twentieth century. But the memory of the scene obscures what the youngsters had accomplished:

First, if the Vietnam War was lost, as it was to be, a major defeat had occurred on the streets of Chicago. "The whole world is watching, the whole world is watching," chanted the youngsters as television lights and cameras carried the scene around the world to Vietnam, encouraging enemy resistance in that Asian civil war which was to end with the victory of a new tyranny.

Second, the Democratic party was to undergo a fundamental change from an unplanned contraption of Old Country blocs to a disciplined party within which separate groups were legally entitled to special consideration. Swept by noise and clamor, punished by television's snatches of the youngsters' sad confrontation with police, the Democrats, in order to mollify the protest, would pass two resolutions to reform the party. These resolutions, designed to purify the way delegates were selected, required every individual state party to give youth, minorities, and women proper representation at future conventions—or be excluded. No matter how ordinary Democratic voters might vote in the future at primaries or caucuses, these groups *must* be guaranteed representation in and of their own right, not as representatives of the general electoral constituency.

The student revolt—a revolt against the war, the draft, the killings in Asia—was one of the shortest-lived phenomena in American politics. It had begun in 1967; had boiled into violence at a dozen campuses; had reached its tragic ending in the Kent State killings of 1970. By 1971, however, "youth" had received its ultimate acknowledgment as full and equal citizens: a constitutional amendment, lowering the voting age in every state of the Union to eighteen. If a man was old enough to fight, ran the reasoning, he was old enough to vote. Swept by this logic, Congress passed, on March 23, and Richard Nixon—very reluctantly—signed this proposal. With record speed it had been ratified by July 1, 1971, as the Twenty-sixth Amendment to the federal Constitution.

The political alarms set off by the youth revolt were over with the passage of their amendment. The consequences of that revolt were, however, longer-lived—as long-lasting, perhaps, as the residue of the G.I. Bill of Rights twenty-five years earlier. Here was a new

generation in politics. Most of the earnest youngsters of the 1968
insurgency of Eugene McCarthy and Robert Kennedy, as well as
most of the youngsters of the McGovern campaign of 1972, would go
on to jobs, careers, homes, and families, with the insurgency only a
romantic memory. But thousands would not give up the memory.
They had developed new techniques of vote-gathering, learned how
brittle were the old machines they had challenged, outwitted the
Old Country politicians over and over again, recognized computorial
analysis and television manipulation as vital tools of the politics to
come. Such veterans would choose to stay on in politics; and would
harden as all insurrectionaries do from managers to professionals. In
the twelve years after 1968, the youngsters of the revolt, Republicans
as much as Democrats, would become the field corps of both the
Carter and the Reagan campaigns of 1980.

Blacks and youth had won their entrance to equality by violence
and demonstration in the streets, as much as by appeal to conscience.
The next group would win, by appeal to conscience alone, victories
that may be even longer-lasting.

These were the women of America.

One must be cautious in writing of women as a group, for they
are as different among themselves as men; but their activists are
sensitive to slight, phrase, and indifference—and their militants violent in response.

One should start with nature: Nature has distributed wisdom
and resolution in equal proportions among both sexes—but has also
subjected women to the special burdens of motherhood, and to certain muscular weaknesses. Of American women, it may be said further that the pioneer history of American life and the indenture to
poverty among the immigrants made American women full partners
in the national life before those of any other country. The first permanent voting rights ever yielded to women in the United States were
granted by the pioneer territory of Wyoming in 1869; and the nation
widened voting rights to all women by the Nineteenth Amendment,
passed by Congress in 1919. (In England, women were not allowed
to vote until 1928; in France and Italy, not until after World War II.)
American women as much as men drove the emancipation of blacks
to a political issue and then on to the Civil War. American women
nailed alcohol as a curse on the national mind, and then on to the
Prohibition amendment. American women, from Harriet Beecher
Stowe *(Uncle Tom's Cabin),* through Ida Tarbell *(History of the*

Standard Oil Company) and Rachel Carson *(The Silent Spring)*, to Betty Friedan *(The Feminine Mystique)*, shaped thinking and issues.

Yet women remained legally and socially unequal. From Thomas Jefferson, who said (in 1807): "The appointment of a woman to office is an innovation for which the public is not prepared, nor am I," to Supreme Court Justice Joseph Bradley, who declared (in 1873): "The paramount mission and destiny of women are to fulfill the noble and benign offices of wife and mother. This is the law of the Creator" —for over a century and a half, women were regarded, if not as chattel, as wards of the state and their families, protected in some cases by law, deprived in other cases of rights by the same laws. Down into the 1960s, women could be denied jobs simply because they were women; they could be denied the control of property simply because they were women; they could be denied access to credit simply because they were women; most of all, they could be denied the most intimate of rights—control over their pregnancies —through laws passed by men.

Protest by women started almost as early as the American Revolution. One can date the protest from a letter written in 1777 by that stalwart lady Abigail Adams to her husband, John Adams, as the first Congress sat down to write law: "I desire you would remember the ladies and be more generous and favorable to them than your ancestors. Do not put such unlimited power into the hands of husbands. . . . If particular care and attention is not paid to the ladies, we are determined to foment a rebellion and will not hold ourselves bound by the laws in which we have no voice or representation." The bitterness runs on and on, like the bitterness of blacks, as a theme in American history. On through the great women's rights convention of 1848 in Seneca Falls, New York, where women declared their cause was as worthy of attention as abolition and demanded not only the right to vote, but the right to testify in court, the right of guardianship over their own children, to equal pay, to control their own earnings, to higher education, the rights of property and testamentary bequests in their own names. On through the suffragettes, who finally won the right to vote in a constitutional amendment ratified in August of 1920.

Protest was always there, because injustice was always there. But the modern push for women's rights begins in the Kennedy administration, with the calling together of a Commission on the Status of Women in 1961; and from there on to the forming of the bipartisan National Women's Political Caucus (NWPC), ten years later. Until then, women had been a claimant group among many claimants on attention, a group recognized sporadically and symbolically by token appointments in government or by the voters in elections where the quality of an individual woman might command loyalties. The National Women's Political Caucus was different: It meant not to plead but to demand; not to beseech but to mobilize power, by votes, at any point of vulnerability in the male power structure.

Here, again, memory pinpoints a place and time of breakthrough—the Democratic convention at Miami in 1972. For there was no doubt that among the many power groups jostling each other in Miami, a totally new, almost irresistible center of pressure was the recently formed National Women's Political Caucus.

An old-fashioned male chauvinist might snicker, as at a bad soap opera, at the scene of their headquarters, the damp, dismal, seasprayed Betsy Ross Hotel, where the charge was eight dollars a night per room. Dank and uncomfortable ("I wouldn't have parked my watch there overnight," said one woman), it may someday become a comic interlude in a television series on women's rights. Phones jammed; elevators were crammed. Around the clock, both curiosity seekers and ardent volunteers wandered through the corridors observing the littered rooms, the unmade beds, dressers strewn with yogurt cartons. One remembers the cockroaches and cooking odors; the mimeograph and copy machines in the corridors, which ran until the hotel's ancient fuses blew; and on the third floor (headquarters), indelibly stained on the old rug in red paint: WOMEN POWER 1972.

But no one could snicker at what they represented, or the force behind them. In a single year, from a standing start, the NWPC had mastered the mechanics of politics. In the continuing endless reform of the Democratic party, 38 percent of all its delegates were now women. The students had fought their cause on the streets, by canvassing and doorbell ringing, had won the primaries for McGovern by their expertise with computers and transcontinental mobilizations in state after state. But the women had learned the craft of politics through years of serving as handmaidens at conventions and headquarters. They had mastered other tricks. They knew how to code names of delegates, how a "boiler room" operated, how to buttonhole, plead, lobby, threaten—and how to move whips about on the floor of an uncertain convention. These skills were now organized. Every one of the state delegations at the more than forty Miami Beach convention hotels was circularized with bulletins, leaflets, news. Every night, blue-jeaned volunteers rode the buses to stuff the mailboxes, or slip reports under the door of every delegate. Their sisters on the floor were identified by cause and issue. They installed their own switchboard to link them to key delegations in the rival Humphrey and McGovern commands. Their famous names could command attention on television, and their whips, obedience from hundreds on the floor.

There were several moments of recognition of this new force in being, this new call to attention:

• First, one remembers the explosion on the convention floor of that issue which torments modern women most—abortion, for the first time publicly debated at a convention in the presence of television. Forced to floor debate by their caucus, opposed by the governing McGovern majority as a political disaster about to happen in an already uphill campaign against Richard Nixon, shouted down by voice vote at the command of McGovern whips—nonetheless, there was the issue, now out in the open. Should not a woman have personal control over her own body's reproductive processes as fully as a man?

• One remembers the instant overnight candidacy of a woman for Vice-President, the campaign of Frances ("Sissy") Farenthold, organized at 2 P.M. on Thursday, breaking through the thicket of rules and credentials so that shortly after midnight Thursday, Farenthold could astound the convention, and even those who voted for her, by gathering 404.4 instant votes.

• One remembers the somersault of Friday morning, when McGovern, bowing to pressure and tears, dismissed Lawrence O'Brien from a proffered appointment, and instead appointed the Democratic party's first national chairwoman, Jean Westwood, who would mismanage the most mismanaged campaign in modern history.

• And one remembers, finally, the triumphant passage of the women's plank in the 1972 Democratic platform, bringing that party out squarely for the nomination of a woman to the Supreme Court (which Ronald Reagan would do) and, far more important, for the Equal Rights Amendment to the Constitution.

At this point we should again pause. Blacks had received their entitling amendments as long ago as the 1870s, but had broken through only in 1964; youth had broken through in 1968, and won its amendment three years later. Women were now demanding theirs. Each group had moved from the fringe of action to the center;

each group had entered with a demand for its rights and freedoms. But each group, no matter what laws or amendments it could force through Congress, would ultimately have to rely on the Supreme Court to decide just how far the enlargement of its liberty might legitimately go—and who else's liberty must be chipped to enlarge its own. The inexorable command of the Constitution makes the Supreme Court the ultimate centralizing authority in American affairs. Each grant of rights to the groups of new claimants placed on the docket of the Supreme Court new decisions for the ordering of American life, politics, and behavior.

None, however, promised to enlarge the Supreme Court's jurisdiction over everyday life more than the Equal Rights Amendment proposed in 1972. If it became constitutional law—and it is still in the process of ratification—it would bring the Supreme Court into family life; would call into question every divorce and alimony right hitherto left to the states, every law on custody of children or protection of women's special privileges. It would equally force the Supreme Court to decide whether the special protection of women, called for by tradition and biology, should be extended to men, who by the same tradition bore other special burdens because of their sex.

The new amendment before the nation concerned a new kind of politics—the politics of behavior and sexual rights. Long ago, a French visitor, Alexis de Tocqueville, had said of the early nation, then shaping itself: "There is hardly a political question in the United States which does not, sooner or later, turn into a judicial one." The supreme judicial authority in the United States is its Supreme Court; and so it is to the Supreme Court, with its record of the 1970s and its invitation for the 1980s, that we must now turn.

One can tangle oneself beyond escape in following the idea of equality through the embranglements of politics to its ultimate result in the growth of the overbearing federalization of authority against which Reagan ran in 1980. One can twist history completely out of shape by trying to make a simple running story, one event following on another, as first Congress, then the courts, then the executive, then the street violence, passed the initiative now to one, then to the other, as the transformation went on. Events overlapped, then bumped into each other, then were re-sorted by Congress or the executive or public opinion as authority changed in character.

Yet, in all these events, the governor and throttle of the motor drives remained the Supreme Court of the United States, as political an institution as Congress or the presidency. The Supreme Court's role in the transformation starts, of course, with its historic decision on May 17, 1954, on school desegregation, known as *Brown* v. *Board of Education of Topeka.* Here, finally, all previous decisions on race, running back through *Plessy* v. *Ferguson* (1896) to the Dred Scott decision (1857), were overturned. Segregation of little children by the color of their skin—blacks to one school, whites to another—was declared to be the denial of equality among citizens. Less noticed in the flow of events was the decision of the court a year later known as *Brown II.* This not only reaffirmed the first *Brown* decision but strengthened its mandate by conferring on all lower federal courts the power of injunction to see justice done.

The Supreme Court is accepted by all as truly supreme. To serve its judgments, even Presidents of the United States must bow, using all national force, up to the army and its paratroop battalions, to enforce the law. Presidents from Roosevelt to Eisenhower have disagreed with its wisdom; but all have yielded. Eisenhower was once heard to observe that he was "convinced that the Supreme Court set back progress in the South at least fifteen years. . . . It's all very well to talk about school integration—if you remember you may also be talking about social *dis*integration." But Eisenhower, nonetheless, sent an airborne division into Little Rock in 1957 to integrate its hate-ridden public schools. Even Richard Nixon yielded to the Supreme Court when ordered to surrender his private tapes, knowing that the publication of those tapes might impeach him.

But when the Supreme Court confers on lesser courts its powers to act by injunction, a quantum devolution of power has taken place. Injunction is the *consultum ultimum* of American justice. The voice of the enjoining judge is the command of law itself. All within its hearing must obey—rioters and bullies, universities and corporations, labor unions and municipal authorities. Before the 1950s, injunction had been used sparingly. Now, in the middle fifties, by the second *Brown* decision, lesser federal courts were invited to proceed by injunction. And federal courts are led not by mysterious, selfless personalities but by individual men and women, subject to all the temptations of power, ambition, and conviction to make law by themselves. And so they moved into those areas of custom and behavior that had previously lain within the authority of the states.

The change happened slowly and had begun well before the Civil Rights Act of 1964. The Supreme Court outlawed segregation at beaches in 1955, segregation at public golf courses in the same year; of buses and bus terminals in 1956; of public parks in 1958. To test these rulings, enough daring blacks were present in the South to throw their bodies and their courage into the legal opening, forcing lunch counters and bus terminals to accept them or flout the law of the land, whereupon the government *must* act. By 1960 and 1961, these testings had become commonplace. So, too, had injunctions.

By 1962, the Supreme Court, which had traditionally removed itself from what it called "the political thicket," had moved forward a notch, ruling that each state must so apportion its local legislature that representation by districts must give each citizen an equal vote; a dissenting Justice Felix Frankfurter called the majority decision "a massive repudiation of the experience of our whole past." By February 1964, the Supreme Court had extended the logic of equality to the Congress itself, ruling that "one man, one vote" must also apply to the apportionment of congressional seats.

So far, so good. But by 1964, with the passage of the Civil Rights Act and the landslide election of Lyndon Johnson, the courts increased their speed. It was Mr. Dooley who, long ago, had said that the Supreme Court follows the election returns. And now, with a vengeance, it did, as the lower courts followed by injunction the lead of the highest court. By injunction, the federal courts gave busing its reach and its wings. City after city, school system after school system, all across the nation, found themselves under court orders; some resisted, hoping for relief in a future election; the Southern states resisted first and then yielded to compulsion. Los Angeles was to resist. Chicago was to resist. North Carolina was to resist. Boston tried to resist and its entire school system was brought under the control of a federal district judge, W. Arthur Garrity, Jr.

Boston was a case study. Its demography had been changing year by year as middle-class whites left for the pleasant Bay State suburbs, north and south. But between 1970 and 1980, Boston was to experience a panic flight of those whites who would not resist busing as did the East Boston Italians or the South Boston Irish. Between 1970 and 1980, Boston's white population decreased from 524,709 to 393,937, while its "minority population" increased from 116,262 to 205,155. Even more dismaying, in its schools—the first free public schools in the nation's history—the proportion of white to minority children dropped from 68.5 percent (in 1968), a few years before the decision of Judge Garrity, to 45 percent (in 1976). By 1981, outside of East Boston, only 24 percent of the city's public school children were white. White families simply refused to send their children into black neighborhoods they considered dangerous; and black families complained that all the burden of busing for equality fell on their own children. Across the nation, the same startling reversal of proportions in big cities repeated itself, as federal courts pressed federal orders on the teaching of young children in their hometowns. The original decision in *Brown* v. *Board of Education* had not been a decision to *integrate* schools but to *desegregate* them—to free black children in any neighborhood where they lived to enter that neighborhood's school, or black students in any state where they lived to enter their state university. Black children must not be shipped from their homes to schools miles away simply because they were black. But by the 1970s, white children could be ordered on buses and directed to leave their neighborhoods for no other reason than that they were white.

If schools were the entering wedge for the courts' assumption of power, that power continued to grow. The logic of equality that applied to schools everywhere was, ultimately, to apply by court order to municipal police systems, to fire departments, to federal and local civil servants, and to reach farther and yet beyond to unions and corporations. Braced by the Civil Rights Act of 1964, the Voting Rights Act of 1965, and all the vast and hopeful legislation of Lyndon Johnson's Great Society, the courts found their mandate for a central ordering of affairs.

What should be signaled in the outreach of the courts is the development of an entirely new jurisprudence—the jurisprudence of class-action suits. *Brown* v. *Board of Education* had concerned itself with a child, Linda Brown, denied access to her all-white neighborhood school in Topeka, Kansas, because she was black. But as congressional act followed congressional act, slowly but definitely, suits brought by individuals against government and institutions gave way to groups suing government and institutions in "class-action" litigation. One cannot mark any precise date when such suits began to crowd the dockets of federal courts. Yet by the early seventies, sometime in the Nixon administration, it had become quite clear that for people who sought a new social or political goal, it was far more efficient to go to the courts than to go to the voters or move through Congress, where every step forward required the building of a new coalition in House, in Senate, in committee staff, in pressure groups.

"The Court," said Bruce Fein, now an associate deputy attorney general, "was part of the zeitgeist of the sixties. Government knows best. . . . With sufficient will and money we will make things work. In the minds of the judges, there wasn't any need to worry about the adverse effects of their policies (though busing ended up creating more racially segregated schools than before by causing white flight). It was hubris. We know what is right, so why not say that the Constitution mandates it? We will reform the social, economic, and justice systems. We don't need the states as laboratories."

Only a legal scholar can relish the drama in those sterile titles of famous decisions that cover twenty years of transformation of the American system: *Brown* v. *Board of Education* (desegregation), *Baker* v. *Carr* (state reapportionment), *Wesberry* v. *Sanders* (one man, one vote), *University of California* v. *Bakke* (affirmative action), *Swann* v. *Charlotte-Mecklenburg Board of Education* (widening busing), *Fullilove* v. *Klutznick* (set-asides for minorities), *Roe* v. *Wade* (abortion). The enormous drama belongs in an intellectual history, a modern American version of Montesquieu's *L'Esprit des lois.* What concerns us here is the role of the federal courts in changing the system and thus the elemental forces in American politics. For the courts were now spraying the United States Constitution into every nook and cranny of national life, draping it about matters best left to state legislatures, or about trivia which in other times might have been left to city halls or town councils.

The Constitution was made by the Supreme Court to address the issue of whether nude dancing constitutes freedom of speech; whether due-process protections must be observed before an unpaid water bill leads to service interruption; whether males have the right to receive alimony; whether males should have the right to buy beer at eighteen instead of twenty-one, if females have that right in the same jurisdiction; whether female soldiers can confer benefits on their spouses; whether private schools have the right to reject a student not to their liking; whether a white homeowner has the right of refusal to sell his home to a black. Matters that once had been left to the judgment of private persons, communities, or states were now raised to national issues in which the national courts imposed their interpretation of the Constitution on state or community.

Such extension of appetite could not but arouse a naturally litigious nation to respond. Public-interest law firms constituted themselves public-interest guardians; they multiplied in Washington and multiplied again. There in Washington, at the bar of the Supreme Court, they could win—or delay—what the public conscience required. In 1961, the Supreme Court had entertained only 1,940 pleadings. By 1978, at the height of its invitation to pursue equality, it was entertaining 4,731 cases, intricate pleadings all, averaging over twenty each working day. It was clearly impossible for any sober judicial mind to grasp them in all their complexity. Thus, perforce, opinions were shaped by law clerks and young lawyers, imbued with the vision of a federal government and a federal court imposing equality and justice for all; and imposing behavioral patterns on a nation that had, previously, thought behavior best left to the communities.

No one can draw a straight line of cause and effect through the bewildering chain of events that changed American politics. All the main actors were caught in the same cultural climate of demands and moralities. But one must go, inescapably, to the Congress of the United States. To leave out the role of the Congress in the transformation would be as unreasonable as to leave out the role of the United States Air Force in the Second World War. Congress, in its twenty-year course, dropped one bomb burst after another on the nation—and then left it to the courts and the regulators to clean up in their wake, as did the infantry and occupying armies that followed the air force into the terrain of the enemies.

A quick backward look sets the stage: Roosevelt had led the nation through two grand emergencies, the Depression and the war, and his Congresses, despite one or two revolts, had been wax for his modeling. It took nineteen years for Congress to regain its old authority after Roosevelt, but by the election of 1964, Congress and the President were partners again. The shock of the Kennedy assassination and the complete failure of the Goldwater campaign brought to Washington the famous Eighty-ninth Congress, accompanied by a President who loved Congress, stroked it, massaged it, twisted it to his ends. Lyndon Johnson meant to accomplish what Roosevelt had begun and what Kennedy had left unfinished. In a country oozing with prosperity and bursting with goodwill, Congress entered into the adventure of transforming the nation with a zeal that far outran its common sense.

The two Congresses of the Great Society still lack their historian. No Congresses since Reconstruction, or perhaps since Roosevelt's Seventy-third Congress of 1933–1934, did more to reorder the nation —and if the Eighty-eighth Congress (1963–1964) and Eighty-ninth Congress (1965–1966) lack a historian it is because their laws were so numerous, so far-reaching, so many of them so divorced from reality as to deny a simple coherence to their actions. For its efforts, in its first year, Lyndon Johnson gave his supreme wreath to the Eighty-ninth: "Tonight the President of the United States is going on record as naming this session of Congress as the greatest in American history. . . . From your committees and both your houses have come the greatest outpouring of creative legislation in the history of this nation. . . . This has been the fabulous Eighty-ninth Congress." But if any artificial logic or phrase can be placed on the Eighty-ninth, the least distortion would come in calling it the Grandfather Congress of Programs and Entitlements. Entitlements to specific and recognizable groups had always been part of American history. Entitlement means that a group is to be rewarded at damn-the-cost for service to the nation. Veterans had always been entitled to their pensions and special treatment since the Revolutionary War. Farmers, too, had been entitled to special benefits—free land under the Homestead Act of 1862; science and specialized research as the Department of Agriculture found its role; parity and price supports. Old people had received their entitlement under Franklin D. Roosevelt's Social Security Act of 1935.

Now the Congresses of the Great Society pressed the government's reach into countless corners of American life where federal dollars and federal bureaucrats had never been seen before. Even the most bare-boned catalogue of the two Johnson Congresses (second session of the Eighty-eighth, first session of the Eighty-ninth) gives only a skeleton outline of their sweep: the grand Civil Rights Act of 1964, to liberate blacks; a major tax cut; the basic antipoverty program; a mass-transit bill for city dwellers; a permanent food stamps program; a program for legal aid to indigents. Followed in 1965 by: Medicare for all over sixty-five; Medicaid for the poor; aid to elementary and secondary schools across the nation; college loans and scholarships; the Voting Rights Act; expanded housing programs with subsidies for low-income families; regional economic planning and development programs; special areas (like Appalachia) singled out for special grants; a new immigration act to erase the taint of racism in past legislation. And in those days of plenty, before the Vietnam War put guns in serious competition with butter, the national budget could push out enough money for programs to please middle-class and special interests as well. For the culture lovers: a national foundation to aid the arts and humanities. For nature lovers: Lady Bird Johnson's highway beautification act. For environmentalists: clean-air and clean-water acts, and crackdowns on automotive exhausts. For the sick and distressed: countless programs, running from those concerned with adolescent pregnancies to regional medical centers for research and care for victims of heart diseases, cancer, and stroke—and on and on. At the root of such programs was the idea of simple equity: *any* citizen who was poor should get Medicaid, not just *some* poor citizens; *any* old person should get Medicare, not just some. But all of the goodwill programs had a political hazard: once enacted, they could not be governed by the annual appropriations process in Congress. As a matter of law, people entitled to benefits could demand them, and Congress merely wrote checks to pay the bill.

No succeeding Congresses, from Nixon, through Ford, through Carter, dared deviate from the path of the Great Society. By 1979, the entitlements and programs set in motion by Congress could not even be summarized in a catalogue. They ran through all of American life: from the seat belt on the automobile, and the buzzer that warned, through programs for hypertension, diagnostic and treatment centers for hemophilia, maternal and child health care, services for crippled children, local facilities for runaway youths, public library services, education for use of the metric system, solid-waste disposal, noise control—on even to a program for urban rat control.

The federal government had become, by 1980, the center court for every group with a cause to plead, good or bad. The federal government simultaneously warned people of the danger of cigarette smoking—and subsidized the tobacco growers to the sum of several hundred million dollars a year. It warned of the dangers of cholesterol in dairy products for those with heart disease—but subsidized the dairy farmers with hundreds of millions more. Willie Sutton, the famous bank robber, asked once why he robbed banks, is supposed to have answered, "Because that's where the money is." The federal government was where the money was, where goodwill could be sharpened to a point where the public attention concentrated and the lance pressed home.

Of the far-flung programs of entitlements passed by the Great Society Congresses and their successors, a number of very serious truths must be stated.

First, each program was pressed through Congress in the name of virtue. No single program could be denounced, vetoed, or buried in committee without the objectors being shamed for their indifference to the call of conscience. Who, for example, could turn his back on the distress of the handicapped—and if a regulation under the

Rehabilitation Act of 1973 required that all urban transit systems (which drew money from the Federal Mass Transit Act) provide ramps, wheelchair lifts, and special aids for the handicapped, who would quibble about what it might cost? Who could object to scholarship loans to college students? Or object to a national recognition of the contribution of artists, writers, musicians, orchestras, dramatists, dancers, actors, to the nation's well-being? Or object to a program to cure narcotics addicts? Or object to the full, final equality to be granted to blacks and other minorities? Who had the courage to choose among all the calls of virtue and goodwill? And Congress, for almost twenty years, chose not to choose, but to enact them all.

There comes next a second truth: All entitlement programs tend not only to grow in cost but, more important, to create their own constituencies. In 1956, Congress passed a disability insurance amendment to Social Security, estimating it would rise in cost to $860 million by 1980. By 1980, it cost more than $15 billion a year. In 1977, to cite an extreme example, a minor amendment to the Small Business Administration's act made farmers eligible for disaster loans. The cost that year was estimated at $20 million dollars; it turned out to be $1.4 billion.

Each act encouraged more, and those dependent on federal money grouped together, while communities organized to demand federal funds. By 1980, twenty-nine states had their own offices lobbying in Washington, claiming money. The National Governors Association, the National Conference of State Legislatures, the U.S. Conference of Mayors, and others all had special pleading offices. New York State now maintains offices in Washington to plead for the governor, the state senate, and the state university. New York City has its own office in Washington; so do seventy other cities. Nor were these the most significant special pleaders. A *Time* magazine survey in 1978 added to these and other classic lobbies the following: fifty-three lobbies for minority groups, thirty-four for social welfare agencies, thirty-three for women, thirty-one for environmental issues, twenty-one for religious groups, fifteen for the aging, and six for population control.

There is a third fundamental truth to be stated about the growth of the federal government, a truth that recalls one of the oldest laws of American politics: All great reforms leave behind a legacy of bureaucracy. These bureaucracies harden all too often from bands of reformers into collectives of time servers, until, usually, they are packed with political figureheads engineered into decisions by their permanent staffs of true bureaucrats, controlled by the interests they were supposed to regulate.

These truths characterized the direction and ultimate results of the programs of goodwill through most of the sixties and into the seventies. But then, so slowly as to be unobserved, the growth of government began to take another form, one to which these universal principles still applied, but which no longer made outright or extreme demands on the United States Treasury.

One can mark no abrupt change in the course of the two decades between 1960 and 1980, except that gradually, as the 1970s wore on and the inflation began to bite, a change in mood crept over Congress. "Throwing money at problems" was becoming unfashionable —so Congress began to throw regulations at problems. Itself swelling with numbers and staff, Congress was slowly encasing itself in its own bureaucracy. Senators and congressmen alike found themselves flooded with paperwork, surveys, studies by their bright assistants, until they were unable to think or legislate clearly; and the quality of much of their legislation, particularly social legislation, became so muddleheaded that the grand purpose was passed on to one or another new regulatory agency to define or to the federal courts to enforce.

A single sample of goodwill muffled in legalese was that of the congressional act setting up the Council on Environmental Quality in December 1969. It states as its purpose: "To declare a national policy which will encourage productive and enjoyable harmony between man and his environment; to promote efforts which will prevent or eliminate damage to the environment and biosphere and stimulate the health and welfare of man; to enrich the understanding of ecological systems and natural resources important to the nation; and to establish a Council on Environmental Quality."

With the enabling authority of such acts, the buttressing bureaucracies could reach further and further into the interstices of American life; and special-interest groups in growing numbers could take their cases to court and demand relief from a federal judge in the name of law.

Agencies grew, and grew again. From twelve in 1970, the social regulatory agencies had grown to eighteen in 1980, and their budgets from $1.4 billion to $7.5 billion. The older agencies of Congress (ICC, SEC, CAB, FCC) had been what students of government call *vertical* agencies: assigned to patrol one industry which had grown so large as to threaten public interest—an industry such as railroading, banking, securities, airlines, or radio and television. The newer agencies were *horizontal*. They could rove and patrol across the board; and regulate and intrude in any factory, any school, any hospital built with federal aid, any university that drew from federal funds or whose students won federal loans and scholarships. And as the agencies grew, the appetite of the regulators expanded. Each day the federal government publishes a paper-pulp volume listing the new regulations of the patrolling agencies. In 1970, the *Federal Register* contained 20,036 pages; by 1979, that number had grown to 77,497 pages. In 1960, the *Code of Federal Regulations* rested at 22,877 pages; by 1970, it had grown to 54,105 pages; by 1980, to over 100,000. No congressman or senator had any but the vaguest idea of what such verbiage meant. But such regulations had the force of law and would be enforced by the courts; only skilled lawyers—and Washington flourished with new law and lobby firms, staffed very heavily by people who had written such regulations—could understand one or another section. Only they knew the corridors or offices in which decision or relief might be found. In the first six months of 1981 alone, no less than 1,056 new lobbyists were registered in Washington.

The decisions handed down by regulators touched every outpost of American sovereignty: from Guam to Alaska, from Miami to Bangor, from San Diego to Seattle. They protected native rights; they regulated the kind of gas one pumped into the automobile's tank; they placed all the coastal zones of the United States under federal surveillance; they decreed how and where a factory might be sited and what emissions were tolerable from its smokestacks. Slowly, the regulators invaded the Internal Revenue Service, so that the spring blight of the income tax's Form 1040 became speckled with complications and deductions, leading on to no less than thirty-six secondary and more incomprehensible tertiary forms and schedules, interpretable only by accountants and bureaucrats.

Goodwill lay behind all these steps to the federalization of the nation's government—and many achieved memorable good. The environmental codes, the Head Start program, the National Oceanic and Atmospheric Administration, the pressure on the cumbersome automobile industry to produce fuel-efficient cars, were wise and, in the result, moved the nation forward.

But one movement in the grand transformation slowly developed, year by year, into a monster whose shadow hangs over all American politics today: the division of Americans by race and national origin into groups, each entitled to special privileges. Beginning in 1964, the purpose of the Civil Rights Act has been twisted year by year, through executive order, judicial fiat, and bureaucratic appetite, into a reverse discrimination never envisioned, and specifically forbidden, by the act itself.*

There were in Washington, by 1980, at least eighteen jurisdictions which police all institutions, private and public alike, in the pursuit of what is called "racial balance." Chief among these were the Departments of Justice, of Labor, of Commerce, of Health and Human Services, the Equal Employment Opportunity Commission, as well as the Office of Management and Budget. All had the power to define and discriminate among Americans based on whether they were a "minority" group or belonged to the nation's majority. The Department of Health and Human Services now lists seven categories of Americans; other departments list five. Generally, however, these are the groups of special racial or ethnic entitlement: blacks (of African origin), Hispanics (sometimes called "Spanish-speaking" or "Spanish-surnamed"), American Indians and Alaskan natives (sometimes subdivided into Eskimos and Aleuts), Asians or Pacific Islanders (sometimes called Orientals), and whites (not of Hispanic origin). Others now knock at the door for special classifications. Hindus, recently arrived from India, do not want to be considered Asians, but seek a classification of their own. So do the growing colonies of Arab-Americans. In August 1980, the Administrative Office of the U.S. Courts went further, insisting that all federal court employees and judicial officers be classified by "race/national origin group." It divided its categories into five, and under "Whites" ("Persons having origins in any of the original peoples of Europe, North Africa or the Middle East"), it required that they be further subdivided and categorized into "ethnics, not religious factors: A. Arabic B. Hebrew." After an outburst of protest, this regulation was withdrawn. But neither Congress nor the courts have ever defined what a "minority," an "ethnic," or a member of a "protected class" is.

One must trace a glide from the old and beginning phrase "affirmative action" to the subsequent phrase "goals and timetables," to the present reality of federally enjoined "quotas." Where the phrase "affirmative action" originated no one knows. It popped up, for the first time in federalese, in an executive order issued by John F. Kennedy on March 6, 1961; and was hardened in September 1965

---

*One of the first and finest descriptions of the change is that by Nathan Glazer in *Affirmative Discrimination* (Cambridge: Harvard University Press, 1976).

by Lyndon Johnson's executive order (No. 11246) ordering all those holding contracts with the federal government "to take affirmative action" so that their employees are treated without discrimination as to "their race, creed, color or national origin."

So far, so good. Affirmative action was, in its purest sense, an effort of the government to remedy past injustices in American life. Ancestors of the blacks had been shipped to America in coffles, without their consent, and broken to slavery. Ancestors of the Indians had been broken in spirit, driven from their hunting lands, penned in reservations. Now, however, "affirmative action" would seize the bureaucratic imagination, and those assigned to enforce it would expand the thought.

It was in 1969 that the term "goals and timetables" was introduced—during the Nixon administration. And with "goals" came the Philadelphia Plan of defining just who is, or is not, to be employed on federal construction projects. From there, goals hardened into quotas, although never acknowledged as quotas. In construction projects funded by federal dollars, a certain proportion of "minority" employees must be hired. The Philadelphia Plan soon afterward was expanded to include New York, Boston, Seattle, Los Angeles, San Francisco, Detroit—in all, eventually, some thirty-one cities. And by the twilight of the Carter administration, the plan went nationwide, with the goals set precisely for all cities rather than targeted areas: Philadelphia contractors would have to employ 17.3 percent minorities, the District of Columbia 28 percent, and so on. Moreover, sixteen affirmative action steps would have to be taken under the new mandate by some eight thousand contractors working on projects funded with federal money.

We must skip lightly over the regulations and court decisions of the years between 1965 and 1980. But one notes that the Federal Office of Personnel Management lists over one hundred critical decisions of the Supreme Court and other federal courts trying to define what the sex, racial, or ethnic rights of equal opportunity are, and to whom they are granted.

These cases, which expanded the idea of affirmative action into quotas, generally fall into one of three groups.

There are the decisions on schools, always the cutting edge in family concerns. Judges attempted to wipe out city and county boundaries in order to import white children to spread among blacks in the inner cities. A whole sequence of orders and decisions attempted to classify little children and their teachers by the color of their skins, abolishing neighborhoods and educational standards in the pursuit of equality of rights. Even New York, that most liberal of cities, rebelled when teachers were ordered to register by the color of their skin so that, as the federal court enjoined, black and white teachers be distributed across the city, away from their homes, in undefined proportions in order that both black and white children might be equally exposed to black or white instruction.*

Next come the decisions on municipal and state employment policies. There is not a single city in the United States that is not, in one way or another, dependent on federal funds. Thus, each falls under federal jurisdiction to determine whether its employment practices flout what the plaintiffs (usually one of the eighteen federal agencies of equal opportunity) consider equal opportunity. This reaches across the board. It has required San Francisco (*Lau* v. *Nicholas*) to teach Chinese students in Chinese, Hispanics in Spanish. It required New York City's school board to come up, within forty-five days, with a plan to desegregate a high school in a district that was 95 percent black. It required the city of Bridgeport, Connecticut, to employ all eighty-four black and Hispanic applicants for its fire department who had failed the written entrance tests given to all other candidates. It required Stamford, Connecticut, to hire one minority-group applicant for every white applicant to its fire department until the quota of 17.5 percent was reached.

Lastly come the executive orders and rulings on jobs in private industry. One by one, the unions and great industries have protested such orders—from the Teamsters Union to Sears, Roebuck. Promotions, training rights, seniority rights, have all fallen under federal jurisdiction, in a series of decisions that stretch from here to endless, all based on race. The decisions, rising to the final judgment of the Supreme Court, come to a climax in a case denominated *Fullilove* v. *Klutznick* (Klutznick being the Secretary of Commerce).

---

*There are many reasons for white flight from the big cities. But in big cities, white families are subject to federal court orders, and those who can afford it send their children to private schools, while those who just get along move to suburbs with more tranquil schools. A sampling of the change in just eight years (from 1968 to 1976), by Professor Diane Ravitch of Columbia University's Teachers College, covered twenty-nine cities. They read the same—the abandonment of public schools by white parents. For example: In Los Angeles, white children in public school dropping from 53.7 percent to 37 percent. In Houston, from 53.3 percent to 34.2 percent. In New York, from 43.9 percent to 30.5 percent. In Dallas, from 61.2 percent to 38.1 percent. In Atlanta, from 38.2 percent to 11.2 percent. In Kansas City, from 53.2 percent to 34.4 percent. All these figures are now out of date; but in every case the trend of abandonment has accelerated. Busing and integration have nullified the desegregation that the courts of the 1950s sought to achieve. Big-city schools are now more segregated in fact (though integrated in law) than ever before.

At issue was one of the first acts President Carter had pushed through Congress, an emergency program of public works—$4 billion to stimulate the economy—of which 10 percent of the contracts must be awarded to "minority business enterprises."

The Supreme Court ruled by six to three that it was legitimate to set aside 10 percent of all contracts for minorities. But who, then, was a minority? As so often before, the dissenting justices posed the real questions. In one dissent, Justice Potter Stewart declared: "Today, the court . . . places its imprimatur on the creation once again by government of privileges based on birth. . . . Because of the court's decision today our statute books will once again have to contain laws that reflect the odious practice of delineating the qualities that make one person a Negro and make another white." In an even sharper dissent, Justice John Paul Stevens asked: "What percentage of Oriental blood or what degree of Spanish-speaking skill is required for membership in the preferred class?"

With its ruling on *Fullilove* v. *Klutznick* in July of 1980, the Supreme Court had passed an invisible mark in the struggle for civil rights. Back in the days when affirmative action was acquiring the force of morality, it had been the great effort of the government to remedy the old wrongs visited by white Americans on blacks and Indians. Now there was a race law, and an ill-defined race law. Americans had visited no harm in past centuries on Chinese who had recently come from Hong Kong or Taiwan. But as Orientals, they were entitled to privileges by birth—even though Chinese-Americans and Japanese-Americans were among the highest-income groups in the United States. Americans had visited no harm on Koreans, whom they had liberated from the Japanese—but immigrant Koreans as Asians were entitled to, and thus given, prior access to privileges. Americans had visited no harm on Hindus, oppressed and denied human rights by their own culture and the British raj. But Hindus also were entitled to privileges. So, too, because of their skill in speaking Spanish, or because of their surnames, were Argentine or Barcelona businessmen now making their way in America. So, too, were the hundreds of thousands of recently arriving Vietnamese.

America was very far away from the Nuremberg Laws of Nazi Germany; those had been laws of persecution. But the American system had now recognized privilege by race or minority—yet not defined it.

Most perplexing of all was the definition of a Hispanic. Hispanics were included in several federal laws simply as "minorities." Yet sometimes they were defined, bureaucratically, as "Spanish-speaking" or people of "Hispanic surnames." But Hispanics were not all alike. In Miami, Hispanics were generally Cubans, upper-level middle-class people. In New York, they were generally Puerto Ricans and Dominicans, the poorest of the poor, except for black families on welfare. In the Southwest, they were generally Mexican-Americans, legal and illegal, blue-collar, stoop-labor workers. Among themselves they were further subdivided into black Hispanics and white Hispanics, and in the Southwest into "Indios" and "Spanish."

Only one act—the Elementary and Secondary Education Act of 1968, designed to help underprivileged children—attempted even to define congressional entitlements for Hispanics. That act declared a child was entitled to public education utilizing the language of his home, and thus, from Texas to New Jersey, public schools were enjoined to conduct classes in Spanish, thereby effectively separating Spanish-speaking children from the mainstream of American life. But a true definition of Hispanics was never made clear, except by bureaucratic or court decisions; heritage rather than color (brown, black, white) entitled them to prior concern by administrative agencies over people of other heritage. Thus, in this perplexity of definition, came to attention the case of Rene Reinecke, a Miami policeman seeking promotion from patrolman to corporal. Only after Reinecke provided proof that his father had been born in Cuba could he win his promotion under the city's affirmative action program.

Other definitions of heritage, ethnicity, or race were just as perplexing. In Detroit, a white woman was fired from her job as secretary-bookkeeper in the city's housing commission simply because she was white; and received a jury award of $750,000 for suffering from racial discrimination against whites. One recalls countless other cases —in universities, in training programs, in union seniorities—in which race or sex was the discriminating factor. I recall the pressure of the EEOC on Harvard, my own alma mater, singling out the departments of history and mathematics as discriminatory because they lacked sufficient professors of black or minority heritage. One recalls a case at Brown University, in Providence, Rhode Island, where a white male Protestant was dismissed as associate chaplain because, in the budget squeeze, it was necessary to cut back, and it was vital to retain both a woman and a black in the chaplain's office; so he was the one to go.

Prejudice has always been a fact of American life. In the kind of country we have made, each new wave of strangers has been warily accepted with suspicion by those already here. Experience had slowly forced older Americans to regard new arrivals as other Americans, and particularly after World War II, when their valor and service in war eroded old prejudices. But now, by the late 1970s, it was not equality of opportunity that was sought, but equality of result, stipulated in goals, quotas, and entitlements, based not on excellence or merit, but on bloodlines.

"Quotas" was a flame word for many, particularly Jews who had suffered under the quotas and the "numerus clausus" of Germany and Eastern Europe. It was now to become a flash word for many others, who found themselves subject to reverse discrimination because they did not have Oriental faces, lacked Indian or African blood in their veins, could not claim Spanish descent, or knew their loins to be crested rather than cloven.

Newer, or "underprivileged," peoples had earned by law, regulation, or judicial fiat particular privileges as "protected classes." Women and young people were also "protected." Such people were active inside the arena of politics; they had claims to advance and new rights to protect. By the election of 1980 they had become separate ingredients of politics, and when they were mixed with older claimants of privilege (farmers, veterans, banks, railroads, oil companies, special interests), American politics could be splintered by identifying the splinters, and then bundling the identifiable splinters into a voting majority.

By 1980, 36 million Americans received their monthly Social Security checks; 22 million drew Medicaid benefits; 26 million more, Medicare; 18 million added to their budgets by food stamps; 11 million received general welfare payments; 15 million received veterans' benefits; 27 million children were nourished by school lunch programs; 11 million drew from the Aid to Families with Dependent Children (AFDC) programs. Most of these categories overlapped, so that there was no way of determining their global numbers. Moreover, there were the millions of young people who enjoyed federal scholarships and loans to go to college; and millions of women who, if denied the avenues to the careers they sought, could appeal to the courts to open the doors. All in all, much more than half the population of the United States depended in whole or in part on federal aid or protection.

All this had happened so gradually that few realized how much the nature of American government and politics had changed. Government had ceased to be, as Franklin Roosevelt once saw it, the umpire between business and labor, between the rich and the poor; it had become the nourisher of dependency. The culture of the previous twenty years, convinced of America's limitless power and propelled by the best of intentions, had pushed the old America entirely out of shape. It was as if one surgical operation here, another prosthesis there, had all set crazily in a body which, if not crippled, had been transformed. One could barely notice the transformation in Washington except for the ugly blocks of curtain-wall architecture pushing west from Sixteenth Street and the White House. These were full of hurrying, briefcase-bearing lawyers, consultants, lobbyists, who smothered Congress and the new agencies with their pleadings and insistences. But out beyond Washington, in the country, these special pleaders had developed constituencies of their own, powerful new voting groups who backed them up. It was these invisible groups who pushed government now this way, now that. No one had planned it thus. But there it was.

For liberals, the melancholy drama was one with no third act, no clear end in sight. They had set out to free everyone and had created a nation of dependents instead. Freedom and dependency did not really go together. For conservatives, the slowly unfolding drama of the previous twenty years had been one of growing menace. They had tried once with Goldwater to upset the trend; they had tried again with Nixon, and he had turned out to be a closet regulator, stretching government's control to the first effective environmental surveillance, to expansion of all things anathema to them, from price controls to grander school lunch programs, construction quotas, new safety and health regulations. This time they were going to try with a true conservative.

The contest, then, in 1980 was to be a new chapter in the old national debate: just what was the nature of the federal government, and what were its limits?

The Democrats built their campaign on defense of the old visions. The challengers built their campaign on a denunciation of such visions—and even more, on their cost. The Great Inflation was under way. That touched everyone. That was to be the main thrust of Ronald Reagan's attack on Jimmy Carter, and so it is to the Great Inflation we must go.

CHAPTER FIVE

THE GREAT INFLATION

Historic disasters usually come labeled with day and year—sometimes even with the hour. Not so with the Great Inflation. October 29, 1929, Black Tuesday, had been the day the stock market crashed and the Depression began. At 7:56 on the morning of Sunday, December 7, 1941, the Japanese bombed Pearl Harbor and America was at war. At 12:30 P.M., Friday, November 22, 1963, John F. Kennedy was shot—and a dream was lost. Before dawn on Wednesday, January 31, 1968, a Vietcong suicide squad burst into the American Embassy in Saigon; the Tet offensive had begun and the Vietnam War was lost.

But inflation has no date of beginning. Inflation is the cancer of modern civilization, the leukemia of planning and hope; as with all cancers, no one can say when it begins or how fast it may spread. It is a disease of money, and when money goes, order goes with it. Inflation comes when a government has made too many promises it cannot keep and papers over the shortfall with currency which, ultimately, becomes confetti—and faith is lost.

It was the Chinese who first, combining their two wonderful early inventions—paper and printing—produced currency. And it was the Sung dynasty almost a thousand years ago which first discovered that the ability to produce and print money at a sovereign's will was a drug that could kill as well as soothe. The Sung dynasty was to die in a burst of paper inflation. So, too, was the Yuan dynasty, which succeeded it. So, too, all other Chinese regimes, down through that of Chiang K'ai-shek, whose chief base of political loyalty was destroyed in 1949 by an inflation which wiped out the savings and hopes of the middle class. Such outbursts of the paper disease have attended the death of Western governments too. The French Revolution died in a blizzard of *assignats*. So did the Confederacy of the United States. The death knell of the Weimar Republic was first tolled in the insane inflation of German currency in the 1920s.

Always, however, inflation comes gradually; is recognized too late; and can be cured only by ruthless political surgery, which, if delayed too long, proves futile. Only two instances come to mind of inflations in modern times that were successfully arrested—both times by autocrats. The first was in the postwar Germany, where, for three years, four occupying powers had been mindlessly spinning the presses that printed money for defeated Germany. Then, in spring 1948, General Lucius Clay of the United States broke with the four-power occupation of the desolate country and, by military command, wiped out the paper marks, imposing an entirely new currency on a nation that could not protest. The second time was when another autocrat, General Charles de Gaulle, seized the French government from the Fourth Republic and simply ordained currency reform. The cruelty necessary to halt an inflation has everywhere else, however, been beyond the reach of any government elected freely by its people, bound at once by promises to its voters and the burdens of defense and statecraft. To stop inflation, many must suffer.

In the Great Inflation of the U.S., we have all lived through an era when the burdens accepted by government at home and abroad have bewildered American understanding. But this bewilderment became apparent only in the decade between 1971 and 1980. The campaign of 1980 was dominated by the Great Inflation, as it altered all values.

It is best to begin the story of those years by postponing the dreary technical terms by which bankers and money market magicians describe the approach of the American crisis. Their colored charts, zigzag graphs, and attempts to pinpoint esoteric phenomena that will not stand still; their peg points like M-1, or M-1b, or other strange M formulations; their prime rates, overnight rates, discount rates—all make digital printouts of ripples and waves which give only monetary measures of a larger reality. And the largest reality of the Great American Inflation is that it is only part of the inflation of the world beyond America's shores—a world we created. This world, for ten years, has been closing in on American life, demanding its "fair share" of resources and comforts, the "fair share" that America, at its peak of power, promised but cannot now deliver or bring itself to repudiate. A "fair share" for the rest of the world means inevitably that their share must go up and ours come down.

A quick afterlook is needed to make events and realities stand out.

The salient result of World War II and American policy was to free billions of the world's people in Asia, in Africa, in the Americas, to dream of the same good things that Americans once enjoyed alone.

The cost of food is a proper place to begin, because it is a cost which, in the modern world, we cannot control. The North American continent, chiefly the United States, is the world's marginal source of food, as the Middle East is of oil. Of Roosevelt's universal four freedoms, "freedom from want" was cardinal. We, as Americans, wanted starving children, their mothers, and their families to be nourished decently. But that American promise to the world was made when no one could predict what medicine and sanitation could do to the world's population. The world counted only some two billion people in 1930. It counts now about 4.4 billion. It will probably count six billion by the year 2000. All must eat. The picture of a starving baby, or of a weeping mother with shriveled breasts, torments our conscience; and our continent, North America, is the chief supplementary source of food to which they can look. Yet another factor enters into the world food picture—a new and ominous phenomenon. The climate of the world seems to be changing; it may, say our best scientists, be warming up. This slight, almost imperceptible, but relentless warming of the past ten years has already brought tragedy, and may forecast worse. The southern fringe of Africa's Sahara desert, the Sahel, has already spread to parch central Africa. A decade of sorrow and starvation has followed. The same climatic change has punished Russian food production—first in 1972, again in 1975, and again in 1981. The Russians (as well as the Poles) must import grain. People around the world have added meat to their diet; so they demand feed grains for their pigs, cattle, chickens. Such feed grains, too, must come from America; the demand from abroad pushes up costs at home and the consumer at the supermarket is faced with this hidden competition from the hungry beyond our shores. In 1980, the United States shipped out $41.3 billion worth of farm products, an all-time record (the largest market was Japan, taking $6.1 billion worth on its own terms). And there is no sign that this demand will ever diminish.

Anywhere Americans shop, they can, if they probe, find the outer world pressing on their prices. What the world has done to the price of paper, for example, is the despair of readers and writers as well as publishers. The first book I wrote cost $3.00. The story of the 1960 campaign cost $6.95. This book, alas, will cost $15.95. The cost of its paper, $920 a ton today, has risen from $300 a ton since 1956. This price jump is due in very large part to the outer world's demand for paper, of which America and Canada are the chief suppliers. In Asia, in Africa, in Latin America, almost *two billion people* have been encouraged by their governments of liberation to learn to read and write. For this, paper is essential. Their local television stations show them the world of consumer products beyond the village, all of which must be packaged with staggering quantities of paperboard cartons. This insatiable demand has made the North American forests, with their pulp and paper industries, the world's suppliers. The two-cent newspaper of prewar American memory has, consequently, risen to five cents, then ten cents, and now, in most American cities, costs twenty-five cents—on its way to half a dollar, perhaps ultimately a full dollar for the daily news. Our policy abroad sought a civilized, literate world; that world now must share our paper.

Take one other ingredient of the many ingredients in the world's demand on us, and our equally critical demand on that world—energy. We Americans alone in the bright years of the 1950s controlled the price and flow of oil—so we built our superhighways, our suburbs, our factories, our shopping malls, in the unthinking belief that every American was divinely entitled to drive his car where or how he chose on cheap gasoline. But Frenchmen, Germans, Japanese, Brazilians, wanted the same privilege; as they produced more and more automobiles and built more and more highways, they jostled the Americans in seeking oil around the world for their cars. Here, then, began a new happening: a handful of underdeveloped countries of the outer world found they were no longer the marginal but the critical suppliers of energy to the automobile peoples. It was only a step from this realization to the action that followed: They would organize *their* cartel to control oil prices. The cost of heating oil, the cost of gasoline and motor oil, the cost of plastics and fibers made from petrochemicals, all would rise or fall depending on their *political* decisions. Sometime in the 1970s it should have become quite clear that for the critical ingredients of oil and energy, the price of life in America was beyond American control—unless we recognized and used our political and military power to bring them under control.

At this point, as we try to trace the Great Inflation, as at other points in this section, we must invite the reader to chew on the juiceless gristle and bones of events, and in particular, on the events of a year of no great memories, 1971. It was then that the President of the United States, Richard Nixon, realized that the architecture of the world he had inherited no longer sheltered America from the demands of the world we had made.

This realization was forced on Nixon; but he accepted it with that strange stubborn courage with which he accepted all confrontations. The postwar world of Roosevelt, Truman, Eisenhower, had been reorganized by the United States in the full naiveté that our victory would last forever. The United States would therefore put an end to the trade wars, the currency jugglings, the nationalistic economic stabs and thrusts which had done so much to heat up the world for World War II. The United States, secure in its mastery of resources and technology, would make a new world—and under its shelter, even the vanquished Germans and Japanese would be invited to share the wealth.

The high moment in this afterlook is the Bretton Woods Agreement of July 1944. Translated from the jargon of those who wrote it, the agreement was a guarantee by the United States that we would police the trade and currency of the world. Other nations' money might fluctuate in value, but they would fluctuate only in relation to each other, while at the center stood the United States dollar, rigid, its strength firmly socketed in gold. Gold was worth thirty-five dollars an ounce—and that was that. If anywhere in the world a merchant or a trading firm could bring yen, francs, marks, or pounds to the bank, that bank could convert them into dollars and those dollars could then be converted by their central banks into gold. The United States held this world stable. Common people around the globe came to eat better, learn better, shelter better, breed more prolifically than ever before in human history. The dominion of the United States was a benign dominion, and of this we should be proud, however hurtful were its eventual results.

By 1971, however, this dominion had run its course and Nixon had to face the end. The nations which had come to thrive under the American system of world trade had adopted and in some cases surpassed American technologies. They could produce cheaper and in many cases better goods than Americans. International politics work by interest, not by sentiment. First the French, under de Gaulle, began to worm out the American promise to redeem its dollars in gold; then the Germans. Then, above all, the Japanese, who under the new rules of world trade found that America was the world's softest trade target; and within that target the Japanese government could pick out, to undermine and destroy, American industry after industry, complacent and vulnerable. It was too good to be true: America provided Japan's defense, yet invited Japan to mount a trade war against it behind that perimeter of defense—a war that used American raw materials and technology to invade and wipe out American industries. And along with the industries went the jobs that American unions had made more and more uncompetitive with Japanese wages.

In 1971 for the first time, a major convulsion overtook the world that the Bretton Woods Agreement had designed. Again, one must use the language of bankers to describe what happened, for they distinguish between something called a nation's "balance of accounts" and its "balance of trade." In the balance of accounts are included all that a nation pays for in invisible transfers; in our case, for what tourists as well as the big multinationals spend abroad, for our foreign aid to backward countries, for services and support to our overseas armies, or, as in the late sixties and early seventies, for the Vietnam War. The dollars flow out and are accumulated abroad, as floating dollars, Eurodollars. This balance of accounts had been running for years against the United States. The balance of trade is a much more solid figure than the balance of accounts; it measures whether a nation's enterprise is selling the production of its farms and factories for more or less money than it needs to pay for what it must buy from abroad. When a country cannot earn enough, by what its workers produce, to buy what its people want, then, sooner or later, it must pay the piper.

In the summer of 1971, that moment came for America. Ever since the 1890s, America had shipped out to the world more than it imported; and the world had struggled with the "dollar gap." In April of 1971, however, the U.S. Department of Commerce posted a morbid figure: a monthly deficit in the trade balance. In May came another deficit, establishing the first two-month deficit in twenty-two years. In June, yet another. In July, a fourth deficit. And thus came the first great run on the dollar, in the summer of 1971. Gratitude is an ephemeral factor in human relations; and in international trade, gratitude is nonexistent. Greed has no morals, financiers few loyalties. If America was losing ground to shrewder, more aggressive trading rivals, if the everlasting American trade surplus was vanishing, it was better to convert American dollars, whether paper or on credit ledgers, to the gold they promised, rather than to hold the dollar as a guarantee. Few emotions are more irresistible than panic; and financial panic pressed bankers and their depositors to unreason.

By midsummer of 1971, the American hoard of pure gold, those golden bars at Fort Knox, Kentucky, had shrunk to only $10.5 billion (from a postwar high of $25 billion). Outstanding against this hoard were a hundred billion dollars in foreign banks and accounts, billions more in American promises, plus the costs of an ongoing war in Vietnam. If those dollars were only paper promises, then the time to grab at the gold they promised was *now*. In the first week of August 1971, the Bank of France received approximately $300 million dumped on it by frightened French traders who wanted conversion to something more certain than the American dollar. In two successive days, the Bank of Japan was forced to accept first $600 million, then $690 million. As the panic grew, the Bank of England reported to the United States that it might have to cover $3 billion in the next week! And all these dollars dumped by frightened foreigners on their central banks were claims against the shriveling hoard of bars in Fort Knox. Later, Richard Nixon was to say that if he had not acted to save the dollar over the weekend, there might not have been a dollar.

But he did act. On Friday, August 13, Nixon had summoned his entourage of house economists to one of the first of those countless conferences which are all called Camp David summits. On Sunday, he appeared before the nation to announce a startling new economic policy. Of this Nixon new economic program, two hard items must be remembered:

First, Nixon declared that America was going off the gold standard. The United States would no longer redeem dollars in gold. Foreigners might play with the dollar as they wished, their bankers setting whatever value they wanted on it. But the United States would no longer give up one ounce of gold simply because it had promised that anyone anywhere with thirty-five dollars in paper could claim that ounce. With that, the climate of world trade changed. Gold was no longer the tether of discipline. Anyone was free to charge in international trade what he could get. It was a long jump of imagination for the ordinary citizen to realize that this esoteric change of doctrine would ultimately lift the price of coffee from ten cents a cup at the counter to thirty-five cents; or a popular Volkswagen from two thousand to seven thousand dollars. We were now free of our obligation to pay in gold what central banks overseas demanded for such floating dollars their depositors might dump on them. Theoretically, we had wiped out speculation against the dollar. But in the next ten years, the float of dollars abroad ran up to $800 billion, and the dollar became the international gamblers' prime vehicle of speculation. It could be protected only by raising interest rates on American Treasury issues to 12 percent, 14 percent, or even higher, to hold those dollars still. And this gave American money strategists the nightmare choice of international crash abroad—or throttling interest-sensitive industries, like automobiles and housing, to a standstill at home. The dollar fell in value nonetheless. Overseas clients were able to buy more and more of American resources— food, sulfur, copper, coal, paper pulp—therefore raising American prices at home. And they were able to charge more, in dollars, for what Americans wanted from overseas—oil, coffee, cocoa, television sets, small cars.

Second, Richard Nixon seized the opportunity to impose on the United States a system of wage-price controls. He had very early spotted the pressure and direction of prices in American life—up, and up, and up—and now, in 1971, inflation was speeding at the then unbelievable rate of 6 percent a year. It *must* be stopped. Nixon decided he must act. He announced that while America would no longer enforce the discipline of gold and trade, he would impose discipline on American prices and wages. There would be a three-month freeze on all wages and prices, to be followed (as it turned out) by another year of price controls until the system of control collapsed.

We were, by the decisions of 1971, all at once adrift in a trade world that had no standards of values except for squeezing the last profit out of the marketplace; and at home, we were locked by a government that felt it could regulate values, from the wages of cannery workers to the price of canned pineapple, from the wages of garment workers to the price of a man's suit. Other nations would soon learn that the American marketplace set a ceiling on prices which they could approach (and undercut) without penalty. And over all this reigned the sense and sentiment of American political thinking. Tradition required us to go on helping the undernourished of the world, tradition required us to continue opening our markets to fair trade.

But already, by 1971, there was under way the unmarked explosion of the American budget, which, like our foreign policy, was subordinate to tradition. Tradition required Americans to approach politics at home with a sense of compassion, with a reverence for equality of opportunity, with a large vision of what the federal government might accomplish for the good of all society, if only its goodwill could be prodded into action. There were, thus, the burdens of American tradition in diplomacy, and the burdens now to be added by changing American tradition at home. These latter burdens are all to be found in the budget of the United States, which, in the next ten years, was to come entirely out of any reasonable control.

No one I ever met has read the entire budget of the United States. It comes in a beige-bound book of seven or eight pounds, over two thousand pages in length, on which computorial printouts have spattered figures beyond comprehension; it would take three months of reading time, and three months of pondering thereafter, to grasp it all. It is possible to locate the nominal source of the budget—on the second floor of the Executive Office Building, directly across the guarded alley from the White House. There, the director of the Office of Management and Budget pulls together figures from all the bureaus, departments, finance offices, and independent agencies of government, and tries to squeeze them into something the human mind can understand. He is served by one deputy director, six associate directors, and a staff of 610, an elite civil service corps, as dedicated to the good of the nation as is the Coast Guard or the National Science Foundation; and equal in quality to that most elite corps in Europe, the French *Inspecteurs de Finance.*

Created in 1921, the Bureau of the Budget was located in the Treasury Department until 1939, when it was transferred to the Executive Office of the President. In 1970, under Nixon, it became the Office of Management and Budget, but its purpose remained the same: to give the President an overall grasp on what the nation needed, what it would cost, and how he must present his proposals to the Congress, which sets taxes. How much for defense? How much for foreign aid? How much for the underprivileged? How much for science? For arts, for humanities, for higher education? How much for farmers? How much for Egypt, how much for Israel, how much for Nicaragua? How much for the sick, the aged, the handicapped, the blacks, the Hispanics?

The technicians of OMB are stern questioners. Each government department and bureau must submit and defend its request for money. Most of the directors in OMB are highly qualified and suspicious people. They expect each program, department, and bureau to ask for more money every year. Ten percent is the generally accepted average padding of demand; that demand may be real, or may be a ploy to insure against a cutback. When the staff of OMB cuts off the fat and leans out the demands, they prepare the national budget, which becomes politics: The President must decide where and how he wants the money spent; he must confront congressional pressure and special interests.

The budget-making process is baffling to common understanding. Two years before a budget goes into effect, the gnomes of the budget bureau are at work on it. In the fall of 1980, for example, their choices of direction were moving up to the President, Jimmy Carter, who, on January 15, 1981, already defeated for reelection, presented a budget called FY 1982—Fiscal Year 1982—which would govern spending from October 1, 1981, to September 30, 1982. The budget, which goes to Congress in early winter, is usually greeted with six or seven months of debate as every interest group in the nation howls, bellows, protests, or demands of its constituent congressmen that its interests be protected from the President's choices. Finally, late in midsummer, the Congress decides which of the President's choices it will accept or repudiate. Then, on October 1 of each year, the budget goes into effect for fiscal year whatever-it-is, all the appropriations and spendings fitted into a giant whole, a hopeful guesswork estimate of what taxes will bring in, and what expenditures will go out.

We can follow the domestic push to inflation by tracing the course of the federal budget; which means, alas, that at this point there is no way of evading figures. In the ten sunlit years between 1950 and 1960, the deficit of the entire decade came to only some $15 billion. In the next ten years, 1960 to 1970, that figure soared to $63 billion. And after that, from 1971 to 1980, the deficits became incomprehensible, mounting to $420 billion! Under Republican and Democratic administrations alike, the demands of conscience and "compassion" forced on the budget more and more attention to good "causes," legally irrevocable "entitlements" or "programs." The federal machinery had become a pump, and anyone or any group that could seize the handle could pump it for more, beyond any power of the President to veto, in good conscience, what goodwill required.

Thickets of figures, so tangled as to be beyond unsorting, cover the ridges of the developing change. Only a few sets of figures are needed to describe what was happening. Food stamps, for example: The present food stamp program had begun as a Kennedy idea, established in 1961 by executive order. The federal government stored huge stocks of surplus food; poor people were hungry; the two circumstances muddled into a tempting idea. Why not distribute food to the poor with stamps they could purchase at a nominal cost? The idea, in its first year, cost only $13 million. By the time of the Great Society, the idea had become law. Twenty years later, in the last Carter budget, when food stamps had become free and served as currency, the budget called for $12.4 billion for food stamps. The school lunch program was just as emotional a political temptation. Time was, before World War II, mothers had packed sandwiches in brown paper bags for children to take to school. But now many mothers worked, and many more felt it was the government that should feed the children. From a substantial total of $338 million in fiscal 1967, the federal outlay on school lunches, for hungry and well-to-do children alike, rocketed to $3.1 billion in fiscal 1980. No person of conscience could object to feeding children. But on the other hand, there was the defense chunk of the budget, the favorite target of liberals. In 1960, the armed forces had absorbed 49 percent of the budget, or $45 billion. Then, slowly, their share declined as a percentage, even through the Vietnam War. By 1973, the armed forces, wasteful as they might be, consumed only 30 percent; by 1977, 25 percent; and by 1980, only 23.8 percent of the total budget.

Where was most of the ever-rising budget going? To those programs that economists call "income transfer" payments, payments by the federal Robin Hood, taken from the middle class to help the old, the poor, the underprivileged. In 1960, those payments had rested at $23.6 billion. By 1980, they had become $271.2 billion! Even after deflating that figure for the inflation of the dollar, payments made to individuals from the federal purse had nonetheless quadrupled in real money. *More than one-third of all families in the United States now receive direct aid from the government.* It was at the beginning of this process that the late Senator Everett Dirksen said, "A billion dollars here, a billion dollars there, and pretty soon you're talking about real money."

There was, indeed, no way of paying for demands of conscience, yet no way of repudiating them. Every beneficiary of congressional intent receives in payment of needs a stiff green paper check addressed to the United States Treasury as payer, and entitling him, her, or it to cash the check at the bank whether he, she, or it be a giant arms corporation or an aging client of welfare or of Social Security.

But what if the United States Treasury cannot pay the check written against it? What if it has not, or cannot, collect in taxes enough money to meet what Congress has pledged?

Then the United States Treasury borrows the money, issuing notes and bonds which the great banks cannot refuse or ignore.

Which brings us to the heart of the theological arguments among the nation's economic thinkers and bankers on the "money supply problem." If there is too much money in circulation, too much credit and too many dollars, prices inevitably go up. The control of this "money supply," which can be understood only in the hieroglyphic language of its priests, rests with the Federal Reserve Board. The board can increase the amount of money in circulation, or squeeze down the amount of money in circulation, by bizarre but effective and usually secretive manipulations in the upper atmosphere of banking and credit. The Federal Reserve Board is an independent government agency, theoretically as independent in its control of credit as the Supreme Court is in its interpretation of law. But when pressure comes to crunch, the President and his Secretary of the Treasury can "lean" on the Federal Reserve Board; can shame it in public by declaring the reluctant Federal Reserve to be the chief enemy of recovery, or chief propeller of inflation. In ultimate analysis, the Federal Reserve *must* create the credit at the banks, against which federal borrowings must be honored, against which the stiff green paper checks must be cashed. The Reserve *creates* money; it simply orders money to *be;* it always does so reluctantly; but it always, ultimately, must make that money available for what Congress requires to be spent.

Once upon a time, back in 1960, Congress required the government to spend $92 billion a year. By fiscal year 1980, that figure had gone up to $580 billion. You will be reading this book, most of you, in fiscal year 1982, when the budget will have gone up to some $704 billion. Meanwhile, the accumulated difference between what the government spends and what the government takes in has risen to a national debt of over one trillion dollars! Interest on this debt amounts to $106.5 billion a year, or 14.4 percent of the entire budget outlay. In short, the federal government is in hock, in unmanageable difficulties, which Ronald Reagan in the campaign of

1980 hopefully promised to sort out, but has not yet been able to master.

The reality is that no one, absolutely no one, can control the budget of the United States—not the President, not the OMB, not Congress. The moral mandate of the sixties and seventies locks expenditures into an ever-rising, irreversible escalation. But the cycle of a free economy reduces or increases tax income beyond any econometrician's predictions, or ability to guess. Ever-rising interest on the national debt *must* be paid; when the Russians push up arms spending, our defense spending *must* go up too. Entitlements rise. Of the national budget, only one-quarter—for all the rest of government—is subject to any reasonable control or slowdown in its rate of increase. This is the reality; and to span the jump between promises and commitments on the one hand and the reality on the other hand, the budget requires a paper bridge of paper money. And thus: inflation.

In Carter's last month in office as President, his chief inflation fighter, that wise and witty economist Alfred Kahn, put it this way:

"Can a democracy discipline itself? . . . We're talking about something really universal. . . . What is it that creates this terrible sense of helplessness which I can't deny? . . . It's clearly something that has to do with the lack of social discipline. . . . If you just say I'm not going to increase the money supply . . . it would sooner or later stop the ability of prices to rise. . . . But the critical question is: What would the costs be, what would the tensions be? The problem in our economy is we have these persistent, well-organized pressures by each individual and group to preserve his or her absolute position regardless of what happens to the country as a whole. . . . [What this does] is create on the part of everyone in society the expectation that no matter what happens to the aggregate, each of us individually is entitled to CPI plus 3 percent, [and] our conception of what constitutes a good life subtly goes up. . . . We are in a sense victims of the success of the American economy; and that success has taken the form not only [of] the perpetual, almost uncontrollable growth of consumption expenditures, but also, of course, in government programs. This is part of the product of the humanization of capitalism. . . . What we've got is these constant forces to increase expenditures, to increase nominal income, to expand government programs, regardless of their automatic escalation. . . ."

Kahn then went on to the fundamental piston thrust of wages upward, ever upward, and the resistance of the unions to any halt or downward flexibility—but that brought us to politics, and the irresistible forces of hope and demand.

At least three more major markers on the way to the inflationary crisis of 1980 should be added to the date of 1971.

The first was the war in Vietnam. Most thoughtful economic historians—with whom I generally agree—feel that it was Lyndon Johnson's war that let slip the thongs of money discipline at home. He had, without the authority of Congress, drafted young men to fight in Vietnam. Almost as important, however, he undertook to conceal the enormous cost of the war by leaching money from the system through deficit financing; Congress was not asked to pay for the war by raising taxes. Until then, for fifteen years, American prices had been relatively stable. From 1965 on, the purchasing power of the dollar began to skid.

The second marker came in 1972, with the indexing of Social Security payments to the cost of living. That story is rather more amusing, and since it is a parable of the conjunction of politics and inflation, it deserves some note. Wilbur Mills, then a congressman from Arkansas, was one of the most powerful figures in the House of Representatives—as chairman of the House Ways and Means Committee, he swung the constitutional authority of the House to set taxes and grant favors. Until late in 1971, he had opposed automatic benefit increases in Social Security. Then a swelling of ambition took possession of him, and on February 11, 1972, he announced his candidacy for the presidency. He learned that New Hampshire, the kickoff state for all campaigns, reputedly counted the second-highest proportion of senior citizens in the Union. Social Security here was a primordial issue. On February 23, therefore, two weeks before New Hampshire's March 7 primary, he announced publicly that he was now *for* automatic annual upward adjustments in Social Security indexed to the Consumer Price Index. By June, Congress had passed his benefit increase (the House by 302 to 35, the Senate by 82 to 4). By then, of course, Mills's presidential campaign had collapsed; he had come in fourth in New Hampshire's Democratic primary, with only 4 percent of the vote, despite his blessing to the elderly. Sometime thereafter, in 1974, Mills was picked up, cut and bleeding, in Washington by U.S. park police, as he tried to prevent his girl friend, a nightclub stripper (Fanne Fox, "the Argentine firecracker"), from throwing herself into the Tidal Basin. Revealed as an alcoholic, he lingered as congressman, stripped of honor, for a few more years, then was retired by Arkansas's voters, though he remained in Washington as a powerful lobbyist. But his short campaign for the presidency, and his power on Capitol Hill, had left a permanent marker behind. Many other "indexings" were to follow, so that some retired people can now draw more from their pensions than they did from wages at the prime of their vigor. From 1972 on, "indexing" meant that benefits and transfer payments would forever follow the course of prices upward. A ratchet had been built into the payments system which would let it move only one way—up—no matter what the budget, the Federal Reserve, learned economists, or common sense required.

The third—and by far the most important—marker was set by the outside world as it tightened a new set of ratchets. That concerned the price of oil, which means the price of energy, and energy is what makes the wheels go round.

So important is this third marker that it deserves a capsule of history all its own.

Oil, in the world of trade today, means oil controlled by the OPEC countries; i.e., oil controlled by the tyrannies of the Middle East. For two thousand years, the Arab nomads had done nothing to develop the oil that lay beneath their rolling sand dunes. But in December of 1936, an American company, Standard Oil of California, had spudded a well in Saudi Arabia, to be known as Dammam No. 7. In March of 1937, the wildcat venture had struck oil—at a free flow of 3,810 barrels a day. By 1940, Standard's geologists had plotted other new fields under the empty sands, and Abqaiq No. 1 came in at 9,720 barrels a day. Three other big American oil companies were invited to join in the adventure—Standard of New Jersey (now known as Exxon), Socony-Vacuum of New York (now known as Mobil), the Texas Company (now Texaco)—and together they formed a company known as Aramco. Other American oil companies followed into the Middle East; and oil oozed, or more frequently gushed, at the bite of their drilling heads. World War II interrupted their operations. But by the first decade of the postwar years, when the oil companies resumed drilling and began to build their bedazzling tank farms, refineries, and installations on the Persian Gulf, it was obvious that the Arab principates sat over treasure which could not be measured in the conventional terms of money. From such resources, American oil companies could once pump oil at ten cents a barrel—and sell it to their customers in oil-poor Europe or oil-starved Japan at twenty times the cost. The American oil companies had, at the beginning, been the masters of this oil. When the Arab countries realized that they, indeed, were the true masters, they expropriated the big American oil installations, and made Aramco and other oil companies their serving and sycophantic agents.

But America, too, was coming to the act of recognition that all other countries had experienced first. Energy was what replaced muscle. Food had once been energy. Coal had replaced it as energy. Now oil was energy. America, under John D. Rockefeller, had introduced the world to this energy that comes from fluid hydrocarbons. Then, without realizing it, America built an independent system of life based on the abundance of cheap energy. This sense of independence eroded only slowly, and then very subtly. It was in 1948 that America first imported more oil than it shipped out—a meager 145,000 barrels a day, chiefly cheap sulfur-contaminated Venezuelan oil for boilers at East Coast utilities. But America then still produced enough "sweet oil" to fuel the American automobiles that took workers to their jobs, families to the suburbs, mothers to the shopping malls, and teenagers down the road for the six-pack.

By the early 1970s, that innocent assumption of enduring American abundance had been totally undermined. America, almost as much as Europe and Japan, was dependent on oil not only from Arabia, but from Algeria, Libya, Africa, Indonesia. It could no longer supply enough of the oil it needed from the diminishing wells of its own Southwest. By 1980, it required an uninterrupted eight million barrels every day from overseas to maintain an entire way of life.

This was a condition that could not be concealed from the rulers of the oil-producing states of the Middle East, so many of whose administrators had been trained in American schools of business or geology. They had learned about America's vulnerability. Thus, in 1973, they closed the noose. The Arab states had long been embittered by American support of their tribal enemies, the Israelis. And so, as Richard Nixon chose to support the Israelis in their war of survival against the Arab states, the Arabs cracked down: They would no longer ship oil to the West unless the United States consented to their extermination of the State of Israel. And with that, the first automobile lines began to appear in the winter of 1974 at American filling stations, and the cost of energy, whether for heating oil in New England winters or for gasoline all over the country, came out of the control of either normal commerce or the American government. Oil was selling on the world market at $3.41 a barrel at the beginning of 1973. It would go to $11.11 in 1974, to $14.54 in 1978, to $28.00

in the spring of 1980, and then fluctuate between $32.00 and $41.00 as 1980 came to its end. America could not swallow such increases. Gasoline had cost $.37 a gallon at the pump in the summer of 1970; it cost $.60 in 1975. It would go to $1.60 by the summer of 1980. And up with the price of oil went the cost of living.

When it was that the Great Inflation migrated from the back pages of the business news sections to the front pages and evening television shows no one can say with certainty. But shortly after the oil crisis of 1973–1974, the Great Inflation had become the obsession of common talk. The costs of a new pair of shoes, of the children's orthodontist, of eating out in a restaurant, of lawyers' fees, of pensions and perquisites, were gloomily accepted as dinner table or cocktail party conversation. The quality of American talk began to resemble what must have been that of the Gauls, the Dacians, the Britons, as they realized that the might of Rome could no longer safely insure them against the future.

The seismograph of the quake—admittedly crude and unreliable—is what Americans have come to accept as the Consumer Price Index, more commonly called the CPI. Of all the many measurements of American economic health, the CPI, imperfect as it is, comes closest to saying what is happening. And so, here again, we must plunge into figures. Sometime during the First World War, between 1917 and 1919, the Bureau of Labor Statistics put together an imaginary "market basket" to reflect the costs of everyday life. It has been revised over and over since then, reflecting American life as it changes, and is being revised once more as I write. By 1980, the Department of Labor was measuring every month some 224 sets of items in some 85 primary sampling communities, and was coming out monthly with its guess of the cost of living. The accuracy of this guess is challenged by many economists, who question the way the CPI is put together, and it is, in truth, put together substantially by theory and extrapolation. But the CPI is more than a theoretical measure—it is a fact, a motor drive, in the cost of government. Over half of the federal budget is now indexed to inflation. Mechanically, automatically, it generates more inflation. Every time the CPI shows a 1 percent jump, between $2 billion and $3 billion more must be spent, automatically, in adjustment upward of direct transfer payments, largely for Social Security. Not only that: wages go up, for the great unions have tied their wages to the CPI; military contracts balloon with each notch, as do pensions of soldiers, sailors, and government retirees, as well as pensions in many private plans. At the rate that the CPI had been rising in 1980, any pension granted a departing workingman would be worth less than half its value in five years—unless the union had built into the pension a COLA, or Cost of Living Allowance. The CPI, in fact, has become not only a description of inflation but a push to inflation.

A quick way of grasping what has happened is to look at what a dollar would buy yesterday and what it buys now. The government gives that measure in terms of something called a "constant dollar" —the purchasing power of the dollar in the year 1967—and then compares against that measure yesterday's prices and today's. In 1913, when Ronald Reagan was a toddler, the "constant dollar" would have bought $3.37 worth of goods. By 1981, the same "constant dollar" could buy only $.41 worth of goods—or roughly one-eighth of what the dollar bought in the last year before the first of the great wars.

Another way of grasping matters is simply to trace what happened in the supermarket in the ten years before the 1980 election. Hamburger rose from $.88 a pound in 1970 to $1.86 a pound in 1980, a loaf of white bread went from $.24 to $.89; and milk from $.28 a quart to $.59 a quart. But what we bought from abroad, where the dollar had been unpinned from gold and linked to the traders' judgment, soared—a one-pound vacuum can of coffee that cost $.91 in 1970 was to peak at $3.69 in 1980, more than tripling in cost. Gasoline at the pump, which had cost $.37 a gallon in 1970, had, as noted, jumped by 1980 to $1.60, more than quadrupling! Even worse was the cost of government. The simple postage stamp of the postwar years, which had cost three cents, was now eighteen cents, a jump of six times, and would go on in 1981 to twenty cents. In a city like New York, where a bus or subway ride had cost five cents after the war, the fare was sixty cents. (It is now seventy-five cents, on its way to a dollar.) Coffee, gas, bus fares, postage stamps, are not luxuries— they are necessities.

The CPI does not distinguish between necessities and comforts. But the AFL-CIO, which represents the large organized unions of the United States, recently broke down the structure of the CPI. Sixty percent of the cost of living in the United States, as reflected in the "market basket" of the CPI, is for four necessities of everyday living—food, medical care, energy (heating the home, fueling the kitchen stove, powering the auto), and housing. The rest of the cost of living goes for comforts, or contraptions; and these have either gone down (like the cost of calculators), or risen gently (like white goods and family appliances), or soared (like restaurant meals). What moves ordinary people are the necessities. The rich have their own set of psychological pinches, mostly in the comfort range. But the poor must go from steak to stew to hamburger to spaghetti as the crunch worsens. In the 1950s, real income had gone up by 37 percent; in the 1960s, by 34 percent. But in the 1970s, growth of "real income" stalled. According to the AFL-CIO study, a real decrease began in the buying power of working men and women in 1977, and for the years since, though their wages go up, their take-home pay buys less and less. Late in 1981, the Census Bureau confirmed this morbid view of American working life in the year 1980: That year, said the Census, the real income of median families, after discounting for inflation, had dropped by 5.5 percent, the largest drop in real income since records had been kept.

By the summer of 1979, no other issue could rival the inflation as a pressure on the American mind, its mood, and family planning for the future.

It is impossible, except for novelists of genius, to recapture the quality of conversation at any given moment in a country's life. But common talk in the checkout line, or in the wash-up at the mines, or at union meetings, or at the parent-teachers meetings, ultimately translates into politics. A good politician is one who can voice aloud and clearly what people know to be their own private resentments. Politicians win when they convert such discontent into issues.

Conversation in the nation as Americans approached the 1980 election was stained and drenched in money talk, by what it cost to live or what it cost to enjoy life.

In the upper classes, one heard cocktail chatter about the cost of a new suit or dress: "I just paid four hundred dollars for a two-hundred-dollar suit." One heard talk about the cost of vacations: Three thousand dollars for a ten-day stay in China! Two thousand dollars for a trip to Egypt! Or occasionally, among the concerned, the cost of a nursing home for an aging mother: "Thirty thousand a year? You're lucky; I pay forty thousand." The astronomical price of summer home rentals in fashionable areas, from Carmel in California to the Hamptons in Long Island: "Remember the first beach house we rented when the kids were little—twelve hundred dollars. It's going for seven thousand this summer, and that doesn't include Labor Day." The new hotel in New York: "It costs five dollars for one cocktail." The impossible bills from lawyers, doctors, psychiatrists, accepted by the rich as a tax on wealth. But the bills from plumbers, electricians, caterers, upset them: "He wanted fifty dollars just to come and look at the dishwasher." Then, the "sticker shock" as the well-to-do as well as the commoner went to shop new cars; and the maids who wanted to be paid in cash "off the books." The meal at the restaurant, with the host sneaking a glance at the tab and, stunned, surreptitiously adding up the figures to verify the total. Or the be-furred lady meeting a friend in line for half-price tickets to a Broadway play: "I won't pay $19.50 to see *Annie* if I can get in for $10.00 just by standing in line." In the Southwest, one heard a new phrase among the truly big rich: "I don't think he's worth more than one or two units," a "unit" implying one hundred million dollars! Or the phrase that sat more comfortably in the Northeast: "They're charging next year's prices this year. I'm not going there any longer." And in California, the epicenter of the real estate inflation, the incessant, obsessive chatter, among gentry and cottage dwellers alike, about housing prices. In that kind of talk, California, as so often, led the nation in style: the house you bought was your main stake in the great gamble, the house financed the children's college, the house was the only safe investment, to have and to hold, as money became a deceit. The first house was called a "starter house," then you traded up and in ten years you might own a house worth seven times as much. Ronald Reagan, reportedly, put down a cash payment of $29,000 for his house in Pacific Palisades. In 1981, after his election, he put it on the market for $1.7 million.

People who talked at this level almost always belonged to an undefined group of the preferred, the smart people, who lived by their services or their wits. They were the ones who benefited from inflation—by talents or skills which could be either medical, legal, histrionic, financial; or else they were the super-elite who played the stratospheric games of resources, conglomerates, securities, communications, real estate.

But the conversation among poor people, among ordinary people, was far more significant. They winced and ached. Some mysterious power was hollowing their hopes and dreams, their plans for a house or their children's college education. They felt the government must do something. It must either protect them from inflation; or it must stop the inflation.

It was more difficult to capture the conversation of such poor. It was the young plasterer saying, "I'm divorced, so I've got to take care of myself *and* my wife and the kids. The kids always need shoes and clothes. Do you know what that costs me?" It was the old lady shopping for morning cereal: "They're charging seventy-nine cents now for a ten-cent box of Quaker Oats!" The poor are mostly mute and rarely quotable. One could see the grimace of an old person buying a chocolate bar which once made a midday snack—now shrunken to the size of a caramel. One could see unlikely people poking through the cans of pet food. One could see a mother reaching to the back of the shelf, where perhaps she could find a bottle of aspirin still marked with the price of six months ago. One could see the lonely old man picking through the apples in the bin, weighing them in his hand, to find the one that felt heaviest, might make a meal.

In the ripples of conversation, one could sense the divisions. One could hear the middle-class shopper complaining bitterly, as she waited in line behind the food-stamp lady whose cart was full of snacks and convenience foods, and remarking loudly, "She's buying junk food with our food stamps. Why can't she buy real food and go home and cook it for the kids?"

What the great inflation had done, by 1979, had been to separate America into layers of different but resentful (or greedy) people. Promises had been made to all of them over the two decades; but now the promises were being redeemed in money which might become as worthless as Confederate dollars. The slick, the shrewd, the smart, the hustlers, had never believed in government promises. But those who had believed those promises, those who still held war bonds, or bought Treasury notes, or put their dollars in saving banks —all those had been cheated. What they saved today would at the 1980 inflation rate be worth half as much five years later. Those shrewd enough to be convinced that the government was innocently lying, or, worse, that it stupidly believed its own promises, knew they must protect their stake by going elsewhere—to land, to houses, to tax shelters, to collectibles like art, antiques, jewelry, and finally, by 1979, to gold. Such people rarely carried one-dollar bills in their pockets, and even more rarely examined one. Nor did the poor. But if an American did look at his dollar bill, he found it promised nothing. On the face of a one-dollar Federal Reserve note is printed the picture of George Washington, who could not tell a lie. The dollar bill used to say it was payable in silver on demand. But no longer. On its obverse side it now makes only one statement, "In God We Trust," which is not a promise of value, but a statement of faith; and faith is what gives any currency its value.

All over the world, except in a handful of oil-rich or stingy governments, faith in all currency was dissolving. No modern state, whether in the West or in Africa, Asia, or the Communist world, can any longer afford to keep its promises to its people, or keep money stable enough to let them plan their way to their dreams. All are pressed by politics or defense to assume burdens they cannot meet. So they print paper money; and the more they print, the more people distrust the promises.

The inflation in the United States had, by 1979, not yet reached panic proportions. Panics, like those of Germany in the 1920s, or China in the 1940s, are bursts of insanity. I remember not only my own madness in the late years of the war in China, but the madness of others. I recall scouring through Chungking, China's wartime capital, in 1944 in a ricksha, with a sack of worthless paper money. I was looking for cheese: only three stores still had stocks of imported Swiss cheese in cans. I bought out their entire stock so as to have enough to last until the war was over. I recall even more vividly the scramble among the younger war correspondents, like myself, to get on the plane that was flying to Japan to witness the enemy's surrender. That was the great professional prize of the war. But several of the older correspondents, wiser than we, hung back. They wanted to fly in to the liberation of Peking. They left for the reconquered city with musette bags crammed with paper currency, to buy valuables at nominal paper value. They returned with bags full of Siberian sables, Chinese mink pelts, and art objects which had piled up in Peking during the war years. They had missed seeing the surrender—but they were rich.

Nothing like this had been happening in the America of the late 1970s. But a contagion of fear had been spreading. A father who, like myself, had gone to college before the war, when tuition at America's best college was only four hundred dollars a year plus a fee of ten dollars, could not but wince for those parents who in 1980 now had to find seven thousand dollars a year to pay tuition and fees at the same college, plus room and board. Faith in one's own planning was dissolving—all across the nation. The bedrock was heaving. And the final disillusion had come after the election of Jimmy Carter in 1976. He had promised so much, and meant so well. And then it soon became apparent that his mind was a battleground between economic theorists—and on this battleground he would be the victim. He was a prisoner of thinking that no longer fit the times. His divided economic councils were of little help; their thinking described but did not explain what was happening. Harry Truman had once declared that he was looking for a "one-handed economist"—because all his economists were "on the one hand, on the other hand" people. Carter, too, must have yearned for a one-handed economist.

We should pause to linger over the influence of economists in American public and corporate life. Economists are not scientists, though they like to think they are. Like scientists, they deal in digits, graphs, computorial models and printouts, but they are really scholars in a branch of history. Historians believe that by reading the past, they are better able to predict the future. Economists believe that by charting the reactions of greed and need to past actions of government, they can predict the reactions of the greedy—which includes all of us—to future actions of government. The laws of greed are, however, no more predictable than the laws of fear. In fear, men may turn and fight—or turn and flee. In the gusts of greed, men may hoard and save—or spend and waste.

Every President since Franklin Roosevelt has had economists in his court. The best Presidents use economists as they should be used —as mapmakers to plot the elevations, the valleys, the contours of the roads the President may choose. Economists are also reporters. They report, essentially, what is happening, whether employment is up or down, whether trade balances are shrinking or rising, whether prices have been stable for the past two months, or how fast they have been rising. Then the President must, politically, decide what he plans to do; what gambles he will take to do it.

A particular phrase occurs to me from the language of the economists—the phrase "fine-tuning the economy," as if government in a free society can indeed precisely control the reactions of hundreds of millions of individuals who think themselves free to make their own plans. "Fine-tuning" the American economy, the last relatively free economy in the world, is an exercise similar to "fine-tuning" a piano when the piano tuner wears boxing gloves. The tuner can hit the lower register and get bass notes; if he hits the upper end of the register, he gets treble. But he cannot play a tune. If a President cuts taxes in the lower register, or increases spending, or both, he can boost the income of the working people. This is a vulgarization of the thinking of "Keynesian" economists. But inevitably then, prices go up, which eventually becomes just as unpleasant as the early spending is popular. If, however, a President cuts taxes in the upper register—so goes the untested and unproved thinking of "supply-side" economists—the rich and the investors will benefit most. This is politically unpopular, but the hope is that industry will expand to provide jobs. "Monetarist" economists believe that fine-tuning can squeeze down the money supply by discipline of the Federal Reserve Board, reducing inflation. But then the probable consequence is that interest rates go up, unemployment goes up, home building goes down. If one examines the thinking of "Keynesian," "supply-side," and "monetarist" economists, or mixes a brew of their thinking, one finds that none know how to fine-tune an economy. No economist yet has been able to prescribe a formula to halt the apparently irrevocable pendulum swings between disasters—between inflation and unemployment. Somewhere, somehow, all the answers lie in politics, for it is not "economics" but "political economy" which governs planning. The inescapable dilemma is that Presidents of the United States are elected for four-year terms; their electors demand quick solutions; but long-range solutions may require six or eight years, or more, to establish the confidence that is the basis of all planning, corporate and private.

Jimmy Carter's economists were just as split in counsel as those of any other administration. But he presided over more troubling times. The Carter stewardship of the economy flipped back and forth unpredictably between conflicting advice. There would be stimulating packages; then there would be wage-price guidelines. There would be one economic program, followed by another program, followed by yet another—until it appeared that the Carter administration had no coherent overall view of how people should make their living, how people might plan to save. And as this became obvious, the erosion of confidence in the American dollar spread from overseas to the American people themselves. Grab now. Get what you can. If you could, try to leapfrog the jump that was coming in prices by demanding next year's wages this year.

The CPI traced what happened in the first three years of the Carter leadership. Gerald Ford had brought the CPI jump down from 11 percent in 1974 to 9.1 percent in 1975, to 5.8 percent in 1976. In the first Carter year, the jump turned up again—to 6.5 percent in 1977, to 7.7 percent the year following, and then to double-digit figures in 1979—11.3 percent. (It would go up further in 1980, to 12.4 percent.) But by then Carter's cause was lost. Prices were now rising faster than ever before in American history; and unemployment was rising also. It had become the time of the grasshopper, as savings dwindled, the bond market collapsed, investment stalled.

It required no public opinion surveys to recognize that Americans had begun to shiver at the way prices were rising. But all polls showed the same fear. By late 1979, one poll was showing that 40 percent of all Americans felt that inflation was the major issue of the next year's presidential race; 20 percent more worded it slightly differently—energy was the major issue. And Carter could apparently do nothing about it.

The summer of 1979 had seen the second of the great oil crunches on American prices. And the Reagan planners had recognized the central theme of their campaign: Prices.

We can date the choice of theme precisely from its very first voicing, in what is marked "Policy Memorandum No. 1" of the Reagan campaign, written by a maverick scholar named Martin Anderson in August 1979.

"By a wide margin," wrote Anderson in his opening memorandum to Reagan, "the most important issue in the minds of voters today is inflation." The Reagan campaign was never afterward to separate itself from this perception. It was to be in many respects a dull campaign, because Reagan had in sixteen years learned one of the central tricks of campaigning: Say what you have to say clearly, say it again, say it over and over, until the theme strikes home. There were many themes to the Reagan campaign—the need for national defense, the need to reduce big government, others. But underlying them all was the appeal to the *Untermensch* of politics: The government is cheating you, inflation is stealing away from you the value of your dollars.

Martin Anderson is worth more than passing notice in the world where ideas intersect with actions. As Theodore Sorensen clothed the ideas of John Kennedy with fact and prose, so did Anderson give orientation to the Reagan campaign. Such idea brokers are as essential to an American campaign as were the power brokers who used to deliver voting packages, and the media masters who now dissect the same packages. Anderson—a shy man of forty-five, slight of build, slow but forceful in speech—graduated Dartmouth College in 1957 summa cum laude, served two years in the army, went on to win a Ph.D. in industrial management at MIT. For six years he had been a professor at Columbia's Graduate School of Business, where he was known as a "libertarian" until he joined the Nixon campaign of 1968 as director of research. Anderson had finally come to rest at the Hoover Institution at Stanford University, a more congenial and conservative assembly of scholars.

There, in California, he had met Ronald Reagan. He was to become Reagan's Seeing Eye dog, guiding him through the labyrinths of academia to that growing minority revolting against the dominant liberal ideas that reigned on American campuses. By 1976, he was the chief resident West Coast intellectual of that year's Reagan campaign. By 1979, Anderson had taken leave of absence from Stanford and moved to Reagan's Los Angeles headquarters, first as a one-man warehouse of facts, then as the scout on the frontier of thinkers, recruiting scholars to funnel ideas, through him, to help clothe Reagan's emotions in plausible programs.

Anderson's policy memo of August 1979 was a montage of minority ideas puckering among intellectuals around the nation. What makes it so fascinating as a campaign document is that two years later, so much of its thinking had become the law of the land.

Taking off from its first sentence, underlining inflation as the overriding issue in the minds of ordinary Americans, the Anderson memo continues:

Compounding the problem for any presidential candidate is the public's pessimism. They believe that there is little that the President, any President, can do about it.

Thus, the economic policy problem is twofold:
1) The development of a valid plan. . . .
2) Convincing the public of its validity. . . .

Inflation is the main domestic problem facing the United States today. . . . And the main cause of inflation is the massive, continuing budget deficit of the federal government. . . . The most effective way to eliminate the deficit is to reduce the rate of growth of federal expenditures and to simultaneously stimulate the economy so as to increase revenues in such a way that the private share grows proportionately more than the government share. . . .

The memo goes on to prophesy how this can be done:

  • *We must speed up economic growth to increase the take-home pay of workers and to provide more jobs.*
  • *Reduce Federal Tax Rates.* . . . We must have a program —of at least three years duration—of across-the-board tax cuts. The personal income tax rate must be cut by a specific percentage every year for three years, especially the higher, incentive-destroying marginal rates. The capital gains tax and the corporate income tax must be cut. . . .

- *Index Federal Income Tax brackets.* . . . While inflation is with us, taxes should be based on real incomes, not government inflated ones. . . .
- *Reduce and eliminate counterproductive federal government regulation of business, education, and the professions.* . . .
- *Federal spending must be controlled.* It is not necessary to cut federal spending . . . but it is necessary to reduce the rate of increase in federal spending.
- *Balance the Federal Budget.*

The memorandum, nine pages in all, is the basic theoretical document of the Reagan campaign. Its message, simply put, is that while man does not live by bread alone, bread becomes very important in hard times.

It is important to remember the principal to whom the memorandum was offered. Ronald Reagan has always fancied himself to be an expert in economics. In 1932, he had graduated from Eureka College as an economics major. What a man majors in at college makes him, in his own mind, forever after an authority on that subject. At tiny Eureka College, Illinois, in the early thirties, the name of John Maynard Keynes was scarcely known. Economics were taught simply: supply and demand, the relation of free enterprise to government, the economic cycle as defined before the New Deal undertook to flatten the curves. Anderson, of course, knew all about Keynes's theory of economics and had intellectually rejected it. Ronald Reagan had never absorbed it. Their thinking fit together.

Two years after the writing of Policy Memorandum No. 1, Anderson would sit as Assistant to the President for Policy Development in the central East Wing at the White House, second floor, where Presidents usually house their personal thinkers. By the fall of 1981, he would have seen most of his proposals written into law, a rare triumph for an intellectual; and had decided, on Labor Day weekend, to resign and return to scholarship. Offered the post of vice-chairman of the Federal Reserve Board, with ultimate promotion to the chairmanship, he persisted in his desire to return to books. There, from the outside, he would watch the troubled passage of his ideas through a storm-tossed economy.

During the campaign of 1980, however, it was Anderson who shaped the overriding themes of economic discipline and political turnaround. But the burden of spreading the message had passed to Reagan and his election managers and technicians.

That message would be transmitted by all the tricks of campaigning and organization. But delivery of the message depended most on the candidate's control of the central arena of American politics—television. So much had changed in the substance and issues of American politics. But nothing had changed more than the stage on which the candidates for the presidency spread the message; and the technology of that change requires us to go now to the story of television, and its impact on the politics of our time.

CHAPTER SIX

THE REIGN
OF TELEVISION

American politics and television are now so completely locked together that it is impossible to tell the story of the one without the other.

Television in modern politics has been as revolutionary as the development of printing in the time of Gutenberg. Once Gutenberg put the Bible in print, and others followed to explain the world to those who could read, neither church nor prince could maintain authority without controlling, or yielding to, the word in print. Television, especially in America, explains the world to those who, if they will not read, can look.

Politicians have always spread their messages wherever people crowded—at county and state fairs, at factory gates, grange halls and union halls, outside the churches and in the lunch-hour crush of big-city streets. But Americans have been gathering for the past twenty years at their television sets. In 1950, only 4.4 million American homes boasted television sets. The next ten years saw an explosion: During some weeks in that decade, no less than *ten thousand people every day* were buying their first television sets. By 1960, 45 million homes in America had television and television was ready to set the stage of modern politics. By 1980, 80 million homes owned television sets—as close to saturation as was statistically possible. And the traditional transcontinental stage of American politics had shrunk to a thirteen-inch or nineteen-inch tube at which, sometimes, as many as 100 million citizens gathered for a single episode.

All politics have changed to fit this stage. The entourages of the presidential candidates have become personal courts where the magicians and wise men are those who know the use and reach of television. The national political parties have been reduced to support forces. The map of politics has changed. The school maps still count fifty states of the Union, each with its fixed number of electoral votes. But the working maps of national politicians now divide the country into sixty-odd ADIs—Areas of Dominant Influence—in which the major television centers control public attention. And this map, for local campaigns, can be further broken down into some two hundred DMAs (Designated Marketing Areas), within which smaller radio and television stations offer audiences at the lowest cost-per-thousand. Computers further break down such audiences by age, sex, occupation, ethnic loyalty. A corps of professionals has grown up that specializes in time-buying to reach the black audience, the Hispanic audience, the evangelical audience, the easy-listening audience, the old-folks audience, the rock-and-roll audience. Other specialists mount, cut, and rearrange tape or film in five-minute, one-minute, or thirty-second commercial spots. Yet others specialize in demography, and the special craft of polling and probabilities. New political advisers have developed whose professional cunning lies not, as it did in the Old Country, in cutting deals among the power brokers, but in manipulating television attention, baiting, diddling, and trying to befuddle those who allot time on television. The once-dominant finance chieftains of campaigning are now the paymasters of the television specialists at court; their chief obligation is to raise the money to buy television time.

The use of television requires two crafts: the production, buying, and spotting of commercials; and the more esoteric craft of provoking news television to report what the candidate wants reported. Under modern financing rules, this becomes very much a game: Do you shoot the wad early to buy enough television for an early lead? Or save the larger portion for a final saturation effort in the campaign's last ten days? And what are the opponents doing?

After the conventions of 1980, by the new federal financing rules, each campaign was given $29.4 million by the federal Treasury to spend as it would. Of this sum, both campaigns invested approximately $19 million in television and radio commercials. The remaining $10 million was to cover travel and organization. But if anything, the spending of this $10 million required more skill and was more important than the money spent on commercials. Campaign travel means mounting a revolving coast-to-coast road show, with schedules arranged to provide the hard news and photo opportunities that tease television producers to air the message.

Every waking day, the average American family has its television set flickering for more or less five hours; and as much additional time is spent listening to radio. The purpose of a campaign now is to capture as much of this audience as possible. Candidates must travel not state by state but from ADI to ADI. The old-fashioned political advance man must now provide not only the proper crowds, but also the proper pictorial sites to silhouette his candidate's personality or proposal; he must, besides, make sure that every important local television or radio station gets anything from a studio visit, to an on-plane interview, to its own airplane-ramp sound bite. Television has made the personality of the candidate central; his quirks, hair style, skin color, voice tone, and apparent sincerity are as important as his themes and programs. It was on television that Ronald Reagan was to be displayed in 1980 as master of the new stage.

A full story of the invasion of America's politics and culture by television would have to pause at this point to marvel at the technology which underbraced television's penetration of the American imagination. Yet the wonders of this technology, both electronic and computorial, will have to be subordinated to the political story of this book. Neither Gutenberg of the printing press, nor Watt of the steam engine, nor Ford of the automobile, had any sense of the information revolution, the industrial revolution, or the mobility revolution they were provoking. So, too, none of the pioneers of the technology of wave radiations had any premonition of the political revolution they would provoke. But it is of the dimension of this revolution in politics that we must talk, skimping with regret the technologies that offered the stirrup for the horsemen of the revolution to come.

One can, for example, simply note that it was in November 1951 that the coaxial cable was completed from coast to coast, thus nationalizing American opinion. One must scant the sense of awe that came over Americans when Edward R. Murrow showed them, in their homes, on their screens, the Golden Gate of San Francisco and the Brooklyn Bridge in New York, live, simultaneously.* One must also skip the story of the new camera technology and floor interconnections at the Republican convention of 1952, when, for the first time, television destroyed one candidate (Robert Taft), and programmed

---

*For both of these events, see *Breach of Faith* by this writer (New York: Atheneum/Reader's Digest Press, 1975), pp. 37–40, where a fuller (but still rudimentary) account is given.

the nomination of another (Dwight Eisenhower). In television history, that episode is to be remembered chiefly by the arrival on the scene of the first anchorman, Walter Cronkite. Anchormen have since become mythical characters, larger by far than the scouts of folklore who led the covered wagons across the trackless plains.

At every step of the way to television's dominance of politics came a jump in technology that spread its reach. But not until the 1960s did television become the atmosphere of politics in which politicians breathed or suffocated to death. Historians will note that television commercials were first aired by Citizens for Eisenhower-Nixon in 1952; they will recall the old-fashioned use of time, the straight-up half-hour face-on-the-camera plea, as in Richard Nixon's famous "Checkers" speech of that year. But in those days of 1952, Eisenhower could give his critical "I will go to Korea" speech in Detroit, aired only on radio; it was left to the newspapers to headline it and score it on the public mind. Times have changed since then.

I have, for many years, been on the outer fringes of the television world, sometimes an adviser, occasionally a fleeting and uncomfortable on-camera face. But my memories begin with the year 1961, a year of considerable disturbance and trouble in the news division of the Columbia Broadcasting System, which invited me to "consult."

My first impression on entering this world was of irremediable schizophrenia. The CBS network truly wanted to give the nation the best, most accurate, most thoughtful picture of the world that it could. But it also wanted to make money. The news divisions of the networks, in those days, were loss leaders, money losers; but they were already, by then, the prestige banners of the corporations that controlled them, the necessary bow to the dictates of public service as imposed by the Federal Communications Commission. The news services nailed down the public franchises on which their parent corporations made their millions—but they did not want to lose too much money pursuing prestige.

Competition had driven the two great networks of the time—CBS and NBC—into a rivalry that was as ferocious as it was unrelenting. In those days ABC was a distant and frivolous rumbling, callously indifferent to news and public affairs beyond the minimum required by law. The competition between CBS and NBC had passed from radio, where CBS had usually led, to television. But there, in the new world of television, the masters of NBC had taken the news lead. They had chosen two young men, Chet Huntley and David Brinkley, as their evening signatures for the news; and the combination of the two—the straightforward, good-willed earnestness of the former, the wry wit and famous irony of the latter—had won them the largest share of the news audience. Moreover, in undeniable fact, NBC, with its in-house computer system, had shamed CBS on election night of 1960. At seven-fifteen that evening, CBS had announced that *its* IBM computers projected Richard Nixon as President over John Kennedy by odds of 100 to 1. The editor of the New York *Herald Tribune* headlined his first edition with a prediction of Nixon's victory based on CBS's report; he was dismissed in short order. So, too, was the president of CBS's news division.

It was at this point, with a new high command at the CBS news division, that I came aboard and learned that CBS News had two main objectives. First, of course, was to tell the news fastest and best. But second, and just as important, was to destroy the adversary, NBC. It was a war without malice; and the target, the objective to be won, was the recapture of the American news audience from the Huntley-Brinkley team. No one at CBS hated either Huntley or Brinkley; but they commanded the ratings and the largest share of the news audience.

Competition is one of the engines that drive television news; from this competition have come many of the most daring forward steps of television reporting. My first exposure to such competition came on the night of the midterm elections of 1962. It was my first time in a television control booth, and I sat at a bank of desks, one tier rising above the other, all of us watching the ten, twelve, or fifteen "feeds" that showed what CBS correspondents and field producers were speeding in from across the country over leased wires to central control in Manhattan. There, producers would slice the feeds into snatches of image and sound, one-minute, two-minute, three-minute bits of clipped reality, to be mixed together by the taste and pacing of the senior executive producer. At the bottom tier sat the technicians, audio and video, with their oscillating dials, their green luminescent monitors. At the top tier sat the men who would, with cool command, shift the election show from "feed" to "feed," from "call" to "call."

Two personalities were to emerge that night. The first was a newcomer, Louis Harris, an intense and dedicated pioneer of numbers who combined the qualities of a scholar and an entrepreneur. Harris had come aboard only recently at CBS, but as a man of imposing reputation. He had been one of John Kennedy's senior advisers in the 1960 campaign, the first personal polling "strategist" of modern campaigns. More important, he had an idea: It was that the story of an election was not told by the totals of the vote; the story lay in how the votes broke down. He had by that night cost CBS some seventy thousand dollars—then a huge sum—making "models" of eight major states, dissecting them into key precincts, precincts of blue-collar voters, white-collar voters, suburban voters, rural voters, big-city voters, Catholic, Protestant, Jewish, and black voters. Americans, he felt, voted by communities of interest. Dissect the communities, and you could not only predict the overall result, but explain it. In each of the eight major states that night, Harris had posted eighty observers, who were to telephone in the precise count from "pure" precincts—all black, all white, all Catholic, all Jewish—all together reproducing the regional, income, and ethnic patterns that made the mosaic of the nation. Both Harris and I were attached to CBS's newly contrived "election unit," headed by a veteran reporter, William Leonard. The election unit, enormously expensive, had been the counterstroke to NBC devised by Richard Salant, then president of CBS News, and Blair Clark, its general manager.

I retain the blurred memory of a vignette. California, where Richard Nixon was running against Governor Edmund Brown, was the most important race that evening. I kept insisting we could not call the race until San Francisco's votes were in—San Francisco always offset Los Angeles in California, as Cook County offset "downstate" in Illinois. The polls had just closed. Harris, a good friend, treated me as if I were as obsolete as Mark Hanna. It was over, he said; the samples from his key precincts were in his hand; Nixon was licked. In the background brooded Blair Clark, an incurable Puritan. Clark had committed the money for this experimental election unit, but he felt it was wrong to divide Americans into blacks and whites, Protestants and Catholics, Jews and blacks. Yet the operational authority to make the call was in the hands of Leonard, later to become president of CBS News himself. His election unit would grow over the years to a corps of scholars and experts as large as any university's department of political science. Leonard, controlling the "call," called for Harris over White, thus for Brown over Nixon. From Leonard the word would pass upstairs to the second star of the evening, Don Hewitt, senior executive producer that night. He, like Leonard, would go on to greater things.

I slipped upstairs to the control booth. Hewitt was "networking." He was like the admiral of an aircraft carrier, surveying his feeds on telescreens, absorbing intelligence from Leonard and Harris below, talking to Cronkite, the anchorman—but also, like an admiral, scrutinizing the enemy, watching the monitors on his two rivals, ABC and NBC. And at this moment, Hewitt struck—Cronkite announced that CBS declared Brown winner over Nixon in California. Hewitt swiveled in his chair to watch his monitor on the chief enemy, NBC. Brinkley was on. Obviously, NBC was monitoring CBS just as CBS was monitoring them. In Brinkley's ear was the tiny earpiece of all commentators who must keep in touch with production control. Brinkley visibly winced as his earpiece told him of CBS's call. Hewitt chortled: "Wry that, you wry son of a bitch, try and wry that one." CBS's correspondent in Sacramento was already in place, ready with his remote, telling the news to Governor Brown, the first to catch his reaction. By the time, minutes later, NBC's crew had caught up in California, Hewitt had switched to another remote, again ahead of NBC in the call. All through the night, as Harris's demographic breakdown proved accurate in state after state, CBS was ahead, NBC catching up. What was happening there in the studio seemed moderately important, even exciting; the true importance was to come later. Politicians, who had always known that Americans voted by community interest, now saw, clearly, that computers could define such interests, measure them, build predictions and strategies on them. If a major network could talk about such matters publicly, politicians too could plan, precisely, on the interaction of those communities.

Such network competition was to go on and on, down to the present, when it has been intensified by the arrival and push of ABC News. Of all forms of competitive journalism, that in television is the most vivid. The networks kidnap stars and producers from one another; they steal plans; they cooperate only when they must. The essence of network news rivalry is speed, and no new technological device is developed by one network to speed news to the New York central but that others, in a few months or a few weeks, have duplicated it.

It was the rivalry between CBS and NBC that produced the great changes in both the commerce of television news and the impact on politics. CBS's momentary victory in calling the midterm election of 1962 more swiftly than NBC was briefly exciting only to political buffs, then a small and limited audience. But NBC, with Huntley-Brinkley, still commanded the larger general audience. And if we follow the rivalry of the two networks over the next few years, we come inevitably to that dominant height of all modern politics, the evening or nightly news.

Until 1963, what was called "evening news" was eleven minutes of news fit into a fifteen-minute pattern of local cutaways and network commercials. "Evening news" was largely a "talking head" show, the anchorman in New York and his producer controlling the then limited inputs of their broadcast empire. A bureau in Washington, a bureau in Hollywood, bureaus in London, Paris, Bonn (still largely confined to radio), fed their news in thirty-to-ninety-second snatches to the limited time slots carved out of the tight eleven minutes. CBS, with its radio tradition, still maintained more bureaus overseas than NBC; but the advantage of their veteran corps was wiped out by film time lag—time to shoot the film, to develop the film, speed it to a foreign airport, safe-hand it to the pilot, view it and cut it in New York. Try as they would, CBS's *Evening News* anchormen, first Douglas Edwards, then Walter Cronkite, could not erase the lead that the personalities of Huntley and Brinkley had built for NBC.

It was necessary for the new CBS command group to take sterner measures. From below, within the organization, had been coming a pressure that they welcomed. The idea advanced by the producers in the news system was that the only way to beat the Huntley-Brinkley lead was to leapfrog NBC—jump the fifteen-minute evening news to a full half hour! But would the nation sit still for a full half hour of news every night? Would the network affiliates clear an extra fifteen minutes of moneymaking time from their lucrative local shows? And with what could the network fill the half-hour show—a half-hour show meant they must fill twenty-two full minutes with news content! Above all, was there that much news content every day? Could a half-hour show take the lead from NBC—and how much would it cost?

The decision-making process was secret. I attended one meeting in the parlor of Blair Clark's East Side brownstone. Those present included everyone with a share in the decision: from Salant and Clark; to the two most vigorous CBS producers, Fred Friendly (who would later succeed Salant as president of CBS News) and Don Hewitt, an irrepressible man, impossible to keep out of any account of modern television; to various other producers and operating executives.

Salant and Clark would have to carry whatever decision came

from this meeting up the stairs of the CBS corporate hierarchy to William Paley and Frank Stanton, chairman and president respectively of all CBS. If they agreed, they would have to force it upon all reluctant affiliate stations, including that owned by Lyndon Johnson in Austin, Texas. The chief purpose of local stations was to make money; they would not easily brook the preemption of local money-making time by the parent network from which they suckled.

Of the colloquy at the Clark house I recall best what Friendly and Hewitt said. The operating proposal had, of course, already been shaped—as most decisions are—by the pressure from an understructure which has arrived at a consensus, and needs only a leadership go-ahead to act. Friendly, one of the great creators of modern television, is a man obsessed by news, by the moralities within it, frenzied in his recognition of the power, for good or evil, of the image orthicon tube. Friendly not only favored a full half-hour evening news show, he was for a full hour of evening news! Whether or not a full hour would work did not concern Friendly; it was good for the viewers, good for the country, good for its own sake. Hewitt was much more practical. Did we realize what this would mean? We would have to fill the whole half hour with news! That meant you could not do it with "talking heads"; you would have to establish bureaus all across the country. A bureau in Boston. A bureau in the Midwest. A bureau in Atlanta. The black revolt was coming to a head there in the South and an Atlanta bureau could probably fill lots of time. But bureaus would also be needed overseas: the Middle East was hot. The technology was there, of course; satellites were beginning to promise instant transmission from the world's trouble spots—no more yellow-helmeted motorcyclists rushing undeveloped film to friendly pilots. But—time! You'd have to give more *time* to stories. You'd have to go from sixty-second snatches to longer stories—running ninety seconds, three minutes, four, maybe five minutes long. You'd have to expand: Filling a half-hour news show would change the whole nature of the news—different thoughts, different strategies, different slicings.

It was clear that all agreed CBS must try to jump NBC by going to a full half hour. The budgets would have to be refined by Salant and Clark, and then they would have to sell the idea upstairs to the corporation.

Nor was there any doubt in the mind of anyone at the meeting that Walter Cronkite would be the signature personality on the show. No one else in television except John Chancellor is more loved by his colleagues, operatives, subordinates, superiors, than Cronkite. The choice of producer, or chief of staff, was equally clear: as between Friendly, who dominated his stars, and Hewitt, who then did not, it should be Hewitt. With the consent of the parent corporation, the half-hour CBS Evening News went on the air on September 2, 1963, its star segment being an interview with John F. Kennedy by Walter Cronkite, focused upon the then distant Vietnam problem. Within one week, NBC, not to be outdone, had also introduced a half-hour evening news. And the reluctant affiliates found their audiences were not "depressed" by news, but hungry for it.

Today, between fifty and sixty million people tune in every evening on one of the three national news shows to find out what the world is doing to them. Some estimates set an unbelievably high figure on the impact of the evening news—they guess that 65 percent of America's people get 100 percent of their news from the evening newscasts. But the reaction in 1963 had been immediate. The Roper Organization has for twenty-two years surveyed and measured the chief public news sources. From time unremembered, newspapers had been the chief source. By the end of 1963, however, the Roper survey reported that for the first time, more Americans relied on television for news than on newspapers.

The blast effect of evening news on public thinking was to be startling. But it would take years for its profound effects to show. It would be a decade before the nation's afternoon newspapers, once the senior forum of American opinion, began to wither. People once rode home from work reading newspapers. Columnists once flourished in afternoon papers. But now morning outlets were preferred. So the afternoon papers slowly died in big cities, because when people came home from work, they could learn in thirty minutes all they thought they really needed to know. It would also take time for politicians to realize what the evening news was doing to their constituencies, national and local. But by 1980, Peter Dailey, media manager of the second-phase Reagan campaign, summed it all up. Dailey was in charge of the commercial buying and presentation of Ronald Reagan's spots. Yet he knew he was secondary in the great game of moving public opinion. "The evening news is the ball game," he said of the campaign. "That's all there is to it."

Nineteen sixty-three had closed a television year of upheaval with the assassination of John F. Kennedy. The ceremonies of laying him to rest made television not only the national mourning place for a weekend but, ever after, the first assembly place of national emotions or national attention to the great events of our times.

Nineteen sixty-four was to bring even more change:

• The Republican convention in San Francisco that year was to mark the end of old-style organization control of a national convention. Barry Goldwater's managers had locked up state delegation after state delegation before the convention ever gathered. The architect of that effort had been F. Clifton White, who held the convention in his hands; from his command wagon, with his electronic floor controls, he could wring the neck of any opposition with a single "all call" signal to his floor whips and captains. But Clif White had not reckoned with television, or how necessary it was to restrain its appetite for drama. What came across on the screens was the hurly-burly of violence, the heroic defiance of the mob by Nelson Rockefeller, the casting on camera of Goldwater as a pitiless Savonarola, and the Republican liberals as martyrs. "If I had had a pint of brains," said Goldwater later, "I should have known in San Francisco that I had won the nomination but lost the election right there." Since 1964, only two other conventions (the Democratic conventions of 1968 and 1972) have been left so completely to the mercy of television. A lesson had been learned by observant politicians: A party convention could no longer be a political marketplace of deals and crackdowns; it was the projection platform from which they must deliver whatever essential image the winning candidate meant to press on the nation. Television's cooperation or control was vital.

• That same year saw, like a clap of thunder, the arrival of the adversary commercial. The adversary commercial was the creation of a mild-mannered, soft-spoken gentleman named William Bernbach, chief of one of Madison Avenue's leading advertising agencies. Bernbach had never been in politics before. He had, however, introduced Volkswagen to the American market, made Levy's Jewish rye bread popular, and knew how to use images on screen. He accepted the responsibility of media manager for Lyndon Johnson's campaign only on condition that he have complete command. Bernbach did not want to be second-guessed by politicians. ("Politics," he said, "is about survival.") Whereupon, Bernbach proceeded to savage Goldwater as no presidential candidate had been savaged before. The first slash of the Bernbach commercials was his Daisy Girl spot: A beautiful child, plucking petals, counting in a high trill, is overtaken in her count by a deep male voice in a missile countdown. The mushroom blast blots out the end of the commercial, with the unspoken message that Goldwater is for bombs, Johnson against them. Ten days later followed the ice cream commercial. A delicious little girl is licking an ice cream cone while, in voice-over, comes a tender, motherly voice explaining how bad nuclear fallout is for children. Then, in lullaby tones, comes the message: "There's a man who wants to be President of the United States who . . . wants to go on testing more bombs. His name is Barry Goldwater. . . ." Such commercials all but branded Goldwater as a baby-killer. Others followed. The one Republicans hated most, coast to coast, showed disembodied fingers tearing up a Social Security card, *your* Social Security card, while in the background a voice repeated one of Goldwater's horseback opinions on the uselessness of Social Security. The commercial made Goldwater the enemy of old people—and old people vote.

The Bernbach commercials were to be imitated each election year with increasing artistry and cruelty until the management, production, and placement of such spots became the last element of solid control over the voters that money could give a national campaign. Most people make little distinction between real news and the commercial messages they see on television. Some scholars* argue that commercials, far more than speeches, carry a candidate's message home.

● There was also in 1964, of no less importance, the moment when the simple commercial and administrative needs of television changed the technical management of vote-counting throughout the country.

That moment came in California's June primary. Primaries then were still fresh as television material, but they were approaching the ultimate craziness reached in 1980. Primaries had even then, however, reached costs that network budgets could not absorb. Both of the dominant rival networks had adopted key-precinct analysis; but the raw count of the actual vote was still the field of desperate competition. The networks would hire Boy Scouts, veterans' groups, members of the League of Women Voters, to call in results from individual precincts, on leased telephone wires at enormous cost, so that one or the other network could flash on its screen the latest

*Notably Professor Thomas E. Patterson of Syracuse University's Maxwell School of Citizenship and Public Affairs, whose book *The Mass Media Election: How Americans Choose Their Presidents* (New York: Praeger, 1980) is a beautiful case study of political analysis.

count in a hotly contested race. In California's 1964 primary, where Barry Goldwater and Nelson Rockefeller were so close that only a wizard could have predicted the results, the stationing of network vote-counters at each of California's more than 31,000 precincts cost almost two million dollars. I remember talking with an RCA executive who was appalled at the cost of NBC's momentary vote counts on screen. "We've got to stop this," he said. "We're going to bankrupt each other."

The cost was no less apparent to CBS executives. And from that California primary came an agreement never approved by the Department of Justice's Antitrust Division. Since no one network could bear the cost of competitive vote-counting in the United States, with all its then sixty-five or seventy million voters, they had to cooperate. The two big networks would invite the third, ABC, to join them, along with the two national news agencies, the Associated Press and United Press International; all five would share the cost. That fall, they devised a cooperative called the News Election Service (NES), which would collect the votes from all across the country and share the tallies immediately. It is the unofficial vote count of NES that one sees on every network and in every newspaper the day after election. NES has since purged vote fraud more than any institution of law; it monitors the results of most of the 180,000 voting precincts of the nation. Gone are the days when in a "squeaker" election, on the late night of the count, the boss of Hudson County (New Jersey), Albany (New York), or Cook County (Illinois) could call a docile precinct captain and say the organization was behind and needed every vote possible. "How many more do you want from here?" would be the usual response. The scrutiny of NES now prevents that. Its semiofficial vote count provides the figures out of which historians and analysts confect wisdom. Schoolchildren will be taught these results for generations to come. But NES sprang from the rivalries of television; and has become, by its integrity and efficiency, the unintended beneficial consequence of commercial competition.

• There remains one other memory of the 1964 election, perhaps the most consequential of all.

I had been in California for the climactic primary of that season's Republican contest. And on the television screen entered a new personality. The personality of that evening in late May was a Hollywood actor named Ronald Reagan. There he was: amusing, yet serious. There he was, in his first flight, pleading that California voters choose Goldwater, the man of American principles, over Rockefeller, the big spender. His was a splendid performance. He was, apparently, doing a fund-raiser.

A few days later, I visited the Goldwater headquarters on Los Angeles's Wilshire Boulevard, a concourse that should be remembered in the history of the Old Country along with such centers as the garment district of New York, Michigan Avenue in Chicago, Blue Hill Avenue in Boston. In Goldwater's Wilshire Boulevard headquarters, a long plank table rested on several sawhorse supports; women sat at it opening envelopes. Out of them came one-dollar bills, five-dollar bills, even an occasional Social Security check endorsed to Goldwater or Reagan. The Reagan personality had tapped a hidden mother lode of money—poor people's money, the contributions of those who must be called the underclass of conservative populism. The Republicans still get most of their money from the big rich and the corporations; but they also get more money from poor people, in driblets of contributions, than do the Democrats, the proclaimed party of the poor.

This discovery of a Republican underclass came with the first appearance of Ronald Reagan the politician on screen in California, in 1964. His appearances in the years since have enlarged his reach and his power. The man understands television, the art of projection. More than any other candidate, Ronald Reagan, a natural artist, has made television his road to power. And this began in 1964.

One other stepping-stone must now be touched: the Democratic convention of 1968, a memorable example of what happens when an uncontrolled convention gathers in the presence of television.

The liaison of a modern convention with the television networks begins just as soon as the two national parties choose the site where they will meet. The parties choose, of course, with television uppermost in mind: the arena (will it hold the television equipment?), the hotel facilities (will it hold all the reporters, who outnumber delegates by ten to one), the access facilities (airports, air contact, buses, highways), and, critically, police control of whatever may burble up to disrupt the proceedings.

The television networks and the national committees are in touch with each other as soon as a convention site is chosen. They need each other. The networks need access to every aisle and back room of the hall, to the podium, to every delegation, to the headquarters of all candidates. They sent, in 1980, some six hundred operatives each, at a cost of $13 million to $14 million for each network. Every candidate now knows that he is at the mercy of the television cameras. Even if his nomination has been set and his rivals foreclosed before the convention opens, his message depends on what the networks will show of his purpose, his policy, and the quality of his delegates and supporters.

But it was in 1968 that the conventions first became the producers' showcase. So large is television's investment of prestige and money in a national convention that the corporate hierarchy of each network descends on the convention center to hover over the news producers who get the show on air. The corporate hierarchy are the hosts of the lavish parties at which so much business of politics is transacted. But the executives worry. Once a convention is under way, no member of the corporate hierarchy comes between the operating producers and the realities; no one intrudes into the control rooms where the cameras, remotes, feeds, oscillators, technicians, do their job.

Lester Crystal, now NBC's senior executive producer, recalls that 1968 convention. He comes of the new breed of younger producers who have never, as older producers did, served their apprenticeship in pencil reporting on the beat. Only a few men like him completely understand the intersection of technology, television, and politics, or can talk its jargon more bewilderingly. They live in a newer world with its own language. By 1968, Crystal had become producer of the nightly Huntley-Brinkley Report. And so he went to his first national convention at Chicago, to preside over the Huntley-Brinkley show from six-thirty to seven o'clock; then he would retreat to watch from central control, where the feeds of all the remote cameras and observation points flickered on the nineteen-inch screens of the many monitors.

"Reuven was running the convention coverage," said Crystal. (Reuven Frank, a major figure in television history, was not only president of NBC News, but executive producer of the convention telecast.) "Reuven would decide when to cut to the podium, when to cut to the speeches, when to cut to the streets [where riots were taking place]. We were reporting something completely out of control." And it was up to the man in the control booth to sequence the simultaneous fragments of turbulence on the floor, beyond the floor, in the streets, into a pattern the mind of the viewer could grasp. Only the executive producer, peering at his feed monitors, could decide how all fit together in the story.

Nineteen sixty-eight in Chicago: Cameras feeding and filming everywhere. Police in the streets of downtown Chicago, windows shattering, mobs jeering. Ribicoff on the podium denouncing his old friend Dick Daley, of Chicago, for "Gestapo tactics." Cut from street to hall. Cut from podium to the delegates on the floor, swaying, screaming, waving their banners for recognition. The delegates become unimportant, all dignity lost. What is the story? There is no time for thought—and the cameras on air must move to show what the producer thinks is the proper pattern of the realities.

I was then sporadically on air for CBS, an occasional foil for wise Eric Sevareid; and I realized in that booth how much power the television camera had over politics. On screen at CBS was the same bewildering mélange of street riot, back room, floor, and podium shots that NBC showed. Somehow Mayor Daley had arranged to place the huge New York and California delegations at the back of the hall. It was the last hurrah of Old Country politics: He wanted to bury their revolt against Johnson-Humphrey. But he could not prevent cameras from closing in on the delegations of these two greatest states in the Union. California and New York had both given their hearts and delegates to Robert Kennedy, now two months dead. California and New York were demanding that the convention nominate in his stead his younger brother, Edward Kennedy. Sevareid and I had both managed to reach Kennedy contacts that evening; I had spoken with Stephen Smith, the manager of Kennedy campaigns from the very first. From a private Chicago club, Smith had said, "It's all bullshit. We aren't running Teddy for President at this convention." Sevareid had received similar reports, and so, in our colloquy, we told the nation and the convention that there was no Ted Kennedy campaign that day, month, or year. The turmoil on the convention floor was imaginary; Ted Kennedy was not running. Then, within minutes, there burst into our locked area a New York politician, brassing his way through the uniformed guards, poking his finger at me. "What are you and Sevareid trying to do in there? We can nominate Teddy at this convention, if only you stop undercutting us. You're *ruining* us!" But we had hard news, and nothing could stop our hard news from reaching the convention floor unless the executive producer decided to cut us off; which he did not.

Another scene: I am sitting, late on Wednesday evening, with Hubert Humphrey in Chicago's Conrad Hilton Hotel. It has been an evening of violence. The producers are trying to bring camera images into a running picture. But Humphrey is imprisoned, as all of us are, in the glass walls of television, seeing what is happening only as the tube chooses to show what is happening. Suddenly the tube shows, once again, the confrontation at the corner of Michigan Avenue and Balbo Drive. It has in fact been several hours since that melee broke up down below, but faint fumes of tear gas are still wafting through the hotel's air conditioning. We, high up on the twenty-fifth floor, do not know what is happening, what is real, what is not, and Humphrey, seeing what the nation is seeing, moans, "Oh, no, not again! Are they starting again?" I dash to the window, look down to the street, and see that it is quiet. I report this to Humphrey; the network is only showing a rerun; but the streets are not the reality, it is television which is reality. This is what the nation will see, this will provoke the reaction that Humphrey will have to fight off for the next three months of his campaign. The affable and amiable man cannot hold back from a rare burst of temper. His set is now tuned to NBC, and he is furious; he shakes his fist at the correspondent. "Don't forget, Vanocur, don't forget I'm going to be President someday. I'm going to appoint the FCC—we're going to look into all this." But the show goes on. Willfully or not, consciously or not, the networks control the nation's imagination.*

One cannot skip lightly from that convention in 1968 to the campaign of 1980 without at least trying to absorb some of the romance of the technologies that underlay the new developments.

There are early benchmarks on the way. One reflects that in the middle 1960s, news from overseas was still flown safe-hand to be edited in New York, until, at the death of Winston Churchill in January 1965, CBS chartered a plane and outfitted it as a studio. There producers and editors could spend their time, on the eleven-hour flight home, cutting and editing film, so that the entire show would be ready for air on arrival. In those days, satellites were just arriving on the scene; before stationary satellite orbits were developed, television broadcasting from Europe was possible for only two hours a day, at the cost of ten thousand dollars a minute. Down the road of time, the day would come when round-the-clock telecasting was possible from a hundred or more spots overseas. Events in the Middle East, or an uprising in Poland, would become instantaneously visible; and upheaval anywhere—from Teheran to Belfast—would be

---

*For a fuller description of this most exciting of all conventions, see Chapter 9 of *The Making of the President—1968*.

enhanced by the knowledge that the whole world would now be watching.

Even more important were the technologies that developed at home, in America, which hastened politicians' awareness of television's power—chief among them the development of the minicamera and videotape. The minicam and tape had been first employed by local evening news shows, which were spreading across the country as piggyback packages tacked to the national evening news shows—and making money. The tape and minicam eliminated old-fashioned, cumbersome film, which took so many precious minutes to develop; the new combination could take you to "the scene of the crime" in an instant. When the tape was married to another stream of technology—microwave transmission and the dish antenna—it changed completely the time frame of those who appeared on the news, and even more, those who produced the news for national showings. A field producer who understood the technology could now originate his show from a dish antenna hung outside his hotel room or, if he had arranged with the telephone company a few hours before, from an antenna hung from a telephone pole. He could flash from a riot in outer Brooklyn to a receiving dish atop the Empire State Building in New York, or from Wilshire Boulevard in Los Angeles to a Burbank receiving station—from which his segment could speed immediately to the national centers in New York.

All these technologies were speeding news judgment, eliminating the filter of time, the pause for reflection. Speed itself forced fundamental judgments to be made in a few hours each afternoon, laced with pictures, spiced with violence, human interest, or the burning oil tank. Speed required fresh pictures to be framed with words immediately. And always the competitive imperative: that the show "march" more quickly, with more dramatic rhythm, thus attracting more audience than the rival networks. What this speed was doing was imposing more and more responsibility, thus power, on the handful of people in New York who fitted the day's events together as they felt they ought to be. In the studios, the senior producers and anchormen had to redesign the world each day. Neither of the two great anchormen of the seventies—Walter Cronkite and John Chancellor—was entirely happy with the power that had fallen to them: the power to set up summit conferences between the Arabs and the Israelis, the power to place Watergate and Richard Nixon before the judgment of the people. But there it was, they could not escape it. "All we are trying to do each night," said John Chancellor once, "is to impose some coherence over events."

Parallel developments in television showmanship—the confrontation shows and the documentaries—were forcing politicians to recognize the vitality of television in moving emotions. The oldest of the great confrontation shows was NBC's Sunday-morning *Meet the Press,* followed by CBS's *Face the Nation,* and by ABC's *Issues and Answers.* Sunday had, thus, slowly become the favorite time of national politicians to reach those interested in politics, and local politicians followed on regional shows that imitated *Meet the Press.* Such shows gave politicians the opportunity to speak for themselves, live, for an uninterrupted two or three minutes, no longer at the mercy of a producer's cutting and splicing. Even more attractive to politicians became the daily morning shows, both national and regional. Here, they could speak sometimes for five or six minutes, uninterrupted. The Sunday programs gathered an important, but very limited, audience of people interested in politics; the morning shows, however, with their puddings of entertainment, fun, hard news, and personalities, invited a larger audience of common citizens. NBC had led the way in the 1950s with its *Today* show, which by the middle sixties was the unchallenged favorite of the Washington executive and political audience. It was followed by rival morning shows, and politicians would fly overnight, or thousands of miles, to appear on them. There, they were faced not with a hostile questioning panel of newsmen, as on the Sunday shows, but by friendly interrogators, grateful for their presence. And the most important of the confrontation shows, one of the prizes of the presidency, was the presidential press conference, first televised live by John F. Kennedy. In the twenty years that followed, the presidential press conference became a bedlam, serious and meaningless reporters reduced alike to jack-in-the-box figures, rising and shouting and sitting and rising, while the President, smiling and supreme, treated them like unruly children. Ronald Reagan has tried to make them more orderly and less frequent—and thus, probably, ultimately more dangerous for him. But the rule remains: No President ever loses at a press conference; he has the last word, the last answer, the final authority in his own place.

All through the seventies and still today, however, the evening news remained the nemesis of the President, who can dominate only his own press conference. A President may appear on evening news for a few seconds preaching brotherhood; but the next slice of the show may show blacks and whites rioting on the street. The President may, in sixty or ninety seconds, be shown talking of the economy or foreign affairs; the networks must give him time; but the following shot may show a spokesman of the rival party denouncing, disagreeing with, or undermining him.

The evening news dominates even the men who mold it. I have spent many hours watching such shows put together at both CBS and NBC, and marveled at the wondrous meshing of technology, drama, and conscience, as in the pressure of late afternoon, anchormen and producers watch the monitors, revise the script on feeds, adjust to the latest agency news bulletins. But they are compelled by events beyond them to report what has happened that day; if they do not, the rivals will. Everyone watches the evening news shows; Lyndon Johnson had three monitors, to watch all three simultaneously. Every President and presidential candidate on the road gets a morning bulletin from his base headquarters reporting the nightly news minutes allotted him for the previous day's effort, giving his score on the road. Foreign embassies watch the evening news and cable summaries to their capitals; some of the Arab embassies in Washington even note down which producers and reporters are Jewish, and which not.

The evening news has thus become a gamesman's field on which professionals of campaigning match wits with the producers and correspondents. They want the evening news to carry *their* message of the day. Correspondents, producers, and anchormen are accordingly suspicious. Time was, before the advent of tape, minicamera, and microwave, when a candidate had to deliver his main message before noon so that film could reach New York in time. Technology now permits the networks to record the noon speech and record the rival's response in some distant place as late as five or six in the evening. The trick for the campaign group is to make its main stab too late for the nets to carry the rival's reply; another trick is to mount the candidate before the proper visual to carry his message. There are a dozen other tricks. The campaign is now a contest between the new professionals—trying to bait, mislead, or compel the correspondents and producers to show what they want to show—and the network staffs, eluding the trap or exposing it.

But television technology is not limited to hardware devices. Technology reaches out to the assembly of information. Louis Harris in 1962 had been a pioneer when he identified the "pure" precincts which, just after the polls closed, were keys to the ways communities voted. But there are now fewer and fewer "pure" precincts in the

United States. By 1973, in the New York mayoralty race, NBC had refined the techniques of "exit polling" (introduced first by CBS in 1968) into an X-ray device. Twice on every election day, morning and afternoon, exit pollsters now question individual voters (usually one out of seven) in key precincts as they leave the voting booths. With less than twenty questions, they can classify each as liberal, conservative, middle class, working class, Catholic, Protestant, Jewish, Irish, Italian, Black, Slav, ticket splitters, or party liners. Before the official polls close, such informal exit polls can be fed into computers; and the computers can predict how communities are voting, defining the bony structure of the uncertainties that move them. The effect of exit polls on politicians is incalculable. They themselves lack the resources to conduct such polls. But what the exit polls say is sometimes as important as the final vote. One of the turning points of the 1980 campaign was to come in Wisconsin, in its primary vote on April 1. There, the exit polls showed the remarkable surge of working people across party lines to vote for Republican candidates. This surge was to influence the Reagan campaign enormously in its final focus on blue-collar votes.

Just as important as exit polling has been simple but massive research. Each of the great television networks has developed a large staff of political scientists and researchers, people who know more than any individual reporter can match. They code the past, they code the present, they code the future. In 1968, CBS first assigned Martin Plissner, now its political editor, to organize a staff to identify the loyalties of each delegate to the national conventions. Week by week, CBS projected who controlled how many delegates. All other networks have since duplicated delegate analysis. But I relish a moment of the 1968 Republican convention when a Reagan operator attempted to switch a vote from Nixon to Reagan. "But I can't switch," the delegate said. "I'm already pledged." To whom? was the next question. And the reply came back: "I told CBS that I'm voting for Nixon. I'm pledged to CBS."

Deep research is now an expenditure only the television networks can afford. Their resources outrun even those of the New York *Times,* the Washington *Post,* or any other printed publication. A great network like NBC maintains more than one hundred news correspondents around the world, with a support troop of over a thousand producers, researchers, and writers, plus technical personnel. Each of the three networks maintains in Washington approximately thirty reporters. We who write must, like everyone else, tune in on their news in the morning and break to watch their news in the evening. All of us are later dependent on network research data; we chew on this data; although we may not understand the algorithms of their election-night projections, we usually accept them.

No single newspaper or reporter can even approach the resources of the networks, for news has now become big business. Rather than being television's obligatory bow to public service, news has become a profit center. The local television stations that so reluctantly accepted network news almost twenty years ago now have their own profit-making news departments; and some anchormen who preside over local news can now draw up to $500,000 a year for coloring the flow of events with their personalities. At the national level, the summit personalities of news can command salaries larger than baseball stars—up to one million dollars or more a year. News had reached its ultimate as big business when, in the years 1980 and 1981, CBS's *Sixty Minutes* was the prime television show in the nation. Conceived and developed by Don Hewitt, it sometimes commanded approximately half of the Sunday evening national audience. A thirty-second commercial spot on that news show cost $175,-000! Its operating profit for one hour each week came to well over $1,500,000. In the ten years of its ascendancy, from 1975 to 1985, if all goes well for the show, it may net the hitherto unimaginable sum of between half a billion and three-quarters of a billion dollars—more than Chrysler Corporation in the same period.

There is one sobering counterpoint in all this swift development. Television has become the stage of all great events—assassinations of presidents and dictators, weddings of princes and princesses, moon launchings and disasters. But then, finally, in the daily unrolling of morning and evening news, it cannot ignore the stuff of history itself, the stuff that challenges the drama of surface events. Was Hubert Humphrey, for example, undone by the televising of the riots at the convention of 1968? Or had he been undone by years of previous presentation on the evening news of the brutality of the Vietnam War, and the consequent revulsion of the American people? For one full year, 1972, Richard Nixon was the prime actor on television news, the cameras showing a miniseries: Richard Nixon in Peking, Richard Nixon at the Great Wall, Richard Nixon outfacing Hanoi, Richard Nixon at the Kremlin. But by 1974, he was undone by something larger—by the seepage of disgust through the evening news, as the abscess of Watergate slowly leaked. The men and women who live by television, or by writing about it, know the penetration of politics by television is irreversible. But they worry. There is, for example, Don Hewitt, who says: "We may be in for a series of one-term Presidents. The Presidents are overexposed, become targets, they get taken apart. They're like a TV series—four years and the people get bored, they tune out. They want a new show every four years."

And there is the more melancholy verdict of Michael Arlen in *The New Yorker* in 1980:

The candidates wander the country . . . perhaps like rock bands, in full view of everyone but seen by no one. . . . Today, both the politicians and the networks are caught up in the same dance of technology. The real power is the power of the men and women who control the montage effects . . . who instinctively under-stand the truth of Eisenstein's statement: "The basic fact was true, and remains true to this day, that the juxtaposition of two separate shots by splicing them together resembles not so much a simple sum of one shot plus another shot as it does a *creation.*" One shot plus another shot; one sound plus another sound: *Creation!* These engineers are the new creators, our political king-makers.

Thus we pause as we come to our times, that period between 1976 and 1980 when network news perhaps reached its zenith, be-fore the advent of cable television, which may undo politics all over again. And we should linger at the phenomenon of Jimmy Carter, who appeared on scene as history, politics, and television all reached a climax.

Nothing is neat about politics; it packs together incongruent realities. One must, however, examine the incongruent realities that confronted Jimmy Carter and television in the campaign of 1976.

There was, first, the eruption of primaries across the country—twenty-nine primaries! Ten serious candidates! How could anyone cover them all? But primaries made drama, and, at least in the early months, people would stay up late at night to find out who would win. Not only that: in the first six weeks of the 1976 campaign, when the opening scenes were still fresh, more people would stay up to watch politics than the CBS late-night movies, or Johnny Carson on NBC, or ABC's *Wide World of Entertainment.* In 1976 came the first major television attention to a ritual now known as the "Iowa caucus"; then came the classic New Hampshire primary, then Massachusetts, then

Florida, then up to Illinois, and so on in the now familiar marathon across the nation. The primaries were, and still are, natural raw stuff for dramatics. There are the candidates in the forefront, as protagonists, chanting; in the background are the people as chorus (the man-in-the-street interview, in either the twang of New Hampshire or the drawl of Florida's panhandle), responding. How the scenes are to be cut depends on the director of the drama, who decides what reaches the camera eye. Since by 1976 it was impossible, even for the television networks, to report on all the candidates, producers had to choose leaders, dark horses, and dropouts. One of the ablest Democratic candidates was former governor Terry Sanford of North Carolina. But network cameras could not afford to report *all* the candidates in the drama; thus, Sanford, though he spent $600,000 in his futile effort, was to be ignored, and in the darkness he became a noncandidate. The candidate of the Democratic center, Henry Jackson, built his campaign on the old structures and packages; thus, he *had* to be portrayed as a candidate of the right, the favorite of the bosses.

Next, the latest technologies had given the networks remarkable new capacities to report events. A television crew need no longer be five people on the road—but three people: the infantryman (the burly, muscled cameraman), the veteran top sergeant (the producer), and the gallant young lieutenant (the reporting personality). One could now double-team the crews attached to a major candidate, a crew for the morning news, another for the evening news.

Finally, in 1976, came a fresh new character: Jimmy Carter, a natural-born hero, a twice-born Christian, a farmer and an engineer. And Jimmy Carter had the acumen, or good luck, to recruit a team who understood television better than any team of troopers who had joined a candidate on the road to the White House before. The Carter organization, to be sure, was able to create events, like the "event" in the Iowa caucuses, or the "event" in New Hampshire.* But his media men were of the new breed, unconnected with old-fashioned politics. They translated events into national television.

First among them was Gerald Rafshoon, a remarkable advertising man who had come up through the bizarre world of movie promotion to become advertising chief of Twentieth Century-Fox; he had salvaged the disaster of Elizabeth Taylor's appearance in

---

*For the actual operation and management of the Carter organization in 1976, Jules Witcover's *Marathon: The Pursuit of the Presidency, 1972–1976* (New York: Viking Press, 1977) is by far the best account.

Cleopatra. Then he had quit, at twenty-nine, to found his own agency in Atlanta, and there discovered that he, a young Northern hustler, was as much an outsider in Atlanta's power structure as Jimmy Carter, a rural state senator from Sumter County. The two "outsiders" struck up a friendship and Rafshoon managed the advertising that brought Carter to the governorship in 1970. "When I first met him," said Rafshoon, "he didn't know which end of the camera to look in. He'd ask, 'Do I look into the camera with the red light?' or 'Do I look at the TelePrompter?' He loved to talk to the technicians. He understood I was a professional and he trusted me."

Affection grew between the two. When Carter stayed overnight in Atlanta, he would sleep at Rafshoon's house and, said Rafshoon, "He'd get up early in the morning and I'd find him cooking breakfast for my kids." It was Rafshoon who carved the first images of Carter on television. By 1974, Rafshoon had a cameraman and a soundman following Carter wherever he went. They would carve snippets of cinema verité of Carter at the farm, Carter in the peanut field, Carter leg over wooden rail, Carter at early campaign rallies. By October 1975, Rafshoon had fifty thousand feet of film, out of which he could carve the five-minute advertising spots he favored, or he could reduce them to one-minute or thirty-second shots as budget required. Rafshoon would show them to the Carter staff, or to outsiders. "A chill ran up and down my spine, the way they'd react to 'I'll never tell a lie.' Some people would say it was corny, some people would say, 'We're gonna lose the liar vote.' But they loved it." The basic Carter commercial of the first-phase campaign was as much a classic as the Bernbach Daisy Girl of 1964.

The commercial ran: "There are lots of things I would not do to be elected, listen to me. I'll never tell a lie. I'll never make a misleading statement. I'll never betray the confidence any of you has in me. And I will never avoid a controversial issue. I won't be any better President than I am a candidate. Watch TV. Listen to the radio. If you ever see me do any of those things, don't support me, because I would not be worthy to be President of this country. But I don't intend to do any of those things. Because my faith and my confidence and my support and my criticism and my advice comes from people like you who don't want anything selfish out of government. And want to see us once again have a nation that's as good and honest and decent and truthful and competent and compassionate and as filled with love as the American people." It was quite clear: Carter was running against big government, against Washington. And most of all he was running for President against Richard Nixon, the man who had lied to the American people.

Next among Carter's television guides was young Patrick Caddell, the boy pollster of the McGovern campaign of 1972. "Carter was the product of Watergate," said Caddell in early 1976. "The country was tired of lying, tired of being torn apart. People needed a sense of restoration, of love of country." The country, Caddell went on, was concerned with basic questions, with what holds the nation together, not with issues like oil divestiture. The campaign should be based on themes, argued Caddell from his polling surveys, not issues. It was proper, in contrast to such Southern governors as Lester Maddox and George Wallace, to speak of love. "We made the decision to use issues only as vehicles to expose his themes, to go for long spots, two minutes and five minutes; better to give up prime time and use off time to give depth and background to the campaign. Jimmy asked us to take a look at religion, he was afraid it was a negative. We tested the theme—it got a tremendous response. This guy *really* believed in *God.* It mattered. It was something no one else could bring to the campaign."

Third among Carter's television instructors was Barry Jagoda, a former CBS producer, who had volunteered his aid. "I knew how you got on air; I knew what happens in the control room; I knew what happens on primary night and who they put on air." Jagoda did not come aboard until January of 1976, but he added the television news dimension to scheduling, urged Carter to avoid the forum debates of the League of Women Voters, for Carter was best at one-on-one confrontations; urged him to make all facilities open to the networks on primary nights; urged him to skip the news producers and correspondents on the road, but to be available at the studios, talking to anchor people directly, in his own words, rather than to put himself at the mercy of the dramatic slicings that evening news demands. Jagoda could "input" advice, such as: On the night of May 25, 1976, with Oregon, Arkansas, Idaho, Kentucky, Nevada, Tennessee, all reporting primary returns, Carter must be available to the networks, not from a "remote" in the field, but in Manhattan, at the nerve center of television. By the time Carter and Jagoda had come that night from the airport to a midtown Manhattan hotel, Carter looked at his watch and said, "I'm going to miss my deadline." Jagoda replied, "You know my job better than I do." And Carter replied, "No —it's my job."

Carter learned television fast. His smile went on as soon as the camera's red light flashed, as if he were plugged in. If the organization, run by Hamilton Jordan, could provide the victories, Carter could stretch those victories, by television, into more and yet more victories. His 1976 campaign, which had begun with organization and television, was short of money by March. From Iowa in January to Pennsylvania on April 19 had been only fourteen weeks. He had organized best in Iowa, and gained the headlines and attention. He had eliminated most of his liberal rivals in New Hampshire; eliminated his Southern rival, George Wallace, in Florida; and had cornered his last serious rival, Henry Jackson, in Pennsylvania. And in Pennsylvania, the Rafshoon-Caddell team had mounted a model of how television must be used in a primary. Cutting up the state into television and radio marketing districts, cross-sectioning it into the Protestant Southwestern vote, the big-city (Pittsburgh-Philadelphia) vote, the ethnic vote, the Lehigh Valley vote, the intrastate rural vote, they threw all their remaining funds ($175,000) into television and radio time for each targeted local audience. They won Pennsylvania handily, which eliminated Jackson; and Carter was home free and clear to claim the nomination, except for the backfield tacklers like Brown of California, or Church of Idaho, who could not stop him.

No candidate had used television better than Jimmy Carter up to 1976—so that what recurs in all our memories of that campaign is largely visual.

• Nineteen seventy-six, in the hotel room with Jimmy Carter on roll-call night of the convention. He is sitting, barefoot, on a sofa with Mother Lillian; Amy, in pajamas, is moving about restlessly; an eleven-month-old grandson, crawling over his knees, is cradled from time to time in his arms. He is facing several television monitors; behind the monitors, three television cameras are lined up and half a dozen reporters cluster behind the cameras. The roll call drones out over television, and as Ohio puts him over the top, there is this strange interaction: Carter leans forward; his wide grin flashes as the red lights go on. He is watching himself on the television screen; and television shows Carter watching himself on television as he "privately" savors his victory and shares it with the nation.

• Next night in the convention hall in New York. This is a convention stage-managed, preplanned for television, the colors of the hall and the podium chosen for their shades of blue. No more old-fashioned rowdy demonstrations. Fifteen minutes is all television will permit. It is like riding in a train looking backward on the history of a party. There in the audience sit past Democratic greats—Hubert Humphrey of Minnesota, Robert Wagner and Averell Harriman of New York—all figures of the past, now members of an invited audience. Lights out for a film of Jimmy Carter's road to the nomination. Lights up. Enter Carter, precisely paced on a chosen path. Choreographed to turn at one aisle, to stride over to Daley of Chicago, the enduring boss, and shake hands. He misses his cue, and Daley, all rouged and ready for the camera moment, winces as Carter turns past him to the podium. Cheers. Carter mounting stairs. Silence. Then the famous smile and the line, "My name is Jimmy Carter, and I'm running for President. . . ."

● It is hot summer in Plains, Georgia, in the weeks between the conventions. There is no news in Plains beyond Carter's private sessions with the noted thinkers who are advising him on his future administration. But Carter makes news for the cameras: There he is, walking through his peanut fields; there he is again, playing softball with the reporters; there he is, one of the common folk, talking to his neighbors; there he is entering the Plains Baptist Church to teach his men's Bible class on Sunday morning. The reporters sweat, scratch, and try to write thumbsuckers. But they are now of the lesser breed. They have already been shepherded at big rallies into enclosures labeled "pencil press." This campaign is being run, not for the "pencil press," but for television. There may be no real news out of Plains, Georgia, for the pencil press. But for television, there are fine photo opportunities; the cameras are carving images for the evening news: of a decent man who will go to Washington to clean up the mess, who plays softball as fiercely as he plays politics.

● A 440-mile rail trip on September 20, 1976, from New York to Pittsburgh, through the industrial East, one of the last bows to the old American tradition of campaigning by train, by "whistle stop." Carter's public opinion lead over Ford has been melting; he has slipped in the polls from a 62/29 margin over the Republican to perilously narrow margins. He is now trying to shore up the traditional Democratic base of minorities and labor on a route that leads from New York and New Jersey through Pennsylvania, and will go on to Ohio, to end in Chicago. Against the background first of clotted cities, then of Pennsylvania's dark Alleghenies, over the hairpin curves by which the first rails were driven across the mountains into the Mississippi Valley, Carter chants his plea: "Roosevelt . . . Truman . . . Jack Kennedy . . . our party . . . help me . . . help me . . . I'll need your help in November . . ." his voice fading away as the train chugs off. Magnificent pictures, but by now the evening news has turned against him. The networks will lead that night not with campaign-trail visuals, but with a *Playboy* interview in which Carter has confessed that he has "looked on a lot of women with lust. I've committed adultery in my heart many times." The interview is months old, but now about to be published. It is hot stuff, and so will wipe the scenic tour from television.

• The Great Debates. Gerald Ford and Jimmy Carter—both preprogrammed and briefed—stand at their lecterns, in Philadelphia, for the first debate. A glitch occurs in the TV audio transmission. Neither will show weakness, or approach the other to say, Let's sit and wait till they get this fixed. For twenty-seven minutes, they remain there, stiff and silent, while technicians work frantically and the nation watches nothing but frozen figures. They cannot move; they are actors in a play without a script. Carter does poorly in this first debate. In the second debate, in San Francisco, Ford in his turn will blow his chance. He burbles that there is "no Soviet domination of Eastern Europe. . . ." Television carries this slip of the mind across the nation.

• Since Carter still leads in the polls, Ford's television advisers (the firm of Bailey and Deardourff) mount a counterattack. They attach to Ford's campaign tour Joe Garagiola, the sports announcer, who will report to preselected audiences, in preselected states, over preselected Areas of Dominant Influence, the day's events as seen by a member of the Ford team. But not even with the help of Joe Garagiola can Ford overcome the Carter lead. Ford is a nice man. So, too, is Jimmy Carter. But Jimmy Carter is running *against* Washington, while Ford, the appointed President, *is* Washington.

• In the last week of the campaign, Sander Vanocur, a major television figure himself, but then, in 1976, the television critic of the Washington *Post*, wrote his summation:

> The show has come to the end of a long run. It began in Iowa in January and it will end election night in New York, where the networks have assembled all their high steppers for the finale. . . .
>
> This campaign *was* television. Those wonderful people in Common Cause, who helped bring about limitations in presidential campaign spending, insured that in the 1976 race the medium would be the machine. . . . if you looked for the buttons, the bumper stickers, the billboards and other forms of political

graffiti that we had come to associate with past presidential campaigns, you could not find them. Too expensive. Save the money for the media.

What you found instead were varying forms of media graffiti, especially on television . . . designed to fertilize the hard soil of a political landscape which, over the past decade, has yielded such a sorry crop. . . . I think this is a burden that television is not equipped to bear. The political process is too complicated, at times even too mystical an experience for a medium that is designed, perhaps unwittingly, to make brief claims on our attention span.

We have heard from the pundits in the press and on television that it has been a lackluster campaign, devoid of issues. But who is responsible? It is not the candidates. They would be fools if they tried to explore issues in a medium that measures out the world in 30-second takes. . . .

But what more can we expect. In an age where the medium has become the political process, it sets the stage, assigns all the roles and tells us when we should laugh and when we should cry . . . mocking any attempts at reasoned political discourse.

It wasn't supposed to work out that way. But it has. . . .

• Carter has won, we come to the inaugural. Inaugurals have always been a new President's call to the nation, but now television delivers the message. The 1977 inaugural is the best yet. A camera shot catches the flag, the vistas; a chorus of black college students from Atlanta is singing "Battle Hymn of the Republic"; a cantor in the cornet voice of the Jewish tenor cantillates a prayer. All faiths are represented. Tip O'Neill, with his gravelly Boston Irish accent, swears in Walter Mondale, the minister's son from Minnesota. At 12:03, the oath of office transfers power from Ford to Carter. Carter speaks. His is not the voice of a trumpeter, it is the voice of the shepherd: the pastor, not the crusader. A biblical rhythm underlines it, and he quotes Micah. It is a good, comforting performance; the sun over Washington is splendid, lighting the horizon over the subfreezing but beautiful city; seventy-five-millimeter howitzers boom the traditional twenty-one-gun salute; in the background, cameras cut to pretty young women moved to tears.

Compassion. Honor. Trust. A government as good as the people. And then, with all ceremonies over, comes the television master-stroke. There is the President, with Rosalynn, and Amy, walking down Pennsylvania Avenue. No limousines. The producers and commentators are surprised. This President is a man of the people. He is proud, and smiling, as the nation watches him walk to the White House. Rosalynn is stunning in her bright blue coat. But Jimmy is the centerpiece. The cameras first learned this kind of artistry following the same hallowed route behind the cortege of John Kennedy from the White House to the Capitol in 1963. Now they are following the new President, back from the Capitol to the White House, hand in hand with his wife, their arms swinging together. There, at the White House, they will together take command, virtue restored.

There could have been no Carter presidency without television. But he who comes to power by television must be prepared to be destroyed by television. For the men and women of television, however hungry for drama and clash in politics, are compelled to report the larger drama of upheaval, change, and erosions of old faiths. Carter was to be undermined not by the malice of television, or by the superior skills of the Reagan television team in 1980, but by history itself. Television, on its morning and evening news, would show a world America could no longer control.

So, then, it is to the Carter presidency we must go next, for though he might control camera attention, he could not control events.

CHAPTER SEVEN

THE STEWARDSHIP
OF JIMMY CARTER

Jimmy Carter was the apotheosis of all the good will and liberal thinking that had made the Democratic party of the United States the majority party for forty-four years.

He had won his presidency as the "outsider," the country-style, small-town boy who had campaigned against Washington and its insiders.

He had proved himself a master of the mechanics of the new primary system and the most successful craftsman in the use of television until the appearance on scene of Ronald Reagan. Yet he arrived in Washington having won both his nomination and his election on personality alone, without an organized party behind him.

It was a combination of these qualities that dominated American imagination and public life for the first few months of his presidency.

Carter had promised, and promised again, and then again, to change the direction of American affairs. A memorandum of 111 pages listed all the promises he had made to the American people in his three-year-long campaign for the presidency. They were fair and decent promises; they embodied every hope of every group and institution that good-willed people had created in reaving the old system. There would be instant registration of any man or woman seeking permission to vote who appeared at any ballot box anywhere in the United States. Cabinet meetings would be open to the press; sunshine laws would purge secrecy from any crevice where sinister special interests did their work. The budget would be balanced by 1980. The income tax, "a disgrace to the human race," would be reorganized. "Big-shot crooks" would be punished. The nuclear arms race would be halted. American troops would come out of Korea. Welfare would be reorganized. The blacks, the poor, the under-privileged, would be comforted. The Third World would be recognized. The environment would be cleaned. The bureaucracy would be called to account and slimmed down to lean-muscled efficiency. No hope any liberal had expressed anywhere at any time would be ignored.

Jimmy Carter had come out of a campaign carrying a garment bag over his shoulder, using symbols on television to press his image home on America. His administration began, thus, as had so many administrations before his, with symbolic action. On his first day in office, by executive order, all draft evaders of the Vietnam War were pardoned. He followed in a few days by slashing to the bone the use of official limousines by White House personnel. The Marine Corps orchestra was silenced as he greeted his first audience in the East Room—no ceremonial ruffles and flourishes or "Hail to the Chief" when Jimmy Carter entered. There was to be no chief of staff; Carter would run his White House as he had governed Georgia. It was a frigid winter in which he took office, so, said the President, thermo-stats at the White House must be set at a patriotic low of 65 degrees to save energy. (Two and a half years later, in the next energy crisis, he turned off White House air conditioning and averred that people could work comfortably in the sweltering executive mansion at 80 degrees.) He had proclaimed, in accepting the Democratic nomination in 1976, "I have spoken a lot of times this year about love. But love must be aggressively translated into simple justice." So people were puzzled as they watched him move into operation—and would remain puzzled to the day he departed, four years later.

Jimmy Carter was always a mystery, this man with the straw-colored hair and clear blue eyes, whose enemies came to despise him while those who would be friends could not understand him. Carter fit no mold nor any of those familiar journalistic diagrams by which political writers try to explore the nature of a presidency through the personality of the President. He could not describe himself, as Roose-velt so jauntily did, as having passed from being "Dr. New Deal" to "Dr. Win the War." Nor could he be described, as was Richard Nixon by so many of us, in the twenty years of Nixon's eminence, as being the "Old Nixon" or the "New Nixon," with new Nixons succeeding one another every two or three years in the public print.

The personality of Jimmy Carter was the same from the day he decided to run for the presidency until he lost it. And that personality, rather than changing from an "old" to a "new" Carter, had to be examined as a set of layers of faith, of action, even of unpleasantnesses. What made it most difficult was that the most important layer of the personality was a Christianity so devout and concerned that political writers found it awkward to write about.

That layer—of true belief—was uppermost and undermost. I encountered it initially before he became President, when I had my first long talk with Carter in Plains, Georgia, in his pleasant middle-class home, surrounded by oak trees—a home comfortable by any standards but by no means the style of mansion so many presidential candidates had acquired. At that time, in 1976, I was pursuing the candidates with a single-track question that might possibly be useful if I was to write a book on that year's campaign. "Where did modern American history really begin?" I would ask, and all had different answers. Jimmy Carter began with civil rights, "the most profound sociological change that's taken place in the country." It was the law as well as Martin Luther King that brought the change in the South, he said. So long as civil rights had been something administered by HEW, and while local and state laws contradicted federal laws, there was this question: "Whose laws do you obey?" But once the federal courts took over, everything changed. The South *wanted* to change, and the federal courts forced it along. Carter rambled on in answering my question and then got to family life. "When I grew up, the family was my community," he said. "I always knew where my mother and father were, they always knew where I was. I never had a problem where there was any doubt or fear except . . . disappointing my family . . . and there was a greater centering of the life in the community, for which our schools and church were the center." He has since been called a "dispassionate President," but when he talked quietly, he could be passionate. And on black rights he was most passionate of all. Sumter County is one of the most segregationist counties of the Old South; but he had led the fight there for integration, had refused flatly, publicly, to join the White Citizens Council or the "segs." To give the blacks their open and equal opportunity was a matter of faith—of Christianity. Somewhere Carter had crossed a line in his past; blacks as well as whites were the children of God.

Much could be said about the archaic fundamentalist underpinning of his Christianity. But it was real. He believed. No other candidate could write, as did Carter, an open letter to a newspaper declaring his belief in creationism.* He taught Sunday school in Plains, held prayer breakfasts in the White House, began lunch, even with such amused big-city politicians as Ed Koch, mayor of New York, by asking permission to say grace. "Why not?" Koch, who had come to plead for aid for his city, is reported to have replied. "We can all use a little extra help."

It was impossible to ignore that motivation of love and mercy which Christianity brought to the administration of Jimmy Carter. He tried to make real all the promises that a generation of liberal programs had substituted for old faith. He ticked off to me the record of previous Presidents, their shortcomings, their lack of faith. Of Kennedy, he said, he "lacked boldness."

Then there was a second layer of the Carter personality—Jimmy Carter the engineer. He had answered my first question by talking of civil rights. Then he gave me an alternative beginning for his reflection on where modern American history began: Sputnik. "Sputnik shook people," he said, "the first dawning of the belief that the Soviets were actually able to challenge us in a world that we thought was uniquely ours from a scientific and technological [view]."

No journalist ever gets to know a President, unless he has known him years before on his way up. Presidents are too busy to spend time on any but those who are useful to them. So a writer must invent the outline of the man he fitfully glimpses. And it seemed to me that one could invent a Jimmy Carter on the model of Sir Isaac Newton. Newton was also a man of science and of God; Newton thought the universe was a clockwork mechanism fashioned by God with some ultimate unfathomed design, and that by exploring the mechanics of things he could bare the larger design.

These two layers of Jimmy Carter's personality intersected. A pilot named Peterson had flown me down to Plains for my first visit. I sat beside him and we talked of Carter. Peterson was devoted to him. He had flown Carter from Atlanta to Plains several times. On their flights Carter would sit beside him, ask him how the plane worked, had learned to understand and operate the instruments in the cockpit. Then Peterson added a catching observation. He and Carter attended the same Baptist church in Plains and Carter would

*"The article in Monday's *Atlanta Constitution* incorrectly states," he wrote in the summer of 1976, "that I do not 'believe in such biblical accounts as Eve being created from Adam's rib and other such miracles.' I have never made any such statement and have no reason to disbelieve Genesis 2:21, 22 or other biblical miracles. . . ."

say occasionally, "Saw you in church on Sunday." But Mrs. Peterson did not go to services. Peterson recalled Carter asking whether he could call on her someday to talk about it. But he could not have been more surprised when Carter did indeed call (this in the midst of a presidential campaign), to talk with Mrs. Peterson about church, prayer, God, and the importance of Sunday services.

The engineer Carter was quite distinct from the Carter of faith. He would rise at five-thirty every morning at the White House and be at his desk before any of his staff. And he worked hard. He seemed to believe that if he could grasp all the facts and figures of a problem, he would understand its dynamics. A prominent New York Democrat, one of the major contributors to the party, visited Carter in midterm and was asked into the private study adjacent to the Oval Office. There sat Carter at his desk, with a pile of papers knee-high beside him. "Do you know what that is?" he asked the visitor. "That's the Air Force budget," said Carter. "I've read every page of it." The astonished executive talked briefly with the President, then made his exit through the office of Hamilton Jordan, who acted as chief of staff. There he sat down to enjoy a good conversation on politics and policy. If was as if, said the businessman later, Carter was the chief researcher, Jordan the chief policymaker. This appetite for swallowing detail went with Carter always. At his summit conference with Brezhnev in Vienna, both were invited to a performance of Mozart's *The Abduction from the Seraglio.* Brezhnev, in his box, tired and restless, would doze, nod, occasionally chat and joke with his attendants. But Carter in his box had brought with him the full libretto of the opera and, turning the pages, followed the score act by act, scene by scene, even making notes in the margins. "Carter," said one of those with the President, "is not exactly a bundle of laughs."

There were also all the other layers of Carter. Carter the yeoman, for example. He knew the name of every tree he saw, and loved them all. I mentioned to him, on my first visit, that I had seen a stand of Southern cypress a few miles south of his home, near the town of Americus. The observation caught him. "That's a climatological line," he said. "North of that stand of cypress you won't find any more . . . all the way to the North Pole." He pulled the last phrase out with characteristic melancholy of tone, for he loved his Southern homeland. Then there was Carter of the primaries of 1976, a first-class mechanic of politics, aware of every county, city, voting bloc he must deal with, enjoying the adventure. Yet however much the public Carter on the stump, at the town meeting, in a student dormitory, seemed warm and outgoing, there was the other, prickly, private man—shy, soft-spoken, occasionally vindictive, withdrawn, unable to entertain give-and-take except with his Georgians, his wife, and Pat Caddell. This was a wary, small-town Carter, peering at the world and the barons of Washington with the skepticism of a country visitor, fearful of being taken in by them as much as they, on his arrival, feared him.

"You have to understand," said one of Carter's White House guard, "that Carter simply did not *like* politicians. He had set his mind on being governor of Georgia, and he got to be governor by politics; he set his mind on being President, and he got that job done using politicians. But he didn't *like* them. He asked Russell Long over to the White House once to ask for his help on a tax bill, gave Long half an hour, and when the half hour was over, he simply got up and said, 'Thank you.' He wasn't offering friendship. We tried to get him to see the older Democrats, the wise men, people like Clifford and Harriman. He tried that twice and then just stopped. We told him he had to make friends in Congress. Of course, he didn't drink, but he played tennis. So we made a list of congressmen and senators to be invited over for a game. He went through the names, played once with each of them, checked them off the list. And that was that."

Carter performed with serenity and grace at his press conferences, always well prepared. But his major speeches to the nation, in which a President must lift and inspire the people, were dry, rustling sermons. He had little sense of cadence, less humor, and his habit was to emphasize a point by lowering rather than raising his voice. Once the novelty of the style wore off, it sounded flat—provoking that biting wit Eugene McCarthy to remark that Carter's speeches had all the "eloquence of a mortician."

Few ever questioned Carter's high purpose or moral integrity. He was going to make the world better. Closest to his heart lay his large causes: to cleanse and purge the environment, to eliminate the threat of nuclear arms, to make civil rights and affirmative action not just the preaching of the righteous but a reality in American life. And above all, he was going to solve the energy crisis, free America from its dependence on the oil dictators of OPEC.

Carter was going to make his programs work, as he had made them work in Georgia, by appealing to the people over the heads of Congress and the entrenched interests.

Thus, the White House, apparently, was never more open. In the first few months came a White House radio program, a two-hour question-and-answer call-in, open to all common folk, with Walter Cronkite of CBS anchoring the broadcast as questions for the President rang in from forty-two people in twenty-six states across the nation. For the rival network, NBC, there came next a special show, starring John Chancellor and Jimmy Carter, showing the President's full working day, taking the people behind the scenes at the White House. No great insights came from such shows; but they were symbols of the open presidency, behind which the true President rested unrevealed. *Time* magazine would also have a full day behind the scenes, both in the White House offices and in the family quarters upstairs. The Los Angeles *Times*'s Robert Shogan would have not only a full working day, but weeks of access to cabinet and staff meetings, to show how the President was going about his duties.* And as if this were not enough, there came the first of a series of his favorite political device, the public town meeting, billed as a "Meet the People" event, where the President, like Harun al-Rashid wandering the bazaars, tried to learn what the people were thinking. Only Carter moved, not incognito, but with a television train following.

Promise followed promise. There would be a comprehensive reorganization of welfare proposed by the first of May; there would be a complete overhaul of the tax system presented to Congress by August; there would be an ethics bill soon; the budget would be balanced by 1980.

Over and above all: the energy program. He had told his energy specialist, James Schlesinger, to have a complete and comprehensive energy program, with a New Department of Energy as its crown piece, ready by April 15. In his second week in office, Carter was off on a helicopter hop to Pittsburgh, followed by the cameras, to show his concern for workers laid off from factories short of fuel, and for the underprivileged who shivered in unheated homes. The cold winter was, of course, not simply an accident of the vagrant climate. The pain came from the underlying energy crisis, which every President, since Richard Nixon, has recognized as fundamental. Energy was, indeed, an immense problem, touching every branch of life, business, and economics. But when the Secretary of the Treasury, W.

---

*Robert Shogan's *Promises to Keep* (New York: Thomas Y. Crowell, 1977) is one of the finest books published recently on White House politics. It is an indispensable reference for anyone who seeks to understand how presidential purpose first collides with the realities of politics.

Michael Blumenthal, protested that neither he nor the chief of the Council of Economic Advisers, Charles Schultze, had any information or input into the master plan being prepared in Schlesinger's office, the President grew irritable. Nor was there then any chief of staff to coordinate matters.

Energy, then, was the overriding thrust of Carter's public effort for his first two months, and by April he was ready to go public with a television blitz. He had begun to prepare the public for the program early in February with a "fireside chat," as he sat in a beige cardigan before a blazing hearth in the White House. On Monday, April 18, he was ready for a full-dress address to the nation, telling the people that: "With the exception of preventing war, this is the greatest challenge our country will face during our lifetimes." Two days later, he was up before a joint session of Congress, presenting his bill. Two days after that, a televised press conference drove the message home.

"The energy bill," said a White House member, "was the single greatest political mistake we made in our first six months. When we couldn't pass it, people got the impression that the President just couldn't manage the government. It came slowly, but we never recovered from that impression." The bill was one drafted in virtual secrecy by unnamed technicians; it had been put together at breakneck speed, much as Reagan's tax bill four years later, and was flawed with technical errors which Congress tried to unknot, in the process finding itself tangled with every lobby in the nation. It was eighteen full months before anything even resembling the original energy bill moved through Congress; and not until the spring of 1980 was a final, comprehensive, and reasonable program pushed through; but by that time it had stalled for so long that Carter won no political credit for his major achievement.

One must try to go deeper to examine that other Washington which Jimmy Carter discovered on his arrival there—not the schoolbook Washington of tradition, but the real Washington, the jungle of special interests, claimants, lobbies, and cause groups. It is difficult to describe this Washington, that shifting menagerie of cold-eyed money men and hot-eyed moralists who shuffle through the marble anterooms of the Capitol, who slink or stalk through the corridors of Senate and House office buildings. The center of their action is the United States Congress, where, in any crisis, they vector in to ambush the President of the United States.

Every President has the unwritten authority, for the first six months of his term, to set the agenda of national purpose. Had Jimmy Carter concentrated all his effort in his first few months in office to make his energy program a matter of supreme national purpose, he might have overcome all special interests and begun his administration with a towering achievement. Four years later, Ronald Reagan began with one primal thrust—the passage of his budget and tax bills —using every artistry of arm-twisting and seduction to force it through. But Carter, in 1977, insisted on keeping all his promises at once, which left him exposed to all those with leverage in the offices of congressmen elected to represent their interests. A single program—his now forgotten "stimulus package"—is thus worth even more attention than his primal energy program. It was to show all the nightmare entanglements a President faces when he attempts to fine-tune the national economy, on which so many dependencies and entitlements have come to rest.

The program was an economic recovery program. Most Presidents begin their administration with such a recovery program. The most famous, of course, was Roosevelt's New Deal. Kennedy had his program, Johnson his, Nixon his. Gerald Ford opened with the War Against Inflation, Reagan would call his, simply, the Economic Recovery Program. But Carter, in 1977, styled his the "stimulus package," with little foreboding of what arguments and disputes the smell of loose money would arouse in Congress and around it. The story of the stimulus package is too instructive and enticing to skip.

Carter had campaigned in 1976 against the unemployment which Gerald Ford's management of the economy had visited on the country. True enough, Ford had reduced inflation to a rate that now rouses nostalgia—a 5.8 percent rise in the CPI. But that effort had apparently caused a rise in unemployment to 7.8 percent. The doctrine of liberals had, however, run with the theories of John Maynard Keynes from Franklin Roosevelt's time to the time of Lyndon Johnson: Government pumps in money at one end, jobs come out the other end. So, too, believed the liberal advisers who had gathered with Carter in Plains in the transition time as he prepared to become President. They felt they must stimulate the economy, and the center of their thinking became something called the "rebate," which might cost anywhere from $5 billion to $8 billion. This "rebate" would be an immediate cash grant of fifty dollars to every taxpayer in the United States. In Roman times, a new emperor repaid his legionary loyalists with a "donative" of silver denarii. But *this* rebate would go to everyone who paid taxes, thus flushing consumption, thus creating jobs.

All economic decisions in any democracy are *political* decisions. The stimulus package could not help but involve politics at its worst: This was handout money! Who would get what share of how much? And with all that money loose, it was every congressman, region, interest, and lobby for itself.

Carter made the first semipublic unveiling of his stimulus package on January 7, 1977, to the House and Senate Democratic leaders, who had been invited down to visit him in Plains. It was a flexible program, with elastic figures: $8 billion or more in immediate rebates, $7 billion in tax reductions, another $5 billion for public works and CETA (the Comprehensive Employment Training Program). The Democratic leaders of the incoming Congress viewed their newly elected leader with awe. He had taken control of the party over their heads. But they, after all, were the congressional leadership and since they had been invited down to consult, consult they would. The senior senators—Long of Louisiana, Muskie of Maine, Humphrey of Minnesota—gave deferential assent, twiddling the figures a bit here and there. But Congressman Ullman (Oregon), who now chaired the House Ways and Means Committee, which sets the nation's taxes, did not like the idea of a rebate at all; it would not sail in Congress. Congressman Foley (Washington) thought the rebate a good idea, though he disagreed with the thinking behind the public works section of the package, declaring that federal public works programs had become "an obscenity, building things like indoor pistol ranges, marinas and other unnecessary projects." But Congressman Wright (Texas) wanted a bigger public works program. Senators Cranston (California) and Byrd (West Virginia) wanted more money for youth unemployment. All, cowed by the new command presence, would, however, go along. But they were by no means of one mind.

On January 25, five days after inauguration, the President met again with the congressional leadership, this time in Washington. This meeting was apparently dominated by the newly elected Speaker of the House, Thomas P. ("Tip") O'Neill of Massachusetts. O'Neill is a traditional liberal Democrat by heritage, inclination, and party loyalty. Now at last he was Speaker and he spoke up, promising all support in the traditional honeymoon welcome to new Presidents. Before the Congress recessed in August, said O'Neill, it would meet the President's goals: not only the stimulus package, but the reorganization authority the President sought, the President's forthcoming energy program, and the President's ethics bill. You lead, he said in effect, we follow. And thus, on January 31, within two weeks of inauguration, Congress received the President's two-year stimulus package, now grown to $31.2 billion, with the famous rebate grown to $11.4 billion; therewith began the President's education in pressure politics. It is as difficult for a President to give away donatives as to cut them, as Reagan was later to learn.

First up, on February 3, was the black leadership. The black leaders were disturbed. They had done so much to elect Carter, but now, say the minutes of the meeting, they felt neglected. They felt they had been allowed inadequate input in forming the new economic recovery program. They wanted, specifically, $2 billion more to go for black teenage unemployment and more black appointments at senior levels of government. The President said this was "discouraging." He had done so much for blacks. He urged them to praise those things he was doing right.

The blacks were only the first of the many groups to become involved in the economic recovery program. Any economic reorganization of the United States hurts or benefits too many vocal groups. The shoe business, for example, moved into the act. Cheap Korean and Formosan shoe imports were wiping out the shoe industry of New England. If there was to be no relief from this flood of cheap shoe imports, so the President was informed, Senator Muskie would vote against the entire stimulus package. Somehow, the President's proposal to raise, or index, minimum wages became involved, So, too, did the President's proposed water-project "hit list," which would eliminate nineteen dams or other water projects dear to the hearts of key congressmen. Then other interests gathered for assault or leverage on the new recovery program—the sugar people, the machinists' union, the dairy people, the bankers —all threatening to scuttle the stimulus package if they were in any way hurt.

One could go on with the bizarre behind-the-scenes struggle over the stimulus package, all the while the President was preparing the public for his energy program. But his authority was hemorrhaging. A summary of the minutes of a ten-day series of meetings in April of 1977 tells the story.

On April 6, the President had invited the senior spokesmen of the American labor movement to a White House luncheon to discuss the economic programs. Among them was George Meany, president of the AFL-CIO, first among equals. Meany was a difficult man, an amiable raconteur among intimates, intimidating to strangers. His private hobby was watercolor painting, an art he had mastered, some felt, with the delicacy of a French Impressionist. But he had started as a Bronx plumber; had risen through the rough and violent gauntlet of New York's construction industries; and learned the application of clout to New York's politics. As president of the AFL-CIO he had become Big Labor's autocrat; he was an honest man, but very tough; and his dealings with U.S. Presidents were no different than his dealings with Bronx borough presidents. He could not be intimidated by anyone.

Meany was in high form that day as he unloaded on the President. The President's stimulus package upset him. The proposed minimum wage left the poor below the poverty level and the proposed indexing was inadequate; of course, none of his union members worked at that level of wages—but he was speaking for the poor. And how about shoe imports? The President's devotion to open foreign trade would put eighty thousand shoe workers on welfare; it was the United States that should be "the client of the State Department, not other countries." Meany went on to color-TV sets: In one year, Japanese imports had risen from 18 percent to 42 percent of the American market. Clothing and textile workers were also being clobbered by imports. The President tried to mollify the labor chief, but Meany insisted there was "no proof wages contributed to inflation"; it was interest rates and unemployment that were inflationary. He felt that business had too great an influence on this administration. Two days later, the President remarked that he never wanted a repeat of the way the labor luncheon had gone.

On April 8, the President met with his Economic Policy Group, an unshaped body, a simulacrum (it was hoped) of what the National Security Council was supposed to be. This body was cochaired by Chief Economic Adviser Schultze and by Treasury Secretary Blumenthal. But neither was in charge. Carter added cabinet secretaries Califano (HEW) and Harris (HUD) to the meeting, and round again they went on the stimulus package. By this time, Secretary Blumenthal, who had for several months been warning of another inflationary surge, repeated once again his stubborn opposition to the rebate and its impact on the budget deficit. Secretary Califano said that budget deficits were *not* related to inflation. Secretary Blumenthal said they *were.* The President allowed that he was still in favor of the rebate, but the party had to be pulled in line. He added that several senators had warned him that in order to get the rebate through Congress, he must balance it with a strong statement against inflation. Then, in the presence of the group, the President permitted himself one of those moments of candor which recalled the original Jimmy Carter of Plains.

The President's remarks, as summarized in the account, reflected his underlying perplexity. ". . . we should inventory the problems that were causing inflation," the summary records him as saying. "Even if we did not know all the answers, we should say here are the causes and there are things that are inflationary. He stated he should be an educator and not claim to know all the answers. . . . There were no magic answers . . . we should simply describe the problem and go with that and sit down with key news people and tell them our purpose in issuing the statement. . . . We should relax tensions if we would all work together, but that we would not abandon the good things such as worker safety and air and water pollution control even though they contribute to inflation."

It was now late in the traditional first hundred days of a presidency and Carter was gearing up for his energy push. By April 12, he told his chief domestic adviser, Stuart Eizenstat, that he was very concerned about the rebate, and was thinking about dropping it. The next day, he met with a key group of advisers to discuss the stimulus package again. By now, Blumenthal was strenuous about withdrawing the rebate; it would push up inflation. But Schultze was equally forceful: The rebate had to go through; it was integral to the stimulus package. The President listened to both sides and concluded the meeting by saying that he had thought he could get the rebate through Congress in April; now it would have to be June or July.

Sometime the same day, on the thirteenth, he made up his mind. He told his Vice-President, Walter Mondale, that he had decided to drop the rebate once and for all.

But he neglected to inform his Secretary of the Treasury, and Blumenthal was to go the next day before the National Press Club, and take a public posture in *support* of the President and the rebate. The President had neglected also to inform Chairman Ullman of the Ways and Means Committee, who had opposed the President's rebate proposal from the beginning but had remained publicly loyal. He had also neglected to inform Chairman Muskie of the Senate Budget Committee.

All three learned only from the press of the President's decision to reverse himself and thus repudiate the public loyalties they had given his rebate, which they privately opposed. When Ullman learned that his support had been publicly repudiated, he said, "It was a little less than fair to those of us who supported it against our better judgment and worked hard to get it passed." Muskie was also furious. "If economic conditions in April justify this abandonment of the course we set two months ago," he said, "Congress has a right to know why those conditions were misjudged in February when the program was proposed."

This was the fourteenth of April. Next day, Schlesinger would deliver the energy program of his experts. And on April 18, the President was to command television, with the energy crisis his prime priority. But by then, the President had lost authority with his own Congress; and that would soon become apparent to the public.

"He was doomed from the start, from early 1977," said Michael Blumenthal, looking back later. Blumenthal continued:

> He had so many admirable qualities, but in sum total they weren't the right combination of qualities and he had done enough things in his approach to people, in his policies, in the way he organized himself, his staff, his cabinet, his relations with others, to make it difficult for him to succeed for any length of time in anything. . . .
>
> There was this deep sense of insecurity. . . . The idea of firing people, even me, was a traumatic thing. . . . He is a completely nonconfrontational sort of person. . . . I would go in to him and say, Mr. President, I really am worried about prices and we have got to do this or that. He would say . . . "huh . . . hum" . . . and he'd look at you, he wouldn't react. It was the most disconcerting experience of my life. He wouldn't ask, Why do you say this?. . . . In the end he would say, That's very interesting, would you write a memo. I'd leave there and I'd be no wiser. He wouldn't agree with me, wouldn't disagree with me, nor challenge me, nor castigate me. . . . At first I thought it was a personal thing. Then I'd ask other people, like Charlie Schultze, and I'd say, "You've just been in there. What's happening?" and Charlie would say, "I don't know what to do with this guy, he just won't react. . . ."
>
> There were so many elements of the personal qualities necessary for organizing people into an effective executive community [he just didn't have], or for understanding the dynamics of being a leader, how decisions are made or not made. . . . Even if we'd chosen the right economic policy, I would say his chances of coming across as an effective President or a popular President or a President who could have been reelected were slim.

Carter had somehow in the first six months of his administration lost the indulgence the nation habitually gives new Presidents.

Nothing was happening. The first to notice was the Washington press corps, that tuning board of national opinion, where, by August of 1977, the mutterings of discontent began to surface in story after story, column after column. Television would pick up this murmuring of dissent soon after. But the most important of the dissidents muttered to each other in the Congress of the United States.

When Carter assumed the presidency in 1977, a new Democratic Congress waited in Washington to join him. He had come to power by preaching to the conscience of a nation aroused by Watergate, wounded by fresh memories of the first war Americans had ever lost in their history. But the same wave of emotion that had brought him to power, with his promise to reshape the nation, had also brought to Congress a new breed of young men and women who, like him, spoke for change.

Superficially, of course, the Democratic Congress seemed to offer the President the same kind of partnership it had offered all Democratic Presidents for thirty years. Yet even at the top, the faces had changed. Two new men had replaced the old leaders of House and Senate: Robert Byrd, a prideful man of West Virginia, had replaced the grave Mike Mansfield of Montana as Senate majority leader; and Tip O'Neill had replaced Carl Albert of Oklahoma as House Speaker. Both had climbed, rung by rung, the slippery ladder of old politics to their eminence. Neither, perhaps, had any greater ambition than to be a large figure in American history, as had Lyndon Johnson and Sam Rayburn when they mobilized House and Senate to support the purposes of major Presidents. But underneath their leadership were new and younger people, and not since the New Deal had Congress undergone a greater sea change than in the refreshment of faces in the elections of 1974 and 1976.

The new people were particularly numerous in the House. Of the Democratic majority of 289 that greeted Carter in his first hundred days, no less than 118 were either first- or second-term members—71 of the famous class of 1974, 47 of the more serious class of 1976. Like Carter, they had run against Washington and the establishment, both local and national. With these on his side, Carter might have found a natural base; but he saw them as the Washington of the insiders; and they saw him as the presidential totem against whom, since Nixon, Congress had revolted. The newcomers had formed themselves into "class" caucuses and, together, they had torn apart the old House establishment—seniorities and chairmanships, procedures and traditions.

Late in 1979, when the reelection of Carter already seemed hopeless, I spoke at some length with Tip O'Neill about what had happened. O'Neill had come up through politics much as Harry Truman had. He had worked the wards in Cambridge, Massachusetts; had made it to the Massachusetts Legislature, and become Speaker on Beacon Hill; had made it to Congress when he took over John F. Kennedy's seat in 1952, as Kennedy moved up to the Senate. Like Truman before him, O'Neill had acquired wisdom on the way, but never lost the old pol's touch for cutting a deal. He was a man steeped in the Democratic tradition, the heritage of Roosevelt, Truman, Kennedy. Moreover, he spoke for his own voters, a motley constituency north of the Charles River in Greater Boston, where Irish and Italian working people, and the liberals of Harvard and MIT, voted in equal numbers. He was thus against the Vietnam War, for Social Security, for the old folks, and loved the dance of politics. He had wanted to work with this new Democratic President as well as with the younger members of his Democratic Congress. But as the new Speaker, he expected respect. It was inconceivable to him that Hamilton Jordan, the President's chief of staff, would not return his calls; O'Neill came to refer to Jordan as "Hamilton Jerkin." Neither the White House nor the younger members of Congress understood politics as O'Neill had come to know the game.

O'Neill began his reminiscence by going all the way back to 1932:

> I start with Roosevelt . . . he made Congress a rubber stamp. The most powerful President in the United States, he was . . . and the power grew, under Truman, under Ike, then Lyndon Johnson. If it hadn't been for Nixon and the impeachment headlines, who knows where it could have ended . . . but then comes this struggle of Congress to reassume its powers, the War Powers Act, the Impoundment Act, setting up our own budget committee. . . . OMB used to send over the budget and we'd follow it religiously, but the founding fathers had expected *us* to set the budget priorities.
>
> So then you had this new element coming in [to the House] in 1974 [after Nixon]. These were highly sophisticated, intelligent, talented people, elected on their own. . . . These guys were

highly educated, scientists, doctors, Ph.D.s . . . there was this diversity. . . . They'd tipped over the Republicans in their districts, tipped over the establishment, they were masters of the arts of the media, of town meetings. They got elected without the aid of the Democratic leadership. These were guys who wanted to change the government. Some of them were elected, like Jerry Patterson, in districts that were six to one Republican!

And they wanted to innovate . . . sending home newsletters six times a year, calling town hall meetings. . . . Congress gives them mobile homes now for offices and they go through their districts talking to people. Gerry Studds can do five town meetings in a day, notifying people in his newsletter.

These people didn't come up through state legislatures, they never ran for city council or county office; they ran against the system. Now they get to Washington . . . they caucus . . . they don't know the arts of politics, or understand the art of compromise. . . . They've been reading about cigar smoke in smoke-filled back rooms. . . . Congress has always been a whipping boy, from Ralph Waldo Emerson and Thoreau to Will Rogers and Art Buchwald. . . . They didn't understand why you go to conference committees, why you cut deals, why compromise and consensus is so important. . . . They didn't understand what our party was. If this were any other party in the world, we'd be five splinter parties, but we try to invite everyone under our tent: ultraconservatives, moderates, progressive liberals, ultraliberals—you've got to take them all into account. . . .

These guys opened up the House . . . opened up the rules . . . no more executive sessions. . . . In the old days when I came, the thirty guys with seniority in the House were the power. . . . Now you have 157 chairmen of committees and subcommittees, each one with extra staff, each one has an agenda, with committee hearings. And they felt they had to show results, they wanted their legislation to reach the floor. . . . We spread the power . . . and they all wanted more assistants, more help. . . . Congress and the media are both overstaffed. . . .

On and on O'Neill went, still loyal to Jimmy Carter, but irritable. He was trying to deliver his Democratic majority to the President, yet was unable to do so. And unable to do so because the President could not recognize his moment in history—recognize that he and the new Congress were at base allies and associates. The same emotions rebelling against the "imperial presidency" and the "insiders" of Washington had brought both him and the new Congress to power at the same time.

A few months after talking with O'Neill, I spent a weekend in Williamsburg, Virginia, early in 1980, with a handful of young congressmen who called themselves "the class of '76," those who had been elected on Democratic tickets the same year as Carter. They were concerned people, they were young, most of them between thirty and forty-five. They had come to this gathering on their own time, paying their own expenses, to think about the state of the nation and the party. They liked old Tip O'Neill, their House leader —but as they would like any well-meaning grandfather figure. Almost to a man, however, they disliked the President who had been elected with them in 1976. He did not function. His people at the White House treated congressmen as they had treated Georgia legislators. These new congressmen wanted to be included or persuaded; but the Carter staff was clumsy, or inefficient. One of the Williamsburg group, along with two other younger congressmen, had been invited to a private stroking session at the White House, at which the President lobbied them to support his medical insurance bill. "But why was he wasting his time on us for that?" asked the young Tennessean. "Didn't he know we were supporting that bill? He didn't have to persuade us on something we wanted ourselves." What irked most was that no one in the White House would return their calls. Said one: "About the only good Teddy Kennedy's candidacy has done me is that now if I call the White House, maybe somebody will call me back." Nor were they happy about Kennedy; they would support the President in the campaign of 1980 rather than Kennedy; the President was a lesser hazard to their own campaigns for reelection. But the President would be no great help, either; and they would keep their distance.

There was, then, at the base of it all, this misjudgment by Carter of the forces at his disposal. The younger people would go along with him, not out of loyalty, but out of conviction. They were to give him the rare victories he won: chopping down the pork-barrel projects of dams and river engineering; overhauling the civil service; supporting his environmental programs; supporting him in foreign affairs; supporting his energy program. But in the last year of his term, Carter had become the first Democratic President in almost thirty years to see two of his vetoes overridden by a Democratic Congress.

Much more could have been done. "We made our mistakes in

the first few months," said one of Carter's White House advisers. "We could have pushed SALT II through the Senate in the first few months by accepting the Vladivostok agreements, and gone on to a SALT III. Ford had signed on, Kissinger had signed on, Baker had signed on; the Republicans were hooked. But he couldn't see it. We could have asked for standby controls on gas prices in the original stimulus package. We didn't need them then, but we could have got them. They would have been vital when we came to the gasoline crisis of 1979."

Carter's natural support lay in the newly elected Democrats of the classes of '74, '76, and '78. But he lacked the skill to mobilize their support into legislation. He ended with no tax reform bill, no national health insurance, no welfare revision, no labor law legislation, no instant voter registration, no energy mobilization board, no Strategic Arms Limitation Treaty. In all these areas, he had entered to do the will of the people; and had ignored his Congress, as sinners and politicians. He had crested on the revulsion of the Congress and the media against the increasing power of the presidency, against the powers of Washington; but he could not redefine the presidency to bring Congress to partnership or meet the needs of the times. And so his major achievements were solitary achievements, the achievements of a President by executive or personal action, for which he must certainly be remembered more kindly than for his shortfall in legislation.

Of the first of his major achievements—the subtle yet profound change in the kind of people who are appointed to leadership in the United States government—it may be said that here, again, Jimmy Carter was inspired above all by good will. And as with so many of his actions, only time will tell whether he was simply catching up with the history of America or whether he overshot the mark.

Carter was determined that his administration would not only seek excellence, but seek that excellence qualified by sex, race, and ethnic origin. No future President will be able to undo his work, for better or for worse.

The changes that Carter brought to climax in his administration had been swelling for over a century—that slow rise to positions of policy of the new groups that crowded the old-stock Americans. It was exactly one century from the year 1877, when Rutherford B. Hayes had named Carl Schurz as Secretary of the Interior, recognizing the new and powerful German-American voters in the Republican party. Twenty-nine years later, Theodore Roosevelt appointed as his Secretary of Commerce and Labor the first Jew in the cabinet, Oscar Straus,* and twenty-seven years after that the first woman cabinet member, Frances Perkins, was chosen as Secretary of Labor by Franklin Roosevelt. From Roosevelt through Truman, Eisenhower, Kennedy, and Johnson, more and more of the cabinet and top White House posts were occupied by people chosen not only for abilities but for origins, as if a "balanced ticket" must be involved in policymaking at the White House, just as in municipal politics.

Carter put it quite candidly in 1979, toward the end of his term: "If I didn't have to get Senate confirmation of appointees, I could just tell you flatly that 12 percent of all my judicial appointments would be blacks, 3 percent would be Spanish-speaking, 40 percent would be women, and so forth." But he had not waited until then to put his convictions to action. In his first three weeks in office, he had appointed more women (eleven) and more blacks (eight), plus one Hispanic, to cabinet or subcabinet level than any President before him. Of his first seventy appointments to top-level jobs, seventeen were of the so-called minorities. And more, many more, were to follow.

His first priority in changing the quality of appointments was based on his conviction that women should be full partners in all phases of policymaking. By the end of his term, Carter could boast, for example, that in all American history only forty-eight women had been appointed as federal judges—and he had appointed forty-one of them! Only three women had ever served as Secretaries of major federal departments in all previous governments of the United States. President Carter was to appoint another three. Three women under secretaries were appointed, four deputy under secretaries, seventeen assistant secretaries. No President had ever appointed a woman inspector general for a department; Carter was to appoint

---

*New York Jews of the old German migration still chuckle at the story of Theodore Roosevelt's visit to New York to address a Jewish group in the days when old-stock Jews still voted Republican. Posing as statesman, Roosevelt told the group that when he had looked for the best man for the job of Secretary of Commerce, he had not asked for a Jew, a Catholic, or a businessman; he had asked his friends simply who would be the best man for the job—and they told him: Oscar Straus. Roosevelt was followed as speaker by that legendary figure Jacob Schiff, one of the dominant bankers of the time. Schiff was then old and very hard of hearing and had not bothered to listen to Roosevelt's remarks. So he began by remarking that Roosevelt had called him and said he wanted a Jew in the cabinet—and who was the ablest Jew that Schiff (himself an Orthodox Jew) could suggest? Without hesitation, remarked old Schiff, the ablest Jew in New York is Oscar Straus—choose him. Embarrassment followed.

five. Only twenty-five women had previously served as ambassadors of the United States abroad; Jimmy Carter appointed seventeen.*

Certain departments soon became almost women's rights departments. Within a year, by January 1978, the Department of Commerce, headed by Juanita Kreps, listed 36 percent of its top appointments as women. The department had already been emasculated in previous administrations by the appointment of a cabinet-rank Special Representative for Trade, taking from the Secretary of Commerce his critical role in a changing world of trade. It had become, when Kreps took over, chiefly a scientific, measurement, and statistical agency, scarcely of cabinet rank. (Its largest component element was NOAA, the National Oceanic and Atmospheric Administration, a scientific agency of peerless quality, which had nothing to do with commerce.) "But," said one department chief, who had served under the larger leadership of people like Elliot Richardson and Peter Peterson, "there was no leadership there. She [Kreps] acted as if she were the hostess of the department, not the leader." The Department of Agriculture could boast 33 percent women in top appointments; HUD, 22 percent; HEW, 20 percent.

The promotion and appointment of women inevitably intertwined with the promotion of minority groups, and here the Department of Defense was a masterpiece of the new politics. Defense is both a managerial and a fighting department; men serve in combat, they hear fire, they are killed. The Department of Defense was to be ethnicized gradually. Two distinguished Jewish scientists were to become, respectively, Secretary of Defense and Under Secretary of the Air Force, both scientists of superb quality and one, Hans Mark, the most creative nuclear physicist in American defense. And then the Secretary of the Army was chosen to represent blacks, the Secretary of the Navy to represent Hispanics. However large or small the quality of these gentlemen, only one, Edward Hidalgo,† had ever heard a shot fired in anger, or seen a man fall bleeding on a battlefield. Underneath the ethnic upper layer stretched more women appointees, officially accepted as the nation's largest minority, al-

---

*If Carter expected political gratitude from women, he was to be disappointed. Feminine activists, like activists of every special-interest group, live by voicing demands; their cry is always: More, not enough. In his 1980 campaign for reelection, the feminist cause-cryers abandoned him, the National Women's Political Caucus refusing to make any choice between Carter and Reagan, the National Organization for Women contenting itself with only a denunciation of Reagan.

†Hidalgo, Mexican born and a lawyer of the Mexican bar, had served with valor in the U.S. Marines and won a Bronze Star in combat.

though women are statistically a majority of all Americans. The General Counsel for the Department of Defense was a woman; so later was the Deputy Under Secretary of the Navy; so, too, was an Assistant Secretary of the Air Force, a former lawyer and professor who had never flown a plane. So, too, were the General Counsel for the Army, the Principal Deputy General Counsel of the Navy, the Deputy Under Secretary of Defense for Research and Advanced Technology, and on and on.

If any group followed women in the priorities of Carter appointments, it was blacks. To the blacks went one woman's cabinet post (Patricia Harris to HUD), and another cabinet post as the United Nations Special Ambassador (Andrew Young); at Justice, Carter named Wade McCree, a first-class man, as Solicitor General; at the Department of the Army, as its Secretary, Clifford Alexander; and as chairman of the National Science Foundation, John Slaughter, another first-class man. Carter went on to appoint more black federal judges (thirty-seven) than all previous Presidents put together. After the election, he said defiantly: "Charlie Kirbo, who is a very wise man, thinks that the major factor against me in the South was the appointment of black judges . . . but it was something about which I felt very deeply, and I must say I don't agree with Kirbo."

Hispanics followed next in all departments, winning leadership of the Navy (Hidalgo); acquiring the post of Commissioner of Immigration and Naturalization (Castillo); being named Under Secretary of Housing and Urban Development (Marrero); and finally, there was the promotion of a United Auto Workers union official (Torres), first as ambassador to the United Nations Educational, Scientific, and Cultural Organization, then to the rank of Special Assistant for Hispanic Affairs at the White House. The White House had always had a special assistant for Jewish affairs since Roosevelt; more recently, always, a special assistant for black affairs; had long had a special assistant for women's interests. But now, responding to the plea of Hispanic-Americans for bilingualism, the White House began to publish a special newsletter on its activities in Spanish, *Noticias Asuntos de Hispanicos,* surmounted by a logo of *La Casa Blanca.*

Ultimately, of course, preparing for the campaign of 1980, Carter was to top all such appointments with the creation of an Office of Ethnic Affairs, headed by an Italian-American, with a staff composed of another Italian-American, a Ukrainian-American, and a Greek-American. "For the purpose of this office," so read the official announcement, "ethnic Americans are defined as persons of Eastern

European, Southern European, Middle Eastern, and Asian backgrounds." The chief of the new office was Dr. Stephen Aiello, who had come to the White House from his post as head of New York City's board of education. As a first-rate historian, Aiello could take a long view of the rise of the ethnics, "a phenomenon of the decade of the seventies." In some sense, he said in an interview, "it is a reaction to the black power movement. They [the ethnics] saw what the civil rights movement had been able to accomplish and they said, 'If black is beautiful, olive is gorgeous.' . . . [It's] a them-against-us philosophy, defined in the 1960s on a racial basis. The blacks seem to get everything, while we get slaps on the back for being good Americans. Politicians come and have a pizza or a blintz in our neighborhoods in election years, and then we are forgotten so long as we pay the bills and our sons fight the wars."

If anything revolutionary was accomplished by the Carter administration, it was this recognition of the various communities which had already changed the quality and composition of American life and thus, necessarily, had to change the quality and composition of American leadership. Here Carter was riding with history, not against it. The fashionable term was "pluralism." "Americans live in a pluralistic society," said the White House announcement of its Office of Ethnic Affairs. "It is essential to develop a public policy that reflects this pluralism. Each of us must learn to live, communicate, and cooperate with persons of other cultures."

It could certainly be argued that all Americans, even before the Revolution, had been learning to live with each other. And the great objective of American life had been to make of these diverse heritages one nation: *"E Pluribus Unum."* The new policy, which would never be reversed, was of value—but of uncertain result. No one could be sure whether it reflected the tolerant philosophy of pluralism or sought to promote it as dogma, whether it would unify the varying and wonderful heritages of the American peoples—or would ultimately divide them. If the prizes and perquisites of high office were to be divided by ancestry and gender, how then could it be guaranteed that leadership would fall to the excellent, on their merits, rather than by lineage? Always, previously, the many communities of America had been protected in their efforts to preserve their heritages by custom and law: the Catholics with their parochial schools, the Jews with their Hebrew schools; the Germans, old-stock immigrants, with their turnvereins; the Japanese-Americans, newcomers, with their own institutions. Still others delighted in their

Saint Patrick's Day parades, Columbus Day parades, Steuben Day parades, or Puerto Rican parades. Should the federal government now finance this plurality of cultures, encourage this diversity, distribute its own power and responsibilities among groups, by group recognition in leadership? Or should it seek to encourage a unity of purpose and culture?

For Jimmy Carter the answer had been clear. He had brought with him from Georgia a commitment to brotherhood worked out in his conscience. Within his jurisdiction, as President and chief executive officer, he would push his goodwill as far as it would go, whatever its consequences, good or bad, on administrations to come. The politics of campaigning hurried him, of course, on the ethnic way, but he was only riding the curve of history in American life. He did not want to resist it; rather, he wanted to encourage it.

But it was in the other dominion of executive leadership, foreign affairs, that history finally overtook Carter, trapped him, and then crushed his hope for reelection.

It is customary now to look back on Carter's foreign policy through the prism of his last disastrous year—the humiliation in Iran, the torment of the hostages, the collapse of the Strategic Arms Limitation Treaty (SALT), so tortuously negotiated with the Soviets. And yet his real achievements—again, solitary achievements—were very large indeed.

The story of the Carter foreign policy should not end with Iran. It should start with his own vision of the world; in that vision, a foreign policy of "human rights" came foremost. He knew that there must, of course, be an adequate defense. But there must also be a new recognition of something referred to as the "Third World"—as if, truly, there were a single, united world of Africans, Asians, Latins, Hindus, all emerging from centuries of repression and exploitation at the hands of white men. Underlying the vision of the world as seen by Carter was the same moral righteousness that had inspired Woodrow Wilson half a century earlier and been repudiated after the First World War, not only by America's allies but by America's Senate. And underlying all was the fundamental flaw in the traditional "righteous" foreign policy—the inability to distinguish between American ideals and American interests, which rarely coincide. For twenty-five years, American diplomacy has been transfixed by the memory of that grand era when ideals and interests *did* coincide, when American diplomacy created the Marshall Plan and NATO and discovered that it served not only interest but conscience. It was an episode that would not come again, but Carter was determined to resurrect it.

He was determined to make the old policies of generosity live, however, in a world that had changed completely. For one thing, the Russians, whom Secretaries of State Marshall and Acheson had cowed by possession of the atomic bomb, were rearming. They had been off on their giant military buildup ever since the missile crisis of 1962. When Carter took office, American arms expenditures had dwindled to 5.4 percent of the gross national product, while the Russians had pushed their expenditures up to an estimated 12 or 14 percent. The Russians had 45,000 tanks, the Americans 8,500. The United States Army had dwindled to a force of sixteen divisions and the Marines added three more. In Europe, the NATO allies mustered eleven armored and eighteen infantry, mechanized, and airborne divisions; the Russians and their Warsaw Pact allies mustered thirty-one armored and thirty-six infantry divisions, and were backing these with a speedy buildup of tactical nuclear weapons that would out-match anything the Western allies could field or had in preparation. Above all: the surly, relentless, ceaseless brutality of Russian diplomacy was pushing everywhere. It was pushing in black Africa, where Angola and Ethiopia had fallen to it; it was in the process of penetrating Yemen; it was devilishly supplying arms to terrorists and client Arab states in the Middle East; it was pushing in America's backyard in Central America; it was to push on later to Soviet military occupation of Afghanistan.

Less conspicuous, but almost as important, was the equally relentless Japanese trade offensive against American industry, both at home and abroad. This was being done under the cloak of Oriental good manners ("so sorry, please") and under the protection of American diplomacy and defense, as if American forces in Asia were mercenaries protecting the expanding perimeters of the Japanese trade empire.

For another thing, the United Nations, originally the creation of the victorious Atlantic powers, was still a high moral symbol of many good-thinking people like Carter; only aging dinosaurs of politics croaked dissent. But the assembly of the United Nations had fallen to the domination of the so-called Third World peoples, united in aspiration only to undermine the white powers. To a large extent, it had already become the world's chief forum of racism: In the General Assembly today, Antigua, with some 70,000 people, has the same voice as America, with its 226,500,000. Of the UN's 157 members today, no more than a handful can claim any practice of human rights as accepted by civilized people; but the Third World majority can always join in chorus against those who they claim abuse human rights, chiefly the United States.

And lastly, perhaps just as important as the Russian offensive, was the separation of Congress from the new President. The old American phrase "politics stop at the water's edge" was obsolete; the bipartisan consensus in Congress that had supported Presidents from Roosevelt through Johnson had vanished under Nixon. Senator Jesse Helms of North Carolina wanted to halt administration policy in Rhodesia, and sent two of his own staff over to London to sabotage it. Carter had promised to withdraw American troops from Korea; Congress simply would not. If Carter wanted to improve American relations with Cuba, or increase foreign aid, or restore relations with Vietnam—Congress simply would not. Congress had been sucked into the Vietnam War by Lyndon Johnson and the war had resulted in disaster; Congress would no longer go along unquestioningly with any presidential foreign policy decision. Congress, in foreign as in domestic affairs, was hostile terrain for Carter.

It is against these new and ominous conditions that one must measure the Carter achievements, all personal triumphs of a dedicated, moral man. It was not until April of 1978 that the first such triumph occurred: the passage of the new Panama Canal Treaty, long overdue, granting Panamanian authority over an obsolete canal, no longer useful to the United States navy or merchant marine. It was followed in September of 1978 by the greatest of Carter's personal achievements, the Camp David summit agreement between Israel and Egypt, an agreement that would have been impossible to achieve except by a person as sincere as Jimmy Carter, who succeeded in convincing both Begin of Israel and Sadat of Egypt that the honor of the American President could permit them to lay down arms against each other. The Camp David accords were followed by yet another triumph: the final restoration of formal relations between China and the United States in January of 1979, made into grand ceremony with a White House dinner and a reception at the Kennedy Center, where Teng Hsiao-ping, half elf and half gunman, looked on in wonder. The enthusiasm of Americans was genuine for an accord which Teng, certainly, sought chiefly as an assurance that the American barbarians would remain either neutral or friendly if the Russian barbarians tried to move on him. One must take a long view to grasp the significance of these China accords. For almost a century, the three chief powers of the Pacific—China, Japan, and the United States—had stalked each other in wars and discord. Now, for the first time since 1895, all three great powers were in harmony and the Pacific, unless the Russians chose to intrude, was a basin of peace. This was no mean achievement, and it was greatly to Carter's credit.

Had he been content with these three achievements, or had history let him rest there at his crest of accomplishment in January of 1979, Jimmy Carter might have gone down as the major architect of a new American foreign policy.

Yet history would not; Carter had come in with so grand a vision of the power of the United States to do good, with so apocalyptic a sense of presidential responsibility, that it was impossible, in foreign affairs as in domestic affairs, to keep all his promises. American foreign policy, he told the United Nations in his initial formal speech to the world, had three main goals: "First, to maintain peace and to reduce the arms race; second, to build a better and more cooperative international economic system; and third, [to] work with potential adversaries as well as our close friends to advance the cause of human rights."

All this he meant sincerely.

And yet, as in his plans for reorganizing the American economy, there was that strange, stumbling quality which could not make the leap from vision to management of affairs.

Carter distrusted the seasoned experts of the State Department as he distrusted Congress; and distrusted that informal collegium of Washington foreign policy veterans as he distrusted the entire Washington establishment.

He had, in effect, three Secretaries of State. The official Secretary was Cyrus Vance, one of the finest of establishment types, a tenacious but cautious man of experience whose interests were chiefly in Western Europe and Asian policy. Without meaning to do so, Carter set up as rival to Vance a National Security Adviser, Zbigniew Brzezinski, a professor and a dedicated anti-Communist, who saw himself as the successor to Henry Kissinger. (Pressed to comment on Brzezinski, Kissinger summed him up as "smart, but not wise.") The distrust between Brzezinski and Vance grew so great that Vance took to writing each night a short memo of events, directly to the President. In the early morning, Vance's memo would be near the top of the President's pile; and if the President would scrawl his agreement (a "good") on a Vance memorandum (as, for example, on the return of Saint Stephen's Crown to Hungary), then the State

Department could proceed with the announcement, despite Brzezinski's last-minute objection.

In addition to the rivalry between Brzezinski and Vance, there was the rivalry of both with Andrew Young. Young, the first black congressman elected from Georgia since Reconstruction, had been an ally of Carter during the civil rights struggle in the South; he had seconded Carter's nomination at the Democratic convention of 1976. And when Carter named him as America's ambassador to the United Nations, he had gone further than announcing a mere cabinet appointment. "I have never said it about anyone else," said Carter, but "of all the people I have ever known in public service, Andy Young is the best. . . . His status will be equal to that of the Secretary of State or the Secretary of the Treasury or anyone else."

Young took Carter's statement literally and was soon firing away in a volley of statements that shook international diplomacy. Even before he was sworn in, he was advocating the admission of Vietnam to the United Nations; he followed with a statement on television declaring that the thousands of Cuban Communist troops in Angola brought a "certain stability and order" to that black African nation riven by civil war. He followed with the public thought that British foreign policy was built on racism. And in an interview with a Paris newspaper, he commented on Carter's effort to persuade Russians to a human rights policy, saying there were "hundreds, perhaps thousands of political prisoners [in jails] in the United States." After a period of some hush, he offered the opinion that Ayatollah Khomeini would be seen as "some kind of saint when we finally get over the panic of what is happening [in Iran]." He finally outran presidential and public tolerance in Washington when, in the summer of 1979, he entered into clandestine negotiations with the Palestine Liberation Organization in New York, and he was forced to resign.

But by then it was too late to pull a demoralized and divided State Department together—and the world was overtaking Jimmy Carter. The forces at large in the new world were closing in on him, and by 1979, it was all about to crash.

Carter's last major triumph in foreign policy had come in January of 1979 with the celebration of America's new and vital relationship with China. But that month had also seen the collapse of the Pahlevi regime in Teheran, and the Shah's flight from Iran. Only a year before, the President and his wife had celebrated New Year's Eve with the same Shah in Teheran, and there, despite the Shah's abominations in the domain of human rights, Carter publicly praised Iran as an "island of stability" in the Middle East. Months of riot, demonstration, and bloodshed had followed, providing television's evening news shows with their magnificent color pictures of total chaos. It was obvious that the Shah would have to go; the President was urged to encourage or unleash the Iranian army in a military coup. But Carter preferred to believe that the Ayatollah, in some strange way, represented the will of his people and that the Islamic republic's revolution would lead to an Iranian expression of democracy and human rights in its own tradition.

The events of the Iranian upheaval would soon ricochet around the world. There would come, first, the choking off of Iranian oil from the world flow of trade; world oil prices would soon rocket—and so would gasoline and fuel oil prices in America, as in Europe. Next, the Japanese trade offensive against the American automobile industry would go into high gear as Americans switched from Detroit's old-fashioned "gas guzzlers" to the neat, fuel-efficient Japanese cars. Gold prices around the world would start their crazy gyrations. The compounding of rising energy prices with the panic flight from the dollar to gold would give the steadily rising inflation at home an afterburst that would crack through all American traditions of saving and thrift.

The last two years of the Carter administration saw all his very large achievements already behind him, and in their stead, an erratic set of actions, some forced on him, some rising from his own distrust and misunderstanding of the apparatus of force and diplomacy he had put in place. He would discover, and announce, the presence of a Russian brigade in Cuba; then, in a few weeks, it had vanished. He would travel the world; but without the majesty that should encircle a President of the United States. There he was, on television, dancing with Yugoslav peasant girls in the streets; there he was in Mexico joking about his running bowels and complaining of "Montezuma's revenge"; there he was, quite innocent of foreign reaction, jogging in a footrace, then collapsing in exhaustion. *The Economist* of London carried the disturbing picture of Carter in physical anguish, and cutlined it, "Joggers to the Apocalypse." His overreaction to Russian treachery in Afghanistan was so sharp ("the gravest threat to world peace since World War II") that he was compelled to withdraw one of his prime achievements—the SALT II pact—from Senate consideration.

Yet, through it all, he remained the same decent man, the same peace seeker. After the 1980 election, I visited him again. I was talking with him this time in another context, about the campaign just ended, and went to one of the journalistic stock-in-trade questions: What did he think were his most lasting achievements? Carter, a very proud man, was at this point melancholy, but firm. He thought a moment, mentioned deregulation and the Camp David accords, and then came back to the center of his personality. "Emphasis on human rights," he said. "[I] printed that commitment on worldwide consciousness. It may have permanent results. . . ."

That remains to me the essential Jimmy Carter statement. He loved humankind—but he gave his love and affection to very few individual members of humankind. He was always remote and distant, and all those who had expected to find in him an effective, avenging saint were disappointed. He was poor-mouthed by those who sought to get close to him—from the stuffy Helmut Schmidt of Germany, to the taunting President López Portillo of Mexico; from his loyal supporter, Tip O'Neill of the House, to his loyal opposition, Howard Baker, Republican leader of the Senate. It is better for a sovereign to be feared than loved. Carter achieved neither.

It was with this record of the presidency that Jimmy Carter entered on his campaign for reelection in the summer of 1979.

What the American people seek when they vote for the presidency is someone they trust, someone who is better and abler than themselves. The President must control matters—must control the Congress, the economy, bread and butter, war and peace, must persuade the people, through the filter of the hostile press, that he is doing their will.

Carter had done his best to do the people's will, to give them, as he had promised, a government as good and decent and compassionate as the American people themselves. His motives were pure; but his thinking was muddled. He was for a government of charity and a government of austerity at the same time. His problem, in essence, was that he could not quite understand the world in which he lived. Nor his party, which he took over in shambles and left in shambles. Nor the Congress, whose partnership he sought yet disdained. Nor the grime and fear of the big cities, whose decay could not be turned about by any call to brotherhood. Nor, most of all, the world of wicked and paranoid men, who were changing the globe beyond the seas. He was a man caught and gripped, then squeezed and crushed, by those stupendous forces of history rising from a world America had once freed and dominated—where now Jimmy Carter's moralities were irrelevant.

A revolution of goodwill had run its course; and now as the

graduate of that revolution Carter was about to face judgment on how he had managed the nation's affairs. Goodwill had not restrained the inflation which terrified all citizens, high and low alike. Goodwill had not mollified America's adversaries in the Third World of the newly freed, or in the Second World of the Communist bureaucracies. Americans were still seeking for something undefined in politics —who they were, where they were going, and whether the nation they had created over the years could still be governed reasonably by the old ideas.

PART III
THE ELECTION
OF 1980

CHAPTER EIGHT

THE REPUBLICANS: ENTER RONALD REAGAN

Among the millions who believed, by 1979, that the United States could be governed better than Jimmy Carter was doing, there were a number of conspicuously ambitious Republican leaders.

They had little to boast about in the Republican record since Eisenhower, for Nixon had erased his public achievements with his personal disgrace. Yet Republicans had been winning presidential elections more often than not; only one Democratic President since Roosevelt had managed a victory that could be called a genuine mandate of the people—Lyndon Johnson's 61 percent victory in 1964. Jimmy Carter had received barely 50 percent of the total vote in a two-man race.

For thirty years, since Eisenhower in 1952, American elections had been swinging between "landslides" and "squeakers." And we should look at the landslides and squeakers of those years, as the Republicans did, for the contrast between them tells much.

An American election landslide is like a tidal wave. It washes out, momentarily, all the well-known headlands of politics. Then, as it slips away, old contours show themselves again in the riptide. Except that after a succession of tidal waves and ebbings, it becomes apparent that the old contours of politics are no longer the same. Unfamiliar but very real new contours have replaced them.

The tidal Eisenhower elections of 1952 and 1956 had been followed by the Kennedy riptide of 1960. Which, in turn, was followed by the tidal election of 1964, followed again by the riptide in 1968; followed by the tidal election of 1972, followed by the riptide of 1976.

And what would follow the squeaker of 1976, in the year 1980? The riptide of 1976 had revealed much. The states of the Mountain West now stood out as the most solid block of electoral votes, a new "permanent" Republican resource. Except in a landslide like Lyndon Johnson's, this solid Mountain West would deliver 42 electoral votes (out of the 270 necessary to elect) for any Republican nominated. On the other hand, there was no longer any such thing as a solid Democratic South. That had disappeared with Franklin Roosevelt, and was embalmed in atlases of history. Strom Thurmond had broken into it in 1948, Eisenhower in 1952 and 1956, Nixon in 1960, Goldwater in 1964, Nixon again in both 1968 and 1972. Carter had carried the South for Democrats in 1976, but he nonetheless had lost Virginia, which could now be accepted as permanently Republican, as Republican as Vermont. And if one examined the Carter vote nore closely, though 90 percent of Carter's thin plurality came from the South, where he had been hailed as a native son, that 90 percent plurality depended more on his huge margin among the blacks of the South than among Southern whites, who had been voting ever more consistently Republican.

A good Republican candidate could thus count on 42 votes from the Mountain states, plus at least half of the South's electoral vote (Texas, Florida, Virginia, totaling 55), putting him into the fight for the Northeast quadrangle and the Pacific states, with at least 97 of the 270 electoral votes needed.

That would be true for 1980—and beyond 1980, with the country tilting like a basin lifted at its northeastern corner and spilling its contents into the Southwest, the Republicans would have an even greater advantage.

Nor was the political geography all that had changed for the Republicans. So, too, had demography, in the Northeast as well as the Southwest. Thirty years earlier, it might well have been said that the Republican party was the party of comfortable Northern Protestants —the very rich as well as the farmers, the administrative classes as well as the suburban homeowners. That was no longer true. Republicans had been winning an ever larger share of suburban Catholics, who were at the same time homeowners and conservatives in family and social values. The Democratic party had espoused the cause of civil rights and the "minorities" in the 1960s; had aroused the conscience of the nation; but then had tangled that cause in such an entrapment of rules and regulations that they embittered not only the ethnic working class but some of the most thoughtful among the intellectual classes.

What had remained solid for the Democratic heritage, after the Carter victory of 1976, seemed to be unchallengeable control of the House and Senate of the American Congress. That control seemed as enduring as any of Euclid's theorems. True enough, looking back, the Republicans since 1952 had controlled the executive most of the time—sixteen years for Republican Presidents, against twelve for Democratic Presidents. But Congress, except for fleeting intervals, was Democratic.

That was easy to understand if one understood the first rule of politics: *Every one, and every group, want more than they deserve, and demand more than they want.* All congressmen and senators are sent to Washington to rip from the national government what their own voters want; but the people as a whole rely on the President to protect them from other people's congressmen. Thus, in the thirty years since Eisenhower, the Republicans had controlled both House and Senate for only two years; Democratic control of Congress seemed as permanent as the faces on Mount Rushmore. In 1976, trooping in with Jimmy Carter, House Democrats outnumbered Republicans by 292 to 143, more than two to one; Senate Democrats outnumbered Republicans by 62 to 38.

Several other significant and subtle developments were also yeasting in demographic and social change, such as, to take one example, the rise of Italian-Americans to political power in the suburbs of the Northeast. Their assertion had been long and slow in coming (see Chapter Two), but now, in an arc that ran from New York's Long Island, through Connecticut, eastern Pennsylvania, and northern New Jersey, Italian-Americans had usurped the dominant influence once held by the Irish. In Long Island, Dominic Baranello had succeeded a long string of Irish names as New York's state Democratic chairman; Joseph M. Margiotta, boss of the Nassau Republican organization, had inherited old Boss Sprague's machine and made it one of the tightest in the country. (It was Richard Nixon's opinion that Gerald Ford's failure to cultivate the Italian vote in New York cost Ford the state in 1976, and thus the election.) In Connecticut, the late Ella Grasso was proving herself the most effective governor in the Northeast; Italian-Americans held mayoralties or county chairmanships throughout Westchester County and through the small towns south and east of Philadelphia; in New Jersey, Italian-Americans claimed that over 40 percent of all voters in the state were of Italian birth or heritage.

Even more important, to take another change, was the rise of the sisterhood of activist women, both conservative and liberal.

Republicans, being richer, had always counted more political activists among their women than Democrats, whose wives had had to
stay home and tend babies. But the rising Democratic group of career women was far more vocal than their Republican conservative
counterparts. They had first broken traces at the McGovern convention of 1972; had been diligently courted by Carter in 1976; by 1980
they would rowel both conventions with their exercise of power.

The primaries and the midterm election of 1978 would produce
no stark surprises. Democratic strength in Congress would be mar-
ginally reduced (to 276/159 in the House, and 59/41 in the Senate).
Yet a slight shifting in local elections in both parties was significant
of things to come: A conservative (Edward King) would overturn a
liberal (Michael Dukakis) in the Massachusetts Democratic primary;
a conservative (Jeffrey Bell) would drive out a classic Republican
liberal (Clifford Case) in the New Jersey senatorial primary; a conservative (Robert Short) would put down a liberal (Donald Fraser) in
the Democratic primary in Minnesota. And when it came to the Far
West, where California voters were being offered a referendum
called Proposition 13, Democrats and Republicans alike voted to
support the proposition, which called for a statewide limitation of
local property taxes.

All this lay in the future, as did the steady increase to critical
force of the newly legalized political action committees; these would
permit corporations and special-interest groups to slush elections
across the nation as they had not been able to do since the 1920s.

But most important of all was something that was not to become
apparent until several years later, in 1980—the development of a
corps of intellectual outriders, absent in Republican politics since
Theodore Roosevelt had given up the White House seventy-two
years earlier. The thinking and scholarly classes of the nation had in
1913 begun to abandon the Republicans, a party founded by thinking
men, for Democratic Professor Woodrow Wilson. They had remained unamused and uncourted by the Harding-Coolidge-Hoover
Republican leadership in the twenties and had come into their own
under Franklin Roosevelt. Then, for thirty years following the war,
they had been reviled and humiliated by a succession of Republican
primitives, from Joe McCarthy to Spiro Agnew. It took courage to be
a Republican intellectual in the sixties and early seventies and stand
against the winds; but now, in the late seventies, Republicans were
mustering a full corps of thinkers, academics, economists, and rumi-
nant idea brokers. From the Institute for Contemporary Studies in

San Francisco and the Hoover Institution of Stanford, California, through the Heritage Foundation and the American Enterprise Institute in Washington, conservative thinkers were furnishing ideas that ran counter to the liberal tide. In Manhattan, William F. Buckley's *National Review* and Irving Kristol's *Public Interest* provided the forum that the liberal *Nation* and *New Republic* had always provided for Democrats. Republican wordsmiths were ready to coin into phrases, essays, and speeches the resentments that twenty years of liberal dominance had incubated. Whether their thinking was better or sharper than that of their liberal adversaries remained to be tested.

Not all of this was evident to the public at large in the first weeks after Carter's victory of 1976. Whether an election is won or lost by the narrowest of margins, we of the press must write the ritual follow-up story, headlined as in November and December 1976: "The 'Profound Inadequacy' of the GOP" (Washington *Post*), "Politicians Find GOP Fighting for Its Survival" (New York *Times*); "Southern Republicans: Their Plight Is Growing Worse" (Washington *Post*); "Ailing GOP May Not Recover" *(Wall Street Journal);* "The GOP: Dying for Real?" *(National Observer);* "Feeble Grand Old Party" *(New Republic).* And finally, the words of one of the Republican party's veteran wise men, John Deardourff, a manager of the Ford campaign, as quoted in the *Wall Street Journal:* "It takes a long time for a party to die or be killed, and I assume there will be a lot of ferment for a couple of years. But the party's prospects certainly are not very bright."

The Republicans had been written off for dead many times—starting with the Roosevelt landslides of 1932 and 1936, on down through the Johnson landslide of 1964, and now again in 1976. But there were a good many Republicans who did not believe they were dead. There was, for one thing, the changed structure of politics, which only professionals could recognize. The Northeast-Southwest tilt was obviously altering the political geography of the country; there was the pressure of new groups, like the homeowners, the right-to-life advocates, others; and added to it all, there was the change in the party process itself.

Belatedly, at four-year intervals, the Republican party follows the Democratic party's "reforms"; and so now Republican candidates could look forward to a national convention won by the mad and open system of primaries that the Democrats had introduced to the nation. The old Republican power brokers were gone; Nelson Rockefeller, the most colorful and able Republican of his time, the tribal chieftain of what used to be called the Northeastern Liberal Republican Establishment, had withdrawn. Richard Nixon, his chief rival for the heritage of Dwight Eisenhower, had eliminated himself. Michigan was the only state still governed by a liberal Republican. And the old primitive opposition was gone too: Joe McCarthy, that symbol of smoldering violence, was dead; Spiro Agnew had been disgraced; Barry Goldwater, ailing, had become a gentle avuncular figure. The new Southern conservatives were unknown. All in all, it seemed an open field—and the prize beckoned to many who could discern the new geography and demography, and were convinced that Jimmy Carter, sooner or later, would mess things up, and push the regnant Democratic doctrine to disaster, either at home or abroad.

This was central to the campaign of 1980: the vivid personal contempt of the Republican contenders for Carter as an incompetent. None had the respect for Carter, say, of a Goldwater for a Lyndon Johnson, a Willkie for a Roosevelt, or all Republicans for a Kennedy. And each of the contenders in 1980 believed that if they could but push through the primaries to the nomination, they could persuade millions of independents and Democrats to support them against a Democratic administration out of control. All had made up their minds well before the humiliation in Iran and the inflation outburst of 1980.

Eight men were serious contenders—a big four and a little four. The little four first: There was Philip Crane, congressman from Illinois. Dark and eloquent, he was at once the most handsome of the candidates and the most learned; he was also the most conservative. A former history professor, Crane suffered from a crippling misfortune: He was not taken seriously by the correspondents in Washington, the ultimate screening committee for all nominations. He was the first to announce (August 2, 1978); the first in the field, he suffered badly from the mismanagment of his guru, Richard Viguerie, a master of direct mail, but ignorant of the media. Crane had a cause, but could not find a hearing for it.

There was Robert Dole of Kansas. Again, a dark, handsome man; of good record in the Senate; of good record as Republican national chairman in Nixon times, vice-presidential running mate with Ford in 1976. Tart, pleasant, with a country way of wisecracking out of the side of his mouth, Dole could boast about his war record with the best of his generation, but would not. He seemed to lack any strategy, either geographically in the primaries or philosophically in his purposes, to distinguish him from a crowded Republican field. Moreover, he lacked the ability to raise money, which is critical. He announced his candidacy on May 14, 1979. He lasted in action only from his resounding defeat in the Iowa caucus on January 20, 1980, to his dropout after Massachusetts two months later.

Another Republican, quickly eliminated, then bobbing back as a curiosity, was John Anderson of Illinois. A handsome white-haired man of delicate countenance, he, too, was a war hero, with an extraordinary combat record. His wares were decency, intelligence, eloquence; but his staff was composed of amateurs until his candidacy was expropriated by David Garth, the media master, and he became an Independent. Anderson had no realistic chance, ever, of being elected President and the television networks wrote him off; it was too expensive to assign another full-time crew to this unlikely candidate; a full-time crew for a major candidate might cost up to ten thousand dollars a week, sometimes more. Thus, Anderson's strongest call to public attention became his unremitting denunciation of the press and the media.

A slumbering presence was Gerald Ford, ex-President-by-appointment of the United States. He had an old score to settle with Ronald Reagan; but he had no base; no strategy; and deep down, no personal lust to shoulder the burden once more.

The big four candidates, however, were to be taken very seriously indeed.

First, at the bottom of an ascending scale, was John Connally of Texas, a man of unquestioned ability. He was significant not only in himself but in what he stood for. A Southerner, a lifelong Democrat, he had become a Republican because a changing instinct had pulled him, as it had pulled millions of other white Southerners, away from his old moorings. A onetime protégé of Lyndon Johnson; Secretary of the Navy for John F. Kennedy; three times governor of Texas, "Big John" Connally had gone back to Washington to become Nixon's Secretary of the Treasury. In a time of disaster for Republicans, he had boldly proclaimed himself a "switcher" and changed parties. Silver-haired and well-muscled, Connally had a burly masculine quality that charmed men and women alike. But his magnetism was shrunk by television's tube, so that on air he looked like a caricature of a Texas politician. Yet he was a solid manager as governor, hard and clear on issues like immigration, and he fostered his state's university system, leaving it one of the best in the nation.

Connally threw off a sense of vitality, and could make one of the finest spur-of-the-moment patriotic orations of any of the major candidates. I once saw him rise to his feet completely unprepared, swagger before one of the most sophisticated groups in America, and hold them spellbound as he improvised. That was at a conference of state governors aboard a luxury political cruise, which both governors and journalists knew could be written off as a legitimate expense. The year was 1967, the Vietnam War was unsettling loyalties, and the governors were debating a resolution of support for Lyndon Johnson's war. Connally listened; became indignant; and knowing the dramatic value of indignation, pushed his way to the microphone at the head table and let go. He called on the flag; recalled the Alamo; reminded his listeners of the War of 1812 and the Mexican-American War; recalled that the students and "the Harvard men" had opposed both those wars. His facts on Harvard, which is a most warlike institution, were wrong. But his central theme was correct: Both the Harvard faculty and student youth were in revolt against the war in Vietnam, which sent young men into the field fighting for the flag. Which side were the governors on? When Big John sat down, he had hushed the audience; and the governors decided, for the last time, to support the flag, Lyndon Johnson, and the Vietnam War as if all were one.

Big John Connally in living flesh and fine voice was impressive. But his campaign had little strategy except to take away the Southern base, first from Reagan, then from Carter, then go on to contest the Midwest and late primaries. But misfortune overtook misfortune. He announced his candidacy early, but went into action as the Iranian crisis broke; his staff mourned for months the fact that just as NBC was about to give Connally its six-minute special segment on the *Nightly News*, the hostage crisis preempted his time. Connally made the mistake of voicing his feelings about Israel in the bluntest of language, calling for an American neutrality between the Israelis and the enemies who sought to exterminate them, which appalled critical supporters in the Northeast. Finally, he was tainted by his association with "Watergate." In the public mind, Watergate has blurred within a cloud that includes break-ins, wiretaps, laundered money, shakedowns—and also the so-called milk scandal. In 1974, John Connally had been indicted by a federal grand jury for having taken ten thousand dollars from the Associated Milk Producers, Inc., in exchange for persuading President Nixon to support a hike in milk price support. The trial, in 1975, lasted eleven days but was meaningless; the jury cleared him after five and a half hours of deliberation. But the smear stuck. Connally languished in Houston; he knew how to raise money, but not how to compel attention. He was to wind up his campaign with the dubious distinction of having spent more money in pursuit of the nomination ($11 million) than any previous candidate; and having garnered but one delegate for all his exertions, Mrs. Ada Mills of Clarksville, Arkansas.

Going up the scale, one came to Howard Baker of Tennessee, another significant Republican. Both the shortest (five feet seven and a half inches) and the youngest (fifty-five) of the major candidates, Howard Baker could not be taken lightly. Seated, he was the tallest man in the room. He was as smooth and well-spoken as anyone in high place, a political professional in the best sense of the word. After fourteen years in the Senate, he could count any number of major accomplishments. He had been elected Senate minority leader by his colleagues. He had married the daughter of the late Senator Everett Dirksen, which put him in the Republican peerage. Most of all, for the public, he was the Republican senator at the Watergate Select Committee hearings who had not deviated from inquisitorial integrity to favor his Republican President subject to charge. "What did the President know, and when did he know it?" he repeated as country prosecutor over and over again. This the public remembered. Among the screening committee of Washington correspondents, he was respected for running for the presidency as a *Washington* politician. It needed a man who knew Capitol Hill and national politics to govern from Washington. Howard Baker was entitled to respect.

But Baker had his drawbacks too. Some were political: He had, for example, voted *for* rather than *against* the Panama Canal accords, which enraged Southern conservatives. Other problems were merely matters of Baker's temperament. His energy was analytical and persuasive, rather than physical and histrionic. He simply would not do the hour-after-hour grind of appearances on the road that most major candidates perform happily. Some enjoy it, some don't. Like Walter Mondale, Howard Baker did not want to spend his best years at Holiday Inns.

Baker's strategy flowed from his position. As minority leader of the United States Senate, he felt he did not have to seek the cameras. His advisers felt that television would come seeking him all through the early months of the campaign year, 1980. The Strategic Arms Limitation Treaty was then expected to move to the floor of the United States Senate by winter, and as the Republican leader, Baker would set the tone of the debate in spring 1980. SALT meant life and death, a dicing with the security and the future of the nation. Baker hoped to appear day after day as a world statesman on the tube, while his rivals were stomping through the snow and ice of the primary states. Consequently, until late in the race, Baker felt he could ignore organization, ignore even the necessary money-raising chores.

Next up the scale of potential was George Bush of Texas, even more significant. Bush, handsome, a lean six feet two, was of patrician stock, of oldest New England heritage. Born in Massachusetts, raised in Connecticut, son of a U.S. senator, he had the easy civility of the best of the upper classes. A man of clean tongue and perfect manners, he also spoke in the diction of good breeding, which, as in the case of William Scranton of Pennsylvania, made strangers think he was soft when he was merely cordial, and petulant when he was genuinely angry. He had been a Yale baseball captain as well as a Yale Phi Beta Kappa. Bush's politics were described as "somewhat to the center of center." To cap it all, he was a genuinely kindly man.

The first problem for George Bush was to shed himself of the image of "elitism" and let people know who and what he was—for he meant to run on his record. Experience *and* leadership would be his campaign theme. His experience was dazzling: He had gone to Texas as a Yankee outsider; cofounded Zapata Oil, one of the first and most successful of the offshore oil-drilling companies in the Gulf; run for Congress from Houston twice, and won; run for the Senate twice and lost; served Richard Nixon as American ambassador to the UN; served Nixon again as chairman of the Republican National Committee and, as chairman, was one of the few bold enough to tell Nixon directly that he should resign for the good of the party. He had then served Gerald Ford as "ambassador" to China, and as that administration came to an end, served as director of the Central Intelligence Agency. It was in that capacity that his duty led him to brief President-elect Carter in Plains on America's strategic secrets. Carter did not greatly impress Bush—impressed him so little that even before the inauguration, in January 1977, Bush had let himself muse with his friend James Baker III about running in 1980 against Carter for the presidency.

For the first six weeks of 1980, the George Bush–James Baker team conducted the best-managed campaign of 1980. That they lost was the fault of both; they ran a national campaign, but they were unable to capture the imagination of the public. Bush's performances were thoughtful, but too often "preppy." They could not match the intuitive performances of Ronald Reagan, who had been stirring imaginations on the screen for forty years. Bush and James Baker had been friends in Houston for almost twenty years. The two men had become even closer during the Ford administration, when both served in Washington. Both loved politics as a game and a purpose. They had first talked seriously of the presidency on a trip to China in the fall of 1977; had awaited the outcome of Baker's own run for the Texas attorney generalship in 1978 (which Baker lost); and then, shortly after Thanksgiving of 1978, having cleared the idea with Gerald Ford, who declared no intention of running in the primaries, sat down with Mrs. Bush and decided that, yes, they were going to make a try.

If the major problem was how to shed Bush's patrician image, the first problem was to get him known at all. For television, Bush was at zero takeoff point, an asterisk in the polls. Until very late in the primaries of 1980, Bush was the public image of a walking stick, or a go-go Yalie. I had seen the difference between the Bush public and private styles early on, during a September 1979 visit to New Hampshire. In an idle hour one afternoon, he had dropped by the hall of the Veterans of Foreign Wars in Manchester for their weekly gathering of beer and friendship. The workingmen who fought our wars recognized the Bush type at once—one of the thin fellows who live on the hill, or in the two Republican wards of Manchester, whose families owned the mills or the plants where the veterans' parents had worked. Bush in an ethnic gathering is as conspicuous as an Englishman in Uganda. He was making no headway as he navigated the bar, the back room, the tables, trying to shake hands. On the way out, he paused at one of the tables for a last stab at friendship and received a bare grunt of acknowledgment to his "Hello, I'm George Bush." Before they could turn their backs on him, he asked where they had served in the war. A good many New Hampshire veterans had served in the navy, and of these, many had joined the submariners; Portsmouth, New Hampshire, had been one of the prime submarine bases of the Atlantic frontier. The two men he addressed had both been submariners. Bush said he had a warm feeling for submarine men—ever since a sub had picked him up when he was shot down off the Bonin Islands. You're too young to have been in the war, came the suspicious reply. No, I'm not, said Bush. I enlisted when I was eighteen. Sit down, said the man, have a beer.

Bush sat and told them his story. He had been the navy's youngest commissioned pilot at the time; he had been shot down in flames, his rear man cut to pieces; he had paddled away on his life raft; an American submarine seemed by miracle to rise out of the ocean; he was hauled aboard, and assumed that the air-sea rescue service was working perfectly. Once aboard, however, he was told that the sub had by chance picked up his Mayday call and surfaced. But they were on their way to the Sea of Japan to torpedo enemy ships and would continue to do their mission as he had done his. So, for weeks, cooped up on the ship, he had watched a submarine torpedo Japanese—he was all for the submariners. By now Bush had the growing group enthralled. It turned out that two of the vets were telephone company linemen; they were working to install the lines the TV nets would need for the New Hampshire primary in February; they wished him luck and meant it. Had there been a camera present, it would have made a marvelous portrait of Bush with the people; but had there been a camera, no such conversation would have taken place.

The central problem of the Bush campaign was, therefore, how to compel the attention of the press, of the opinion-makers, and above all, of the television networks, to the man, his record, and his personality. On the national scene, Bush was an unknown, though among the administrative class of the East Coast, as onetime chief of the CIA, onetime UN ambassador, onetime special envoy to China, he was already admissible to the junior class of elder statesmen. How to compel attention is the problem of all outsiders. Bush and Jim Baker had decided after reading the books on the 1976 election to do it the winner's way, which, in 1976, had been Carter's way. The candidate creates events, in order to capture or compel attention. He invests his resources in capturing the early primary contests by victories in the field; such victories compel the daily press, the weeklies, the networks, to turn and pay attention to the man who makes the news.

So, then, the Bush campaign would be focused on the *early* primaries; and he would make, as would all the others but one, his major effort in the Iowa caucuses.

I make these Republican candidates sound, I know, like a Child's Garden of Candidates. But I know no evil of them. I know that most of them were conservatives—some frighteningly so, some reasonably so. But they looked good and sounded good. Three (Dole, Anderson, and Bush) were authentic war heroes, to be saluted for gallantry; one was an authentic intellectual (Crane); two others were men thoroughly experienced in government (Baker and Connally). There was neither a proven crook nor a certified idiot among them. Line them all up for the television cameras—as was done in Iowa for the first debate of 1980—and they were the most impressive six Republicans that the old party had offered the nation since primaries first let people pick candidates.

Except, of course, that there was one more candidate, who had been advised not to appear that opening night in Iowa but who would soon be called, by the attendant press corps, the O & W (the Oldest and Wisest), taken from a tag pinned on him by Jack Kemp, congressman from New York.

The O & W was the oldest serious candidate to run for President in American history. If elected, he would be sixty-nine when he took his inaugural oath, and seventy, two weeks later. He had been both a professional actor and a professional politician, but his fervor was unfeigned—the fervor of a man consumed by ideas. His were simple ideas, to be sure, but they more vividly repudiated the dominant ideas of his time than those of any other candidate since Barry Goldwater.

It is this last Republican—Ronald Reagan—whom we should now follow into the contest of 1980.

Ronald Reagan had been running for President for a long time by 1980—longer than anyone else. He had been running for President at least since 1966—and perhaps even before then in his own mind.

The Reagan biography reads like folklore: the boy born in Tampico, Illinois, population 1,200, a town caught in the same time warp as Tom Sawyer; his boyhood a Horatio Alger story of onward and upward. He had first tried out for drama and football in high school; but from his first attendance as a college freshman at a performance of *Journey's End,* he had known, as he wrote in his autobiography, that "my heart is a ham loaf." He unfolded in the presence of an audience like a tulip in the sun. From Eureka College to radio sportscasting in Davenport, Iowa, and then in Des Moines; and from there, on to Hollywood, where he became not only a major actor but a major personality.

A good actor, Reagan knew his trade—from how to kiss a woman before a camera ("Just touch your lips to hers; if you press you'll flatten her cheeks and push them out of shape") to the victimization of screen actors by their studios. It was in Hollywood that Reagan entered politics. Accepted as a naif in the movie business of the thirties, in an industry whose unions were raddled by factions of right and left, as well as by thugs, he was nominated president of the Screen Actors Guild; but instead of becoming a puppet of faction, he took his job seriously. As an innocent discovering sin, he discovered simultaneously that the Communists had wormed their way into the film industry through the talent unions, and that on the other flank of the talent unions were the operating unions, controlled by goons. His abiding suspicion of both Communists and underground crime dates from his six years as president of the Screen Actors Guild. So does his obsession with politics. As a reserve officer in an Iowa cavalry unit, he was called to service; because of poor eyesight he was given "limited duty" and assigned to a Hollywood unit making training films for the Air Corps. But his absorption with politics grew through the war years, so much so that his marriage to the actress Jane Wyman eventually broke up. "There was nothing in common between us," she said, "nothing to sustain our marriage."

By 1954, the once-young actor was approaching his middle forties, his screen career fading. His agents found for him the role of host of the weekly *General Electric Theater,* an early television prestige show. From that he moved on to be General Electric's spokesman, lecturing on what he calls "the mashed potato circuit," and found that live audiences were even more rewarding than studio audiences. They wanted him to talk of Hollywood; he talked of Hollywood but also told them that America was going to hell. As a public speaker, he polished his lines to sharpness. He had already learned, as an actor, how to wait for applause; as a public speaker, he learned new rhythms, the hesitation, the toss of the head, the style that he claimed had been inspired by watching Franklin D. Roosevelt. Above all, he projected sincerity; he meant what he said, and that could move others.

I did not meet Ronald Reagan in the flesh until the fall of 1966. By then, his conservative friends in Los Angeles were convinced they could make him governor—and, moreover, they would finance him in a race against Governor Edmund G. ("Pat") Brown. He invited a handful of the press to his Santa Monica ranch for the announcement, and it was spread out for television, as have been most of his appearances since. One of the cowboy stars of the then popular horse-and-oats serials stood behind a trough of glowing charcoals; steaks sizzled; the cowboy star speared out the steaks for us and introduced the candidate, who, in a graceful little patriotic statement of duty and crisis, explained why he was running. It was so pleasant a performance that I found myself following him for days thereafter. He was engaging in any audience, from the silks of Beverly Hills to the housedresses of Orange County. He was self-deprecatory; he warned his friends not to be overconfident. He used, over and over again, as he did down to the campaign of 1980, his favorite lines, about welfare, about waste, about spending, and above all, about not trusting the polls. ("I was just on the telephone with President Dewey," he would say, "who told me never to trust the polls.") There was always the charm of the man; and then, always, the persistent, undeviating, unchanging theme: Americans must be unyoked from government. He was convincing; and was elected by the astounding majority of 993,000 votes to become governor of the largest state in the Union and begin a new experience in learning.

About Reagan's eight years as governor of California there is no large debate among California political observers. His first term was a political bumble-shoot exhibition; his second a success. Two of the shrewdest men in California politics agree in the assessment. Lyn Nofziger, one of Reagan's first mentors, said: "In his first term we had to divorce him from the romance of politics and introduce him to the reality of government." Richard Bergholz, chief political writer of the Los Angeles *Times* and now senior observer of Southland politics, said: "His first term was a disaster. He hadn't learned how to yield or give. . . . In his second term he began to compromise, to make things happen. He liked issues reduced to the simplest, most precise statements. He had this theory he had professional people around him, he wasn't going to do everything himself. . . . The education of Ronald Reagan was to pick people on their ability. He flubbed around with a finance director until he came to Cappy [Caspar Weinberger], a liberal. . . . the question was: is he a prisoner of his staff or not, can he hear more than one point of view?"

Reagan's second term was substantially more successful. Re-elected in 1970, by less than half his first majority, he had learned how pressures interlock. Dealing with a hostile Democratic legislature, he had to compromise; and doing so, was responsible for some remarkable legislation. In his first term he had approved a notably liberal abortion law; in his second term, he launched a first-class mental health program; and in a working partnership with Democratic legislators, pushed through a comprehensive reform of California's welfare system. Reagan had come in with a state budget in deficit; he left a surplus, having increased taxes in the interim. He was irked that the Eastern, or national, press still described him as a Hollywood actor. He had come to office expressing California's resentment at the students of its great university, middle-class youngsters mostly, who were receiving the benefits of education from a system they persistently denounced; he had quipped, "Their signs said make love, not war, but they didn't look as if they could do either." He had been reviled and, with Nancy Reagan, spat upon on one of the university's campuses; but he had doubled the university budget while squeezing as many other programs as he could. It bothered him that his defense of the university was not recognized by the academic-media complex, which so influences the news system of the nation.

Very early in his governorship, Reagan had decided he would try for the presidency. That decision was made on November 17, 1966, within two weeks of his election, at a meeting at his home in Pacific Palisades. He had acquired the national services of F. Clifton White; was well under way for the large try when a scandal in his own staff burst. Reagan seems prone to staff troubles. But this one concerned a trusted lieutenant, revealed as homosexual, who was packing the governor's office with other homosexuals. Reagan then suspended his immediate presidential ambitions. When, in 1968, his appetite for the presidency revived, the effort was more comic than impressive. In clandestine alliance with Nelson Rockefeller, governor of New York, Ronald Reagan, governor of California, proposed to deny the Republican nomination of 1968 to Richard Nixon, former Vice-President of the United States. But since the two governors had never agreed on how they would divide Nixon's corpse between them and who would claim the nomination of the Republicans once Nixon was disposed of, their alliance collapsed. It was only when Nixon was forced out of the presidency six years later, yielding it to Gerald Ford, that Reagan's ambition surfaced once more. With a more experienced staff, and relieved in 1974 of the burden of governing California, Reagan was free to put full time into the adventure of unseating Gerald Ford as President. He lost; but the very closeness of the 1976 primary race run by this outsider against his own party's President tantalized his imagination. Had he been defeated overwhelmingly, Reagan would surely have resigned from politics. But the contest had been so close!

It is impossible to pinpoint exactly where, and when, the Reagan campaign of 1980 began. Each person involved gives a different starting point, as each met with Reagan alone, or in a group, and thrust the question at him. I, personally, prefer the story of the luncheon held at Reagan's home in late November of 1976, a few weeks after Jimmy Carter had put down Gerald Ford. Those present were all of the inner circle, and while her husband listened, Nancy Reagan presided. She was bitter at Jerry Ford. Reagan's long primary struggle with Ford during the year and their close-run contest at the Republican convention had left the Reagan team not only wistful, but vengeful. Had they been a shade sharper, a touch luckier, they might have carried the nomination—and then the election. Nancy Reagan asked the question at the table: How many had voted for Jerry Ford? Only three hands were raised. The conversation then went on to who might run in 1980; and hung inconclusively, as it broke up, with the general assumption that Reagan would, if he could, try one last time in 1980.

The organization of Reagan's 1980 campaign was by no means one of those smooth operations which go down as textbook classics. It was, from the beginning in 1977, down to the convention of 1980, split; riven with feuds; disjointed. And it is by taking the campaign apart at the joints, by examining its interlocking parts, that we can best clarify the nature of both Reagan's leadership and the Republican party.

At the center, always, was Ronald Reagan himself—with his crusader's idea to remake America. Second in importance to Reagan, ignored by no one who understood the dynamics of the campaign, was Nancy Reagan. Pert, handsome, immaculately groomed at all times, Nancy Reagan with her doll-like prettiness can mislead strangers into thinking she is simply the comely actress Ronald Reagan married. To the contrary, she is as strong an influence in the White House today, and was all through the campaign of 1980, as Eleanor Roosevelt in 1932, or Rosalynn Carter in 1976. Nancy Reagan was, and is, a woman of politics. To cross Nancy Reagan or to offend her is to tempt fate; her judgments of men are measured, sure, and merciless. Reagan himself reads clippings and magazine articles; she reads books. If one watches them unobserved, it is quite obvious that she loves him, totally; and he trusts her, totally. The central Reagan command meets in bed at night.

Presidents of the United States can have no friends except for those who are useful to them; and Reagan was to prove himself particularly adept at sorting out his political friendships into those who were useful to him and those who showed themselves troublesome.

At the core of the 1980 Reagan campaign team, as it began back in 1977, were three of his oldest and most trusted political veterans. Richard Wirthlin, to whom we shall return, was a polling master of enormous technical skill, never challenged by any rival throughout his years of service. Senior to Wirthlin in terms of service was Michael Deaver, custodian of the candidate's personality, caretaker of his time and energy level since his days as governor. All candidates have such a person in their entourage, as Kennedy had a Kenneth O'Donnell, and Roosevelt his Louis Howe. Deaver's loyalties ran directly, personally, without qualification, to Ronald and Nancy Reagan. Third of the old campaign team that had seen Reagan through so many contests was Lyn Nofziger, a pudgy, rumpled, smiling man, whose grooming occasionally offended the dainty Mrs. Reagan. But Nofziger's wit was sharp, his perceptions accurate, and his disdain for the press and media was shaped by his own years as a reporter and correspondent. Nofziger was an unabashed conservative, much farther to the right than his candidate with the exception of the one issue of abortion. There, Nofziger held for woman's right of choice against the zealots of right-to-life. Nofziger was the essential bridge by which Southern and Midwestern conservatives made their way into the campaign.

An intellectual team was also part of the Reagan operation. First among them was, of course, Martin Anderson. Following came Reagan's foreign policy adviser, Richard Allen, also a scholar, but not without political ambition himself. Third, perhaps most important, was the sparkling personality of William F. Buckley, author of *Up from Liberalism*, whose writings so affected Reagan's thinking. Alone among the intellectuals, Buckley could claim an affectionate personal relationship with both the Reagans; they visited at each other's homes in Los Angeles and Manhattan when one or the other made the transcontinental journey. Buckley was in no sense operational, but when Reagan was disturbed, he would call Buckley and be comforted.

The basic problem of the Reagan campaign was that it had two rivals for managerial hegemony of the 1980 adventure: Edwin Meese, who commanded the California base as Los Angeles chief of staff; and John Sears of Washington, who commanded Reagan's national organization.

The rivalry between these two is instructive, not only for its impact on the Reagan personality, but for what it told of the nature of American politics. Both wanted to manage the entire campaign— but the control of a presidential campaign in modern times holds out the prize that with victory, the dominant manager will control the White House, its staffing, and the executive branch. A campaign is a strike for power. Ever since William the Conqueror swooped on England and, after victory, distributed the dignities and spoils to his Norman lords, those who originally surround a conqueror on his adventure will surround him in power. Meese believed he was the chief steward of Ronald Reagan; Sears believed he was the chief guide. Had Sears won, he, rather than Meese, would now sit in the White House managing national affairs. And so, because the inner history of a presidential campaign determines the nature of the administration that comes out of it, we must explore the parable they offered.

Edwin Meese III is an affable, ever-courteous man, of old California stock. His great-grandfather had come to America in the German migration of 1848 and trekked west by wagon train in the gold rush; his grandfather had been Oakland's city treasurer; his father had been Alameda County treasurer. His own bent was thus, naturally, to administration. He had graduated from Yale, served two years in the army, graduated thereafter from Boalt Hall, the University of California's law school in Berkeley; and become an assistant district attorney in his hometown, Oakland, where he proved himself an outstanding organizer. Meese is, by training, a man of law and order, an old-fashioned patriot (very proud to see his son graduate from West Point), and a tireless worker. He is one of those apparently bland, round-faced men, deceptive on first meeting, with an endless capacity for absorbing and sorting out detail. He had come to Reagan's attention, in Reagan's first term as California's governor, as a very intelligent student of cops and violence; by the end of Reagan's second term, Meese was, in effect, deputy governor. He knew when to wake Reagan in a crisis, and knew when his authority let him deploy state police and fire fighters to quench a forest blaze without waking the governor. Though he is entirely pleasant, his devotion to orderliness makes him a formidable and cunning opponent. When crossed, he strikes back—hard. He does not like his turf invaded.

Meese had come to politics through administration, as so many do. But Sears had come to politics through politics; and at the top. After graduation from Notre Dame (where he had been a leader

among undergraduates in the Kennedy for President wave of 1960),
John Sears had gone to law school, then found a place in the Wall
Street firm that came to be known as Nixon, Mudge, Rose. Nixon had
found Sears promising; at twenty-seven, Sears had been assigned to
delegate roundup for Nixon's push at the 1968 convention. There he
had matched wits with Reagan's convention manager, the masterful
Clif White, and won. Dismissed from Nixon's victory because his
ambitions so irritated John Mitchell, Nixon's Attorney General, he
resurfaced in 1975, this time as campaign manager for Ronald Reagan. He then took the Reagan campaign of 1976 from ground zero
to touching reach of the Republican nomination. Depending on
whether one favored Ford or favored Reagan, Sears could be described either as the Machiavelli of the 1976 convention or Peck's
Bad Boy. Sears had passed beyond the mechanics of politics he had
learned from Nixon, to a loftier level. He had acquired a touch and
taste for the newer politics, which depend on media. No other Republican politician could make the media blip so responsively to his
will; few others could use a press conference more effectively. His
talents were so large that it was odds-on that Reagan would use him
again in 1980, this time as campaign manager.

"Sears," said one of his companions of the 1968 Nixon campaign,
"suffered from an excess of talent. He was a born principal with an
ego to match." Sears displayed apparent contempt for local politicians. He was far, far beyond them; they were to be used. He had
come to see issues as most important; and Reagan was his vehicle.

Sears could make a better presentation of perspective to newsmen than anyone else in the Reagan campaign. Two years before the
election, in 1978, I pressed him: Why was he for Reagan? His response was of a man thinking high. "What counts," he said, "is can
you put events in a historical perspective. Ever since World War II,
circumstances always sided with the Democratic party. Now circumstances aid us. America lives in the future, but the future now looks
grimmer than ever in the past. . . . Hope is the one permanent feature
of American life, so maybe this pessimism can be turned around.
. . . Politics are always played against a cultural perspective, and from
FDR on, the cultural perspective has been with the Democrats. But
now they're through. . . . Nineteen eighty will be a culture coming
to an end." "The old system," he observed in another conversation,
"forced each candidate to speak to the party leaders, who judged
whether he would make a good President. The old system forced him
to deal with people who were tough bargainers. This system forces
a man to perform before an amateur audience."

For Sears, this was a campaign against the Democrats; and it was obvious that he was involved in an enterprise larger than the election of Ronald Reagan. It was also obvious that this would inevitably bring him to clash with the Reagan loyalists, and with Ed Meese, major-domo.

Sears's power base was his Washington connection. From Washington, he twitched the attention of television and press. From Washington, Sears put in place and commanded the field organization of the Reagan campaign. From Washington, Sears commanded and extravagantly overspent the campaign budget. From Washington, Sears began his push against the Los Angeles base headquarters commanded by Meese. A consummate intriguer, Sears peeled away, one by one, the men on whom Reagan and Meese had depended for so long. First, in 1979, was Lyn Nofziger, Sears's only court rival in understanding the connections between the media and politics. Using Nofziger's old friend Mike Deaver as an ally, Sears forced Nofziger's resignation. Next he turned on Deaver, the man personally closest to the candidate, and forced a showdown which brought Deaver to resign. Sears closed next on Martin Anderson, the theorist —and Anderson, rather than fight, withdrew from Los Angeles to Stanford, putting himself on standby for a recall to the campaign if any recall came.

What Sears wanted, and made no bones about, was total control of the revolution he foresaw. If indeed, as he thought, an era was coming to an end and a new cultural epoch beginning, then nothing was more important than assembling the proper thinkers to think through the decades ahead. Few practicing politicians have paid as much attention to thinkers or paid them better than did Sears. In complete administrative control of the Reagan budget, Sears began to build his own rival issues team. Rumor set his consulting fees for some scholars at fifty thousand dollars a year; and for individual position papers, ten thousand dollars each. In the field, he had already built a formidable transcontinental net of political professionals in eighteen regional offices, counting some two hundred men and women, most more loyal to him than to Reagan. But as he built and spent, campaign money was running out—a matter which increasingly annoyed Reagan, and upset Ed Meese, the administrator and chief of staff. On the outcome of the quarrel between Meese and Sears would, ultimately, depend the organization of the Reagan White House, its staff, and its policies.

In the first week of January 1980 began a series of climaxes. Reagan assembled from both East and West his key advisers to discuss not only such grand issues as inflation, deflation, Iran, and the Panama Canal, but also the immediate tactics of the nomination. Less than three weeks over the horizon lay the opening public act of the campaign: the presidential caucuses in Iowa. Should Reagan fight it out there, or stand aloof? The Californians present thought Reagan must go into Iowa and fight it out. Sears, the master strategist, thought otherwise. Reagan, he felt, should take no part in a scheduled six-man debate. He should present himself as front-runner, above the pack, beyond the pack. It was, said someone, very much like Jimmy Carter's Rose Garden strategy—except that Reagan had no Rose Garden. Sears prevailed; and Reagan was to lose to George Bush's intense first organization drive. Of all the mistakes he made, said Reagan later, Iowa was the first: ". . . a strategy was planned in which I would campaign almost as an incumbent, and I saw that fail in Iowa; and I . . . said, 'I'm going to go into New Hampshire . . . and talk to the people and I'm going to open myself up to questions and answers.' "

The Iowa defeat was the catalyst, thus, of what was about to happen. Sears had been skirmishing with Richard Allen, Reagan's foreign policy expert. Allen had taken their quarrel directly to Reagan, asking whether Reagan wanted him in or out. "I know what Sears is doing," Allen remembers Reagan as replying. "He's closing in on us one by one. He's after Ed Meese next." Sears had met with Wirthlin in Washington and secretly tried to enlist him in the coming coup against Meese. Wirthlin held his tongue—but would not play. Sears approached Nancy Reagan and suggested that someone else be brought in as chief of staff to sit over Meese in Los Angeles. But she would not play, either.

It was quite obvious to Meese that it was either him or Sears—and Meese controlled access to Reagan. Thus, then, on Friday, February 15, less than two weeks before the New Hampshire primary, the inner group met at a Holiday Inn over the border, in Massachusetts, to plan the countercoup. Ronald and Nancy Reagan, of course; also Richard Wirthlin, also Ed Meese, also Richard Allen. As they met, they awaited the arrival from New York of a Wall Street lawyer named William Casey. Casey had begun his apprenticeship in the Republican party serving Tom Dewey's campaign in 1948; he had gone on to serve both the OSS in Europe and the Marshall Plan in Paris after the war; was a familiar figure on the fringes of the Eastern foreign policy establishment; and had served in Washington as Nixon's chairman of the SEC. He had been scouted, felt out, was willing to take over the campaign. He did not want to share high policy; he was content with Reagan as Reagan, governor of California ("the only man I know who turned things around," said Casey, explaining his loyalties). He was adamant only about the administrative authority he must exercise—complete control of budget, management, operations. These having been granted him, he would take over.

It was now up to Reagan to put the word to Sears. "I don't fault his ability at political analysis," said Reagan of Sears, "but he wanted to do *everything*. And when I wanted to bring someone in to really handle an office situation where the morale was at zero . . . he delivered an ultimatum . . . that he would leave if that was done. So I just knew that it could not go on that way."* Reagan went on to other matters and then came back to Sears again, as if to make his point clear. "There was . . . a feeling that I was just kind of a spokesman for John Sears."

The timing of the beheading was nicely set, as Reagan chose the day: ". . . election day of New Hampshire, actually, for his sake, because if I waited until afterward and lost New Hampshire, then it would seem as if I was blaming him for the loss, and therefore I wanted to do it before we knew the result from New Hampshire." Shortly after lunch on primary day, Sears was summoned to the Reagan suite, this time at the Holiday Inn in Manchester, New Hampshire. Sears arrived with his chief lieutenants, Charles Black, political director of the field organization, and Jim Lake, Sears's official press spokesman. Reagan had brought along Nancy Reagan and William Casey. Sears had apparently treated the candidate with the same affection that a jockey extends to his horse; this had displeased Mrs. Reagan, and she must have listened with prim satisfaction as her husband sliced neatly into the matter at hand. As Sears recalled it, Reagan began by saying something like: "Well, you know we've been having some basic problems," and then gave the Sears group a statement which began: "Ronald Reagan today announced that William J. Casey has been named . . . campaign director of his presidential campaign, replacing John Sears, who has resigned to return to his law practice." Sears handed the statement to his two lieutenants, and

---

*These political observations by Ronald Reagan, here as elsewhere in this book, are taken from an interview after election. We were talking politics, not policy, ticking off high points in the campaign. It does not make a consecutive story, so I do not reprint the full text. Reagan had, by then, learned to be wary of newsmen, so we only touched stepping-stones.

muttered, "I'm not surprised." Then withdrew. And Ronald Reagan was in charge of his own campaign, no longer a spokesman for any subordinate.

Instead of a Sears team, he would now have what was announced that evening as a "management team," its governing triumvirate three men—Meese, Wirthlin, Casey. That night, Wirthlin telephoned Nofziger and asked him back on board; a telephone call asking Deaver to return followed shortly. But Reagan, upset by the beheading, telephoned all the way to Italy, to his friend William Buckley, to explain what he had done and why. And Buckley supported him.

It was Deaver who later explained why he felt the removal of Sears was a turning point in the campaign: ". . . that decision did something to the entire campaign all over the country. The grass-roots people knew that Ronald Reagan had once again—was in charge of his own destiny. He was not a captive of someone, and I can't tell you what that did all over the country." For years, Reagan had set the tone for Republican conservatives; all other Republicans, except Nixon, had been forced to run against, or with, the image of Reagan. For some he had become the von Hindenburg of the Republican party, a figurehead. But with the firing of Sears, Reagan had repossessed his own image and was master in his own house. Other managers and revolving pressure groups would contend for his ear for the balance of the year and on into his presidency, where the continuing differences of his advisers would rowel his administration. But none would challenge him as Sears had done for control of purpose in the Republican revival.

The Republican revival was a matter of spirit, a call of instinct to a people confused and wandering between old values and new values. The Republican party is as dissolute and unorganized as are the Democrats; it is, like the Democratic party, less a disciplined organization than a state of mind. But the ideas that were to move the rest of the campaign were the ideas of Ronald Reagan. They were simple, almost simplistic ideas. But so, too, had been the ideas of Herbert Hoover, Franklin Roosevelt, and Dwight Eisenhower. Simple ideas win campaigns; they do not necessarily make great Presidents. Had Sears won his campaign struggle, the ideas of the Reagan administration would have been the ideas of John Sears; the vapors of "supply-side" economics might not have filtered into government policy, for Sears had a cold eye for ideas as well as men. But Reagan would have been a puppet President; and from New Hampshire on, he had established himself as the man in charge.

It was to be a campaign dominated by Reagan's ideas, Reagan's image, Reagan's mastery of television. Against these simple ideas Jimmy Carter would have to run while he, the sitting President, wrestled with the realities which confronted and contradicted all accepted ideas, both Democratic and Republican. So it is time to look at what was happening on the Democratic side of the divide.

CHAPTER NINE

THE DEMOCRATS:
THE PARTY THAT LOST
ITS WAY

The Republican party had come out of the election of 1976 a defeated and divided party, yet one that still held some inner coherence. The Democratic party, on the other hand, had come out triumphant—yet with a historic incoherence.

By 1980, the Democratic party as the midcentury had known it was gone. There were so many Democratic parties that not even a three-dimensional chart could link them into a cohesive national party. They had left far behind, and totally repudiated, the philosophy of their founder and patron saint, Thomas Jefferson, that eloquent advocate of states' rights and minimal government. As he reflected on the upheaval of the French Revolution, Jefferson wrote of the French monarchy: "Never was there a country where the practice of governing too much had taken deeper root and done more mischief." In its long history, his own party had done just that. All that now bound together the interlocking power groups of the Democratic party as they approached the election of 1980 was their common belief that the purpose of government was—to govern! The struggle among the factional groups who called themselves Democrats locked on how government should share its benefits and entitlements among the deserving and how far it should push its way into community life.

The most responsible of these Democratic parties was the Congressional Democratic party, where Tip O'Neill, the House Speaker, and such center senators as Henry ("Scoop") Jackson and Patrick Moynihan maintained a defense perimeter around the heritage of

Roosevelt, Truman, Kennedy. This Congressional Democratic party sought to preserve as much as possible of what had been achieved by the revolution of the previous decades. But it was like a border patrol, guarding abroad the limits of the global protectorate set by Roosevelt and Truman; and at home, trying to restrain its parade of great triumphs, like civil rights, from being stampeded by the insurgency over the cliff to the crash of absurdity.

More restless, however, was what can be called the Convention Democratic party, child of the insurgency of the sixties. This shapeless group had sprouted from the field that reformers had opened and plowed. In the sixties, it had recruited the best and most ambitious of the young, who had grown in professionalism until they dominated the primary elections which selected the presidential nominee. By the time these convention players had chosen the nominee, the conventions as nominating bodies had become farces, forums where "cause" groups and special-interest groups engaged in spirited battle over issues and emotions—ethnic rights, pollution, abortion, women's rights, unemployment rights, nuclear moralities —and over other theological and imperial matters. This Convention Democratic party had only the most remote connection with the Congressional Democratic party. It had surfaced as the insurgency in 1968; pushed through to its first victory with McGovern in 1972; followed with Carter's victory in 1976.

The Convention party was vaguely connected to the high priesthood of the Academic Democratic party, warden of the cathedrals of scholarship, which pumped ideas into the political process. So great a debt did all the Democratic parties owe to the scholars, so real had been their contribution, that success had addled many of their wisest heads: they had acquired the arrogance of truth multiplied by virtue. Great honor was indeed due the scholars; the party and the nation owed them much—not only for atomic bombs, nuclear power, radar, and astronautics, but for the fostering of culture and art, the triumphs in American medicine and research, the first primitive definition of credit as an opportunity that should be open to working people as well as the rich. Brilliant as they were, however, the members of this priesthood were snobs; they could not recognize where their own diagnoses and prescriptions had gone wrong. To the power of their thinking they added access to the media, which made their names standard reference points in all debates about the public wisdom.

These three Democratic parties all lusted for control of the presi-

dency, the Executive Democratic party, which was the most important. But now, as 1980 approached, the Executive party, the White
House command staff, was being challenged by the other Democratic parties. This was remarkable enough—never before had a
sitting President, an *elected* President, with command of both houses
of Congress and the party machinery, been so challenged by his own
people. What was even more remarkable was the nature of the challenge—a charge of incompetence. No grand and different visions
divided his rival candidates from the President as candidate; no dispute over race, over sexism, over tariffs, over war or peace, separated
them from him. They insisted simply that he had mismanaged the
country and they meant to take their case first to the party, then to
the people. Personalities and ambitions played their usual inescapable role in the contest about to start. And behind the candidates
trooped the usual ragtag array of hustlers and visionaries, cause people and job seekers.

Foremost of the Democratic candidates was the President himself. His assets were formidable—control of the White House, of
patronage, of punishments; also the ability to dominate the news
when he wished; to which he added another, unrecognized prime
asset, the team of young professional politicians whom he had trained
and blooded in the primaries of 1976. Together, these young men
made up perhaps the best team of primary and convention mechanics fielded in modern times.

Next came Senator Edward M. Kennedy, eloquent and vigorous,
with the heritage of Camelot behind him.

Next came Jerry Brown, governor of California, certainly the
most thoughtful of all the candidates of 1980, but a man arrived
before his time.

All three came of that streak in American politics which can be
called the Humanitarian Overcall, the desire to present and to prove
oneself as a greater humanitarian than any other, a man with heart.
Whichever of these candidates won the Democratic nomination, it
seemed certain that a conservative Republican could make the race
into the clearest ideological contest since Goldwater and Johnson
faced off in 1964.

First, then, Jimmy Carter.

No Democrat would have dared raise a voice against Jimmy
Carter had he been clearly successful, or more vengeful—or even
moderately lucky. But by 1979, all the sweet memories of the win-

ning Carter of 1976 had faded. The lingering image of Jimmy and Rosalynn walking home, hand in hand, from the inaugural to the White House had been bleached by repetition; his promise of a government as "decent and competent as our people" had curled at the edges; and the personality in the White House perplexed the American people.

As early as October of 1977, with Carter just ten months into office, his private pollster, Patrick Caddell, had reported that the President's personal popularity was holding high and steady, yet his polling also showed Carter's "job rating" going down—"like a skier on skis going two ways at once." For the next two years, Caddell, reaching the President usually through the First Lady, was to be the bearer of bad news, the house Cassandra of the administration. Caddell's reaction to the title was acute: "Cassandra was not a madwoman, she was King Priam's daughter; she sat at the table."

But Caddell was not the only one in the Democratic leadership who was disturbed. So, too, was House Speaker O'Neill, examining his own polls. So, too, were Senators Moynihan of New York, and Ribicoff of Connecticut. So, too, was the party apparatus, even the President's newly appointed chairman of the Democratic National Committee, John C. White. Said White of his party in April of 1979, when he could already see a challenge to the President for renomination: "We knew our role in the Depression . . . the problem was unemployment. But here we are so prosperous . . . and the problem is inflation. Carter's position is that we have to give our program time to work, it'll take eight or nine months. . . . Inflation is the strongest issue. To ensure that the President is re-elected we've *got* to do something about prices . . . we never had to live with this before . . . our old answers don't work."

The first serious warning signals, however, flashed, as they do these days, on the radar screen of the pollsters. The signing of the Israeli-Egyptian peace treaty in Washington on March 26, 1979, before the cameras of the world, should have been followed, as normally happens, by a spurt in presidential popularity ratings. Instead, it brought Carter no more than a four- or five-point upward blip— a measurement that brought glee to Richard Wirthlin, Reagan's pollster in Santa Ana, California, and consternation to Caddell.

Convinced that Carter's survival as President was at stake, Caddell brought his poll findings early in spring to Jody Powell, the President's press secretary. Together, they decided they must somehow break through to the President's imagination, and their best avenue was Rosalynn Carter. A two-hour breakfast with Caddell on April 9 convinced Mrs. Carter that affairs were indeed at peril—that something even more disturbing than prices was on America's mind, that it was seeking something, a purpose, that it could not find in Carter. At Mrs. Carter's urging, Caddell had produced by April 23 what became known to all who read it as the "Apocalypse Now" memorandum—for the President's eyes.

The memo opens bleakly: "America is a nation deep in crisis. Unlike civil war or depression, this crisis, nearly invisible, is unique from those that previously have engaged Americans in their history. Psychological more than material, it is a crisis of confidence marked by a dwindling faith in the future . . . there are no armies of the night, no street demonstrations, no powerful lobbies. . . . *This crisis is not your fault as President. It is the natural result of historical forces and events which have been in motion for twenty years. This crisis threatens the political and social fabric of the nation.* . . . The pessimism has extended to the elites; the young, the college educated, and the higher income groups. . . . Everywhere there is a groping tentative swirl of discussion among the most intelligent elites from many fields over these matters. . . . 1 out of every 3 Americans see their own lives going straight downhill. . . . [This] is a psychological crisis of the first order."

In short, reported Caddell, with immense polling data on expectations, on pessimism, on fall-off in voting, the President's reelection was in danger. And, by May 20, a Sunday evening, the sense of urgency provoked by Caddell had caused the President to gather his inner circle on the Truman Balcony of the White House, overlooking the South Lawn. The President was in search of something beyond specific bills and laws, beyond prices, petroleum, programs. He wanted to understand what was wrong with the country.

It is perhaps good to look more carefully at this group. No more than these six were ever in Carter's true inner circle, although for the purpose of campaigning Robert Strauss was later occasionally admitted and, because of rank, personality, and affection, Vice-President Walter Mondale. This May evening, the original six sat together: the pensive, conscience-burdened President and his wife; Hamilton Jordan, a man in love with the art of politics, pragmatic, always Carter's true chief of staff; Jody Powell, a man at once courtly and rude, who claimed to "occupy the middle ground between the President and Hamilton"; Gerald Rafshoon, the team's media mastermind, who had carved the President's original 1976 image; and Patrick Caddell, who would call himself a "conceptualist," the longest-range thinker of the group. These six were still what Washington operators considered "outsiders." But the men who had created the Carter presidency were no little surprised to hear their leader say, "This country is going to hell. This government has fucked up from end to end." Then, realizing Rosalynn was with them, he apologized. She said it made no mind; she had heard the word before. And they went on to discuss what must be done about the "crisis of confidence" in the nation.

Whose idea it was to assemble a handful of leading American intellectuals ten days later is obscure. But both the President and the First Lady felt they should hear from men above politics, at the intellectual edge of this crisis of spirit and morale. And so, on May 30 they assembled.

Present were two genuine intellectuals, Professor Daniel Bell of Harvard *(The Cultural Contradictions of Capitalism)* and Professor Christopher Lasch of the University of Rochester *(The Culture of Narcissism);* television personality, Bill Moyers; Washington editor, Charles Peters; black leader, the Reverend Jesse Jackson; Haynes Johnson (of the Washington *Post*); John Gardner, professor and public conscience of liberals; Caddell; Powell.

There is little disagreement among all assembled about how the evening went. For the White House members, the evening was a total fiasco. At one knot of the group, Jody Powell was overheard to say, "we *know* how to get elected, we asked you here to tell us what's wrong with the *country.*" For the thinkers it was a puzzlement and a perplexity. "If we had some foreknowledge, I suspect that the dinner would have been more focused and useful," wrote Bell later. After dinner (a mixed seafood appetizer, lamb chops, and asparagus), the President had begun by saying that what was on his mind was the state of America itself . . . the feeling that somehow things had gone wrong in the country . . . a loss of trust, a failure of will . . . that was why he had asked this group this evening, to find out how they read the American temper. Caddell led off with his polling results on American pessimism. Editor Peters said the American people must be told the hard facts. Reverend Jackson spoke of the disintegrating effect of television. Gardner spoke of the multiplicity of interest groups in the society. Bell said the administration was being bogged down in detail, the President must provide a framework so that people could understand the entire situation, why Americans by and large had the feeling of distrust.

The President was called out of the room at that point, and Mrs. Carter commented that she had hoped for more discussion on the problem of values in American society and how we could rebuild them. When the President came back, Moyers took over the discussion. "The real problem," he said, "is inflation," and continued with the danger of a succession of one-term Presidents, and said aloud there was a real danger that Carter, too, would not be reelected. The President asked for specifics as to what he should do, and Moyers, nonplused, said perhaps he should invite more people to the White House. The evening broke up at eleven—the White House group and the thinkers group equally bewildered and unsatisfied by this summit meeting of minds. On their drive from the White House, Bell asked Gardner what the purpose of all this had been? Gardner replied: "I think that Mr. Carter is quite perplexed as to what is going on in the country. . . . Jimmy Carter listens but he doesn't always hear."

"The problem," wrote Bell later, "was obviously [for the White House people] not that the President was doing anything wrong, but that the people were wrong."

Perhaps no President since Lincoln has probed so deeply into the metaphysics of spirit that makes America a nation as Jimmy Carter tried to do. But Lincoln had music in his ears; sought out few scholars; and was faced with only one stupendous clash of interests. Carter was faced with so many clashes of interests that he could not sort them out. But he tried, with almost reckless personal expenditure of energy and emotion, to master and unravel the details that encase the spirit. He was searching, always searching, for the proper course; but could not pose the questions.

It was the very intensity of his effort, perhaps, that doomed the Carter presidency. Somehow, he had come to Washington believing that the spirit was buried in the flesh; and he could free the spirit to soar if only he worked hard enough at detail to disembody the spirit. Here was a man who wanted to get to the bottom of things; and in his self-imposed application to duty, in his sixteen-hour-a-day busyness, he absorbed more information than his mind or politics could digest. Yet now, in late spring of 1979, his own spirit was to be mired in two matters of bewildering complexity and detail—the energy crisis and the agreements with Russia on restraining nuclear holocaust.

In June 1979, duty thoroughly punished even Carter's sturdy constitution. Off he went, on June 14, to Vienna, a seven- or eight-hour time jump on the sunrise side of the clock in America. There, for three days, he parleyed at a summit conference of immense importance—the SALT II peace treaty—with his archrival, Soviet leader Leonid Brezhnev. Back home from Austria, on June 18, he scheduled himself to a week of total exertion, as if his energy were limitless. He addressed Congress on the overriding importance of SALT II; he entertained an uncounted number of citizen groups in the East Room, briefing them and pleading with them to support his treaty; he monitored but did not cope with the spreading gasoline shortage; and then was off to Asia the next week to confer on matters of summit economics with the leaders of the industrialized democracies. Asia is a twelve-hour time jump on the sunset side of the clock in America. Almost no one's body can take such a jolting of the circadian rhythm in so short a time; jet lag addles the senses, the perception, the mind. Most travelers break the Pacific jet lag curse by an overnight in Hawaii, but Carter flew directly to the Asian negotiations, having allotted himself a four-day vacation and recovery in Hawaii on the way back. That, however, was not to be. Get your ass back here as fast as possible, cabled Pat Caddell, watching the polls, to his buddy Jody Powell, traveling with the presidential party. And back Carter came directly, for it needed no pollster to tell him that the discontent the polls had first reported in early spring had now surfaced growling on the streets—or at least, at every city and suburban gas station.

The gas panic of 1979 was under way.

As a case of mass hysteria, whipped on by television reporting, the Great Gas Panic deserves its own chronicler. As in all such large stories, its roots could be traced anywhere; ultimately, of course, it ran back to Eisenhower's decision during the campaign of 1956 to yield Western control of the oil lanes of the Middle East to the Arabs. But by 1979, the entire social system of America rested on the innocent assumption of everlasting availability of cheap liquid fuel—from the commuting suburbs to the farthest reach of the interstate highway system that had spawned them. The fuel system was, however, delicately balanced to a precision of supply and demand that no layman could comprehend. The seven great oil companies of the world had computerized time and resources, exploration and pumping, storage and refining, so that a miscalculation of 3 percent, or even 2 percent, in supply and demand or overall transoceanic oil lift could result in exactly what did happen in the spring of 1979—shortage. Then concern, then alarm, then panic, then anger.

Far beyond the ken of America's motorists, the crisis had begun when the Shah of Iran had fled his country on January 16, 1979. The Shah, tyrant though he was, had been an ally of the United States and Western Europe. He pumped oil into the Western world in defiance of his fellow Moslem oligarchs—and oil from Iran had satisfied more than 10 percent of the needs of the non-Communist nations. When he fell, chaos had followed. By early spring of 1979, the interruption of oil exports from Iran had upset all the nicely computed strands of oil flow around a world hungry for energy. And by May, halfway around that world, in California, had come the first choke of the oil shortage, an arrhythmia of circulation, almost like a blood stoppage or a heart attack, as the governor put California's filling stations on restriction of gas sales. Carter had taken the occasion to lecture the nation, insisting that "the American people refuse to face the inevitable prospect of fuel shortages"; and with his scolding, the alarm moved into panic gear. If there was going to be a fuel shortage, as the President said, then it was every man for himself—and out to fill the family gas tank!

Whether it was the President's scolding, or the marvelous opportunity for television to be at once serious, dramatic, and entertaining on the evening news, the next three weeks were a study in the sociology of unreason. The gas crunch had been a phenomenon, chiefly confined to California and Florida in the first fortnight in May. In Los Angeles, the first weekend, gas stations simply closed on Sunday. Then followed thuggery—as, for example, a Cadillac driver crashing a gas line in Hollywood, brandishing his pistol, to hold off manager and queued motorists while he filled his tank. Through May, state after state experimented with odd-even days; with sale limits ranging from three to ten dollars; with red and green flag systems indicating availability; with speed limits. By Memorial Day weekend, the traditional first long weekend of holiday driving, the crisis had surged east. In June, President Carter set his Domestic Affairs Assistant, Stuart Eizenstat, to work on a new comprehensive energy plan; while he himself, preoccupied with matters grander than oil shortages, was off to Vienna to seal the apocalyptic negotiations on strategic arms. And then was off to Asia, for his summit meeting with Asian and European leaders, now restyled a conference on the energy shortage. And while he was away, his political base came apart, crumbling first at the gas stations, then at the polls.

California and Florida had been first hit by the shortage; next hit was the nation's capital, Washington. And then, in domino style, followed the rest of the states, until by June the shortage closed on

New York City, the capital of communications, where the television networks make their home. Auto lines snaked in and crawled out of the city's filling stations, defying both red and green lights, clogging traffic, and making neighborhoods hideous with their honking. Young feature reporters of press and television now had their tryouts in a situation where they could not miss—a "lady" offering her body in return for a tankful of gas in Queens; a Shell Oil Company tank truck hijacked, its driver bound and blindfolded, while the hijackers delivered its contents to a gas station in Brooklyn; brawls. Indeed, shortly, a shootout in Brooklyn when two irate motorists tangled over priority in the gas line and one was killed.

While the summit conferees met in Tokyo to discuss the world's energy crisis with Jimmy Carter, his own people were far more involved with the simple difficulty of getting ready for the Fourth of July weekend. Would there be enough gas? Emergency regulations cascaded from governors commanding gas stations to stay open on the weekend, even if they had no gas. The statistical summary: 90 percent of all stations in the New York metropolitan area closing for the big weekend; 80 percent in Pennsylvania; 50 percent in Rhode Island.

The gasoline shortage of 1979 would have been at all times manageable by a severe, disciplinary government. The overall short-fall of approximately 3 percent from the previous year's summer gasoline consumption had struck the country unevenly. The pin-points of acute shortage, as in growing states like California, pro-voked anxiety and panic; and the panic provoked the gorging of gas in jerry cans by frightened motorists. The consequences of the panic were to be great; there would be the slow, sensible adjustment of Americans to the realization that the age of plenty was over, that energy was not for cheap buying. But there would come also the sudden widening of the breach that the small Japanese cars had been making in the American automobile market as early as 1971, and no one could predict that the pinch of the purse on gas-guzzling Ameri-can cars would smash the automobile industry of the Midwest a year later.

The political consequences were to show in 1980; but the first of the common impressions was that no one was in charge in Wash-ington; and after years of turbulence, it was this sense of strong leadership that the American political system craved more than ever. The gasoline panic was soon to abate. It would be over by Labor Day. Already, by July 1, it had begun to come under control, first in

California, where it had started, later on the East Coast. But the President, returning from Asia that July 1, like Sheridan on his gallop from Winchester to rally his troops, was greeted by a Washington *Post* headline: "Gas Crisis: Color the White House Blue," and a prescient dispatch by its correspondent Martin Schram: "The Oval Office and much of the White House West Wing are empty now as President Carter travels to another summit—but among those Carter loyalists who remained behind, a feeling has set in that is far gloomier than emptiness. It is despair. A genuine political despair, perhaps unmatched in any modern White House, except in those very last days of Nixon. It is a despair that Carter may have been so severely crippled by the latest gasoline crisis—and by a public perception that he is not coping with it—that he may be kept from re-election."

The story of the next two weeks is bizarre, meshing politics and American purpose, and should serve to introduce the next of the Democratic candidates, Edward Moore Kennedy—except that to make clear the entry of Kennedy, one must examine at length another episode at Camp David.

Ever since Jimmy Carter arrived in Washington, the struggle for his mind, his soul, his thinking had been the central battleground of his administration.

It is best to follow two men into the events of July 1979. One was Stuart Eizenstat, an Atlanta lawyer, once on Johnson's White House staff, a man of highest decency and as omnivorous for work as his President. Eizenstat believed that government's job was to deliver services to the people at the most effective possible cost. He was an idealist—but in the Carter White House he was considered a pragmatist. If there was in the White House a philosophical rival to Eizenstat, it was Pat Caddell. In his own mind, Caddell was as much an idealist as Eizenstat—but where Eizenstat dealt with programs and facts, Caddell dealt with people and the moods his polls reflected. In Carter's absence, Eizenstat had been wrestling with reality to pull together a comprehensive energy and gasoline policy on which Carter could base a speech of program and leadership to the nation. At the same time, Caddell had been wrestling with what the polls told him—that confusion reigned, dismay was rising, that the nation was passing through a crisis of faith in itself as much as a crisis of gasoline at the pump.

The President had come home to Washington on Sunday, July 1. While Carter was in Japan, the OPEC nations, with what must have been some sense of relish, twisted the screws a bit tighter, raising the price of oil 16 percent, to twenty dollars a barrel—60 percent more than at the year's beginning. At the pump, gas already had gone up about a penny a gallon every week. Carter lingered at the White House for two days. Discontented not so much with Eizenstat's energy program as with the speech drafted for him on the basis of the program, he had, late on July 3, helicoptered off to Camp David for reflection. From there he announced on Wednesday, July 4, that his previously announced and eagerly awaited speech on gasoline was canceled. Even so loyal a Carter supporter as Abraham Ribicoff was appalled. When the senator heard of the cancellation on the radio, he burst out angrily, not realizing he was being overheard, "Why . . . the man doesn't deserve to be President."

At Camp David, the tired President was undergoing the pain of decision. On the one hand, he had to weigh the collective wisdom of his domestic council, passed up through Eizenstat from all the energy experts in the government, on a program that, though it would lift no spirits, was genuinely reasonable. With it came the draft of a speech. On the other hand, here was the opinion of Caddell, based on a superlative polling apparatus, reporting the cynicism everyone knew to be true, also accompanied by a script for a speech, a call for renewal of faith.

What followed is difficult to describe in believable terms: The President's closest advisers were about to gather to discuss the spirit and faith of a questioning nation. In the court of almost any other contemporary sovereign, the attempt would be material for comedy, except in China, where such doctrinal disputes end in tragedy.

On Wednesday, the Fourth of July, three days after his return, the President had canceled his speech on energy. On Thursday morning, as his most intimate advisers, Jordan, Powell, Caddell, lounged by the pool at Caddell's Georgetown home, they were instructed to meet the Vice-President, from whose pad at the Naval Observatory a helicopter would lift off for Camp David. Stuart Eizenstat and Jerry Rafshoon would join them. It was a short but gloomy flight. Hamilton Jordan, depressed, muttered once, "We gotta fire people." Eizenstat was depressed also, and reported to them that since the energy speech had been canceled, the dollar had, that morning, fallen in value on the world market; he added, "I hope you're happy."

The group met first at Camp David's Laurel Lodge, before the President arrived, and they broke immediately into the cleavage lines that ran not just through the Carter administration but through American politics. Caddell handed around a polling survey and a new memorandum which went far beyond his April 23 report. But the theme was the same: America was afflicted by self-doubt, its people no longer had the old patriotic spirit, they were too self-centered. To which Eizenstat, normally a very understated person, blurted out, "Bullshit." "In four years," said Eizenstat later, "I was never in so agitated a meeting or state. I made the point in the most vigorous terms that what was wrong with the country was not the American people themselves . . . they felt their government was the problem; and to turn the tables, like the Czar of Russia, and say 'You're the problem' would not fit well." Eizenstat thought that the problem was due to external factors, primarily the energy revolution, and that the President had to talk about the crisis of the gas lines.

The President and the First Lady arrived shortly later, the President in good spirits. He obviously had been swayed by the Caddell memorandum on purpose and spirit, and pronounced it "brilliant." Powell lined up with the President, Mrs. Carter, and Caddell: This was a crisis of spirit, not gas, and they might as well go with that theme. He added that in Washington, no matter what you said or did, "they'll fuck you but they won't kiss you." Eizenstat now spoke up against the Caddell theme, and Caddell compared the accumulated trauma of the nation to the accumulated trauma that finally breaks a man down. As the discussion grew bitter, Vice-President Mondale attempted to mollify the dispute by talking about jet lag, how people feel terrible a whole week later, but was cut off by Carter's rejoinder: "I feel fine." At which point, the Vice-President, raising his voice, declared that this discussion of "social psychology is a dry hole," adding that Caddell's memorandum was "crazy." The Vice-President, himself the son of a Methodist minister, felt that what the nation needed was not a sermon but a statement on gasoline. To which the President responded that he had thought this through; he was with Caddell "100 percent"; and was going to speak to the nation on spirit and faith. The group broke for dinner, later watching TV and laughing at the commentators, so publicly puzzled by what was happening up in the Catoctin Mountains. The President went off for a walk with Mondale, while Mrs. Carter took Caddell for a ride in a golf cart, and told him *his* speech was replacing the energy speech. An evening meeting followed, less concerned with the national mood than with the personalities of the cabinet. It was decided that Secretaries Califano (HEW), Blumenthal (Treasury), and Schlesinger (Energy) should be fired. After which, Vice-President Mondale and

Domestic Counselor Eizenstat, who objected, were offered a helicopter ride back to Washington, while Jordan, Powell, and Caddell were invited to remain.

Thereafter, and for the following two weeks, something very disconcerting happened. At deep bottom, the President wanted to speak to the nation about his driving concern; somewhere, though never voiced, the problem was that the American nation could *not* be governed without a common faith of Americans in one another, and a readiness to sacrifice for a common cause. But for such a restatement of American purpose, no great occasion offered itself for another Gettysburg address. To arouse the nation, it would be necessary to "produce" the occasion, with attendant theatrics, ceremonies, mysteries, and clearances, in the game called "touching base."

Thus, then, a ten-day production. On Friday, eight governors flew up to the mountain to consult with the President on the crisis. On Saturday night and Sunday morning came a group called the "wise men," for their national eminence as thinkers: Clark Clifford, adviser to Presidents from Truman to Johnson; Jesse Jackson; John Gardner; Lane Kirkland, of the AFL-CIO; Sol Linowitz, lawyer and one of the creators of Xerox, a skilled public negotiator in diplomacy; Barbara Newell, president of Wellesley College. It was a classic convocation à la Carter—black and white; women and men; labor and business; Christian and Jew. Sunday was the day for energy, an assembly of experts. Meanwhile, senators of the proper committees had been coming and going, both Republicans and Democrats. By Tuesday, matters of spirit and flesh had locked. A memorandum had arrived from Vice-President Mondale, pleading that the President not address the nation in the spirit of Jonathan Edwards, as "sinners in the hands of an angry God." Rafshoon supported Mondale. But in the morning, the economists, men of matter, held forth; and in the evening, the men of God. The evening gathering included Terence Cardinal Cooke of New York; the Reverend Theodore Hesburgh of Notre Dame; Claire Randall of the National Council of Churches; two lay spirituals, Professors David Riesman and Robert Bellah, respectively of Harvard and Berkeley; and Rabbi Marc Tanenbaum. That Tuesday evening had the quality of a revival meeting, and was described by some as "the best of all the meetings." Cardinal Cooke was the star, talking of fundamental values, and how a nation could not live without them. It was left to Rabbi Tanenbaum to make the closing prayer, and the President suggested as the spiritual evening ended that they hold hands, as brethren.

The week continued from there, with bulletins dropped from

Camp David on the news system from time to time, further confusing the citizens, who were clouting each other on gas lines, hoarding
gasoline, and wondering, simply, who was in charge. Every now and
then, the President would reappear in semipublic, dodging cameras,
darting from his hilltop to consult with common citizens in their
parlors (at Carnegie, Pennsylvania, and Martinsburg, West Virginia),
sampling pulse. By Friday, the irrepressible Mondale had checked in
once more, with the support of two Georgians, Eizenstat and Jack
Watson, Secretary to the Cabinet, insisting that the President must,
simply *must,* say something about gasoline and repeating their view
that this quest for a new faith in the nation was a disaster. Later that
Friday afternoon, the President summoned the most important
columnists and television commentators of the Washington press
corps for one of their rare entries into Camp David, and spoke to
them for two and a half hours on both energy and spirit.

By now, he had touched all bases, and by Sunday, July 15, Carter
was back in Washington; he had gone to church in the morning, had
been closeted with his wife most of the day, going over his address.
At 10:00 P.M., the President went on air with a speech immediately
dubbed the "malaise" speech, although that word was never uttered.
Carter's eyes were fixed unflinchingly on the camera, his expression
unsmiling, and he spoke as "sincerely" as Presidents do when announcing war or disaster.

The climax speech was divided into thirds—the first part anec-
dotal, entertaining, quoting from the citizens, high and low, whom
he had surveyed in search of meaning in the past ten days. This part
was speech writers' art. The next third, the core of the message, was
inspirational: ". . . a crisis of confidence. It is a crisis that strikes at the
very heart and soul and spirit of our national will. . . . The symptoms
of this crisis . . . are all around us. . . . Washington, D.C., has become
an island. The gap between our citizens and our government has
never been so wide. . . . We simply must have faith in each other.
Restoring that faith and that confidence to America is now the most
important task we face." The last third spoke of the oil crisis and the
measures Carter, as President, would implement starting immediately to free America from the "intolerable dependence" on OPEC
oil. He closed with a ringing Churchillian call: "Let us commit ourselves together to a rebirth of the American spirit. Working together
with our common faith, we cannot fail."

No President since Abraham Lincoln had spoken to the American people with such sincerity about matters of spirit. What Carter

had said was true, and long overdue in the saying. His delivery had been impressive; it had almost veneered over the carpenter's jointing between the professional speech writer's opening, Caddell's deep concern about spreading cynicism, and the Eizenstat-Mondale urging that the nation was worried as it should be about energy.

Whatever gain the President may have won by sincerity, however, was erased only two days later by theatrics. His White House suddenly announced that Carter had called for the resignation of the entire cabinet and White House staff—and within forty-eight hours the announcement revealed itself as the cheapest of publicity gimmicks to cover the firing of three cabinet officers who particularly annoyed him.

Moreover, whatever political gain Carter may have won from Congress, the national impact of his speech was overtaken by his own behavior. The President's party leader in Congress, Speaker O'Neill, had not even been informed in advance of the gimmick of mass firing, or the technical liquidation of cabinet members. Additionally, the President had called in his speech for national unity and renewal of common purpose; in pursuit of that goal he had invited to the Oval Office Senator Howard Baker, seeking cooperation. Baker, Republican minority leader, had sacrificed much of his own Republican base in supporting the President on the Panama Canal Treaty. Their talk was candid: If the President wanted to talk to the Republican party in the Senate, he, Baker, was the party's chosen leader. To invite three Republican senators to Camp David, as the President had just done, without consulting the party's leader was—well—"Don't do that again, Mr. President, or I'll bust your balloon." Carter promised candor and cooperation, and then, as Baker left the White House, he was accosted by news people, who asked him what he thought about Carter's firing of the whole White House staff and cabinet just that morning. "I looked like a fool," said Baker, who had not been told.

Here were two Jimmy Carters—the earnest and devout Carter, the slick and gimmicky Carter. And for the next two months, these twin candidates contended with each other. In August, the gimmicky Carter took over. Down 650 miles of the Mississippi River he floated for one week, attended by the cameras of the local and national news programs, aboard the steamboat *Delta Queen,* urging the citizens at almost fifty stops to support his energy policies. The scenery was good, the visuals for evening news shows outstanding. People shouted and waved at their President, babes in their arms, hailing him as national leader. And thus into the fall season, until, by September 13, the NBC News/Associated Press poll, one of the nation's most reliable, showed Carter, as President, with an "approval" rating of only 19 percent, less than one person in five approving his conduct of the presidency.

By then, of course, a Democratic contest for the nomination of 1980 was out in the open. It had begun in the gas crisis; had festered in several minds as the President's authority leaked away; and had come to a head, a direct and pointed challenge, man to man, a week earlier, when the President had asked Senator Edward Kennedy to lunch with him at the White House.

It is to that lunch we should now go to look at how Ted Kennedy came to enter the campaign of 1980.

There was something unreal about the Kennedy campaign from the very beginning. For months, his reflex answer to every question had been: "I expect the President to be renominated and I expect him to be reelected and I intend to support him." The statement was unqualified, but I explored it with Stephen Smith, the senator's brother-in-law, a man of candor. We lunched in May of 1979, and Smith explained: There was no Kennedy campaign, there would be none. Teddy, he said, had no issue, not the way Bobby had had with the Vietnam War in 1968. Teddy also had problems. The Chappaquiddick problem was still there; there was the problem with his wife; there was a problem with the family. Even if Teddy won the nomination, said Smith, he would split the party and lose the election.

And then had come the gas crisis of July. Down, down, down went Carter in the polls, until by mid-July, a New York Times/CBS News poll showed that Democrats preferred Kennedy over Carter, 53 percent to 16 percent. Added to which was the presence of Jerry Brown, governor of California, who by mid-July was making the unmistakable noises of a serious candidate. If the presidency of Jimmy Carter was collapsing, it seemed as silly for Kennedy to let Brown claim the nomination as it had been unwise, in retrospect, for Robert Kennedy to let Eugene McCarthy claim the nomination in 1968, when Johnson's presidency was collapsing.

When Kennedy decided to run is uncertain even to him. He had spent a tranquil summer weekend at Cape Cod, boating with his children, in July; but on Sunday evening, July 15, he had flown back to Washington. There, at home, according to his recollection, he had watched the President's speech to the nation. "That speech," he said later, "was so completely contrary to everything I believe in that it upset me. I was alone watching it. I didn't talk to any political reporters for three weeks before; you know how political reporters are—they keep coming around to take your pulse. . . . [Then] I spent four weeks making a *personal* decision, not even talking with key people you respect."

Steve Smith picked up the story from there in a later conversation, in October. "There were always two areas in Teddy's mind," said Smith, "the public and the private areas. When I talked to you [in May], I had no sense that he'd begun to address the private area —Joan, his mother, the family. Teddy keeps his own counsel in that process. . . . He talked with Joan, with the children, with his mother, he explored how they felt about it, what the impact on them was. He found a real sadness, but the underlying sense that he ought to go with it. . . . Put it in the balance of what was happening across the country . . . old and new friends saying they would help, and the public and private process began to come together. . . . I didn't see or talk to Teddy all of August . . . then we took a week at the Cape, and while he was there, the President called."

For three weeks, leaks from the Kennedy camp had been steaming out into the press, encouraging response and volunteers from all over the country. The polls were adding to the pressure. Even in California, in a three-man trial among Democrats, Ted Kennedy ran first—59 percent for Kennedy, Brown 17 percent, Carter 16 percent; and in a two-man race in that state, Democrats favored Kennedy over Carter by 72 percent. None of this had been hidden from the Carter staff, and sometime in August, they decided to force Kennedy's hand—he must be persuaded to renounce his candidacy, or be pushed into the open as a rival, and thus be a target to attack. Go-betweens felt each other out, and finally, on the Thursday before Labor Day, the President had telephoned Kennedy at the Cape, and suggested they talk. The earliest convenient time for Kennedy to meet with the President was lunch on Friday the seventh of September. And so they met.

The lunch, with Mrs. Carter present, was cordial enough and the conversation revolved around one of Mrs. Carter's favorite subjects —mental health and retardation. Then Mrs. Carter withdrew and the two men settled to business. Both agreed the meeting would remain private, that not even their closest associates would hear the details. The President firmly suggested that what he wanted from Kennedy was a Sherman-like statement of complete withdrawal.

Kennedy let the President have it then, quite quietly: He was reconsidering his earlier position of the spring. When pressed, Kennedy will say only that he had the impression Carter was "surprised." As soon as Kennedy had left the White House, the President called Hamilton Jordan with the news—Jordan, who had feared just this contest with Kennedy from the first Carter campaign planning in November 1972. Kennedy had haunted the plans of the Carter staff for almost a decade, just as he had haunted the scheming and planning of all other presidential candidates—for Edward Moore Kennedy was more than a distinguished senator. Ted Kennedy had inherited a legend along with his name and he was almost as much trapped by the legend as propelled by it. The legend was very large, perhaps the largest part of the Kennedy candidacy of 1980—and it was rooted in reality, the triumphs of John Kennedy.

Americans had been abused by history since 1963. Looking back —across the disaster in Vietnam, the breach of faith at Watergate, the runaway inflation, the seepage of squalor in public life—looking back on all this, the last President in the great line who had given Americans a sense of control of their own destiny had been John F. Kennedy. He had faced down the Russians in the missile crisis; he had opened the gates for the blacks; he had established standards of open opportunity measured by merit and excellence. Not least, he had maintained a stable economy in which working people grew comfortable and the rich got richer; if a man made a dollar, it was worth a dollar and he could save a dime. All in all, John F. Kennedy had been not only the last good President but a superior one—he gave the nation a sense of new direction. The tag "Camelot" had been placed on the short Kennedy term, but it was Alfred Lord Tennyson who, a century earlier, had explained Camelot best: "The city is built/To music, therefore never built at all,/And therefore built forever." Ted Kennedy was the sole surviving heir to this immense political legacy.

Great families run all through history; they come into events, like the Churchills of England, as actors, and remain as symbols. Perhaps the closest parallel to the Kennedys of Boston were the Gracchi of the old Roman Republic. The Gracchi, as tribunes, had used their leadership to defend the Roman soldier families, the peasants who were being wiped out by the economics of empire. What rooted the Gracchi in the hearts of so many Romans, however, was the tragic death of both brothers—Tiberius in a riot in 133 B.C., Gaius by suicide in 121 B.C. Their memory and their causes rang down through Roman history, creating a party of the *populares,* which dominated politics to the days of Caesar, himself a declared *popularis,* who found the republic too decayed to be saved.

Tragedy of a similar kind hung over Ted Kennedy like a shawl. He was the last alive of four brothers. His oldest brother, Joseph P. Kennedy, Jr., had died a hero, flying a death-defying mission into a Nazi submarine pen on the Channel coast. Joe junior was not only a conservative but an ideologue of the right. The next brother, another hero of the war, was John F. Kennedy, the model of an enlightened Tory, a superlatively civilized man, so neatly situated at the political center as to make his older brother, Joe, seem like a hard-rock reactionary. Next had come on stage Robert Kennedy, with a public reputation for ruthlessness, but of a personal kindness, forgiveness, and fun-loving mischief that made him, to his friends, the most lovable of the clan. Then, last, had come Edward Kennedy, only twelve years old when the oldest son died in the war, thirty-one years old when his brother John, the President, was assassinated; thirty-six when his brother Robert, as candidate, was murdered—and he himself, still young, bearing alone, as the last surviving male, the weight of the legacy.

In his own generation of four brothers, the political progression had been from Joseph Kennedy, Jr., closest to the conservative tradition, to John and Robert Kennedy, who had moved steadily closer to the humanitarian goals of the new politics—to himself, Edward Kennedy, the man of the unabashed liberal extreme. Concern for the sick, the aged, the black, the underprivileged, had become, by 1980, his central cause. One of the famous anchormen of television went down to Washington to interview Kennedy and came back saying it was useless. "If I had asked him any question, he would have replied the same way. If I had asked him about the weather, he would have said, 'When I think about the weather, I think first about the sick, the black, the old people, the underprivileged.'"

If his politics had moved far beyond that of his brothers, he had nonetheless inherited many of their qualities.

First, of course, was personal grace. He had matured now and was a graver person than the young Teddy Kennedy who could do a daredevil schuss on skis down a Wyoming slope to draw attention to his brother John's campaign in 1960. He no longer did the imitations that enlivened so many Washington parties, mimicking Sheriff Manton of some forgotten West Virginia county, mimicking President Carter in public rallies, mimicking even this reporter's awkward television appearances. But he could, when the mood stirred him, make any party come alive, as when he attended the wedding of Kenneth O'Donnell, John Kennedy's aide, and, lifting his tenor voice, led all the guests in Irish songs so that the wedding became a blessing in the memory of all there.

Secondly, he retained the family sense of the politics of issues. In the seventeen years since he had come to the Senate as a young man, Kennedy had become a skilled parliamentarian, a master of congressional committee tactics—not only a dedicated champion of causes, but one who knew how to translate a simple cause into twelve pages of cogent legislation. He loved government, its mechanics and practices, and thought he knew how to make government work for the people.

It is this latter quality—his own infinite love of government—that comes closest, I think, to being the genesis of the Kennedy campaign of 1980. No real difference of politics separated Kennedy from Carter. What did separate them was, very simply, the growing contempt Kennedy developed for Carter as a national leader, the contempt of a master machinist for a plumber's helper.

Kennedy's exasperation with Carter was so great that, at times, he simply spluttered. I went to visit him in November of 1979, shortly after he had announced his candidacy. I wanted to know precisely where it was he differed from Carter so strongly that he must run. He said that a President must *direct* the government, has to give it vision. I pressed him for hard specifics. He said they differed about a "fundamental view of how this institution works. Congress *wants* to see a President do well, Congress can be used by any President who's prepared to put Congress out front." He became more irritated as I pressed: Well, how, specifically. There then burst from him a cascade of annoyances. "A President," he said, "has got to stay ahead of the curve. The one institution in this government that has the ability not to be crisis-crushed is the presidency of the United States. You can't wait," he said, growing angrier, "until the crisis is upon us—like Chrysler or the Rock Island Railroad. Look. He makes this speech about the energy crisis being the moral equivalent of war. Then he does nothing. Nothing!" And from there Kennedy was off into a stunning discussion of just how laws are passed, of how Carter's amateur lobbyists had messed up program after program by odd legislative couplings of unsorted programs. Then, details cascading from him more and more rapidly, he concluded in an outburst of frustration: "We wanted the same things . . . [but] this . . . this *outsider* can't solve our problems. . . . Even on issues we agree on, he doesn't know how to do it."

He was angry, personally, with Jimmy Carter. He was outraged by what he considered a clumsy "outsider" mishandling the powerful and delicate instruments of government. The Carter address of July 15, which Kennedy insisted on calling the "malaise" speech, had misread the nation. The job of a leader, insisted Kennedy, was to uplift the people, to sound the call—not to mourn in public, not to find fault with the people. Carter was acting, though Kennedy did not say so, in a way offensive to the entire family tradition, offensive to the heritage of governing skills in which he had been brought up. And again, though Kennedy did not say so directly, the impression left was that Kennedy felt it his duty to run.

If Carter had misread what the Kennedy family had learned of government, it could not be denied, as the next few weeks unfolded, that Kennedy had forgotten what his family had learned in almost a hundred years of politics. Rarely has any campaign been so mismanaged as the Kennedy campaign of 1980 in its first two months.

The Kennedy campaign was, from the beginning, historically preposterous. What the senator proposed to do was to destroy the chief of his own party, the President of the United States. Having undermined the President, he would then have to pull the Democratic party together again and face the Republicans, defending a record he had spent a year denouncing. If he succeeded in destroying the President, that would come at the convention in August. Thus, Jimmy Carter would be publicly castrated—yet officially remain as commander in chief of the United States Armed Forces, national spokesman on foreign policy, for another six months. He would be the silhouette of impotent authority, not even a lame duck, but a limping capon.

The Kennedy campaign lurched into action in early November as if from a cold start—without organization, with no clear lines of authority, without the blooding of experience in the changing tactics of field campaigns that had developed since 1968, the last time the Kennedy team had tried the race.

There was no doubt that it had spirit at the beginning. The legend had drawn a corps of young volunteers, as romantic and ambitious as the original volunteers of the Kennedy campaign of 1960. Housed in an old automobile agency, hastily partitioned into cubicles, the youngsters had come expecting veteran leadership, a plan, a strategy of conquest. But only two men present had learned the techniques developed in the seventies—Richard Stearns and Carl Wagner—and both were overworked. Stearns, for example, had volunteered for Kennedy on the thirtieth of October; the candidate had announced on the seventh of November. But the new headquarters had no telephones until days later, and Stearns, who had masterminded the McGovern delegation operation in 1972, was appalled, not at disorganization, but at no organization. He would within a week ship out twelve organizers to prepare for the Iowa caucuses; but these twelve would have to mobilize at least three thousand volunteers who, somehow, must in the next eighty days recruit and energize thirty thousand Iowa Democrats to come vote at the caucuses. Nor did anyone understand the politics and manipulation of television.

Kennedy had counted on a warm reception from the press. A friendly press was a Kennedy legacy, and in the collective of the older reporters, those who cherished John and Robert Kennedy had always outnumbered their adversaries. Not so in 1980. Kennedy's first jolt was his interview with Roger Mudd of CBS, long considered a friend of the family. On air, however, Mudd became a reporter driving for answers, leaving parlor companionship behind. The interview was a disaster, as Mudd bored in on Joan Kennedy's drinking problem and Chappaquiddick, while Kennedy squirmed. Mudd asked the senator why he wanted to be President, an opening to any candidate for a long base hit if not a home run. Kennedy replied: "Well, I'm—were I to—to make the—announcement . . . is because I have a great belief in this country, that it is—has more natural resources than any nation in the world . . . the greatest technology of any country in the world . . . the greatest political system in the world. . . . And the energies and the resourcefulness of this nation, I think, should be focused on these problems in a way that brings a sense of restoration in this country by its people to . . . And I would basically feel that—that it's imperative for this country to either move forward, that it can't stand still, or otherwise it moves back."

An equivalent disaster was the *Reader's Digest* cover story just before the Iowa caucuses, bannered *"Chappaquiddick, the Still Unanswered Questions."* The *Reader's Digest,* the largest periodical in the world, savaged the youngest Kennedy; and then followed with a series of nationwide promotion broadcasts on television, scoring on the minds of mothers, truckdrivers, family people, that Kennedy had not only left the scene of an accident, leaving a girl behind to die, but lied about it. Younger writers, determined not to be caught in a show of affection for Ted Kennedy, as their elders had been caught barefoot in their affection for his brothers, were determined to tell it as it was, whatever it was. It had been open season on Carter, from the spring of 1979 to November. Now it was open season on Kennedy. Tom Shales of the Washington *Post* wrote, summing it up when Kennedy had lost the Iowa caucuses: "For the past three months the network news departments have had a field day playing Get Teddy. They have turned the election process into the Wide World of Politics. . . . 'It's the new sociology of news,' says one of the most respected TV newsmen. . . . 'They forced Teddy to declare for the nomination, and then the minute he declared they started saying, "What good is he?" ' "

Over all hung the major crisis: Iran. The President was the Flag, and people rally around the flag. Privately Kennedy could, and did, criticize Carter for lack of any contingency plan on Iran. But to speak criticism of the Shah in public, as Kennedy tried but once, was to bring down on himself all the criticism of patriots.

Underneath was the monstrous problem of money. In the old days, it had been possible to finance an election out of the pockets of half a dozen rich contributors—or out of the purse of a single family, as had Nelson Rockefeller, and John and Robert Kennedy both. New laws made that impossible. But the Kennedy campaign spent as if money were as loose as it once had been; except that everything cost more. Young volunteers were no longer content with peanut butter sandwiches; and the handful of veterans needed money. Said one of the lawyers: "I'm in my thirties now. I have a wife and a baby. I *can't* be a volunteer again. People like me need at least thirty thousand dollars a year to support a family." The old Kennedy campaign plane, the *Caroline,* had been a family indulgence in 1960. Now the new campaign plane was a regulated accountable expense. Aloft and flying, it consumed over twelve thousand dollars a day. It cost five thousand dollars just sitting on the ground. The expense of flying with the Kennedy campaign reached the point where news people were charged 225 percent of the cost of a first-class flight from point to point. They groused. But they were caught in the squeeze. Whenever a candidate alights for a major campaign stop, a platform now has to be built so that the television cameras can have a vantage point for showing the action. Campaigns have to pay for such momentary infrastructures, and such platforms *must* be union built. The cost of providing television vantage for each stop must then be cranked into campaign overhead; and the overhead is distributed in charges to all correspondents, pencil men and video men alike.

By the evening of the Iowa caucuses, January 21, the money had run out. The Kennedy campaign had by then collected about $4.1 million and spent all but $160,000. The Kennedy staff had reduced its goals in Iowa, hoping to come within ten points of the President, whose victory they had sensed coming for weeks. Over 200,000 Iowans voted at their caucuses, each party drawing about 100,000. And Iowa Democrats chose the President over Kennedy by 59 percent to 31 percent.

The technical blunderings of the early Kennedy campaign are, largely, irrelevant. Something much more important had become clear by the Iowa caucuses. Ted Kennedy had nothing, at this point, to say. Whatever he had to say echoed back to the 1960s and the popular insurgency of that time. In a troubled country, this was no longer enough.

His brother John had made the underlying Kennedy theme clear from the very beginning in 1960: new leadership for a new decade. After rubbing this theme to a high gloss on stump speeches across the nation, he had stated it as eloquently as has ever been done on the last night of that long-ago campaign in their hometown, Boston. "I do not run for the office of the presidency," said John F. Kennedy, "after fourteen years in the Congress with any expectation that it is an empty or an easy job. I run for the presidency of the United States because it is the center of action and in a free society the chief responsibility of the President is to set before the American people the unfinished public business of our country."

So had spoken John Kennedy. The early campaign of Ted Kennedy had picked up the words of the theme. But he had not defined, as his brother had, what was the "unfinished public business of the country." No message had come clear enough to remove a sitting President from leadership. The rest of the Kennedy campaign was an exercise in personality—an effort of the challenger to redefine his themes and heritage in more positive terms than simply "leadership." He would not find his tone and theme until the Democratic convention in August. By then, of course, it was too late and the Democratic nomination was Jimmy Carter's. The contest between Kennedy and Carter, meanwhile, had completely obscured the third of the Democratic candidates—Jerry Brown of California. Among those trying to redefine directions for the confused Democratic party, he is worth more than passing attention, for he was a man of ideas.

Edmund G. Brown, Jr., governor of California, forty-two years old, was a man who could be described as neither a liberal nor a conservative; he belonged somewhere in the future of the eighties or nineties, when, perhaps, his ideas might find a national echo. Like Kennedy, he came of a political family; his father had been governor of California for eight years. But the senior Brown was an old-fashioned Democratic politician, while his son was as different in style as John Kennedy had been from his father.

It was the personal, rather than the political, style of Jerry Brown that piqued the curiosity of the press, and Brown suffered from the same handicap that all governors of California suffer. The fact of their dominance of the most dynamic political state of the Union calls instant attention—but that attention is filtered through the lens of the twin East Coast news centers, New York and Washington. And in these centers he had already been tagged as a "flake," Governor Beige, Governor Moonbeam, Governor Mork.

Jerry Brown the flake was more publicized than Brown the governor. Refusing to sleep in the governor's mansion built for Ronald Reagan during Reagan's eight years in Sacramento, Brown instead slept on a mattress on the floor in an apartment nearby. In San Francisco, he would overnight at a Zen Buddhist meditation center. He openly cultivated and campaigned for gay and lesbian votes. He liked late night work and midnight conferences. He interrupted a critical campaign swing through Boston to visit Indian Swami Mukhtananda; he made no secret of his close companionship with singer Linda Ronstadt.

Of his record as governor, moreover, there was not much to put forth, not nearly as much as had come out of Reagan's two terms. No great legislation had marked Brown's first five years in office. But he had done more to adjust politics in a state of boiling ethnic upheaval than any governor of the old polyglot Eastern states. In his first year in office he had appointed fifty-seven new judges—among whom were nine blacks, nine Chicanos, four Asian-Americans, six white women. By 1979, well into his second term, he had pushed to the limits the politics of appointment by ethnic and minority groups. Out of 3,500 supervisory or leadership jobs filled, he had named 1,007 women, 341 Hispanic-surnamed, 258 blacks, 146 Asian-Americans, 33 American Indians. He had proved an untidy or indifferent admin-

istrator, but a trailblazing policymaker. Most of all, in what he was
doing he was speaking for the new California, the most rapidly
changing constituency in the country—and they liked what he was
doing. Elected by a thin margin of 178,000 votes in 1974, he was
reelected in 1978 by the thumping margin of more than 1.3 million.
By spring of 1979, he was openly out to take the presidency away
from Jimmy Carter, whom he had beaten in five of the seven late
primaries of 1976.

I went to see him early in the fall of 1979, to measure the "flaky"
governor of the Union's largest state, and found myself intrigued by
the conversation of one of the most thoughtful men in public life. He
fit no known mold. He was exploring, he said; he'd been exploring
himself since his first adult decision to go to a Jesuit seminary at the
age of eighteen. There he had learned frugality and community.
Being governor since 1974 had been another learning experience. In
his first four years he had come to his themes: "frugality, a theory of
limits, planetary realism." He was for a balanced budget but was
being attacked for his sponsorship of a constitutional amendment to
require one. Balanced budgets and conservation of resources were
part of one whole, he thought. He spoke of his California, where in
the great Central Valley 400,000 acres had been mineralized and
salted, other arid areas rendered almost useless by wind erosion and
overgrazing. We were overloading our system with greed, he said,
our lakes with waste, our air with acid rain. "You've got to stop this
throwaway society . . . this massive pumping up of credit! Excess!
Love Canal! . . . People are driving with OPEC oil to buy Australian
hamburgers on credit cards!"

And the political system, he continued, was fragile. Fifty percent
of Americans didn't vote, and those who did had no stability. "I won
the primary of June 1976 in California by a million votes, and then
by November of 1976, my popularity had gone. Why? My behavior
at the convention, my support of Chavez's Proposition Fourteen. In
five months I went down from being a hero to being a schmuck.

"I'm trying," Brown continued, "to get a theoretical framework,
to understand monetary, physical, transportation theory. I start at a
high level of abstraction, but I come right down to specifics." Inflation was the peril: a nation whose growth rate had been 3 percent
a year could afford to share the wealth around, but now the growth
rate was down to 1 percent a year; limits had to be set on waste, on
consumption, on government expenditure. Leadership, he continued, will always flow to someone who deals with real problems;

solutions start with a definition of problems. Coalitions are formed by ideas, rules flow from ideas. He would organize his campaign around ideas; his task was to redefine the goals of America in a nation whose resources were no longer limitless. "My principles are simple," he said. "Protect the earth, serve the people, and explore the universe. . . . An election is to decide something."

I compress his thinking here, but it made more long-range sense than I have heard from most candidates in twenty years. And yet, somehow, his futuristic ideas did not connect to the mechanics of politics in 1980. The primaries set forth a knifing schedule. New Hampshire was first—and Brown planned, he said, to send the organizers of Cesar Chavez, the vaunted champion of California's stoop-labor farm workers, up to New England. I wondered aloud how the Chicano style for organizing migrant farm labor would work in industrial New England; but Brown had no doubts. Kennedy had not yet announced and Brown did not at all realize the nature of the threat. When he did, his staff prepared a series of absurd radio commercials attacking Kennedy as the candidate of the big oil companies. But the imminent Kennedy candidacy had already cut off Brown's money flow, and by December his campaign was faltering. Having organized late for the Iowa caucuses, he pinned all his hopes on a three-way debate there with Carter and Kennedy, where he could speak his ideas to a mass audience. When Carter withdrew from the debate, Brown's Iowa campaign collapsed, at which point the major news organs withdrew their attention from him; his ideas were smothered; he was a nonperson as he went on to New Hampshire.

In New Hampshire, without media attention, Brown campaigned in a vacuum. I recall my last glimpse of him on the Sunday evening before the New Hampshire primary of February 26. It was at the Wayfarer Inn, where the high baronage of the press and television had made their camp. The governor of California, attended only by a swarthy bearded man in padded coat, was lounging idly in a hallway. Wondering what he was doing, I stopped to ask. He said he was on his way to a rally in the little town of Keene. I did not want to hold him up, but we talked briefly. We got onto the problem of New Hampshire's Merrimack valley. Brown was heartily in favor of using the waterpower of the Merrimack to turn the mills; that was nonpolluting energy. A knot of students gathered around; one asked what Brown thought of "heuristic autonomy." Brown answered. A passing correspondent, Martin Nolan of the Boston *Globe*, stopped, asked whether the governor was going to the bar. The governor said, Why, yes. It suddenly occurred to me: Brown had scheduled nothing for his campaign on that critical evening. He was there soliciting attention from the media, and as he entered the bar, he joined first John Chancellor of NBC to exchange ideas, then was joined at the table by Walter Cronkite of CBS. But no one quoted him or put him on air, or gave him the public time for which he was so forlornly begging in the marketplace of media merchants.

In the Iowa caucuses, Brown had won not a single delegate; in New Hampshire he drew only 10 percent of the vote. And so in February he decided to bypass all the intervening primaries and concentrate his last effort on the Wisconsin primary of April 1.

The correspondents who followed Brown to Wisconsin remember his last evening as something out of fantasy. Academy Award winner Francis Ford Coppola (of *The Godfather* and *Apocalypse Now*) had flown out from California to "produce" for his governor this climactic event, which would take place in the square fronting the Wisconsin capitol in Madison. It was cold; students lit bonfires or burned wood in drums around the square. On a side wall of the capitol, Coppola had hung a huge white screen for film clips. Overhead flew a helicopter, filming. As the candidate spoke from the podium under spotlights, the film clips on screen intercut scenes of Brown's gubernatorial record with the "now" of the evening. It was hoped that a live thirty-minute broadcast of all this would go out to the voters of the Badger State. But nothing worked: no sync; the voice of the candidate drifting out now and then, then lost. It was, wrote Carl Leubsdorf of the Baltimore *Sun,* "one of the more bizarre events" of the entire campaign; and a total fiasco.

The voting on primary day brought in Carter with 56 percent of the vote, Kennedy with 30 percent, Brown with 12 percent. Hollywood techniques had failed to salvage a fading campaign based on serious ideas. The Associated Press filed its overnight lead as the primary results came in: "California Governor Edmund G. Brown, Jr., the maverick who waged a Presidential campaign based on protecting the earth, serving the people, and exploring the universe, said goodbye Tuesday to his 1980 White House ambitions. . . . 'It is obvious that the voters have spoken and have given their verdict on my 1980 campaign . . . ' said Brown."

All three candidates for the Democratic party's nomination had been products of the insurgency of the sixties and seventies—

Kennedy nostalgic, Carter contemporary, Brown futuristic. But by April 2, the nomination was securely Carter's, and for the rest of the primaries he would have to point the direction in which the party must go; which he did not; which is as much the fault of the primary system as of Jimmy Carter himself. And it is to the primary system we must now turn, as it unfolded in both the Republican and the Democratic parties.

CHAPTER TEN

THE PRIMARIES OF 1980: THEATER OF THE ABSURD

There was a terminal madness to the primaries of 1980—the madness of a good idea run wild.

The idea had been simple and straightforward when the progressives first advanced it at the turn of the century: Let the people, not the bosses, pick delegates to the national conventions; let them choose by open vote, in primaries.

The idea was gutted rather quickly as it became obvious that the bosses and organizations that controlled local elections and nominations could easily use their machinery to pick the primary delegates. Thus, at the conventions, for the next fifty years, the same old people would bargain out their interests; and by their judgment of their party's strongest contender choose the two national nominees. Delegates were handpicked. Big money paid hotel bills for entire delegations; hacks and luminaries alike were rewarded for docility and loyalty by the honor of a few days' frolic at some city where their betters told them how to vote.

Not until the 1950s (with Eisenhower in 1952 and Kefauver in 1956) did primaries first bite into the political process;* and since then, as they have spread, they have become that feature of the presidential process most despised and denounced. A pageant of paradoxes has contradicted the dreams of the progressives who introduced the concept. Delegates, who were once creatures of bosses, are now captives of candidates; in some states delegates are chosen

---

*See Chapter Three.

without ever having had their name on a ballot. In the Democratic party, an unfamiliar and un-American racism dominates the choice of delegates, as does a mechanical division of Americans by sex. Special interests, from the most greedy to the most idealistic, pour more money into politics than ever before, finding the primaries the most vulnerable point in the American process. The number of primaries has grown from fourteen to thirty-six, exhausting candidates, attendant press, and public interest alike. An entirely new breed of professionals has grown up, voyaging like Gauleiters from state to state, specializing in get-out-the-vote techniques, cross sectionings, media, ethnic breakdowns, and other specialties of psephology. Most of all, delegates, who were supposed to be free to vote by their own common sense and conscience, have become for the most part anonymous faces, collected as background for the television cameras, sacks of potatoes packaged in primaries, divorced from party roots, and from the officials who rule states and nation.

How this came about is of some interest, for the history of primaries in recent years is a classic example of the triumph of goodwill over common sense—and it is best to follow the story through the adventures of the Democratic party, where excess of good intentions has been most disastrous.

That story would begin, of course, at the Democratic convention of 1964, where the black revolt crested in the seating of two black delegates from the Mississippi Freedom Democratic Party.* More important, however, the black revolt forced a masterly compromise: that in the 1968 convention and forever thereafter, the Democratic party would seat no delegation from any state where citizens were denied the right to vote because of race or color.

We should pause over the compromise of 1964, for at that time its effect was incalculable. Until then, the great American parties had been patchworks of diverse delegations, each state choosing its delegates by its own rules, sometimes slated entirely by one man, sometimes bought out by one big corporation (as Republicans from South Carolina), sometimes the marionettes of one great labor union (as Democrats from Michigan). Now, however, for the first time, a national party imposed binding rules. States must obey—or their delegations would be excluded from the choice made at national conventions. But if the new rule insisted on the inclusion of blacks—why not in the future Hispanics? Why not women? Why not youth? Why not,

*See Chapter Four.

finally, every group that party reform committees would designate as especially entitled to treatment as a privileged category? Instead of a *ban on exclusion* of American citizens from political participation, the idea would glide to an *insistence of inclusion* of each group given irrevocable entitlement by the mood of reform.

The next step was to come in 1968, in the roaring violence that surrounded the Democratic convention in Chicago. There the insurgents had brought in a minority report for revision of party rules. The minority report demanded that all Democratic voters get "full, meaningful, and timely opportunity to participate in the selection of delegates" to the next convention. With the support of Hubert Humphrey, it passed. A reform commission was set up to rewrite party rules; and with that the reshaping of the Democratic party began, soon to be imitated halfheartedly by the Republican party.

Committees and commissions operated on the body of the Democratic party for the next twelve years—a McGovern-Fraser commission, followed by a Mikulski commission, followed by a Winograd commission, all dominated by activitists, idealists, and people of single causes. In their years of back-room labors, ignored by all but the new professionals, the commissions not only incubated the multiplication of primaries, but also strangled their results in a net of rules that no one, even today, thoroughly understands. The rules, refined and again refined, divided Americans by sex, race, origin, and surnames, effectively turning the Democratic party into the party of quotas. Moreover, a Compliance Review Commission was set up to police obedience in every state; if voters voted the wrong way, the state's delegation might be excluded from national conventions. And the Supreme Court, in one of its watershed decisions *(Cousins* v. *Wigoda),* affirmed the party's power to do as it wished; a national party, it declared, was a free association of private citizens, thus privileged to make its own rules, all state laws to the contrary notwithstanding. And the new rules came into effect over the years in which television was achieving its dominance of American political thinking—demanding simplicity of drama while reality became more complex.

The heart of the thinking of all the good-willed commissions was that the primaries must be open to the equal participation of all. But that was defined as participation not for individuals but, more important, for groups, never carefully defined. These groups must have their share of delegates, whether elected at the polls or not.

Cardinal to the primaries of 1980, however, was the final abolition of an old principle of American politics—the unit rule, the winner-take-all principle that governs American politics, from the practice of the electoral college down to the selection of city councilmen. The abolition of the unit rule was to change strategy. Under the new rules, there could be no winner-take-all victory anywhere. Every state, and each congressional district, would now have to divide its delegates in proportion to the votes the candidates had won, and then the candidates would own the anonymous delegates chosen in their name as if they were property. No large state like New York or California would exercise decisive power at the conventions; but in effect, no small state fragmented by proportional voting would have any say at all in the choice of candidates; the primaries would become nationwide serial plebiscites. Practically, it meant that no state was worth a candidate's full exertion, yet no state could be safely ignored. Each candidate would have to fight everywhere, in all thirty-six primaries, because even a landslide loss, like Carter's in New York and California, would net him a substantial loser's share of delegates —118 delegates from his New York defeat, 139 in California.

One boggled, in the spring of 1980, as one reported across the country, on the complexity of the new system:

• New York. New York has been changing its primary laws every four years. In 1972, New York had elected delegates district by district, without the name of a presidential candidate on the ballot. New Yorkers thus voted for local delegates, hoping those delegates would choose at the convention a candidate who suited the voters' tastes. By 1976, delegates appeared on the ballot committed to specified candidates. By 1980, only the names of candidates appeared on the ballot—the delegates to be chosen later, at caucuses attended by a few hundred here, a few hundred there.

New York in 1980 was, moreover, bound by rules made by unnamed people in distant commissions. No matter how its citizens voted, the delegates would have to come out as the rules fixed: 19 percent black, 50 percent women, 7.2 percent Hispanics. Suggestions for quotas for Native Americans and for Asian-Americans were finally put down. And since no delegate names were on the ballot, it would be up to the candidates to adjust the names of their delegates to what the Compliance Review Commission would accept as proper quotas.

• Michigan. Michigan lay at another extreme of the political madness. Under the first interpretation of the Democratic party's 1968 mandate for "full and timely" participation, the 1972 primary had produced results which astounded Michigan's liberal leadership. George Wallace, a Southern populist of the meanest streak, had clearly won no less than 51 percent of the Democratic primary vote—chiefly from working people and union members who perversely vibrated to his primitive vision of America. By 1980, liberal leadership had jiggered the rules so that only "enrolled" members of the Democratic party could vote at their caucuses. And in all Michigan, only 41,717 Democrats could enter the caucuses—after having paid a new kind of poll tax called a membership fee, costing two dollars for retirees, three dollars for students (some of whom were too young to vote), and up to ten dollars for ordinary citizens. Of these 41,717 enrollees, only 16,048 appeared at the caucuses, less than 1 percent of the 1,661,532 Democrats who voted in November. They gave Kennedy 71 delegates, Carter 70, and Michigan's role at the Democratic national convention was reduced to zero.

- Arizona. A small state, Arizona had had its voice eliminated by the new rules. I quote from John Frank, a distinguished attorney and writer, a dedicated Democratic liberal. As counsel to the Arizona Democratic party, he wrote to Arizona's state Democratic chairman, former governor Sam Goddard, shortly after the 1980 election to protest the abolition of the unit rule:

"I propose that Arizona withdraw from participation in the nominating process until, if ever, substantial changes are made. . . . There are approximately 3600 Democratic delegates. We are about 30, less than one percent of the whole. Since our [delegate] margin this year was only three votes (16–13), our actual weight in the result is under .1 of 1% of the total. . . . Given the present procedures, we make no difference. . . . In 1960, under the unit rule, Arizona at least got a Cabinet member who greatly affected Western resources. . . . The present system is utterly destructive of party. . . . This contributes to the withering of party organization, the very opposite of what we need."

For a small state like Arizona (population 2,718,000), riven by ethnic clefts between Anglos, Hispanics, and Indians, the cost of a major primary campaign, out of which comes a split delegation giving the state zero influence at a convention, is preposterous. But the new rules forced it on Arizona.

- Pennsylvania. One must not think that the anomalies of the new order were limited to Democrats. Pennsylvania showed what the new system was doing to the Republicans, although in much lesser degree. There, in his finest primary campaign, George Bush won, decisively, over Ronald Reagan: He had spoken best, organized best, found his tone of attack, and won his primary by 50.5 percent to 42.5 percent. The rules of the new game, however, gave Reagan 35 delegates to Bush's 17. Instead of a comeback, perhaps a turning-point victory, Bush had won a trophy in popular votes but lost the hard number of delegates that would once have been his.

I could go on. But from Massachusetts to California, each state delegation had to conform to the "outreach" rules of the Democratic party, which required different minorities in each state to be given precise proportions of that state's delegations; and in both parties reigned the doctrine of proportional representation. There was no longer any way of making a simple generalization about how Americans chose their candidates for the presidency. What was worse, no school, no textbook, no course of instruction, could tell young Americans, who would soon be voting, how their system worked. And if we of the political press had to cram such rules into our heads as we moved from state to state, each with two parties, and each state differing—how could ordinary voters understand what professional observers had such difficulty grasping?

The effect of the reforms in both parties produced another unintended consequence—among delegates. Delegates to the conventions of 1980 would be bound to vote willy-nilly for candidates who had, sometime in winter–spring, approved of them. But delegates cherished more than ever the urge to express themselves on programs and platforms where they were free to speak for their special-interest constituencies—whether right-to-lifers, rifle-bearers, gays, or women determined to purge their enemies of all party support and aid in the fall elections. (This urge would disrupt both national conventions, as we shall see shortly.)

A new set of imponderables was at work—all of them throwing more power to press and media. The Washington correspondents surveyed the hopefuls early in the race. This family of reporters was one of radiating influence. They proposed candidates for the attention of national television. But television time is limited by the inflexible passage of the fleeting minutes. Television is compelled to render down to a few minutes each evening, or half an hour on primary night, all the complexities of rules and minutiae. To capture early attention by victories in early primary states became, thus, primordial strategy. The primary marathon must now begin with a sprint.

The maximum exertion must come in the early pace; that gains headlines and television time. Such victories in spring will influence the voters in the later states, who will then choose among the leaders and survivors of the first spring rounds.

Mired in such detail, one had to seek an overview. How did this system of choosing a President connect, if at all, with what lay before America? Looking for such an overview, I found the most thoughtful from Walter Mondale.

The Vice-President, normally a bubbling and cheerful man, was somber. It was early in November of 1979, and Kennedy had just announced his candidacy; soon the dreary primary trail would be hustling Mondale out of the spacious grounds of the Naval Observatory, where Vice-Presidents make their home.

The revolution in the party's nominating process," he said, "has weakened the presidency more than people perceive. In the old days a Truman could bring his influence to bear on the standing leadership. But that subtle ability of a President to do unpopular things is gone. The terrible thing is that a President has *got* to do unpopular things, knowing the party is not responsive, that you have to face the uncontrolled fury of the people in the primaries. . . .

But there's been this whole sea change of issues. In the early sixties you had a stable dollar, increasing employment. You could stimulate the economy, reduce taxes, the pie grew. . . . For twenty years there'd been this pent-up frustration to do something—for the blacks, for education, for the environment, for legal services. We passed the whole thing in the Eighty-ninth Congress. And now we find serious problems implementing them. There's waste. There's intrusion on private lives. There's unanticipated costs.

Now we're in the midst of a total unexpected inflation, with no time to think of anyone else's problems, and we don't have a good answer for inflation, and we've got to legislate to protect people from inflation. Then add to this the energy problem. Then add growing Soviet military might; they've been adding strategic and conventional arms. It's passed the point where you can ignore it, so we've got to put more resources into our own defense. It's going to cost like hell. And to get a tight budget, you've got to cut all the programs we Democrats supported. The choices are just awful.

We have to think beyond today—and Teddy Kennedy is going to try to revive the nostalgia of 1960 and 1964. That's the setting of this campaign. And we've got to put it to them, make them face the realities of 1980, with all this disastrous running around, people running around giving us advice on leadership, people who don't have to live with their advice.

We were talking, then, off the record, and he permitted himself the only criticism I ever heard him make of the President:

"Carter's largest weakness has been his failure to adapt, to exploit the public-education role of the President. He doesn't like to do it, he resists the use of the 'bully pulpit'; it's only half occupied when it should be fully occupied. He's done poorly at that. I'd rather give up the veto than the bully pulpit. The first thing we did bad was the mass firings in July; we were grinding new bedrock in the polls; and then Teddy Kennedy found it intolerable that Jerry Brown would jump in—he would preempt the position." On Mondale went into the mechanics of the primary contest of 1980, the states that would be battlegrounds, the problems in each, concluding: "The oddest thing is that Teddy Kennedy has galvanized us."

The effort that had been galvanized in the Carter campaign was, at once, the defense of a failing faith and a civil war among the faithful.

Between the two levels, meshing their needs, stood, always, the figure of thirty-five-year-old Hamilton Jordan. Jordan, having matured over years in the White House to something beyond strategist and tactician, was a link between Carter's purpose and Carter's needs. His memoranda of planning are historic papers.

The Carter strategy of 1980 was defined by Jordan's now well-known memorandum of January 17, 1979, marked "EYES ONLY: To: President Carter. From: Hamilton Jordan."

The memorandum reflected all that Jordan had learned of politics as a one-time political science student, now acidized by experience. The title was: "The Myth of the Incumbent President," and it began thus: "Over the two-hundred-year history of our country, the myth developed and was sustained by events that incumbent Presidents are always re-elected." Jordan's memo went on to demolish the myth. The fragmentation of party power by new rules, the presence of television, the performance of the President in a world of apparently insoluble crises, would generate new concerns. The memorandum urged the President to prepare immediately for a challenge within his own party. Gerald Ford had not foreseen his problems, recalled Jordan; he had tried to wheedle Reagan out of the 1976 nomination contest; had, consequently, not organized in time for the challenge; and almost lost his renomination. Therefore: Organize now; field an organization to sweep the early primaries and crush any potential rival, say Brown or Kennedy. "Our potential opponents," wrote Jordan, "will have the latitude and the luxury of deciding the time and place where they will make their challenge." Therefore, he continued, in an eleven-point strategy, it was vital for the President to perform as President.

"We will be re-elected or not re-elected based largely on your performance as President," said Jordan, concluding his list of action points. "While displaying basic political confidence in our prospect for re-election, we should not be perceived as taking the Democratic Party or the nomination for granted." What Jordan sought was authority to put his troops in action. He reminisced briefly, when we discussed his strategy. He recalled the action of 1976 and his captains. "We were a guerrilla corps in those days," he said. But now, from the White House, he commanded an army.

The troops at Jordan's command, as marshal, were among the most accomplished professionals of their time and they should be examined, not for the precise role they played, but as a cross section of what a new generation had produced.

Of these organization troops, the field commander was Tim Kraft. Kraft, mustachioed and curly-haired, had the appearance of a college romantic and the skills of a tested organizer. He had graduated from Dartmouth in 1963 with a B.A. in government; had volunteered for the Peace Corps in Guatemala; and when he returned, enlisted as a free-lance political organizer in California, Indiana, and then New Mexico. He enlisted for Carter early in 1974, organized for Carter in Iowa and Pennsylvania in the early rounds of 1976. He was now, as he entered the campaign of 1980, very tough—and he had learned every craft and trick of moving voters to the polls. By late 1978, two years before the election, Kraft had begun to plan operations.

By midsummer of 1979, while Kennedy was making up his mind to run, Kraft's headquarters team had fielded its outcountry primary staff. The trick of organizing primaries is easy in principle, tedious in practice: It is to find and identify leaders or volunteers, who will find and identify other volunteers; who will reach out and set up committees, either hungry for spoils or moved by the message of the candidate; and these teams must get the voters to the polls. By July 1979, as the gas crisis struck, the organization Kraft had put together already had three headquarters in the early states that Jordan's memo insisted must be swept: New Hampshire, Iowa, and Florida. Each had a staff of seven or eight people; in August 1979, the Florida staff was doubled to fourteen, to dominate, organize, move the buses that carried voters to Florida's meaningless caucuses, which would command early headlines. By that time, a steering committee of twenty-three members was in place in California, under cochairmen Jesse Unruh, state treasurer, and Dianne Feinstein, mayor of San Francisco. And all across the country, other key operatives were being put in place.

The young were most interesting as specimens of the change in politics and several will do to present a cross-sample:

• In New York, Kraft had installed Joel McLeary, a young man of utmost charm, only thirty-one years old. McLeary had been a flower child of the seventies, whose wanderings had carried him to the gurus in India, where he taught American history in high schools. As he passed from a seeker after truth to operations, he had been named the youngest treasurer ever of the Democratic National Committee. But McLeary, rather than becoming cynical, had developed an almost anthropological amusement at the people he met. As a North Carolina youngster, now the President's surrogate for New York politics, he found New York politicians an entertainment beyond belief; he could tell of their meetings with a narrator's relish of rich material.

• Then there was Evan Dobelle, another bright one, thirty-four years old, who had raised two million dollars for the Carter campaign fund by the fall of 1979. Dobelle's career had spanned generations. He had been sixteen years old when John F. Kennedy was elected. "It was like a gift," said Dobelle, "like my father giving me a bicycle for Christmas." He had moved into politics in Massachusetts, where he managed campaigns, as a professional, for Republicans, then ran himself as candidate for mayor in Pittsfield, and was elected at twenty-eight. He enlisted for the Carter campaign of 1976, and after victory, had been appointed Chief of Protocol for the State Department, then appointed chairman of the Carter-Mondale committee for reelection, then removed. He still nursed the belief that his own generation, the Kennedy generation, had entered politics to make life better. As for the younger men in the Carter campaign of 1980: "They still have the same rimless eyeglasses and beards we had ten years ago," he reflected, "but they're different. They're all junior Dick Daleys, they're in it for themselves. The first question they want to get answered is: What piece of the turf is mine if we win? They look the same. But they aren't."

Of such young men, thoroughly experienced, was the machine made. But they were all troops. When Dobelle, after his nomination as campaign chairman, met the President, Carter admonished him, "I don't want you calling me up on matters of substance, about Iran or the Middle East. You tend the machine."

Such young people tended the Carter machine across the country. In New Hampshire, the critical first primary state: Christopher Brown, only thirty, a veteran of the McCarthy-McGovern insurgency, seasoned in politics from New Mexico to Washington, an expert assembler of names at pressure points. In the capital: Tom Donilon, only twenty-three, a political science student, fitting together names that controlled delegates and delegations for the disposal of Kraft and Jordan. In Chicago: Bob Torricelli, only twenty-nine, planning the wipeout of Ted Kennedy in Illinois. Such young idealists, now grown crafty, were the Carter organization. They had learned a new trade—and against such veterans Kennedy pitted himself, with no organization at all, with nothing more than a legend to sustain him.

"If nothing else," said Tim Kraft, reflecting on the undermining of the Kennedy campaign, "we meant to use all out the power of the presidency."

The power of the modern President is prodigious. A total of $80 billion now goes in grants from the federal government to states, counties, and cities across the nation, much of it entirely discretionary. But all of it, even that ordained by statute, is subject to timing, to announcement, to the credit calls of favored local officials. And by midsummer of 1979, the entire apparatus of Carter politics, directed by Jordan and Kraft, was moving to make sure that federal money greased its way through the primaries.

"We will tax and tax, spend and spend, elect and elect," Harry Hopkins was supposed to have said, explaining the strategy of the Roosevelt administration forty-five years earlier. The Carter team were lineal descendants of Hopkins, who had converted the WPA into a support organization for Roosevelt's administration. Florida, for example, would be coming up first with a meaningless Democratic straw poll, whose roots would be planted in October 1979 caucuses. In September, the government announced an unprecedentedly swift $1.1 billion loan guarantee to an electric cooperative in northern Florida, whose application had been received only in July. To Dade County (which is Miami) went a $19.9 million grant for public housing in the same month; as well as $6 million for Tampa; and $4 million each for Polk, Orange, and Hillsborough counties; plus $31 million for housing projects for the elderly throughout the state; plus a grant for hurricane aid; plus a grant for tourism in Miami, and plus and plus.

New Hampshire would be first on the calendar of primaries. The slushing of New Hampshire began in January, with a $34 million grant for a four-lane highway from Manchester, the population center, to Portsmouth on the coast; followed in early February with a Small Business Administration set-aside of $100,000 for New Hampshire's ski resorts, hard hit by a snowless winter; followed just before the primary by an announcement from the Department of Transportation that it would fund a special commuter train from Concord, the state capital, to Boston, less than fifty miles away.

Money fluttered down over other primary states. For Massachusetts, a special grant of $3.3 million for the city of Lynn, once the shoe capital of America, to rebuild its decaying downtown; the Speaker of the Massachusetts House, Tom McGee, came from Lynn, and he promptly came out for Carter against Kennedy, his home-state leader. For the blacks across the nation, an announcement of $2 billion for disadvantaged youth. For dairy farmers across the nation (just before the Wisconsin primaries), a decision not to carry out a scheduled cut in price supports for milk products. For New York, grants announced by every visiting member of the administration: new hospital support for Brooklyn; a promise of an Urban Development Action Grant to build a new building for the American Stock Exchange—and to balance that promise to the stockbrokers, a promise to Congressman Rangel of Harlem to build a new World Trade Center in Harlem, which would give New York *two* world trade centers, one for the blacks uptown, one for the whites downtown. And for those who might raise resistance to the Carter drive: cutoff. In October, Mayor Jane Byrne of Chicago was told by the White House that U.S. Air Force facilities at O'Hare Field would be relocated to allow Chicago to expand its major airport. But on October

27, Mayor Byrne announced her support of Kennedy against Carter in the Illinois primary. Retribution was swift; less than a month later, the Secretary of Transportation revealed that the cabinet had lost "confidence" in Mayor Byrne, and would look for opportunities to deny transportation funds to Chicago and its mayor.

So the political team of Jimmy Carter prepared to enter the primaries, buoyed by the reflex reaction of Americans in support of their President, as he grappled with the atrocities of Iranian politics.

Despite the fact that the Democratic primaries stretched so long and so far, their story can be briefly told. They were like a long gray smear across the political map, lacking bold colors or flashing issues.

Carter's strategy was simple: to act as President sheltered in the White House, appearing on the evening news as a nonparticipant from his Rose Garden, while his team crafted each primary victory, one after another, with all the skills they had acquired in years of campaigning. Kennedy had no strategy until the primaries were almost over; and no staff worthy of the name until New York, when it was too late.

It is best to separate the Democratic primary contest into rough chapters.

The first chapter was quite short, and was over by the first primary, New Hampshire. Kennedy had that opportunity that comes to every candidate, which is to hold the attention of the American voters for a brief span of concern. This opportunity he had blown in November and December. He could find no issue to proclaim except leadership. Muzzled from an attack on Carter's foreign policy by the surge of patriotism that followed the Iranian kidnappings, he stuttered—for he suddenly found himself the issue.

"We don't have to attack him on his character," said one of the Carter people, "the press will do that for us"; and so the press did. Kennedy's disorganized volunteers and faithful had tasted dismay even before the Iowa caucuses in January. Iowa's Democratic voters had moved out from him weeks before. "It was like they were moving to the 'Battle Hymn of the Republic,' or 'rally round the flag,'" said Frank Mankiewicz, chief theoretician of Robert Kennedy's 1968 campaign, now, as an elder statesman, a fringe-watcher of the younger brother's effort. Iowa was a disaster for Kennedy. New Hampshire, a month later, was worse. Of the four regional areas into which New Hampshire may be divided, Kennedy had carried only one—the suburban belt of expatriate Massachusetts flightlings on the southern border. The rest of the breakdown of New Hampshire gave little consolation. Kennedy lost working-class Manchester. Even more important, he lost the Merrimack valley. The Merrimack River flows from the old Manchester cotton mills, through the electronics and other technology plants of southern New Hampshire, crosses the Massachusetts border and then turns east through a similar industrial belt. It is crammed with the same kinds of workers who inhabit Chicago, Toledo, the industrial communities of the Midwest—family people, Catholics, Irish, French, Polish. To lose them meant that Kennedy had lost the loyalties that had always sustained his family's victories. He lost them and lost New Hampshire by 37.3 percent to Carter's 47.1 percent.

Kennedy himself probably knew it was over then. A few days after the defeat in New Hampshire, after he had spent a grueling morning campaigning among old folks and on the ice-cold docks of Boston's fishing pier, I joined him at lunch. We looked out over the rime-coated vessels and he commented on what fishing life was like these days—the skippers making $75,000 to $100,000 a year, the crew $35,000 to $40,000, depending on the catch. Kennedy had done more to revive New England's fishing industry than any other senator of recent times. Then, after this excursion into the past, he asked me what I thought of his campaign, what the long view was. I knew his campaign was hopeless. But I did not want to depress him, for he was aching with the pain of his injured back, which he had put to torture in the rounds of New Hampshire. I urged that he carry on at least as far as the New York or Pennsylvania primaries, so as to keep faith with his supporters. And after that, quit. He listened moodily, looking out over the bay, and said that Florida, coming up soon, was already lost. And what would you do, he asked, if your own polls in Illinois showed Carter 72/36 ahead? I had no answer except to repeat that he carry on a few weeks longer, then recognize reality.

In the Florida primary, on March 11, Kennedy was annihilated: in the popular vote, Carter over Kennedy by 60.7 percent to 23.2 percent; in delegate count, Carter 74, Kennedy 25. In Illinois, the week following, he was again humiliated. Carter's team took the Illinois delegation by the almost unbelievable margin of 165 to 14.

So as Kennedy entered New York for its March 25 primary, his serious campaign was over. The younger Kennedys, the nieces and nephews of the next generation, weaned and raised on politics, met at Trader Vic's in New York one evening for a debate on how Uncle Ted should get out—whether he should make a clean withdrawal, or a withdrawal with an endorsement of Carter as President. Jacqueline Kennedy Onassis, fond of Ted and one of the guardians of the Kennedy heritage, called together in her apartment a group of older friends to explore some graceful way of getting her brother-in-law out of the hopeless campaign. No one could help but be overwhelmed by the showing of the polls: the *Daily News* poll conducted by Louis Harris showed Carter over Kennedy by 61 to 34! Even though its last pre-primary poll showed that lead narrowing to 56/36, the gap was apparently insurmountable. And the in-house Kennedy polls, ten days before the primary, showed that Carter would carry the state by eighteen points.

And then, in New York, began the second chapter of the Democratic primaries, running roughly from mid-March to the voting in Pennsylvania, April 22. In the first chapter, Carter had been the national leader, carrying the flag, while Kennedy, cursed by Chappaquiddick, had been running against himself. Nothing went right for Kennedy. But by New York, perspectives had changed. In this second chapter, almost nothing went right for Carter. Now the President was running against himself. Since Kennedy had been all but eliminated, a vote for him was no longer a vote for Kennedy for President, but a protest vote against Carter. And as the protest accumulated, there came one of the most remarkable demonstrations of voter volatility in American politics.

Events destroyed the President, as New York Democrats came to vote. On the front page of the New York *Times*, a picture of the brooding Shah, hastily ushered out of Panama to refuge in Cairo. On the economic pages, the response of the stock market to Carter's hastily improvised plan to cut credit and squeeze the budget—his fourth anti-inflation plan in three years. On Monday, a week before the primary, the stock market was off by 23 points; off again the next day; the next day; and the next. In the ten days before the primary, the Dow Jones average had fallen from 811 to 765. Investors were frightened; so were ordinary shoppers: Easter was coming and Washington's hasty new credit rules were clamping off credit-card buying.

Capping all was the bedlam of American policy at the United Nations. For almost a month, a series of grotesqueries had succeeded one another, all revolving about that emotional problem the Middle East, of transcendent interest to New York's Jews, who vote more heavily in primaries than any other ethnic group. The U.S. ambassador at the United Nations had voted to deny Israel authority over its holy city and capital, Jerusalem. It was a vote to placate the Third

World, but one infuriating to Jews everywhere. Worse, the White House claimed the President had not been informed of the vote; and then, worst of all, he repudiated it. On Thursday and Friday, before New York's primary, local television displayed the discomfiture of the Secretary of State as he tried to satisfy first a Senate committee, then a House committee, which sought the answer as to just who was making American foreign policy. Apparently, no one was in charge.

Of the Kennedy campaign in New York, it may simply be said that it was lost by the President.

Of my recollections of New York's Democratic primary, one vignette remains etched in mind, as the coincidence of tactics with history. Kennedy, the morning before primary day, made the ritual trip that all candidates take in New York: a subway ride attended by cameras. In the packed train he rode for almost two miles, from Fifty-ninth Street to Ninety-sixth, aides plowed their way through the crush of press and cameras to present the candidate with authentic subway riders. As microphones poked in on each conversation, Kennedy explained that he would do more for New York, promising help to fix its decaying subway system. He left; and then later the same day, at precisely the point where he had descended into the subway, a portion of the roof of the Fifty-ninth Street station fell in, lethal chunks of rotting concrete dropping on the platform, barely missing passengers. That night, the television producers, irresistibly tempted by reality, juxtaposed the shots. Kennedy had demanded help for New York's subways; a few hours after he left, a subway roof fell in.

The results of the New York primary showed that no amount of organization could overcome the disarray of a world outside. That world was troubled, and growing more so; if a vote for Kennedy was the only possible protest, so be it. And the vote ran 58.9 percent to 41.1 percent for Kennedy over Carter, 164 delegates for the contender, 118 for the President; as it did the same day in Connecticut: 46.9 percent for Kennedy, 41.5 percent for Carter, Kennedy winning 29 delegates, Carter 25. Carter would have to conduct his presidency for the next two months with one eye always on his party rival; and Kennedy could not quit. "We were always looking for a clean opportunity to get out," said one of the Kennedy inner circle. "We said, if we lost in New York, we could get out; if we lost in Pennsylvania, we could get out. But we won in both, so we couldn't get out."

The second chapter spanned four weeks, Carter completing his sweep of the eleven states of his native South, his total on the eve of the Pennsylvania primary running to 975 delegates to Kennedy's 480. And then Pennsylvania imbrued the chapter with bitterness.

The climate had changed by the eve of Pennsylvania's April 22 primary; prices were now wild, gasoline up and climbing, interest rates crushing home-building, the Japanese drive against America's auto industry in high; and the President, it seemed, powerless. In the changing atmosphere, Kennedy turned savage. Always a character just a bit too "hot" for the cool of the television screen, Kennedy, from one end of Pennsylvania to the other, let himself go on the stump—jabbing, sarcastic, flailing, his favorite target now the President. A sample, from his climax rally in Philadelphia: "What this country needs is a brand-new Democratic party. . . . The presidency of the United Sates doesn't belong to one man alone. . . . We aren't going to turn our backs on the poor, on the elderly . . . when your gas prices have gone up fifty cents in one year, when your home heating oil has doubled . . . when we carry Jimmy Carter out of the White House, I say we aren't going to turn our backs on the young people either. . . . Those policies didn't work for Herbert Hoover, or for William McKinley, or for Richard Nixon. . . . I come here tired of listening that the problems are too difficult to solve. . . . I say: No more hostages, no more high inflation, no more high interest rates, NO MORE JIMMY CARTER! No more surprise foreign policy. . . . He's *surprised* [the word long-drawn-out to emphasize the point] by Iran, he's *surprised* at Afghanistan, he's even *surprised* at the United States vote in the UN. . . . So, if I have your help, we'll give Jimmy Carter a surprise!"

The Carter command responded. At ten points behind in their private polling, they had known ten days early that they were hemorrhaging votes; and that they must meet nastiness in kind. Since the press had now run the Chappaquiddick incident into boredom, it was necessary for the Carter campaign to remind the voters, with adversary commercials recalling Kennedy's "character." Rafshoon hastily put together a standard form of political commercial, a paste-up of clips of man-in-the-street interviews, in which the people themselves, not a rival, snap the arrows at the target. Sample: Man: "I don't trust him." Woman: "I don't believe him." Man: "I would definitely go with Carter myself, I trust him." Woman: "You're taking a chance with Kennedy," etc. By the time the Pennsylvania primary rolled around, Carter had pulled almost even, but he was wounded as in no other primary contest. Kennedy squeaked in with a 45.7 percent to 45.3 percent win, gaining 93 delegates to Carter's

92. That same day, Carter's organization had carried off a coup at the Missouri caucuses, to win 54 delegates to Kennedy's 10. The score now read, nationwide: Carter 1,207 delegates, Kennedy 667. There was no hope of denying Carter the 1,666 delegates needed to win the nomination, and thus the third chapter of the Democratic primaries began.

If it can be said that in the second chapter of the primaries almost nothing went right for Carter, then, in the third chapter, almost everything went wrong—starting on April 26, four days after the Pennsylvania primary, when Americans woke to read that the previous day's desperate attempt to rescue the hostages in Iran by helicopter had crashed in failure and flame. The third chapter unrolled over a six-week period, from the end of April to Super Tuesday, June 3, when eight states, including three of the big ten (California, Ohio, New Jersey), held the last primaries of the nation.

Few good men have ever known such humiliation as Jimmy Carter was to endure in the weeks preceding and the ten days immediately following Super Tuesday. The catalogue of misfortunes is almost endless. Abandoning the Rose Garden strategy, he left the White House. On May 30, he whirled through a one-day campaign trip to Ohio, announcing that we had finally "turned the corner" on the dizzy downturn of the economy. The following day his Council of Economic Advisers announced that the downturn of economic indicators predicted the sharpest recession in years. He had ordered the expulsion of three Libyan diplomats from Washington as terrorists; they refused to leave. Miami was being flooded by both genuine Cuban refugees and the criminal offscourings from Cuban jails. Carter had welcomed the first wave with "an open heart and open arms." Less than two weeks later, he called out the coast guard to protect Florida from the invasion. He demanded a ten-cent-per-gallon increase in gasoline prices; his Democratic Congress refused to pass it. Abroad, India's Prime Minister, Indira Gandhi, had ignited India's first nuclear bomb in violation of all agreements with the United States, India's chief supplier of nuclear fuels. The United States protested; Madame Gandhi flounced her skirts. In Europe, seeing the crumbling of the President's authority, the chief powers of the European Economic Community decided that the Common Market would give legal recognition to the terrorists of the Palestine Liberation Organization.

The last Democratic primary, on June 3, was a primary of eight states simultaneously—which meant, fortunately, that a thoroughly bored nation would have to spend only half an hour at its TV set, if it still cared. Of these last primaries, Kennedy was to win five, Carter only three. In the key states, Kennedy was to win California and New Jersey, Carter only Ohio (although losing that state's industrial belt on the Great Lakes). But across the nation, despite the fact that Kennedy had on this last day polled 2.6 million votes to Carter's 2.4 million, the arithmetic read inexorably: Carter now had 1,971 delegates to Kennedy's 1,221. The nomination was Carter's.

Though the nomination was his, and the convention in his hands, neither control of public opinion, nor his own Democratic party, nor the ultimate victory, would be Carter's. The discontent with the way the country was moving had come to rest on him. And the man who would harvest this vast discontent was Ronald Reagan, who had just concluded a victorious primary war of his own.

On the Republican side the primary story was different and simpler.

Time had erased the old hatreds among Republicans. For the most part, the Republican party, as Goldwater and Taft had meant it to be, was the party of the conservatives, and the 1980 primary contest reduced itself more swiftly than anyone had anticipated to a contest between two of them—George Bush, a gentleman–Ivy League–center conservative, and Ronald Reagan, a covered-wagon, or homestead, conservative. Each, in modern campaign style, like Jimmy Carter before them, had made his drive for the presidency a full-time occupation—Reagan since he had given up his governorship of California in 1974, Bush since 1978.

It is best to start the story of the Republican primaries with Bush, for if Reagan was accepted as the "incumbent" candidate, Bush was the challenger; and if one starts with Bush one cannot separate him from his alter ego and closest friend, Jim Baker. Together, they had put together an eclectic team of tacticians from all wings of the Republican party, which, if it lacked the continental spread of the Reagan organization, was no less in quality. Both men had "class," the one the scion of a great Connecticut family, the other the scion of a great Texas family. Bush had spectacular credentials, but no natural voting base to use as an echo board. His steering committees in the key states came of the best people; "they looked," said someone, "as if they'd been picked from the Harvard and Yale crew rosters of the past twenty years."

Both Bush and Baker were shrewd and effective men, playing

a long shot. They picked, as their strategy, that made classic by Carter in 1976: to compel attention by creating an event, a set of victories in the early contests; with that would come press and media recognition; on that they could ride through the early and middle rounds of the primaries, to win out at the end. The Bush-Baker organization had organized superlatively for Iowa, for Puerto Rico, for New Hampshire. With those victories they felt they would carry New York, the Midwest, Pennsylvania. But only nominal organization existed in New York and in Pennsylvania. In the South, not even Texas, their home state, had been organized. And Bush disdained, as a gentleman, any cultivation of the hard-rock primitives, so large a part of the Republican revival. As a civilized person, he could not, or would not, court the Moral Majority, the right-to-life movement, the National Rifle Association.

Bush's victorious drive in the Iowa caucuses, by 31.5 percent to Reagan's 29.4 percent, compelled the attention he anticipated— full-length profiles or cover stories in *Time* magazine, in *Newsweek,* even in that "smart" magazine *New York,* whose correspondent Michael Kramer had an irrepressible taste for class.

But neither Bush nor Baker knew what to do with the attention they had sought. Thus, their first blunder. Like Ted Kennedy, they had lost their moment of national attention, with nothing to say. Carried away by the euphoria of his Iowa victory, Bush let himself be badgered by correspondents to respond as a Yale baseball captain might respond before the Harvard game. He had momentum going for him, he said—the "Big Mo." But the programs and the philosophy concealed in his head remained concealed. By New Hampshire, he had been outlined as a cartoon; and in New Hampshire, Ronald Reagan had mousetrapped him in the Nashua debate.* He was to lose New Hampshire, then Vermont, then Florida, then Illinois, then the Southern states, one after the other.

It was never easy to explain Bush's themes, for he could not see the country's problems as easy. As director of the CIA, he knew more of foreign affairs than any other candidate except Carter. He was no less hostile to Russia than Reagan; but he had no easy response to that problem. For the problems of illegal immigration, Bush confessed that he "honestly" did not know the answer. Inflation, also, was too complicated to lend itself to the one-line solutions his rival Reagan proposed.

It was not until the Pennsylvania primary that Bush regained, in

*See Chapter One.

public, some of his natural private poise. He spoke well and eloquently about national issues; he drove hard on Reagan's economics. The thought that one could cut taxes and thus increase revenues, all the while jumping the defense budget to new heights, was, he said, "voodoo economics." He won in Pennsylvania by 50.5 percent of the popular vote to Reagan's 42.5 percent. But Reagan's team had organized and carried away the delegates by two to one. In Michigan, on May 20, Bush won another signal victory in popular votes, speaking his piece on what an enlightened conservative policy might do for the country. With the naiveté of a novice, he welcomed the event that night as a turning point—only to find that the television counters had added up the arithmetic, that Reagan now controlled a majority of the Republican delegates and the victory was meaningless. Five days later, Bush withdrew from the contest; he had been doomed since the Nashua debate.

If he was to have any share of the Republican victory that he felt was certain, he would have to humble himself before the man who could wring out of the people an echo louder than his—Ronald Reagan. Very early on, Jim Baker had put to Bush the hard question: If they lost the nomination to Reagan, would Bush accept second place on a Reagan ticket? Bush had said he would. They could, then, only wait for that decision to be made by those who surrounded Reagan, and swayed his thinking.

Ronald Reagan had a very clear message. The confusion of his staff and the reshufflings of management amused almost everyone who reported the campaign. But the message was so elementary it could not be misunderstood—and it was what the American people wanted to hear, what they voted for.

The Reagan primary campaign had been designed by three people: Richard Wirthlin, Edwin Meese III, John Sears. When Reagan had discarded Sears early in the campaign, it had been like a missile discarding its booster rockets. But the organization Sears had put together remained in place, the design fixed—and the candidate was now in free orbit on his own.

Tracking Reagan's campaign is simple. It lurched off to a dismal start in the Iowa caucuses; pulled itself together in the New Hampshire primary; stumbled in Massachusetts; and then certified its irrevocable victory in the South. South of the Mason-Dixon line, Reagan was to win every primary by spectacular margins. Even in Texas, Bush's home state, Reagan carried 51 percent of the vote to Bush's

47.4 percent. Beyond Michigan, to the west and south, Bush was not to carry a single state.

One could, if one wished, see Reagan's triumph as a matter of demography—the Sunbelt coming into its own. One could, alternately, see it as a triumph of an organization that had put down its grass roots four to eight years earlier. Yet the triumph was more than that—it was the triumph of a man with a message that stirred restless forces.

A reporter's eye could note outcroppings that were disturbing. In the Iowa caucuses, the right-to-life zealots did their best to pack meetings and offended enough center-road Iowans to give the caucus victory to Bush. In New Hampshire, the National Rifle Association threw all its strength to Reagan; and across the nation, in other primaries, surfaced those incoherent groups for which the Moral Majority was the commonly accepted rubric. These could be seen as a movement in American culture that went back as far as the Prohibitionists—dedicated single-issue people, a minority in a minority party, exercising maximum leverage by concentration of votes.

But underneath lay a more important, less vocal tier of Reagan votes—votes that surfaced first in the New Hampshire primary. There I could find no one who gave an apter description of this Reagan majority than the chairman of its campaign, Gerald Carmen. Carmen was a Jewish businessman who had made his small stake in Manchester, and moving up, moved in on the strife-ridden local Republican party. Who are we? he asked, repeating my question. "Most of us," said Carmen, "are the first generation of our community or family who went to college. Our people are on the make. We're middle class. Bush has the elite, the old Yankee aristocracy of the valley; but ours are people who've bought the first house in the family, who want to get ahead; and they don't want the government to take it away. I'm at home when I talk to Ronald Reagan."

Another, and seriously important, answer, came from Reagan's Northeast director, Roger Stone, twenty-seven, himself of Italian heritage. Stone, already a consummate technician of the same veteran skills as Carter's centurions, directed Reagan's campaign in New York and Connecticut. In the Northeast, the campaign had made its axis of thrust the ethnic vote, particularly the Italian-American vote. "These people," said Stone, "are suburban now. They have homes; they hate taxes; and there's a social component to it. Italians are very family-oriented, conservative in home life. Reagan is against taxes, he's for family life." Stone compared the compositions of the

Bush and Reagan steering committees in Connecticut. The Bush committee was salted with *Mayflower* names, overwhelmingly Protestant. Of the five names on Stone's Connecticut committee for Reagan, three were Italian-American. When voters came to vote in the Republican primary, Connecticut chose Bush, for Republicans in the Nutmeg state are still largely Protestant. But where it counted, in a quintessential sample of industrial America, the factory town of Bridgeport, working-class Republicans chose Reagan over Bush.

The Reagan message came in two parts. The first part was the message of the personality. In a season of melancholy his good nature pleased. The camera stimulates Reagan as catnip does a cat; he loves, as a television personality does, the one-line quip. He could quip about Carter's call for national austerity: "A man who tells you he enjoys a cold shower every morning will lie about other things." Or about the difference between a depression ("when you lose your job") and a recovery ("when Carter loses his"). In private, the quip could be more barbed: "Carter is the South's revenge for Sherman's march through Georgia."

But the second part of the message was the theme and was more important: that government itself was choking the American people, wasting their money, forcing up prices, poking its nose into local affairs.

The message was so simple as to become monotonous. In the years I had followed Reagan's campaigns, the speech had changed but little. A few new quips were added now and then, but quips so banal that television would not carry them; and they therefore seemed fresh and unworn to his live audiences, who chuckled along with him as once they had with Jack Benny of the Jell-O show. Reagan would, of course, decorate his standard speech for the news media with a flaking of facts, sent on to him each day by his research base. Reagan liked such fact flakes as he liked jelly beans. If sometimes they were wrong—as they frequently were—he could always correct them the next day.

Let me quote from a typical stump speech. It is May 30, 1980, the last weekend of the long primary campaign. He is driving hard now on his electoral strategy: the winning of the industrial Midwestern states. He is in a public square in Cleveland, one of the centers of steel and automobile country. Rain is about to fall. He must hurry, no quips; he goes directly into the attack on Carter. There floats across my tape recording the essential phrases of Reagan on the stump:

. . . when he [Carter] took office, inflation was 4.8 percent and he said he was going to do something about it, and he did. It's now averaging 16.4 percent. He was horrified that gas was selling at fifty-eight cents a gallon, and he said he'd do something about that. And he did. It now averages $1.20 a gallon. . . . He has betrayed the automobile workers, he has betrayed the steel workers . . . time to turn this country around . . . everything that's been done means more taxes, more inflation, more unemployment. . . . Why don't we try to leave more money in your hands for you to spend the way you like. . . . Income tax cut over a three-year period . . . reducing cost of government . . . deficit monster! . . . Federal aid to education has become federal interference. . . . I see the rain is coming down a little bit harder. Why don't we get to the closing point, so we can all run for cover. . . . This administration has depleted the great arsenal of democracy, left us vastly inferior to the Soviet Union. He tells us we must sign the Salt II Treaty because no one will like us if we don't. I think it's time to tell we don't care if they don't like us or not, they're gonna respect us again. . . . No more Taiwans, no more Vietnams, no more betrayal of friends. . . . God bless you all. . . . Thank you, and I need your help on June third.

The rain is pouring down now, the band plays "Glory, glory, hallelujah," and the crowd cheers.

The Midwest is a Reagan strategic target, and he is punishing himself. He has been up at six this morning in Toledo, Ohio, addressed a breakfast rally, led a parade complete with live Republican elephants for the cameras, gone on to Cleveland for this noon rally, will give a press conference, and will close the day in Canton, Ohio, whose major heavy industries are also suffering hurt. Up early again the next morning, he is off to Saint Louis, to address the Missouri state Republican convention. Reagan enters wearing his cowboy hat; but the speech is the same as in 1976, or in Manchester in late winter, or in Cleveland the day before. One must listen closely to see what new fact flakes adorn the old screed, but it is only an extended version of the speech: ". . . people on welfare are *not* no-good people. They are trapped by a bureaucracy that needs clients to keep their job." Or Carter's policy: ". . . unemployment . . . a betrayal of the working people . . . need of strong national defense . . . thank you."

Then off again, back east to New Jersey to attend a Ukrainian folk festival, an appeal laying the groundwork for the big ethnic drive of his election campaign. Ukrainian dancers, in native costumes, perform for Reagan. Ukrainian delicacies are served. It is late afternoon when he directs the caravan back to Newark's airport. There, because the money has run out, he is booked on a commercial flight to Los Angeles, and home.

On this last leg of the primary campaign, from the ethnic East to Pacific Palisades and the ranch, Reagan is accessible, since no staff closes him off in a forward compartment, as in a chartered plane. Throughout the campaign, he has been so amiable and charming that I have come to like him as a person; he is a decent man; and I ask to speak with him.

Reagan comes to sit beside me. As he talks, I realize that his personal charm conceals a political indignation as deep as Barry Goldwater's. He means what he says, and he has said it over and over again since 1964: The bureaucracy is the enemy.

He had once been a devout Democrat, a union leader—and I asked him, when did he turn? "Oh," he said, "the turning began back there in the fifties, when I began to warn against the growth of permanent institutions of the government, they were beyond the control of the elected representatives of the people. Even back then, our party, the Democratic party, had bought the New Economics, which rested on a theory that a little planned inflation would not get out of control . . . but you can't plan a controlled inflation, it's like radioactivity, cumulative. . . . There was a time back there when I said to Nancy, Every four years I've got to go out there for these people and I don't go along with them."

Reagan went back to his political breakaway. "But out of the New Deal, interrupted by the war, came, I think, a permanent structure of government that had in mind, not, as I believe Roosevelt had in mind, a temporary medicine for the ills of the Depression—they had in mind a permanent change in government. The federal government would usurp functions which properly belong at the state level. . . . They acquired that strength that has made them almost more powerful than those we elect to office. The massive staffs of Congress are now definitely part of the bureaucracy. We hear that the people call for these things, [but] you know, the truth is I can never recall the people ever asking for any of these things. Most legislation is born in the departments of government . . . then they look around by way of a congressional staff, or a congressman, or a senator, who will sponsor the legislation. . . . Once a congressman came up to me and told me what would happen if he took on an important agency or opposed its budget: The first time your secretary calls that agency for any help, for information, they say, 'We don't have the manpower to do that.' "

Reagan ran on, in a narrative interrupted by the buzzing of the plane, calls from the plane's captain. He had supported Helen Gahagan Douglas in the famous campaign against Nixon, sat on the platform with her but not made any speeches. He had liked John Kennedy, but decided to lead Democrats for Nixon. Kennedy had upset him, especially the Bay of Pigs incident: "We landed those men there and then we abandoned them."

Between interruptions we went on. Why or how, I asked, had he acquired his reputation in the East as a reactionary; could he explain it?

The answer came rambling out. "On inauguration day when Jack Kennedy took office, I was in an automobile from Chicago to Bloomington, Illinois. I was scheduled to address a business group in Bloomington. . . . Now, I was on my way to make that speech, listening to the inaugural address on the car radio. . . . I'd been making the speech for years. The theme was always the same warning against the growth of big government, the same things I'd been saying when a Republican was President, since 1955. And forty-eight hours after I made that speech in Bloomington, a national labor paper had me on the front page as some kind of 'right-wing fascist' . . . this began to circulate . . . of course, having been opposed to the left-wing takeover of Hollywood [I was already attacked]. But then in '64, when I so wholeheartedly supported Goldwater, then I was a Republican. I was wholeheartedly in the enemy camp. . . . [Then, when I was governor of California for eight years] what received the most attention was, of course, 'Cut. Squeeze. Trim' . . . no one paid any attention to the rest of my record. . . . In '76 [the campaign against Ford], I found when I crossed the Mississippi River coming east, the horns began to grow out of my head, at least in the minds of [those] people. . . . It's much less today . . . they've learned about my record as governor and they've found out the record does not bear out that I'm some kind of right-wing nut."

We went on to talk of issues.

Illegal immigration? He preferred the term "undocumented aliens." He thought about it more in terms of refugees. He believed in what it said on the Statue of Liberty. Immigration was a broader problem than the United States could solve by itself; it needed an international understanding. "We're all ethnics," he said. "You and

I are too. . . . My grandparents came here in the potato famine, fleeing Ireland . . . on my mother's side they came from England, where they picked up broken bricks at a brick factory, and built an oven and baked and sold bread door to door so they could get the money to come here steerage."

Busing? Flatly, he said, "It's a failure, it didn't work." And had created more bitterness than it had eliminated. Busing was a "waste of resources."

I had held him now for a goodly time, and I began to realize that the man, despite his courtesy, was exhausted, not just from this talk, and this day, but from five months on the road.

But one more question: Where did *he* think Jimmy Carter had gone wrong? Reagan groped for a reply, but the venom of the campaign was in him and the answer came out this way: "Well . . . what I think went wrong with him, his hunger was so great for the job and the office that he said anything to get it. . . . The administration came in with no economic plan of its own, and I think his principal moving force was the desire to hold office. It was not a desire to say, I want to do this, I want to do that. . . . I wonder whether he's confusing some of his own statements with having come from God."

I urged him off then, for we were into hard politics and I did not want to invite more confidences from him than I could, as a reporter, decently handle. We had talked for, perhaps, an hour; and he was so tired. He was now homewarding at the end of what had once seemed an endless primary campaign. Sunday and Monday would be for resting, the following day would be Super Tuesday, with the last eight primaries closing at once. He settled down beside his wife to watch the movie, Neil Simon's *Chapter Two*. Mrs. Reagan, bone weary from her hundreds of pert and dainty campaign experiences, let herself relax and drowse. But Reagan remained alert. Movies had been his business; he could not conceal his enjoyment. He would nod approval at some technical cut in the film, at a remark well-timed. At a bad cut he would frown or shake his head. Finally, he too drowsed. At Los Angeles airport he stalked off vigorously, but rather stiffly, into the night, to the limousine that would carry him home to Pacific Palisades, sixteen miles away, where he would prepare for one more staff reorganization and the final election round against Carter.

On the evening of Super Tuesday, Reagan appeared, tanned after two days in the sun, neatly barbered, handsomely tailored as always, showing no signs of the wear and tear of five months on the road. He dropped by at a two-room hotel suite, converted by NBC into a makeshift studio. He had sat through the television ceremony of the half-hour evening primary roundups countless times this year, and was entirely at ease with the routine, waiting for the camera to turn to him as the calls came in from other states. The room was hot, steaming with television lights, crowded with twelve technicians; Nancy Reagan and their daughter, Patti, perched together on one small seat in a corner. But there was no video monitor in the room, and none of us could see what was happening elsewhere in the country. Nor could we hear; only two earpieces were available to monitor the sound—one for the director of the show, one in Reagan's ear. As we shifted restlessly, in ignorance of what was going on, Reagan took over. His head cocked to one side, his earpiece catching the broadcast, he slipped into the patter he had learned so well when, as a radio sportscaster, he broadcast games blind from a Davenport, Iowa, studio years before. "And now," said Reagan, talking flawlessly from the earpiece report, "Teddy Kennedy is coming to the plate. Kennedy has hit for five out of eight in the primaries today. Kennedy looks loose. . . ." The audience of technicians began to laugh, and Reagan, always an entertainer, went on with a joke about "Strangler" Lewis, the onetime heavyweight champion wrestler, then another joke.

Then the director behind the camera pointed the command finger at him, and instantly Reagan transformed himself for the national audience beyond. He was *on*. Twinkling, yet serious, he fielded the questions; and then later, with the lights off, joked with the crew before sauntering off down the corridor to join the victory celebration below.

Downstairs, that celebration was in full swing—a band playing Reagan's favorite songs, suburbanites pouring in. It was not like a Kennedy victory party, where the unwashed used to mingle with the politicians, and the "beautiful people" mingled with both. These were ordinary people, the men in business suits, trousers more often baggy than not, the women in their best department-store dresses.

I recall telling Lyn Nofziger a day later that it was the frowsiest crowd of frumps I had ever seen at a victory party. "Yup," said Nofziger, "that's us. We're the middle class."

CHAPTER ELEVEN

THE CONVENTIONS: ON STAGE AND OFF

Nowhere in the Constitution is it written that there shall be conventions—or political parties. The founding fathers feared parties and factions above all—but since power never falls to those who will not reach for it and since government is power, it followed by the laws of nature that political parties would develop to grab for the power and would have to climax their own internal power struggles in convention.

For one hundred fifty years—from 1832 on—the conventions were the great national meeting places of politics; out of them came the nation's leaders. But by 1980, their function of choosing leaders was a fading memory. National candidates were now chosen by the serial plebiscite of the endless primaries. The candidate was the survivor. Yet the conventions in 1980 remained exciting; there, new constitutional issues were debated, new social issues driven forward through committee to platform, the nature of the parties themselves reshaped. At the conventions, the delegates, chained in the discipline of candidates' whips, worked off their fury, energy, and ambition in either the pursuit of a momentary burst of publicity or the advocacy of private causes. These causes expressed far more vividly the changing mood of the nation than did the keynote openings of the orators or the classic acceptance speeches of the candidates.

What was happening in the nation was reflected in the convention settings of 1980—in Detroit, where the Republicans met, and in New York, where the Democrats met, both cities grim examples of the urban devastation that racked the country. Not since the pioneers and the covered wagons trekked west across the plains had so great a change been so clearly visible as in the crime-infested streets and the ruins of such great Northeastern cities. In the safe centers of Detroit and New York, the delegates convened.

Detroit was a paradigm of industrial dismay. Once a city of transplanted Southerners on the bank of the Detroit River, it had, as the census revealed, lost 20.5 percent of its population in ten years. Of those who remained, 63 percent were black; the whites who remained were mostly Southerners or Slavs too poor to find homes in the suburbs. What had hit Detroit was the undermining of its great automobile industry, which had put the nation and the world on wheels. In all Detroit, not a single plant rolled out automobiles as the delegates gathered. "Motown" was as anachronistic a nickname as was "Knickerbocker City" for New York. Unemployment in Detroit ran at 18.4 percent, approaching the levels of the Depression; automobiles carried bumper stickers: "Unemployment—Made in Japan." As the Republican delegates set out for the convention, they could read in their papers a United Press dispatch of the preceding week: "The Japanese automobile association today announced that for the first time in history, Japan this year has surpassed the United States in automobile production."

I shared a cab one day with a disconsolate businessman, a member of Detroit's host committee. His assignment was to keep the Arkansas delegation happy; but so short was hotel space and so little the clout of Arkansas that the delegation had been housed across the river—in Canada! The Arkansas delegates wanted to visit one of Detroit's famous automobile factories, the factories of legend. None were working; their host was upset he could not show them American cars coming off the assembly line. "So what are you doing?" I asked. He replied, "I've arranged to take them to a Polish picnic instead."

The delegates who went to Detroit were to meet in a downtown rectangle called Renaissance Center, one of those strange developments conceived by promoters and funded by federal moneys to revive a city in trouble. But like so many of the great urban renewal projects of the past twenty years—Harborplace in Baltimore, the new downtown Boston, Independence Square in Philadelphia—it was a cultural and commercial project, which sucked away money from the homes and needs of ordinary people who lived in the ever-more-shabby peripheral inner city. Two luxury hotels, the Pontchartrain and the Detroit Plaza, and a convention center—Cobo Hall and

Joe Louis Arena—pegged out the corners of the stockade in which it was safe for the Republican delegates to wander.

Only from the top of the towers at the Renaissance Center complex could one see the reason for, and the beauty of, Detroit. From the plaza's Renaissance Club, Lake Huron was visible in the hazy distance, as was the water passage between Lake Huron and Lake Erie; on the Canadian side of the passageway stretched the original narrow strips of land the French had laid out to give every colonist access to the great water passage. The placid waterway is still magnificent, explaining the roots of Detroit's industrial greatness. Such waterways once brought to Detroit the iron ore of Minnesota, the coal of Pennsylvania and Illinois, the steel of Indiana and Ohio, gathering the Midwest's natural resources in one of the world's great natural sites for industry. At all the fashionable convention parties for the famous, particularly those at the Renaissance Club, one might stand bemused at the grandeur and beauty of the prospect—but after four days of parties, one realized that only an occasional freighter had been seen passing through the once-crowded passage to the once-throbbing cities of the Great Lakes. From the sky-top windows one could not see the dingy city of those who still lived, hoped, and wanted jobs in Detroit.

New York, where the Democrats met, differed in scale and nature from Detroit—but it, too, was fighting a desperate battle against decay. New York had once been a city of almost eight million people; now there were only seven million, and of these, only four million were whites. The full impact of the new wave of immigration caught one in New York as sharply as in Los Angeles: Caribbeans, tan and black, speaking Spanish in the streets; puckering new colonies of Chinese, Koreans, Hindus; and blacks were now a full 25 percent of the city's population. Crime was not as bad as in Detroit or Houston, but to sensitive New York, with memories of other years, it was terrifying. In the New York of 1980, more than five people were murdered every single day; in the 1950 city, substantially larger, the average had been one murder a day. Years before, the massive West Side Highway had simply begun to rot away, dumping a truck one day to the cobblestones below; four years earlier, at the Democratic convention in New York, its reconstruction or replacement by a $2.3 billion "Westway" had been under debate. "Westway," in 1980, was still under debate, and the old highway still ended in a broken stump, as do the ancient Roman aqueducts in Europe; bridges and underpasses were rotting and rusting away too. At the piers of what was once the greatest harbor in the nation, the liners and freighters had stopped coming; not a single pier handled cargo on the North River, although one four-block area on the East Side still did; some Brooklyn piers still worked too; but the commerce of New York had passed to neighboring New Jersey, and what was once the Port of New York could now, correctly, be called the Port of New Jersey.

New York City still offered visitors a thriving downtown and midtown center—but unlike Detroit's center, New York's was the creation of private enterprise, a vibrant community throwing up monument after monument to celebrate the city's determination to remain the world center of finance, investment, and entertainment. For the executive class, New York still offered the finest restaurants in the nation, the blaze of American music, theater, opera, dance, at its best. But for ordinary white people, the blue-collar workers who had humped cargo, tunneled out subways, erected high steel, done the intricate needlework of the garment industry, the city had become less and less friendly a place to live in. New York had never received its proper share of federal money; it had been too proud to beg when it reigned over the greatest state in America, and its congressional delegation too stupid to exercise leverage when the city held maximum clout. The result of neglect—urban, state, and federal—was visible in the burned-out, abandoned stretches of the south Bronx and central Brooklyn. New York, proclaimed its housing experts, had no lack of housing—only a lack of *safe* housing. The decay was eating away even at the fringes of Manhattan. The great hotels that ran from Central Park South to Forty-second Street still marked a belt of civilized living; SoHo on the lower East Side was being repossessed by the artists and strivers who had once made Greenwich Village the outpost of American nonconformity; that, too, was still safe. But on the West Side, the convention center, Madison Square Garden, pegged out the limits of safety. The police had done their best to arrest and clean out the prostitutes from the *corso* of Eighth Avenue. But as they emerged from the convention hall, strangers to the city were told to look for cabs on the Seventh Avenue side, rather than on Eighth. Beyond was danger country—head shops, hookers, derelicts, and the dangerous bus terminal, where unfortunate old "bag ladies" and degenerates congregated.

To these problems sprawling about them the two conventions paid only formal attention, a bow to their gravity, and substituted hopeful aphorisms for answers. There would be no answers until the thinking leaders of the country came to an analysis and offered intellectual options.

Over both conventions reigned the presence of television. The national conventions are television's World Series. There, on the floor, reputations are born, young stars squirt to fame, and maximum deployment of every resource and ingenuity is commanded. To win the ratings game at conventions means millions and millions of dollars, and the continuing millions that come when one network pulls ahead of another in the news shows. Edward R. Murrow had lost his crown to Walter Cronkite as America's leading broadcaster at just such a convention. John Chancellor had won his crown for his charm, wit, and inexhaustible energy at just such a convention. No single newspaper can compete with the three great networks when they go all out in rivalry as at conventions. Together, at the conventions alone, the three networks probably spent $50 million—apart from the untabulated millions that they had spent or would spend on the primaries and the election itself. For the great election race, the federal government allotted each candidate only $29.4 million.

Television news, as we have seen, is the bastard offspring of history and drama. While election night returns are the maximum competition between the networks' computer and data analysts, conventions are the maximum competition in dramatics. Constantly, producers and correspondents are tugged and torn between the needs of history and of drama. The huddled delegates below the broadcast booths are a faceless sea in which the floor correspondents fish for interviews with recognizable names; producers in control centers weigh the catch, and arrange the feed of patterns to the anchor booths. Producers and correspondents alike are caught in the network competition for audience shares beyond any power to resist what the reality of television demands.

Nor are the two parties able to resist the reality of television. Television will spread their message to the nation. The parties must, therefore, rearrange their schedules, cut their agendas, choose their podium personalities, to catch and hold television's attention. They must, also, do their best to mislead or cast dramatic bait to television's fishermen on the floor. On the floor, the delegates are lost, caught in a hall of echoes, relaying to one network interviewer as their opinion what they have just heard from another network. The delegates bounce, oscillate, vibrate to television signals, disciplined only by the word of mouth they get from back-room floor whips.

For there are still back rooms in any convention. What the public sees is the pageantry, punctuated by the attempt of correspondents to tease the ritual and ceremonies into meaning by preplanned interviews or random news breaks. What the public does not see is the clash of causes and wills in the back rooms, where matters are too intricate, dull, or concealed for television to define in its chase for drama.

Under these circumstances, then, in 1980, the Republicans gathered in Detroit, the Democrats in New York.

The old Republican war between progressives and conservatives was over by the time the party assembled. If there were to be any new wars in the foreseeable future, the foreshadow was discernible only in the rift that was opening between the straight-out conservatives of Ronald Reagan's majority, and the primitive conservatives who felt that Reagan was just a bit too soft and must be stiffened by pressure from the right.

The preamble to their platform statement put the case of the Republican party of 1980 most simply:

> . . . America is adrift. Our country moves agonizingly, aimlessly, almost helplessly into one of the most dangerous and disorderly periods in history. At home, our economy careens, whiplashed from one extreme to another. . . . The hopes and aspirations of our people are being smothered.
>
> Overseas, conditions, already perilous, deteriorate. The Soviet Union . . . is acquiring the means . . . to blackmail us into submission. Marxist tyrannies spread more rapidly through the Third World and Latin America. . . .
>
> These events are not isolated, or unrelated. They are signposts. They mark a continuing downward spiral in economic vitality and international influence. . . . History could record, if we let the drift go on, that the American experiment . . . came strangely, needlessly, tragically to a dismal end early in our third century. . . .

Under this roof statement were detailed the planks, programs, promises, that embodied the "New Beginning" pledged by Ronald Reagan. His overarching slogan was: "Family. Neighborhood. Work. Peace. Freedom." After this slogan came seventy-five pages of platform specifics, where in the fine print was embodied what had gone on in the back rooms weeks before the convention convened.

Of all the back-room fights, it is most important to signal one as the first thrust of a revived force making its way back into the arena of Republican politics—the thrust of the messianic movement that now called itself the Moral Majority and which at this point pinned its battle on a definition of family values, women's rights, and, specifically, abortion. These forces had long been there, but for twenty years had been submerged.

Most of the Republican platform was entirely acceptable to the conservative and center majority that Reagan had put together from the South, the West, and the suburbs. Where centrists and conservatives split was on moral postures. The Republican party had been born in the moralisms of preachers who found black slavery intolerable. It had opposed the entrance of Utah into the Union until Mormons gave up their way of family life and outlawed plural wives. Their great cause in the early twentieth century had been Prohibition—the dictation of how, when, where Americans could sip cocktails or guzzle booze. That moral cause had culminated in the Eighteenth Amendment and the Volstead Act, both later repealed by Democrats; and the Republicans had ever since held themselves aloof from intrusion in private lives. Now, from out of the past, buried deep within the Reagan delegations, surfaced the old forces, led by the right-to-life moralists, who believed, as faith, that government should, and must, dictate how women should control their bodies. It was their back-room skills, the same as those once practiced by the Anti-Saloon League, that dictated how the Republican platform should be written on that most sensitive issue, abortion.

"Abortion," said James Brady, later press secretary of the Reagan administration, "was one of those underground issues we didn't recognize. But it moved the magnetic needle as you passed over it." Reagan himself had signed into law, as governor of California, one of the most enlightened abortion statutes of any state in the Union. Of his inner circle of advisers, my own coarse system of direct questioning showed that only one out of the six favored a platform denying a woman the right to choose, with the advice of her doctor or husband, how her body should be used. But the right-to-life movement had been one of the stronger supports in the Reagan primary campaign. And its people had packed the platform subcommittee as skillfully as any single-purpose zealots had ever done.

Platform drafting had been the province of Senator John Tower of Texas. His democratic procedure was to let all members of the platform committee list their first, second, and third choices for subcommittees. The zealots against abortion had listed as their first choice the Subcommittee on Human Resources; most had won their choice and dominated the subcommittee. "Fascist baby-killers," screamed one at the cowed opposition. They demanded, and wrote into their first draft, a pledge that the President would not appoint to the Supreme Court any justice not committed to outlawing abortion, demanded that the government deny federal funds to pay for abortion for needy women; they went further, seeking to withdraw traditional commitment of the Republican party to an equal rights amendment for women.

"What were we to do?" asked Brady, explaining the strategy of the Reagan leaders at the convention. "We were like a ship crossing the North Sea in a storm, and we didn't want to take a torpedo." He added, "There were forces there completely beyond our control."

It was quite impossible politically to throw open the convention to a floor debate on abortion and women's rights, which television would seize on as the high peak of drama. It could be as explosive as a debate on homosexual rights, which the Democrats were trying to avoid. So in the full platform committee, where Reagan controlled a majority, the language was massaged and wrestled into a shape acceptable to both the moralists and the centrists. Thus, there emerged the language on rights which begins with the flat statement: "We oppose any move which would give the Federal government more power over families," and concludes, ". . . we affirm our support of a constitutional amendment to restore protection of the right to life for unborn children. We also support the Congressional efforts to restrict the use of taxpayers' dollars for abortion." Gone was the anti-abortion loyalty oath for prospective appointments to the Supreme Court, and instead the compromise language: "We will work for the appointment of judges at all levels of the judiciary who respect traditional family values and the sanctity of innocent human life."

By voice vote, the full platform committee approved the language and the Republican party was committed to a federal intrusion in family life deeper than any the Democrats had ever dared propose. That week the traditional women of the Republican center would parade through Detroit, in the traditional white dresses of the suffragettes of fifty years before, to protest the reversal of their party's course. Two senators, Mathias of Maryland and Javits of New York, joined them in their parade.

One had the sense, trying to follow the diffuse and concealed debates over family and women's rights, that here was the stuff of drama yet to come. But for real, actual, ongoing drama, there was little to compare with the struggle over Reagan's choice for Vice-

President. There, politics and history interlocked cleanly, lifting the struggle to the nature of the Constitution. And though it was worked out privately on the tower floors of the Detroit Plaza, it could not be concealed from television, which amplified it for the nation. It was, for a full day, the central action of the Republican convention.

For over twenty-five years, the choice of a Vice-President has, more often than not, been a familiar madness of American political conventions. Kennedy had decided, overnight after his nomination, to pick Lyndon Johnson, rather than one of the two candidates— Henry Jackson and Stuart Symington—his inner circle favored most. Then, persuaded by other forces, he decided in midafternoon to reverse himself and dump Johnson; then, when Johnson refused to be dumped, television went on the first of its vice-presidential frolics. By 1964, when television dominated conventions, Johnson spent an entire day teasing national attention while he played Caligula, and left Humphrey, the natural choice, fuming and fretting for two days in public. By 1968, Nixon, on the night of his nomination, found his advisers deadlocked; Nixon out of desperation reached for a convenient ethnic, Spiro T. Agnew. In 1972, after an all-night session with his exhausted advisers, George McGovern was persuaded to accept a man unknown to him, whose background none of his staff had thoroughly checked. That choice resulted in the Eagleton affair, and the erasure of McGovern's already almost hopeless candidacy.

The choice of Vice-President at the Republican convention of 1980 included many of these elements of madness, but elevated the episode to a dimension it had never approached before.

Only three candidates for Vice-President had ever been seriously considered by the Reagan group—all men of the center, for Reagan meant not to repeat Goldwater's mistake of 1964 and split the party by moving his candidacy to the far right. First was Howard Baker; but Baker two weeks before the convention had flatly eliminated himself, for family reasons, in a private telephone call to Reagan. Next was George Bush, the candidate most acceptable to the convention delegates. (An NBC poll at the opening of the convention showed Bush with 47 percent of the delegate preferences, the other aspirants scattered.) But Bush had fought a bruising adversary campaign in the primaries, had tagged Reagan again and again off base. Finally, there was ex-President Gerald Ford. Ford had declared in early March that Reagan could not possibly win the election; this rankled too. But Reagan had made a dutiful pilgrimage to Ford's home in Rancho Mirage two days after his final primary, felt out Ford, been told flatly that Ford did not want to be considered for the vice-presidency.

The matter could not rest there, however. Wirthlin's polls showed that none of the several potential running mates added strength to the Reagan ticket, except for Ford; Wirthlin urged that Ford be given one more chance to say no. The Reagan entourage— Casey, Meese, Nofziger—agreed. Ford first; if not Ford, then Bush. Enter Henry Kissinger, once Ford's Secretary of State. He had met with several senior Republican senators just before the convention and been asked to feel out Ford again. Had Ford locked the door or only closed it? Kissinger felt out Ford, reported back that there was only one chance in a thousand that he would accept—but there was that chance.

The Reagan entourage moved on from California to Detroit, where the senior Republican centrists converged on Reagan, urging Ford, Ford, Ford—the "dream ticket," Reagan-Ford. By Tuesday of the convention, July 15, the idea was fixed, and Kissinger was asked by William Casey, Reagan's campaign manager, to see him "immediately." He was met by Meese, Nofziger, and Casey, whose message was straightforward: They needed Kissinger's help to get Ford; they would offer almost anything, even to a Ford veto on cabinet posts, or to name Ford Secretary of Defense, as well as Vice-President. But they needed an answer quickly.

It was midnight before Kissinger could meet Ford in the former President's palatial suite on the seventieth floor of the Plaza Hotel— just one floor above the Reagan suite on the sixty-ninth. With his mastery of diplomacy, Kissinger began by admitting that the vice-presidency was a "lousy job"; but went on: This was a national emergency; Ford must consider the Reagan offer seriously. Ford was reluctant. He had been both President and Vice-President; the relationship between the two was always difficult. Moreover, his wife had only recently recovered from a serious case of alcoholism; he did not want to put her under Washington pressure again. Finally—he just didn't want to do it.

At this point, after a forty-five-minute private meeting, others entered, chief among them Alan Greenspan, who had served Ford so well as chairman of his Council of Economic Advisers. Greenspan raised the conversation to another level. "They had the power," he said of Reagan's staff later. "We had the experience." He, Kissinger, and the others in the room knew the complexity of the presidency;

there was no question that the burden on the modern President was absolutely staggering. What useful role could a former President play when reduced to Vice-President? Said Ford: "Construct a definition." It would have to be, said Greenspan, something Reagan could live with. Said Kissinger: "You can't make a treaty with a President." For two more hours they debated, as if in a seminar on government.

What they were debating was central to the American system—the powers of the presidency itself. Greenspan offered the thought that the Vice-President might act as chief of staff to the President—an analogue roughly to corporate life, where a chairman of the board is chief executive officer, and beneath him there is a chief operating officer. The President, thus, would be the Chief Policymaker; but the Vice-President would be the Chief Operator. They discussed the operation problems of the White House, which they knew so well. A Chief Operating Officer (i.e., Ford) should have jurisdiction over the Office of Management and Budget, over the National Security Council, over the State Department. All agreed that the next morning Ford's councillors would meet with Reagan's and see if a new definition of the roles of President and Vice-President could be worked out.

It was now almost three in the morning; all were tired; and Ford had a heavy schedule the next day—a self-imposed exposure to the media. He would be up at dawn on Wednesday to appear on NBC's *Today* show. He would go from that to a breakfast with the editors of *Time* magazine. He would then grant the New York *Times*'s national political correspondent, Adam Clymer, a private interview, followed by lunch with *Newsweek* editors. In between, he would be meeting with deputation after deputation of senior Republican senators, all pleading with him, pushing him to accept second place on the "dream ticket."

The next morning, Wednesday, then, as Ford made the media rounds, Ford's negotiators met with Reagan's—with campaign manager Casey and William Timmons, a veteran of both the Nixon and the Ford White Houses. Ford's spokesmen put the Greenspan concept to Timmons and Casey; there was no conflict; Casey undertook to draft a summary of their talk on the nature of the presidency and the "enhanced role" of the Vice-President. By one o'clock, a two-page memorandum was ready, presented to the Ford group by Meese; the memorandum apparently accepted the "enhanced role" of the vice-presidency, placing under Ford's jurisdiction, as Chief Operating Officer, both the Office of Management and Budget and the National Security Council. The President of the United States, once elected, would share operating power with his Vice-President. If the concept was accepted by both Reagan and Ford, the nature of presidential leadership would change.

By early afternoon, the memorandum was shown to Ford. "Had we written it," reported Greenspan, "it would not have been materially different"; and, for the first time, Ford budged. He was now cross and tired after a sleepless night, and the day's exhausting rounds with the media. Everyone is trying to make me do something, he complained, to give up my life. If I give up my life, he asked, turning to Kissinger and Greenspan, will you give up yours too? Will you come back to government again? Greenspan remembers gulping, but agreed. Kissinger agreed too. Thus, the stage was set for the climax meeting at about five o'clock between Reagan, the putative President, and Ford, the once-President. They met alone; what they said to each other is only hearsay. Several of the Ford negotiators have stressed again and again that Ford was tired—that he had either overplayed his hand or was trying to find a way out. He could not, Ford is reported to have said, go back to Washington alone; he would have to have his own people around him, to help him—namely, Kissinger and Greenspan. This request, both Kissinger and Greenspan felt, was stronger than they would have advised. Both had insisted to Ford that he not make their names a subject of the negotiations.

Meanwhile, at the convention, it was already nomination time and the floor rocked with every new rumor. Bands played, speakers spoke, orators orated, and Ronald Reagan's name was placed in nomination; balloons drifted down from the roof. The California delegates for Reagan, in golden cowboy hats, the Texas delegates for Reagan, in white cowboy hats, and the New England delegates for Reagan, in yellow fishermen's slicker hats, all rose to demonstrate. Suddenly there appeared, at seven o'clock on CBS, with Walter Cronkite, the figure of Gerald Ford, who had just come from his talk with Reagan. Ford had not informed Reagan that he was en route to another national television appearance—perhaps because he had been so tossed and pummeled by the media that day that it had not appeared important to him.

It was one of Cronkite's best interviews. He bored in. Would pride prevent Ford from accepting the vice-presidency after having been President? Ford dodged. Cronkite put the question another way: "It's to be something like a co-presidency?" Ford replied,

"That's something Governor Reagan really ought to consider . . . the point you raised is a very legitimate one. We have a lot of friends in Washington. And the President-to-be . . . he has to also have pride. And for him not to understand the realities and some of the things that might happen in Washington is being oblivious to reality." The transaction of the vice-presidency had now been raised to a new level.

From the booth of CBS, Ford circled the high rim of the amphitheater to the ABC booth and repeated himself. He had now touched all the bases of the networks, NBC in the morning, CBS and ABC in the evening, and was making his way back to the Plaza Hotel, where his negotiators were still trying to reduce the understanding of the two principals to specifics.

On the convention floor, no other news circulated but that of television's instant communication system. From the command headquarters to the floor whips came the instruction: Keep the nominating demonstration going. The band played "Oh, the monkey wrapped his tail around the flagpole," "Stars and Stripes Forever," and any other tune they could think of, while the delegates tuned in their portable radios or TV sets to pick up the freshest rumor, which, coming from the floor, was only an echo of their own confusion. The decision on the vice-presidency was not theirs: it was the nominee's decision as always, and he was making it alone, torn by the confusion and divisions among his advisers. What they were trying to define was the nature of the presidency that Reagan would have in November—and whether it was worth the extra help a joint Reagan-Ford ticket would guarantee for an election victory as against the change in nature of the constitutional office.

The Casey-Timmons memorandum of understanding on the new definition of the vice-presidency had begun to circulate on the Reagan staff floor, the sixty-eighth, of the Plaza early in the afternoon. Among those who had the nominee's ear and were privileged to read the memorandum, opinion split sharply. Wirthlin was appalled. He was against it. So, too, was Michael Deaver, who insisted that Reagan must not agree to anything that "would limit his power to govern." Also furious was Richard Allen, who had played a major role in the Nixon campaign of 1968, only to find himself eliminated from any prize of victory by Rockefeller's favorite, Kissinger.

They had disputed among themselves all afternoon until Ford had met with Reagan. Upstairs and downstairs between the sixty-ninth and seventieth floors trotted emissaries. Immediately after the unfortunate five o'clock meeting, Kissinger had gone directly to

Casey and Meese and withdrawn his name from any consideration for a high post. There were other uncertainties, however; Kissinger wanted more clarification on the meaning of the phrase that the Office of Management and Budget would "report through Ford" to the President. In the absence of a full Ford staff, how would that work? Ford had now come back from his last television appearances; he had had a tiring day and wanted to "sleep on" his final decision.

It was late now, and the convention seethed. Reagan was with friends in his suite, watching the tube. Without forewarning, he had seen Ford's appearance on CBS, and was astounded. Wirthlin was observing Reagan as Reagan observed TV. There was a moment, said Wirthlin, when his expression changed—when Ford announced his willingness to accept a "co-presidency." "It was like two ships passing in the night," continued Wirthlin, "and the searchlights pick up the silhouette of the other. What it did was illuminate the distance between them."

In an interview later, Reagan picked up the narrative: "I sat there ... watching ... television and I saw this out-of-control thing, when I saw one commentator on the floor, when the booth called down to him [Dan Rather], saying that he absolutely knew that he [Ford] and I were on our way to the convention floor to announce this. And I'm sitting there in my hotel room ... and by this time I realized that it was totally out of hand, and I said, 'No.' I said, 'There's no way that I can give away the prerogatives of the presidency, and you tell them [the Ford group] that. And I need to know right now.' "

At ten o'clock, Reagan had dispatched Casey upstairs to the Ford suite to bear the message. "You decide in fifteen minutes or it's off," Casey recalls himself saying. Any acceptance had to be based on faith and understanding; it could not be a written compact.

In a short while, before eleven, Ford had made up his mind and was down on the Reagan floor, withdrawing himself from consideration. As Reagan recalled it: "He said, 'This just can't go on. I feel stronger than ever, inside me, that it is wrong and I shouldn't do this [take the vice-presidency]. ... I want you to know, though, that I'll do everything I can to help you get elected. ...' He put his arm around my shoulders and he said, ' ... I want you to know that I hold you in affection and respect and meant what I said: I'll do anything I can to get you elected. ...' So then I just went to the phone, because I had also realized that other than this so-called dream ticket, from all the input, that George [Bush] was the choice of the party. And I went to the phone and called him."

At the hall, the foreordained nomination of Ronald Reagan went on. The band again played "Stars and Stripes Forever"; then "California, Here I Come," "I've Been Working on the Railroad," "God Bless America"; and on and on it played. The signs waved on the floor: SHELL THAT PEANUT, RON TURNS US ON, WASHINGTON STATE ERUPTS FOR REAGAN, ELEPHANTS EAT PEANUTS. An indecipherable banner in Chinese. LIFE LIBERTY AND THE PURSUIT OF REAGAN. The roll call of states proceeded; then ended; but television had a more important story than roll call. Rumors bounced—that the Secret Service was tracking down the private telephone number of George Bush, of Guy Vander Jagt, of Jack Kemp, of others. That Reagan had seen Ford at five o'clock, but had not seen him since. That Bush was getting a haircut, that Bush had just been out jogging, that Bush was in his suite. That it was Ford, Ford, Ford. The band resumed after the roll call: "From the halls of Montezuma," "East side, west side," "Onward, Christian Soldiers." In his suite, Reagan's advisers could see that to quell the convention pandemonium, a decision must be made immediately, quickly, on the vice-presidency; that Reagan must go to the convention to show himself master of his house. At about eleven-thirty, Reagan's call went to Bush's suite.

Bush had been waiting for the call for days. He had begun the week as a Reagan team player, circulating the caucuses, genial yet proud as always. In his suite on Monday, with his wife and a few friends, he had shown a rare irritability. The decision on the vice-presidency should be made by now, he felt, but there was no way of campaigning for it. He was perplexed, too. He did not go along with Reagan on women's rights and abortion; the Republican platform, he thought, was fine, except for those two points, on which his conscience disturbed him. What should he say if he was called in? He pondered language of acceptance should the call come. In any event, he had had it; he had chartered a plane and would fly on Friday, from the convention, back to his old family summer home on the coast of Maine, to rest up. There was nothing more he could do but wait. He had waited, thus, all through Wednesday, into evening, and was still waiting, fretting at television and the wild reporting from the floor, when the call came from Reagan. There was no elaboration. Reagan had one question: Would George Bush support this platform? Bush said he would, enthusiastically.

Within minutes, the word was out, the decision relayed to the command wagon; from the command wagon to the floor whips, who raced through the convention; on the floor, Chris Wallace of NBC was first to pick up the blurted words of a Reagan whip, and as NBC broadcast the word, it was now concluded. Reagan would be coming to the convention; he was on his way; he was arriving; and there he was, in the flesh, on the podium dressed in a dark-blue suit, announcing, quite gracefully, that Gerald Ford and he had talked over the possibility of joining the ticket: ". . . we have gone over this, and over this, and over this . . . and he believes deeply that he can be of more value as the former President campaigning his heart out, as he has pledged to do, and not as a member of the ticket. . . . I am recommending to this convention that tomorrow when the session reconvenes that George Bush be nominated for Vice-President."

Thursday, Acceptance Day, was sedate, orderly, and efficient, Reagan reaching the podium in prime television time, with balloons dropping once more, the band playing, and then the hush, as he began.

His acceptance speech was straightforward, spoken simply and clearly, no gimmicks except at the very end:

> Never before in our history have Americans been called upon to face three grave threats to our very existence, any one of which could destroy us. We face a disintegrating economy, a weakened defense, and an energy policy based on the sharing of scarcity.
>
> The major issue of this campaign is the direct political, personal, and moral responsibility of Democratic party leadership— in the White House and in Congress—for this unprecedented calamity which has befallen us. . . .
>
> We are taxing ourselves into economic exhaustion and stagnation, crushing our ability and incentive to save, invest, and produce. This must stop. We *must* halt this fiscal self-destruction, and restore sanity to our economic system. I have long advocated a 30 percent reduction in income tax rates over a period of three years. . . . A phased reduction of tax rates would go a long way toward easing the heavy burden on the American people. But we should not stop here. . . .
>
> The first task of national leadership is to set honest and realistic priorities in our policies and our budget, and I pledge that my administration will do that. . . .
>
> When we move from domestic affairs and cast our eyes abroad, we see . . .
>
> • A Soviet combat brigade trains in Cuba, just ninety miles from our shores.

• A Soviet army invasion occupies Afghanistan, further threatening our vital interests in the Middle East. . . .

• And, incredibly, more than fifty of our fellow Americans have been held captive for over eight months by a dictatorial foreign power that holds us up to ridicule before the world.

On, then, to quote Tom Paine, to quote Franklin Roosevelt, and: "The time is *now*, my fellow Americans, to recapture our destiny, to take it into our own hands."

Then, finally, after coming to the end of his prepared text, he changed personality. With a cock of the head, a purse of the lips, in a quavering voice, he asked the convention to share his dilemma. "I'll confess that I've been a little afraid to suggest what I'm going to suggest—I'm more afraid not to—that we begin our crusade joined together in a moment of silent prayer. God bless America."

And with that, the convention rose, bowed its many heads, and silently prayed.

The Republican convention was at its end. The audience ratings on television had not been spectacularly high; but the polls that rolled in were unmistakably clear. An NBC/AP survey showed Reagan's convention had pushed him up to 55 percent over Carter's 24 percent; in the Harris poll, to 61 percent over Carter's 33 percent.

It was hot and steaming in New York as the Democrats gathered—reminding everyone that New York is still a low-lying cluster of islands which becomes in August a subtropical archipelago. The garbage mounded in the streets; 3,000 members of its reduced police force of 22,400 had been deployed to protect the convention and its visitors; but geraniums had been planted on the highways from the airports. The central city glistened. The famous hostesses and the dominant media invited the great and near-great to revolve from party to party all through the introductory weekend. Caucuses of the arriving state delegations met on Sunday to get their tickets and bus passes, to be warned of pickpockets and other street dangers, to hear roving Kennedy and Carter surrogates plead for support, while the committees met to hammer down rules and polish phrases.

If one followed such parties, caucuses, and committees, one would be trapped in glitter and confusion. But if one studied the official documents, one could be even more trapped. The official call to the convention proclaimed, according to the reformed rules, that there would be 3,331 delegate votes, divided by formula. "The formula is expressed mathematically as follows," read page one:

$$A = \frac{1}{2} \left(\frac{\text{SDV '68, '72, '76}}{101, 276, 222} + \frac{\text{SEV}}{539} \right)$$

To read further was futile. That way madness lay. Puerto Rico, for example, which could not vote at election, had more delegate votes (41) than either Oregon (39) or West Virginia (35), one of only six states that *did* vote Democratic in November. A strange new category, listed as "Latin American Regional Democratic Party," had four votes; this represented what had once been the U.S. Canal Zone but was now officially part of the sovereign Republic of Panama. Guam, with 70,000 people who could not vote in the election, also had four votes, one-third as many as Vermont, with 500,000 people. If the Republicans had eliminated their political center in Detroit, and fought their muted civil war between hard right and paranoid right, the Democrats, too, had eliminated their center. Their war was between the liberals of the Carter administration and the humanitarian left of the Kennedy cause. The structure of the convention party had also changed. There had been seventy-eight Democratic congressmen as delegates to the Democratic convention of 1968. In 1980, only thirty-seven congressmen had been chosen. In 1968, thirty-nine senators had come; in 1980, only eight. And half the delegates, as stipulated by the new rules, were women, compared to 13 percent in 1968.

Yet matters of great moment were to be exposed at this convention, and the matter of greatest importance—the function of a representative in a democratic system—was the first. It was engaged, as so often happens, by a power struggle—in this case the desperate effort of Senator Edward M. Kennedy to overturn the verdict of the primaries and, by so doing, throw Jimmy Carter out of office, at the Democratic convention, on its opening night, Monday, August 11.

The power struggle bannered itself as the call for an "open convention." It was the same rhetoric that Democratic liberals had used since 1964 in their quest to achieve justice and opportunity for all, all the while tangling the quest in a Laocoön of rules. Technically, the struggle hinged on a dreary clause called rule F3(c), rammed through a committee packed by Carter forces earlier in the year. It bound each delegate to be faithful to the candidate he' was elected to support. The Kennedy forces had gradually through the long primary campaign spun off the faint of heart, the discouraged loyalists, the realists who read the arithmetic of the primaries, and found Carter's lead in chosen delegates insurmountable. But those who remained closest to the senator still believed, as did he, that the delegates could even now be unlocked from their binding commitments, that rule F3(c) could be overturned by the full convention— and that by appeal to conscience, they could wreck Carter's majority the first night, go on to sweep the convention by Kennedy mystique, and Wednesday night take the nomination from Carter.

The issue involved, however, was deep. What was a delegate? Did he represent his conscience? Was he sent to exercise his judgment? Or was he bound by his pledge and commitment to speak, at least on the first ballot, for the people who had sent him to the convention? The effort to unbind delegates from the packages which the old machines had deposited like chips in a poker game had gone on for twelve full years. This long, untiring effort had resulted in an anomaly. Only 18 percent of the delegates present had ever had their names on a public ballot. Most had been chosen at caucuses of the candidates who had won their proportion of the popular vote; and had been pledged at their caucuses to vote for the candidate, who was entitled to discard them at will. So read rule F3(c), which permitted the candidate to punish any violator of loyalty: "Delegates who seek to violate this rule may be replaced with an alternate of the same presidential preference . . . at any time up to and including the presidential balloting at the National Convention." This, said the Kennedy forces, was a "jerk and yank" rule, which must be overturned by their call for an "open convention."

Of all the floor debates in both 1980 conventions, this debate on representative government, on Monday night, was the most illuminating. First to the rostrum was Edward Bennett Williams, once the treasurer of the Democratic National Committee, a moving force in the effort to unseat the President. "You came here free," said Williams. "You are free tonight. In the name of reason and liberty . . . reject the chains of F3(c). . . . I say to you, Mr. President, trust us, trust the delegates. Be strong. Be confident, and let your delegates be free. Let them vote for you in freedom and not in compulsion. Only then can a victory in August mean a victory in November."

He was followed by Connecticut's Senator Ribicoff, a man of uncommon common sense. Ribicoff had spent eighteen years in the front ranks of Senate liberals, had been a friend of the Kennedy family since he and John Kennedy had been junior congressmen together, and now saw the undoing of twelve years of party reform in what was proposed by his old friends among the Kennedys. "The issue we are debating is one of fairness," said Ribicoff. "It is not fair to change the rules now. It is not fair to the nineteen million Democrats who voted. It is not fair to the candidate who won the most delegates. It makes a mockery of the Democratic process." He was followed by other pro and con speakers, the most notable of whom was Senator George McGovern. In 1972, McGovern had won his nomination over Hubert Humphrey by insisting that the convention be bound by the rules under which California had given all its 271 delegate votes to him. He had argued then that no one could change the rules in the middle of the game. Now he argued the contrary: "Delegates who are trapped in the time capsule of decisions made months ago cannot carry out the present opinion of the people." Therefore, said McGovern of 1980, arguing against McGovern of 1972, the delegates must be freed of the rules adopted by the party.

"When you have the votes, you've got to use them," had said John White, chairman of the Democratic National Committee, shortly before the convention opened. White was a disillusioned loyalist of the Carter camp; but the game was power, and he surveyed what was about to happen on Monday evening with reluctant approval. Carter would exercise every leverage to win on the rules, to hold the delegates elected in his name. And the Carter command was prepared, with a mastery of convention technology that had developed over twenty years of politics and floor communication.

Now, at this convention, the Carter off-floor headquarters was a circle of six trailers, about which buzzed the crowding press, while command by telephone and walkie-talkie went out to fourteen floor operatives, ten regional floor leaders, and some two hundred whips, all dressed in shimmering green vests. They meant to ensure control of their votes, or yank the troublesome by direct voice command. The Kennedy command post—an 1,800-square-foot area called the "triangle"—was outgunned as it had been in primary after primary. One hundred twenty floor whips, recognizable by blue baseball caps, were assigned to shake loose the few uncommitted and a larger number of unhappy Carter delegates. One could follow the commotion on the floor as a clash of blue and green colors; but control had passed, as it usually does, to the back rooms.

Thus, then, the balloting began shortly after seven-forty on Monday night, in a tense but glum atmosphere. Carter delegates waved their green banners, Kennedy delegates their blue. New York hoisted its slogan: IMPORT PEANUTS, EXPORT CARTER. Carter delegates chanted: "Four more years, four more years." Kennedy placards displayed a red circle, within which was a robot, then a slash, then "F3(c)." Simpler placards read: WIN WITH TED. Clearly, on the floor and for the television cameras, the visuals ran for Kennedy. But as balloting began, it was clear in ten minutes that the Carter command had the numbers. By five minutes to eight, the "yes" votes (for the Kennedy minority report) were outnumbered—214 yes, 435 no. By ten minutes after eight, it was 549 yes, 1,031 no. By the time Pennsylvania had voted, at eight-twenty, it was 1,708 for Carter, and 1,174 for Kennedy; the President had carried his party. An hour later, from his suite at the Waldorf-Astoria, Senator Kennedy, with full grace, withdrew from the contest that had been hopeless from the beginning, and the fight for the nomination was over.

Yet not the convention. The convention was no longer a nominating body—but it had become a forum where all the new pressures first surfaced, then joined or clashed, hoping for attention.

Television at conventions focuses on the junction of events on the floor, snaring personalities, displaying the pageantry, switching now and then to the podium, where speakers ache for attention. What television cannot do is define those forces beyond the floor trying to shape causes into demand. Such causes are the future, and to observe them at the Democratic convention, it was necessary to leave the convention hall and walk across the street to the Statler Hotel. There one could see what had happened to the Democratic party, and how the call for full participation had divided both the party and American life.

The Statler is a dingy, shabby hotel which has seen better days. Its cramped rooms offer multiple housing to those who must be conveniently located near Madison Square Garden, and as in the convention of 1976, it housed the press, pressrooms, committee rooms of the party, as well as caucus and press conference halls. Its bank of twelve elevators soon clotted, then thickened, then froze with crowds trying to reach the operational floors. So it was necessary to force, shove, or climb one's way to the seventh floor, to see the display of what "participation" had brought forth.

On the lobby of the seventh floor—dank and dreary, its brown rugs stained by many visitors—corridors split in T formation, and where they joined hung the hand-lettered signs. "Middle East? Visit NAAA," pointed one, indicating that the National Association of Arab Americans, which claimed two million voters, was now a pres-

ence. "The Democratic Agenda" pointed another way. Still another
sign pointed toward the New Democratic Coalition. Other signs
pointed to the American Indians, the International Association of
Machinists, the American Federation of Teachers, Dellums for President, the Joint Center for Political Studies, "Gay Vote '80," "Campaign for UN Reform," and more, as one discovered in a walking
tour. To the left from the T, the National Organization for Women
and the Coalition for Women's Rights, which included the National
Abortion Rights Action League. To the right, the National Democrats for Life, vehemently opposed. Then the Congressional Black
Caucus and the National Ad Hoc Coalition of Black Democrats. And
on and on.

Everyone had learned over the previous twelve years to play the
convention game. The cause lobbies and political action committees
had moved into the primaries, elected their delegates, named them,
organized them. There had always been an AFL-CIO lobby at conventions; and the railroads, once a power at conventions, still poured
free drinks for reporters at the Railway Lounge. But now they were
overwhelmed by an array of interest groups, in continuing cellular
multiplication, that sought to control, not the results of the convention, but its commitments.

The blacks, the largest minority group at the convention, now
claimed between 470 and 480 delegates. The Hispanics claimed 333,
up from 46 in 1976! American Indians claimed 31. The Asian/Pacific
Americans caucus now claimed 79 delegates and alternates, up from
22 in 1976, including Mr. James Nhon Do, a Vietnamese refugee
naturalized only five months before. NOW—the National Organization for Women—claimed to control 200 delegates; the Women's
National Political Caucus claimed 400. The gays declared that they
had 46 delegates openly out of the closet, up from 2 in 1976; their
strength was particularly great in the New York, California, and
Minnesota delegations. Individual unions had long since freed themselves from the discipline of the AFL-CIO, which once controlled the
most solid bloc of votes at a Democratic convention. The United
Automobile Workers claimed 100 delegates/alternates of their own;
the Communications Workers claimed 53, the American Federation
of State, County and Municipal Employees 64, Machinists 91. But far
and away the most important organized groups were the teachers.
Teachers had come to politics late, being at once both shy and talka-
tive. They had considered themselves for years as professionals of
dedication, like doctors, learning only recently that doctors have

lobbies too. Now the American Federation of Teachers (pro-Kennedy) had 94 delegates/alternates and the National Education Association (pro-Carter) had 464—up from 265 in 1976. ("The Carter delegation," said Senator Moynihan of New York, "is a wholly-owned subsidiary of the NEA.") And beyond such large, measurable groups stretched the letterhead and direct-mail groups, organized by cause promoters, whose members consisted of earnest people devoting their efforts to calling attention to solar energy, the nuclear threat, environmental cuases, stopping the draft, the reform of the United Nations.

One could poke around, visit their press conferences, and savor the rhetoric. At the black caucus, Jesse Jackson, in beige trousers and open-necked shirt: ". . . we have the key to the White House door. And we should hold that key until we get more judgeships. We should hold that key until we have at least three cabinet members. . . . We are the difference." At the press conference of the National Organization for Women, its president, Eleanor Smeal, a short, strong-willed woman, with just a touch of gray in her hair, whose voice can reach high decibel level at the microphone: "We have been fighting for years for equal division between the sexes. And now we have it. The convention, when it convenes, will be the first major institution of our society that will be one-half female. . . . If we are ever going to pass the ERA, the Democratic party has got to discipline its members who do not support ERA. . . . The Democratic party at the presidential level cannot take for granted the support of women's rights activists. . . . We could opt not to participate in that election, and instead work in congressional and local elections for those who support us."

Yet not all the pressure groups were united. Blacks were split between Kennedy and Carter. Hispanics were divided between Puerto Ricans, on the one hand, and Mexicans and Cubans on the other. Puerto Ricans did not want to be included among Hispanics; they were born citizens; they were themselves confused about federal aid in block grants to their island. Would block grants help general economic development more than would the ongoing food stamp program, on which 55 percent to 60 percent of the island's population depended? Mexican and Cuban Hispanics were more interested in immigration laws. Chicanos were irritated by many injuries to pride, as for example in California: California's Democratic party, by its quota system, had allocated 15 percent of its votes to Hispanics, so that no less than 42 members of that state's delegation were ostensibly Hispanic. But the powers of the state party had slipped in Greeks (Greeks!) under the Hispanic allotment. Asian/ Pacific Americans were not yet strong enough to split among themselves. There were, they claimed, already four million of them in the United States, half of them newly arrived since the Immigration Act of 1965. But they had learned. "Our top priority has been raising money. We had to do it with money," said Joji Konoshima, cochairman of the caucus. "It has given us access to the White House and we are using that to get our share of grants and appointments. . . . We don't expect them to help us because they like us." On and on went the demands of the groups, most piquant being the gathering of the American Indians, one with his hair in braids, another with feathers in her hair. They did not like their classification by liberals in the Democratic party as "Native Americans." They wished to be recognized as "American Indians and Alaskan natives (Eskimos)," because that phrase would give them "legal clout and power." If they were classified as "native Americans," Hawaiians and Puerto Ricans might start feeding on the entitlements they sought. "If the Asians and Pacific Islanders need their own programs, they can come to us and we would support legislation for them," said an American Indian spokeswoman, "but they should not piggyback on our programs."

All the recent past of the Democratic party had invited these groups to participation. No man had done more for women, for blacks, for minorities, than Carter. Yet now the client groups of the Carter coalition were leveraging for more. In a memorandum for the President, Hamilton Jordan had, on July 22, choreographed convention proceedings for television to sustain the coalition. For example: "Recommended Speakers for the Tuesday programs are: Blacks: Parren Mitchell, Pat Harris. Hispanics: Mayor Ferre, Cesar Chavez. Catholics: Senator Moynihan. Jews: Phil Klutznick." And: "We will search for generally unknown delegates to speak who represent these groups." Then, for nominators of the Vice-President: "Doug Fraser (unions), a female and an Hispanic." But neither Jordan nor any of the convention staff had expected the dynamics of participation to emerge as they did.

The entire convention had been planned for television impact. But what if some uncontrolled surge from the floor caught the camera eye? The gays wanted to nominate a candidate for Vice-President and had been gathering petition signatures; if they could reach the podium and unfurl their banners on the floor, the television nets would gleefully highlight the demonstration. That must be stopped.

Ronald Dellums, congressman from California, wanted to be nominated for President; the signatures on his petition, the Carter command felt, were invalid; but Dellums was black and, as a black, could not be challenged in public or denied access to the podium. That could be handled—Dellums would get his moment on the platform, with the required three seconders; and then, he agreed, he would withdraw so as not to complicate the balloting. The women felt that the bottom line was ratification of the Equal Rights Amendment; some suggested the clearly impossible idea that all grants and federal aid be cut off to states that had not ratified ERA. That was stopped before it reached the floor and television. But the women had at least two other minority planks on the platform, on which they would not yield, planks 10 and 11. Moreover, at least thirty-six protesting minority reports had also come out of the Carter-controlled platform committee, which had met in Washington in mid-June. Each was entitled to a roll-call vote; debating such measures, the convention might waste its prime time and thus abuse the attention of the nation, repeating the blunder of McGovern in 1972. If Ted Kennedy chose to do so, he could force the convention to debate each of the minority reports, hour after hour, as the nation droned off to sleep. It was essential, therefore, to have an understanding. Carter had wanted the convention to be the public display of his themes for the election campaign; Kennedy had wanted attention focused on his minimum demands, the springboard for what he had hoped would be his seizure of the nomination.

Thus, then, on August 5, a week before the convention, both sides had signed a confidential agreement—Hamilton Jordan for the President, Paul Kirk, Jr., for the senator—signed, sealed, stipulated in an eight-page compact with riders attached. Prime time would be precisely allotted on the matters that must be debated; all minority planks but five were withdrawn—two on the rules, three on the economics of the nation. No one, of course, could resist the combined forces of the Kennedy-Carter alliance except, of course, the women, whose demands would cut across factions.

The Carter people, from the very beginning, had understood television better than Kennedy's team. They had preceded the convention on August 5 with a presidential press conference—a dignified and somber performance by a President publicly aggravated by a squalid brother who had taken $220,000 from the terrorist Libyan government. Carter had handled it well and lanced a boil. His staff had been studying the Republican convention and calculated that the cameras stayed on the podium for no more than eight minutes out of every hour, cutting away the rest of the time to famous personalities and floor reports. They had studied floor layouts, the movement of television's reporters down corridors and aisles, and now proceeded to strew dignitaries and cabinet members through the aisles on the floor. There, accidentally, the scurrying floor reporters would meet the people they had been seeking and could interview them forthwith, or send them off, if they were eminences, to be interviewed in the anchor booths. For the country press the Carter command had arranged specials. While the nation might focus on the national networks, there were thousands of local television and radio stations in the outcountry whose correspondents had never enjoyed the company of Washington's mighty. For these, members of the cabinet and the President's staff were available from special broadcast and taping booths at Carter headquarters, a few blocks up the street. "Whoever heard of Dayton interviewing the Secretary of Defense live?" asked a Carter staffer. "But he was there for Dayton, and Saint Louis, and Boston, and all the others too."

What Carter could not control, however, was the live drama on the television time allotted to Kennedy—and on Tuesday evening, the senator from Massachusetts brought the convention alive.

The mystique of the Kennedy family is part of the invisible but solid furnishing of American politics. Of this mystique, Ted Kennedy had displayed but little during the campaign of 1980; now he was to recapture it.

Kennedy had begun, the weekend before the convention, to polish the speech drafted by Robert Shrum and Carey Parker, his two most loyal aides. It had been combed out by the family's two senior intellectual advisers—Arthur Schlesinger and Ted Sorensen—and it was to be, as fortune would decide, either an acceptance speech of the nomination or a rallying cry of the party against the Republicans. Kennedy had tried out some of the lines at the California caucus on Sunday, and his attack on Reagan had drawn them to their feet, united. He had rehearsed it twice on the TelePrompTer in his suite at the Waldorf, then once again on the TelePrompTer at the convention hall.

When he strode to the podium, the magic was finally on him— he had caught the Sense of the Occasion. The Sense of the Occasion is one of those mysterious intuitions that come to a political leader when he knows the moment and the mood will amplify words.

Churchill had it. Roosevelt had it. John Kennedy had it. Now, at this convention, the senator's loyalists bounced as they waited. The curious, and the Carter loyalists, were ready to give Kennedy a moment too. They were to hear great oratory:

"My fellow Democrats," he began, "I have come here tonight not to argue as a candidate but to affirm a cause. . . .

"Our cause has been, since the days of Thomas Jefferson, the cause of the common man and the common woman. Our commitment has been, since the days of Andrew Jackson, to all those he called 'the humble members of society—the farmers, mechanics, and laborers. . . .' "

He was now in full golden tone, and the delegates hushed. Then he was into Reagan:

"The same Republicans who are talking about the crisis of unemployment have nominated a man who once said, and I quote, 'Unemployment insurance is a prepaid vacation plan for freeloaders.'

". . . a man who said, and I quote: 'I have included in my morning and evening prayers every day the prayer that the federal government not bail out New York.'

". . . a man who said just four years ago that participation in Social Security 'should be made voluntary.' And that nominee is no friend of the senior citizen of this nation."

Now they were roaring on the floor, Carter and Kennedy delegates alike.

". . . a man who last year made the preposterous statement, and I quote, 'Eighty percent of air pollution comes from plants and trees.'

". . . a man who said in 1976, and these are his exact words, 'Fascism was really the basis of the New Deal.' "

Now he had them rising from their seats and, like a great orator, lifted them up, sat them down, lifted them again, as if they were dancing to his words.

". . . We are the party of the New Freedom, the New Deal, and the New Frontier. We have always been the party of hope. . . .

"For me, a few hours ago, this campaign came to an end. For all those whose cares have been our concern, the work goes on, the cause endures, the hope still lives, and the dream shall never die!"

At this, as he stood on the platform waving, the convention exploded. It had heard one of the great convention passages of all time—easily the equal of Adlai Stevenson's acceptance in 1952, the Eugene McCarthy address of 1960, the taunting grace of Nelson Rockefeller in 1964.

Stirred, I went down to the convention floor to join the demonstration—for it was an authentic demonstration, as authentic as the Goldwater demonstration at San Francisco in 1964. The floor had coagulated; the aisles were jammed; one could only inch through the processions. Old Senator Warren Magnuson of Washington, tottering, seemed to be caught in the jam and I tried to clear a way for him by pushing through the crowd. It was then I realized how different it had all become. I was pushing women; it was women who were dominating the floor, bouncing on their chairs, waving banners, shrieking, "Go, Teddy, go. Go! Go! Go!" An old lady of the South Carolina delegation reached out, I noticed, to touch one of the younger women, as if to show affection for a sister displaying the will to claim her rights.

Above, on the rostrum, Tip O'Neill, Speaker of the House, was gaveling, then calling for votes on the disputed platform resolutions. No one on the floor could hear him, no delegate knew what was going on unless he had a portable radio and could hear an explanation from the networks. It was all to be by voice vote, as per the agreement of August 5, and on the podium, the Kennedy and Carter representatives, in touch with their back rooms, policed their deal. It would be to yield to the Kennedy minority on all economic programs except for their demand that the next administration impose wage-price controls. O'Neill called for the ayes and nays above the noise, gaveled as instructed, and proclaimed that he had heard both ayes and nays, deciding the issues already decided in the back rooms.

No other event of magnitude happened on Tuesday, the second day of the convention, except for the revolt of the women, an event of exceptionally large magnitude. Beyond all deals between the Kennedy and Carter camps, the Democratic women had decided to demand a floor vote on two minority reports of their own: first, that the federal government finance abortions for the poor out of Medicaid; second, that the Democratic party "withhold financial support and technical campaign assistance from candidates who do not support the Equal Rights Amendment." On these resolutions, caucuses and lobbies cross-locked beyond candidate control. The teachers, both those for Carter and those for Kennedy, joined together; the black delegates joined with them; as did almost all the women seated in the 50 percent of the seats allotted them by party rules. By voice vote, their resolutions were approved. Said Tim Kraft, Carter's organization manager, the next day, "We were dealing with forces completely out of control," echoing almost exactly the words of Reagan managers in Detroit, facing their women a month before.

Wednesday, then, was to be the day for the renomination of

Jimmy Carter, a ceremony. Carter's name was to be put in nomination by three speakers, carefully chosen. First was Governor D. Robert Graham of Florida, to voice the Southern white vote—still, it was hoped, Carter's base. Next came symbolic characters who gave double credit on the platform. Following Graham came Coretta King, widow of Martin Luther King, Jr., representing both blacks and women; and then Sol Chaikin, president of the International Ladies' Garment Workers' Union, representing both Jews and labor. With that, the stage was cleared for Carter's acceptance speech the next day.

The stands and galleries had been almost empty Wednesday evening. The parties rolled on, from Windows on the World, at the southern tip of Manhattan, to the zoo, on the outer north of the Bronx. At private parties, along Park Avenue and down into Greenwich Village, convention proceedings were watched on television. And so the next night, the convention officials, in order to provide the appropriate background for Carter's acceptance of continued leadership of his party and country, papered the auditorium with passes, so much so that delegates and reporters who arrived late were turned away when Madison Square Garden was closed by the fire department, which felt it had now been packed to danger point.

A full throng was waiting for Carter when he rose to speak on Thursday night. It had been a trying week for him. As usual, his advisers were in conflict. He could give a "hard" speech, attacking Reagan and the Republicans; or a "soft" speech, proclaiming the difference in vision between the two parties. But Kennedy's oration on Tuesday night had been of such thunder that the "hard" position had been preempted; and the basic memo of the campaign, written by Jordan (which held that the election would be won not in the trench pits of the cost-of-living index but by a difference in "vision"), was out of date. Carter, as he had done in the gasoline crisis, tried to patch the two concepts together, and left it, as so often before, to his skilled but hard-pressed speech writer Hendrik (Rick) Hertzberg to fit the prose to a compromise.

"I am proud to run," he began, "on a sound and progressive platform."

At this point, the sound of firecrackers bursting in a corner of the platform terrified those close enough to hear, and the police hustled out a young woman in a black dress. But Carter, with perfect aplomb, continued.

"We will win because we are the party of a great President who knew how to get reelected—Franklin D. Roosevelt," he said. And on through the litany of Democratic greats—Truman, Kennedy, Johnson, down to, unfortunately, "Hubert Horatio Hornblower." Recovering from the fluff, he went on to plead for Senator Kennedy's help: "Ted, your party needs—and I need—your idealism and dedication working for us."

He turned to the theme of different visions, which Hamilton Jordan had advanced.

"We're Democrats. We have had our differences, but we share a bright vision of America's future—a vision of good life for all our people—a vision of a secure nation, a just society, a peaceful world, a strong America—confident and proud and united."

Then on to the other vision, that offered by the Republicans.

"But there is another possible future. In that other future I see despair—the despair of millions who would have to struggle for equal opportunity and a better life—and struggle alone. . . .

"In their [the Republican] fantasy . . . inner-city people, farm workers, and laborers are forgotten. Women, like children, are to be seen but not heard. . . . The elderly do not need Medicare. The young do not need more help for a better education. Workers do not require the guarantee of a healthy and safe place to work. . . ."

On to national defense, peace and strength, the menace of the Soviets.

"A President must act—responsibly. When Soviet troops invaded Afghanistan . . . I suspended some grain sales to the Soviet Union, called for draft registration. . . ."

At this point, some black Kennedy delegates began to boo, and stood up, holding thumbs down on the draft, but they were overcome by cheers of applause from Carter delegates. Soon he was speaking of his efforts in black Africa, and in creating a Middle East accord, then he returned to his domestic record.

"We have slashed government regulation. . . . We have increased our nation's exports dramatically. We reversed the decline in basic research and development. We have created more than eight million new jobs—the biggest three-year increase in history. . . ."

At the mention of jobs, the entire convention broke into hearty and prolonged applause. Then on he went to the continuing vision and enterprise of the 1980s to come, his effort to strengthen family life, another denunciation of the Republicans, as the "party of privilege." On to praise teachers, "eager to explain what a civilization really is." On to his concern for minorities: "I want minority citizens fully to join the mainstream of American life, and I want the blight of discrimination forever wiped away from our land." At this the convention burst into its longest applause.

"Above all," Carter concluded, "I want us to be what the founders of our nation meant us to become—the land of freedom, the land of peace, the land of hope."

On the floor, the banners waved: REAGAN—EAT MY GRITS. BEAT REAGAN—BUY AMERICAN. Southerners stood and waved the Stars and Bars. Pro-life and pro-choice women waved their banners. And up above, in a planned sequence for the television cameras, two huge nets of colored balloons were about to drop. The first balky net slowly tilted, and the balloons trickled out, one by one; the second net was tugged, and tugged again; it would not let go. On the platform, the Carter family appeared, then the Mondale family. Then Carter's campaign chairman, Robert Strauss, began to call to the podium the famous: Coretta King . . . young John Rockefeller, governor of West Virginia . . . Tom Bradley, mayor of Los Angeles . . . Senator Daniel Inouye of Hawaii . . . Dianne Feinstein, mayor of San Francisco . . . John White of Texas . . . Patricia Harris, Secretary of Health and Human Services—a marvelous polychromatic panorama of the Democratic coalition. The band played, Strauss announced the famous, the delegates waited: Would Ted Kennedy appear or not? There are two traditional pictures at the close of every convention: the nominees for President and Vice-President holding hands with arms upraised; then the nominee and the defeated rival hugging each other.

Carter's face was gaunt as he waited for Kennedy's appearance; then the burst of shouts of "We want Ted, We want Ted," announced that the senator was coming. Kennedy's appearance was quick and crisp—what politicians call a "drop-by" to the headquarters of a ward leader who needs a lift. He shuffled onto the platform for a minute. Carter clasped his hand, but Kennedy dodged the traditional hug and greeting. He lifted his hand in a seigneurial wave of goodbye, as if he had appeared at the wedding of his chauffeur, and was gone.

The Reverend King senior gave the closing prayer. The band now played in triumphant rhythm the hymn of black liberation, summoning up those hopes that had stirred the country for twenty years. To the strains of "We Shall Overcome," the conventions were finally over.

Both candidates and both parties would now go on to discuss whether "liberation" meant liberation from government, or whether government was the agent of liberation. But they would be speaking to a nation that had changed from the nation of 1960. And there is no better guide to those changes than the bewildering figures of the Census of 1980, still being sorted out and measured.

CHAPTER TWELVE

WHAT KIND OF PEOPLE
ARE WE?
THE CENSUS OF 1980

Had a satellite from space been cir-
cling the earth every ten years since the coming of colonists to North
America, it would have beamed back a startling panorama of change.
But no more significant change would have shown than in that belt
of fair land between the forty-ninth parallel and the southern gulfs
which came to be known as the United States of America.

The satellite would have shown first the unpeeling of the forests,
the murmuring pines and the hemlocks along the Atlantic shore,
then the clearing of the hardwoods that forested both slopes of the
Appalachians. Then would have followed the squaring of the green
prairies and plains into sections and quarter sections, then the speck-
ling of the valleys with villages that grew into cities. Then, the trac-
ery of iron rails linking east and west coasts, until finally, in 1890, the
satellite would have shown that the entire country below was so
traced by the marks of men that there was no longer any frontier of
settlement.

But only the United States Census could have described what
was happening in those cities below in 1890, what kind of people
lived in them, how they made their livings. And only a historian
could later have described the jolt to the imagination when Americans realized that the frontier had vanished and felt that the land was
full—even though it counted, then, only 63 million people.

But the satellite, in its ten-year orbits, would have kept circling,
picking up more wonders as it went. Lights strung out from city to
city below, from coast to coast. Concrete highways replacing iron

rails, then airplanes blinking, day and night, across the continent. The cities would throb and grow as the countryside emptied—then pulse, then wince, then push out, then withdraw, like amoebae, by their own laws.

By 1960, the satellite would have reported a puzzling new development. The cities were spreading across the horizon in huge metropoles. But, though they were thrusting up the spikes of spectacular tall towers, they were simultaneously spotting with raddled open spaces. By 1980, there could be no doubt: Everywhere in that vast patch of American civilization, from the Atlantic coast to the point where the Mississippi joined the Missouri, rubble, scabs, and tumbled hulks of inner cities were spreading, as if by leprosy. From Boston to Chicago, from Saint Louis to Philadelphia, the large cities of what is called the Northeast quadrangle were being burned out and abandoned. The satellite could not pick out the plumes of smoke or the flares of fire by night; nor could it notice the shattered windowpanes, the desolate streets, the lurking dangers in the areas of abandonment. But nowhere else in the world was there any such sight for the satellite to pick up—of cities gutted and hollowed while no war raged. Down there below was a civilization now undergoing a convulsion like no other in modern times.

The satellite would not, of course, define what was happening in 1980—nor why it was happening in the rich Northeast of the United States, while the Southwest, parched for water, scanty of foliage, seared by a relentless sun, was, apparently, thriving.

That was the job of the United States Bureau of the Census, which was supposed to probe into the innards of change—not only what was happening in the cities, but what was happening to women, to blacks, to families, to the quality of American life, and, in 1980 for the first time, to the entirely new categories in the ethnic composition of the American people.

The census is an American institution supposedly above politics —as is, for example, the Internal Revenue Service, or the United States Army, or the United States Geological Survey. It lies at the opposite extreme from the Supreme Court, always an institution of political judgment masquerading as a council of priests.

The census is, by tradition, supposed to measure, not to judge. In its almost two centuries of existence, it has become the world's finest statistical agency; almost all modern techniques of data retrieval derive from the U.S. Census. In Europe, punch cards for data processing are still called Hollerith cards after Herman Hollerith, the boy genius of the 1880 U.S. Census, who found its data too overwhelming to be counted except by machine. For the 1890 census he developed a punch card system, linked to electric scanning, which revolutionized tabulation. (Later, he founded his own company, one of the roots of today's giant IBM corporation.)

By 1980, the census had gone far beyond Herman Hollerith. Some 275,000 people averaging four dollars an hour in pay would be collecting data on 86 million forms—5,000 tons of paper. These would be reduced to microfilm; and FOSDIC machines would scan the microfilm data at the rate of 900 forms per minute, each family form or individual form scanned in 37 microseconds before being sped electronically to the bureau's computers in Suitland, Maryland, to be sifted for meaning.

But the census by 1980 had grown so important, in a country that lived by measures and quantifications, that it was deep in politics. Its figures determined how the federal government would share approximately $50 billion with cities and states. They would determine, as always, how Congress would allot its seats among the states, and thus determine the shape of the electoral vote. The census determines, by defining neighborhood tracts, how local political districts are drawn, and thus shapes the politics of each state and city. It defines regions, districts, urban centers, by race, income, growth rates. It would cost $1 billion to take the Census of 1980—and all its data would be available on request to marketing agencies who told Japanese how to distribute Yamaha motorcycles, or Germans how to spread Mercedes-Benz dealerships across the country. No other nation was so lavish in inviting strangers to penetrate its markets, or understand them.

The census was under particular new pressures in 1980. Since so many of the huge federal programs of benefits and entitlements were shared by kinship groups, all such groups insisted that the national census count them collectively in their groups. Previously, the census had counted Americans in two chief categories: White and Black/Others. In 1980, however, under immense political pressure, one-fifth of all households counted would be asked to identify themselves by ancestry—as English, or Ukrainian, or Irish, or Chinese, or German, or Lebanese, etc. This left no category for the largest group of all, the undefinable Americans: the children of Irish who had married Italians, Anglos who had married Germans, Lithuanian Jews who had married New England Protestants, and all the others who had cou-

pled to make of their offspring a new American nation. The census
made it clear that no one was compelled to answer the question of
origins; and the complicated results may not be tabulated until after
this book is published. But, said Vincent Barabba, director of the
1980 Census, himself of Italian heritage, ". . . what used to be a
statistical account is now become a social accounting of our society
. . . we've moved to a more pluralistic society where people are now
spending more time identifying themselves with their various heritages and seeking from that either an inner or an outer strength.
. . . Where can we find out about ourselves? Where can we assure
ourselves that we get our fair share? . . . You put a dollar sign in front
of that number now . . . and it's not only a monetary dollar sign, it's
a psychological dollar sign."*

It is best to start with the gross numbers of the 1980 accounting
of the census, for these are the least controversial.

On April 1, 1980, so said the census, there were 226,504,825
Americans. This was a jump of 11.4 percent from the 203,235,298
Americans counted ten years earlier—the smallest percentage rise in
total population since 1940. Of these 226.5 million Americans, 188
million were white, 26 million black, 3.5 million Asian, 1.4 million
Indian, and 7 million others unclassified.

Within these figures were buried some of the grand movements
of American history, most important of which was the Frostbelt-
Sunbelt migration. The states of the Northeast had grown during the
decade at laggard rates and several, for the first time, had shrunken.
The states of the South and West had boomed. The result, according
to the census figures which determine such matters, would be a shift
in political power measured by the allotment of new seats in Congress for the eighties. Seventeen congressional seats would be relocated, with an almost inevitable gain for the Republicans, who dominated the new Sunbelt. All the winners of such seats (eleven states)
were of the South and West, with Florida the biggest gainer (plus
four), Texas next (plus three), California next (plus two). All but one

---

*The 1980 Census, directed by Barabba, was probably the best ever. But political
pressure pushed it beyond reason. Much of its information may be useless nationally;
but in local politics, its figures define clout. "I go to Detroit," said Barabba, ". . . to meet
with the mayor at Dearborn and there's an Arab community sitting in a room . . . it's
a major community . . . they absolutely have to know how many of them there are
so they can understand the extent of the problem. . . . How well off are they? [Should
we] bring in special educational programs? Is it a community that requires special
treatment? Is language a problem? See?"

of the ten losers lay in the Northeast quadrangle. The biggest loser, by far, was the State of New York, which would lose five seats (four in New York City, one in Buffalo). Pennsylvania, Ohio, and Illinois would lose two seats each. At one time, New York had dominated the Union as much by its political weight as by its financial and cultural leadership. Starting in 1810, it had sent the largest of any state's delegation to the House. For years, its forty-five congressmen had held more than one-tenth of all House seats. In 1970, California for the first time outstripped it. By the 1980 Census, New York would have only thirty-four congressmen, and California would have forty-five, a quarter again as much. *Sic transit gloria.*

New York is worth lingering over, for in the 1980 Census it stood out as a disaster area of American demography. Americans had always moved restlessly and had seen various states lose population in previous census counts—but these in times past had been Southern states, Northern prairie states, or Appalachian states. In 1980, however, the only two states to lose population were Rhode Island (down 0.4 percent) and New York, a staggering 3.8 percent, down from 18,241,000 to 17,557,000, a loss of 684,000 people—a loss greater than any ever sustained by any other state in the entire history of the Union. What had drained New York were its promises. Except for the United Kingdom, no political community had ever made such promises to its citizens. But New York could not meet those promises, except by taxing the working and middle classes. New York City's taxes had become the highest in the Union. Simply by moving across the border to Connecticut, a corporation could give every executive a tax saving equal to a 10 percent to 15 percent raise in salary. So people had moved, corporations and individuals alike, writers and artists, executives and clerks, mechanics and machinists, to Connecticut or New Jersey or Pennsylvania—or farther, to Dallas, Houston, Los Angeles.

It was not that New York State was bankrupt. Up the Hudson Valley and around the Finger Lakes, population still grew. Farmers produced an agricultural bounty of milk and dairy products, sweet corn, sour cherries, apples, grapes, vegetables. Outside New York City and other stricken cities, the state's factories produced airplanes, spaceships, paper products, electronic devices, business machines and computers, and myriad wizardries of modern technology. But it was in such centers as Buffalo (down 22.7 percent in population), Rochester (down 18.1 percent), and New York City (down 10.4 percent) that a disaster had taken place. These were the cities that had been penetrated by newcomers who were entitled to the services that the white middle or working class could no longer sustain. New York could not be viewed as one state any longer. New York was several communities—a thriving suburban civilization, a prosperous farming community, and, finally, a desolate, almost helpless system of urban communities.

From the plight of New York, the figures of the census led on to the plight of the other urban centers of the Northeast, where American civilization seemed powerless to reverse the crumbling going on.

Spot the finger anywhere on the map of the cities of the Northeast: what was happening was almost too complex to describe. One could start at the western limit with Saint Louis, once the fourth-largest city of the United States, where the Mississippi and the Missouri join under a stainless-steel arch which is a masterpiece of American architecture. Saint Louis surpassed New York in misfortune. It had dropped from a peak population of 857,000 in 1950, to 622,000 in 1970, and then to 453,000 in 1980—a falloff in a single decade of 27.2 percent! Cleveland had dropped in the decade by 23.6 percent, Baltimore by 13.1 percent, Pittsburgh by 21 percent, Detroit by 20.5 percent, Philadelphia by 13.4 percent, Chicago by 10.8 percent, Washington, D.C., by 15.7 percent, and so on across the map of the Northeast.

To describe what was happening, the census limited itself to bare-bone figures. And those figures showed that the internal changes in the cities, the changing nature of the population, the new waves of migrants both legal and illegal, were persuading the white working people to leave their communities. New York City, for example, had lost only 10.4 percent of its total population, down from 7,895,000 in 1970 to 7,071,000 in 1980. But that population was utterly different in street sound, and street color, from the old population that had lived there a generation before. In 1950, whites had made up 86 percent of the population, "nonwhites" only 14 percent. By 1980, black population had risen to 1,784,000, Hispanic to 1,406,000, and in a single decade, Asians had more than doubled (from 94,500 to 231,500). But between 1970 and 1980, New York City's white population had dropped by 30 percent, from 6,091,000 to 4,293,000. Census and city officials disagreed in their figures of social change, since the census was condemned to sort people out both ethnically and racially, and missed hundreds of thousands of minorities and "illegals." Depending on whose figures one accepted, a minimum of 2,000 whites or a maximum of 4,000 had left New York

City *every single week of the decade.* White flight was an overbearing phenomenon everywhere, but figures were starker in other cities. In Detroit, for example, 838,800 white people had been counted in 1970; by 1980 only 413,700 remained. More than half had left.

From Los Angeles on the west coast, to Boston on the east, the pattern of changing population repeated itself. "Los Angeles," said Dr. Franklin Murphy, one of the sovereign wise men of that city, "used to be a dull gray city of transplanted Midwesterners. Now it's an Oriental carpet of colored stripes." By 1980, the white population of Los Angeles had dropped to 1,816,500, while its black population had risen to 505,200, its Hispanics to 816,000, its Orientals to 644,900 (more than a fourfold increase in one decade). In Los Angeles's public schools, only one-fifth of the children were white—122,500, as against 257,500 Hispanics, 120,400 blacks, 40,700 Orientals. In Boston, which, over the century and a half since the Protestants burned down a Catholic convent, has alternately been a citadel of intolerance and a bastion of liberal hope, the white population in the decade had dropped from 524,700 to 394,000—while blacks had grown to 126,000, Hispanics to 36,000, and Asians to 42,850. Boston was still fundamentally a white city, due to its student population and the tenacious Irish and Italians. But Baltimore was no longer a city of white majority; nor was Detroit; nor Washington; nor Atlanta; nor Chicago; nor San Antonio; nor New Orleans; nor half a dozen smaller cities. There was no way of avoiding the recognition: blacks, Hispanics, and Orientals would put the white population of all other central cities into a minority within years. Of the ten largest cities in the United States, none could evade this prospect in the next decade unless policies changed. But if one attempted to change policies, one would have to ask the beginning question: Is it good or bad to have metropolitan centers dominated by minority cultures so different from the general culture outside them?

These, then, were the clearest of the figures of the Census of 1980. Such figures are the handbook of politicians, the bible of political scientists. These, perhaps, were the most important figures for analysts planning the 1980 campaign. But such naked figures had to be clothed in meaning and further sorted to give some sense of the shapes emerging and divisions widening in a universe of 226 million individuals struggling, as Americans always had, to become a nation.

To provide such meaning, thus, the United States Census also prepared and published in December of 1980 its long-awaited study of the Social Indicators of the United States, attempting to describe the new trends developing, new problems rising over the horizon, the quality of life changing.

It is best to begin with the simplest matters when we approach something as indefinable as the quality of life. Culture always cups politics; and so, in the culture of America of the seventies, the most sweeping force moving on politics, as unsettling as the entry of the blacks into the arena in the 1960s, was the entry of women into the mainstream of American life.

The entry of women was more penetrating, more subtly disruptive of old values, than in any other country in the world. Not Israel, not Britain, not any country of the West, could match the speed with which American women were asserting, and gaining, their demand for recognition and leadership.

For the director of the census, Barabba, this surge of women was the most significant change the census would report: "What women are doing with their lives . . . once they've decided they're going to do things other than be housewives, it has an unbelievable ripple effect . . . relative to employment, relative to the number of kids being born, relative to the number of . . . schools you need, relative to the number of housing units being formed, a whole mess of things. That one event . . . has tremendous impact."

But statistics only faintly reflected what was going on in the decade. By 1976, women could count two elected governors—Dixy Lee Ray in Washington, Ella Grasso in Connecticut, both Democrats. By 1980, two women, both Republican, were sitting in the U.S. Senate. Women could count, as we have noted, half the delegates at the 1980 Democratic convention (29 percent at the Republican). The first women presidents were assuming leadership of American universities and colleges. Almost every major American corporation— or so it seemed—had set out on a frantic chase for symbolic females to sit on their boards. Organized religions were yielding. Conservative Jews now counted women in the ceremonial *minyan* or quorum of ten required for worship. Female rabbis were moving into the pulpit. By 1976, the House of Deputies of the Episcopal Church had authorized the ordination of women as bishops and priests. The Conference of United States Catholic Bishops declared in Rome that the Church must acknowledge that "men and women were equal in the eyes of God and of the Church."

The armed services had fallen into step. In 1972, the first coeds were admitted to Reserve Officer Training Corps across the country.

By 1976, President Ford had signed into law a bill abolishing sex discrimination in the service academies, and so West Point, Annapolis, the Air Force and Coast Guard academies admitted their first female plebes and cadets and set them on their way, they hoped, to eventual high command. By 1977, the army had opened missile and combat-support duty to women in what, in war, would be zones of danger. By 1978, the navy shipped out its first seaborne women ensigns. That year, too, the White House honor guard included women in the same dress blues as men, with the same weapons training. By 1981, the first woman Justice would sit on the Supreme Court. In 1950, only 23 million women had ever worked outside their homes, a figure inflated by the transitory war need for woman power. By 1978, that figure had grown to 48 million and was ever rising.

It was impossible to measure the change that had come in American life with the thrust of women toward careers and identities, nor give the color or fragrance of the change—and thus the census was reduced to figures in measuring the surge of women in American life.

The first and most glaring of the measurable changes began with the family—and babies. Americans had lived through a baby boom for fifteen years after the war, the peak birth count coming in the late 1950s, with 4.3 million babies a year. In those days, American girls married young. Now American women were marrying later and later, having babies as often in their thirties as their twenties; by 1978, they were bringing to life only 3.3 million babies each year, lowering the birthrate from a postwar high of 23.7 per thousand to 15.3.

This baby dearth could be regarded either as a sadness or as a phenomenon of liberation—but when cast against the aging of the population as a whole, it forecast a convulsion in the Social Security system. The Social Security system had expanded again and again since its establishment in 1935, always against a perspective of growing population, rising production and productivity. But in 1950, for every hundred children under fifteen, there were only thirty old folks over sixty-five. By 1978, there were forty-seven. Most of the old people were dependent on pensions and Social Security. But just as surely as the postwar baby boom had pumped up the working force paying into Social Security, the baby dearth of the seventies would reduce that force. The number of Americans sixty-five and older had been only 12,334,000 in 1950; the number in 1980 had grown to 25,544,000. The number would be half as large again twenty years hence. If the number of working people declined, who would pay for the growing number of elderly? (It was in his attempt to confront the reality of the Social Security problem that Ronald Reagan was to suffer the first defeat of his new presidency.) By 1980, the life expectancy of an American female had grown to an unprecedented seventy-seven years. These old ladies could be expected to grow in numbers and unhappiness; but proportionately, they voted more than any other group in America. If the system could not provide the love and warmth of children and grandchildren, it nonetheless must care for the aged. Grandmother care would become one of the saddest problems of the eighties and nineties. Their families were finding it more and more difficult to care for them, for families were growing smaller, and the extended family, where grandparents, parents, and toddlers all lived together, was a vanishing phenomenon. In 1970, the census had reported the average American household as 3.11 persons. By 1980, the average was down to 2.75 persons, the smallest figure ever.

Now, what was a household? The sexual revolution had caused a total change of definition. In every big city, developers were building "singles" barracks, where young people lived alone. Even more significant, both young and old of opposite sexes were living together as unmarried couples. The number of such couples doubled in the decade. By 1981 the census would report that, for the first time in history, less than 60 percent of households would shelter a married couple under the same roof.

The figures the census offered were vivid with understated drama. In 1940 (in a country slightly more than half its present size), the census had counted 1,596,000 marriages and only 264,000 divorces—count six for love, and one for hope betrayed. By 1948, as the postwar marriages settled down, the count was 1,811,000 for marriage and 408,000 for divorce, four and a half to one. By 1975, it was 2,153,000 for marriage, 1,036,000 for divorce. And by 1978, it had become two for troth to one for parting. Way back in 1910, when the census first began to measure marriages and divorces, the figure had been ten for love, only one for parting.

There was no doubt that marriages were no longer considered permanent, and as a corollary, families were ever more shaky. Nature had not lost its lovely human magnetisms; men and women wanted to be together; most still wanted babies. But women were tugged and torn by the developing economy and the expanding horizons of education. The nation was moving from a blue-collar production economy, where muscle counted, to a service economy, where brains, training, and personality counted. Skills counted most, and education offered skills. By 1980, the census could report for the first time that women were pursuing higher education with an ardor surpassing men's: There were now 5,480,000 men in colleges but college women numbered 5,900,000. Nor did these women want to be burdened by babies as their older sisters had: Young married women in 1979 expected (or wanted) only 2.2 children; only twelve years earlier, they had hoped for 2.9 children.

The census did not explore causes for this revolt of women. Rosie the Riveter of the World War II working class had, probably, liked her job and, more important, the pay and the companionship of the shop. She had passed on such memories to her daughters, who found the stitching of computer circuits more rewarding than stitching patches on the pants of toddlers or teenagers. The young women of the seventies whose parents had sent them to college in the turbulent 1960s had found their talents equal to those of the young men they met there; and they meant to use those talents to seek an identity more their own than that of housewife.

The effect of this devouring change showed everywhere. Fast-food chains spread all across the country because women who worked all day (and 43 percent of all women with preschool-age children did work in 1979!) were too tired to come home at night and cook for man and child. On weekends, these fast-food establishments were overwhelmed by families, whose tired mothers claimed the right of relief from housekeeping on their weekends. On television, the decade of the 1970s had enjoyed the arrival of women as news personalities—not just any women, of course, because television chooses only the pretty ones to show on air (plain women are, perhaps, the most discriminated-against subgroup in America). Their arrival, first on local shows, then on national networks and morning, noon, and evening news programs, had given them (whether brilliant and pretty or stupid and pretty) an authority which enlarged their personal self-esteem and the status of women generally. And as more and more women went off to work, the daytime soap operas, on which politicians had advertised their wares, shrank in audience. Politicians had to reach these new working women on the terms they set themselves—as citizens, clamorous with their own demands, even though these demands might contradict each other, as did the men's. The "liberation" of women had changed the thinking of America and of American politics more than any other force except the rise of the ethnics—and it would take years to sort out their demands, from the real and necessary to the fanciful and preposterous.

The silent majority of women still wanted marriage, still tended children, still felt that the design of a child's life was as rewarding as an architect's design of a new building. But this domestic majority could not outvoice the growing minority of women who felt that their identity lay beyond the kitchen, the home, and the playpen. And the chief victims of this growing dissolution of family were not the lonesome old people, but the children of the dissolution.

Few figures are more poignant than those on one-parent households. The sterile term "one-parent household" conceals the anguish of mating breakups. It almost always means a family in which the mother alone takes care of the children (and sometimes holds a job as well), the father having left, or been dismissed. In the decade of 1970 to 1979, such one-parent family groups soared by 79 percent! In 1970, only 11 percent of all families were headed by a single parent, almost always the mother. By 1979, that figure had almost doubled to 19 percent. In the America of 1978, 22 percent of all children under eighteen were growing up in such homes. And as we sift the statistics, we come upon the tragedy of black children, a tragedy impossible to ignore. In 1960, 31 percent of all black children were growing up in homes with only one parent caring for them. By 1978, that figure had swollen to aching dimension—56 percent of all black children were growing up in fatherless homes. For them, the street was school, the asphalt the jungle, the love that must warm children as the sun does flowers was generally absent.

Yet one must add a happy footnote to the otherwise dismal statistics of family life. Though marriages were breaking up faster than ever before, those who remained married displayed a comforting counteropinion. When asked in a 1978 survey to rate their range of satisfaction with life, 84 percent of the still-married respondents declared that their area of greatest satisfaction was their marriage. (It should be noted that the lowest area of satisfaction of those queried was their savings, a reflection of the devastation of inflation.)

Skimming the figures in the census's massive outpouring of data, one could note only here and there other changes in the quality of life that politicians had to heed in 1980.

In education, Americans had made one of their greatest of all exertions; the proportion of the gross national product spent for primary and secondary education rose from 3.4 percent in 1951 to 7.7 percent in 1976. It now cost something more than $1,800 a year to educate each student in a public elementary or secondary school. Education at all levels was the largest enterprise in the nation—63.8 million Americans were either students or teachers. The teachers had become, thus, as potent a political force in both parties as, say, the Teamsters Union; a politician would disregard them at his peril. And the teachers had much to defend. Elementary school enrollments were dropping with the birthrate; but the number of teachers had increased by 337,000 in the last twenty years (slimming down the average class size from 28.4 pupils to 21.7). To protect and advance their interests, teachers had extorted from the Carter administration a new cabinet Department of Education.

In health, the indicators also showed rewards. The percentage of the gross national product spent on health and health services had risen from 5.9 percent in 1955 to 8.8 percent by 1977. But life spans had increased, and the poor and elderly particularly were getting better and better publicly supported nursing and medical attention, despite the gross inefficiency of the two great new programs, Medicaid and Medicare. Public health education and government programs scored real successes in the past decade. Americans, wary of heart disease, had learned to beware of cholesterol. They ate, per capita, 10 percent fewer eggs than twenty years earlier, 28 percent less butter, 21 percent less milk and cream. The number of adults who exercised regularly was up 92 percent. They smoked substantially less—28 percent fewer smokers among adult men, 13 percent fewer among adult women.

Environment, along with education and health care, was another of the sacred causes of the 1970s—a concern scarcely present outside Los Angeles twenty years before. The federal government had spent $3,701 billion to protect and police the environment in 1973; by 1978, it had pushed that figure to $11,024 billion. Here there was occasion for some rejoicing. The chief polluters of the air are automobiles, with their carbon monoxide and particulates. By 1980, the air was visibly clearer, though the census reported that the scientific measure of air pollution was only "slightly" lower than at the beginning of the decade. As for water pollution, no conclusive results were evident, although spot observations of coho returning to Lake Michigan, of salmon running along the Atlantic coast into the rivers of New England, the return of aquatic life to the once "dead" Lake Erie, were signs of hope. In measuring environmental quality, it must be remembered how rapidly the postwar boom had fouled the air and water of America. Instead of getting worse, the national effort had at least arrested, and possibly reversed, the deterioration. Moreover, the American people approved of the effort. By 1978, 52 percent of those surveyed thought the federal government was spending too *little* on the environment. What Americans now complained of most, in the metropolitan areas, was noise pollution and inadequate street lighting.

Beyond such statistical measures of quality of life were vaguer figures, and disturbing guesses. One could guess, as the surgeon general's office did in December of 1980, that teenage pregnancies would burden the nation for years to come. Every year, a million teenagers, two out of three unmarried, became pregnant, producing poorly cared for children. This resulted in an 80 percent school dropout rate among the mothers, thus condemning children and mothers alike to the cycle of poverty. Already, one out of every ten children in America was being nourished by the federal welfare program Aid to Families with Dependent Children. What the cycle would do in coming decades to this enormous and growing problem was unpredictable. While pro-choice debated pro-life advocates in the middle classes of America, the underclasses continued to produce a larger share of unplanned babies in a diminishing baby total; the federal government would have to pay for their care.*

Of the other changes in American life which politicians would have to grip, then formulate policies, there are few, or rubbery, measurements. No measurements, for example, for the rise in the population of gay men and women, which, in such cities as San Francisco, dominated politics, and in other cities, like New York

---

*The general tables on rising illegitimacy over the past decade are startling. In 1970, 398,700 children had been born out of wedlock. In 1979, that figure had grown to an estimated 597,800. Though white women were increasing their rate of illegitimacy faster than blacks, black women still bore almost six times as many babies out of wedlock per 1,000 childbearing women. In total, white women gave birth to 263,000 out-of-wedlock babies, black women to 315,800.

The social and cultural import of this difference between the races in mating styles frightens the imagination. In several states, the development of a fatherless black cohort of young people is startling. In Delaware, 63.1 percent of all black babies were born out of wedlock in 1979; in Pennsylvania 66.3 percent. In cities, the problem grows sharper. In Washington, D.C., whose population is 68 percent black, 64 percent of all black babies were born out of wedlock. In New York, in central Harlem, 77 percent of all children were born out of wedlock; in Mott Haven of the South Bronx, an area of Hispanics and blacks, 65 percent of all babies were born out of wedlock. By comparison, in Flushing, Queens, predominantly white, only 7 percent were out-of-wedlock births. All of these children must be nourished, cared for, and loved. The state must, in the interest of its tranquility, assume this responsibility.

and Boston, developed increasing influence. No real measurements of the uses of increasing leisure time, which, apparently, was still concentrated at the end of the decade (as at its beginning) on television.

There is one last hard measurement that must be included in the changes in the quality of life, the most morbid measurement of all, that of crime, fear, and violence—always a sharp-edged political issue.

Americans have been called a violent people—all too often. But Americans had had to fight their way across the continent, each settler defending his cabin or homestead with rifle and determination against the "hostiles." The firearm was once a tool of living, because it provided not only safety but also hides, fur, and meat for the family. But the gun had now been turned against other Americans, along with the knife and other instruments of violence.

Americans had increasingly, in the 1970s, both grumbled at and demanded more anticrime measures. The public had been annoyed when, in 1972, Richard Nixon had set up electronic gates and scanning booths at every airport to eliminate the menace of hijackers of airplanes, which now carried 80 percent of all public intercity passenger travel in the United States (as against only 3 percent in 1940). But the measure had worked and air travelers now accepted the momentary delays as necessary and even good. Electronic search had proved the most effective mechanical anticrime device in all the arsenal of law enforcement, second only to the self-enforcing stop-go, red-green lights that regulated street traffic. But no mechanical device could protect Americans from what they feared most—the random violence in their neighborhoods, parks, suburbs, and cities. No one could untwine the roots of the senseless crime, the drug-crazed crime, the racially inspired crime, the crime of passion. But here, in their home places, Americans' quality of life had deteriorated, in some places to nightmare. The census had collected various survey measurements of fear of crime. In 1967, one in three people had reported that they dared not walk alone at night within one mile of their home. A decade later, that figure had grown to 45 percent; and by 1980, for which data is not yet available, the figure was probably approaching half.

The fear was justified. Murder is usually taken as the most solid index of crime, because the action leaves a body behind. Most analysts focus on New York City: its police figures are probably the best in the nation. New Year's Day of 1980 opened the presidential year in New York with no less than eleven people killed. By the end of the year, 1,814 people had been killed, an all-time record, in a city which during the decade had lost 10 percent of its population. But New York was far from the most murderous city in the country. That ugly honor was held by New Orleans, followed by Houston, then by Saint Louis, with New York ranking a lowly thirteenth in killings per capita among America's killer cities. By all odds, the most dangerous city in the United States was Saint Louis, first in muggings and knifings, second in robberies, third in murder per capita. It was not at all coincidental that Saint Louis had suffered the largest loss of population of any major city of the United States, although Miami, writhing under the inpouring of Cubans, Haitians, and illegals, was approaching a condition of violence that soon might make that once-tranquil city into the nation's worst. Miami had counted 134 murders in 1979; by December of 1980, the count was 235, and rape was up by 200 percent.

The overall national picture was bleak. Between 1960 and 1978, the number of violent crimes (murder, rape, mugging, robbery) had multiplied three times. Where fear most sharply stabbed at perception and provoked flight was in the big cities. And there, inescapably, one could not blink at the reality. Where minorities—blacks and Hispanics—congregated, violence spurted. True enough that most black crimes were perpetrated against other blacks in the big cities; true that the homicide rate was 60 per 100,000 among black males, and only 9 per 100,000 among white males. But an inescapable conclusion rose from the figures—that the speeding breakup of black and minority families was putting on the streets young people who were a danger to all.

The plague was everywhere. Colleges reported an increase in on-campus rape. Bank robberies increased. On August 30, two weeks after the Democratic convention had left New York, the city suffered no less than eleven bank robberies in a single day, raising the total for the convention month to 137. Car thefts were now everyday events across the nation, up 2.6 times since 1960; but burglary and larceny-theft were even more common, according to the FBI's *Uniform Crime Reports.* Suburbanites now carefully locked their doors at night, and even in rural areas, people were installing burglar alarms; the market value of stocks in companies producing such security systems rose almost as fast as those of the fast-food chains. The *Uniform Crime Reports*—compiled nationally by the FBI—are considered unreliable by everyone, including the Department of

Justice, which does its own special surveys to measure crime unreported to the FBI. But the Gallup Poll produced its own figures in November of 1980—and its sampling indicated that one of every five American households had been hit by crime of one kind or another in the past year.

Crime, by 1980, was a universal pestilence. Crime ran through Congress (six congressmen and one senator were convicted in the Abscam trials alone); crime ran through state legislatures and city halls; crime infested the unions and the banks; crime ran through the white-collar bureaucracies and the new computorial elites alike. How much was due to inflation, which as it devalues money opens an invitation to all forms of cheating; how much was due to films and television, which feature violence as the high point of drama; how much was due to the values of new arrivals in the culture of American cities—all these were debatable.

No amount of learning could unsnarl the figures. It was certain that handguns were responsible for most killing crimes, and the handgun and the knife together for most threats of crime. The first and most necessary step in crime control was gun control. But politics were powerless to enforce that truth. The gun lobby controlled district after district, where its single-minded advocates could make or unmake congressmen. Even the President of the United States, himself nearly killed by a handgun, would not challenge the gun lobby. Behind the hardware—100 million handguns in private hands—were attitudes of mind. There were all those poor and underprivileged who watched the world of fashion and comfort unroll on the television screen—and yearned for their share of cash or notoriety. There were the veterans of the Vietnam War, unhonored and unrecognized, resentful yet combat wise. There were the mentally unbalanced, heated to action by private stimuli.

Learned commissions and stately investigations examined the condition. For twenty years, the humanitarian view had prevailed, from the Supreme Court to the police beat—reducing penalties, restricting police action, seeking remedies for crime in gallant crusades against poverty, discrimination, and ignorance. But none of the humanitarian remedies had slowed what seemed an endemic and worsening condition of American life. A salient fact stood out—we were a country with more violent individuals than any other Western nation, and our crime rate ran higher. The second most violent of the world's main nations was Canada—but our murder rate was four times as high as Canada's, and ten times higher than that of Ireland, of Italy, of the United Kingdom—source countries of American origin.

We come then to another underswell of change in America and what could become catastrophe—the tide of immigration, legal and illegal, pouring into this country.

For this underswell, neither the census nor any other authority can provide fully reliable measurement. One starts with the obvious: that the United States has lost one of the cardinal attributes of sovereignty—it no longer controls its own borders. Its immigration laws are flouted by aliens and citizens alike, as no system of laws has been flouted since Prohibition. And the impending transformation of our nation, its culture, and its ethnic heritage could become one of the central debates of the politics of the 1980s.

The debate must touch every one of the many-twined roots of American nationhood, and hurt—for it is a matter of conscience against reality, of tradition against facts, of right against right. For this writer, whose father came to America as an immigrant boy of sixteen almost a century ago, it is particularly painful. Ours, as John F. Kennedy wrote, is a nation of immigrants. To reexamine, reverse, or discipline that tradition must wrench all our hearts.

One must begin with several overwhelming conditions: The first is the outside world. That world seems to be doubling in population every thirty years, some nations even faster. In the arid countries of the tropics, in the paddy fields of Asia, in the forest clearings of the world, in the villages where people still lug buckets from muddy wells, where children die from contaminated water and the old die of malnutrition, the pressure is on: to move. To the pressure of hunger is added the other force of thrust: the terrors. Ours is a truly free country, and a generous country. Those who flee in leaky boats from Haiti, those who slip across the passage from Cuba to the Florida Keys, those who escape or are pushed off unwillingly by the racist regime that governs Vietnam, those who wriggle their way out of the Soviet tyranny—all know that the place of refuge is the United States, where the streets are paved with gold and free hospitals for the sick. To these conditions is added the heraldry of modern times—the television that lures people to the golden land, and the airplane which gets them there in a few hours' flight. The earlier immigrants from Europe spent weeks trekking to ports, and then more weeks in the steerage of tramp steamers, to reach the promised land. A modern immigrant can be here in three or four hours from any airport in the Caribbean, in fifteen hours from Asia. A ticket from Asia costs under $1,000, a ticket from the Caribbean only $200 or $300. It once took years of work and savings for an honest man to buy passage for his family to join him. Now, after six months in the United States, a diligent immigrant can afford air passage for all the rest of his family.

The result has been a stampede, almost an invasion. The United States accepts twice as many immigrants—counting legal immigrants only—as all the rest of the world combined. By 1979, the United States had accepted 373,747 Vietnamese refugees—while Japan, a highly prosperous country, had taken in only 276. Half of the entire population increase of the United States in the past decade came from the tide of immigration. And immigration is now running at a higher total than in any other decade of American history. By the law of 1978, only 270,000 immigrants in quota categories were allowed to come to the United States each year; but the President was permitted to admit any number of "refugees" above that. In 1977, the United States admitted 462,000 legal immigrants and refugees; in 1978, 601,000; and in 1980, an estimated 808,000.

It is only for such legal immigrants that we have reliable figures. But these figures are startlingly significant as a change in the ethnic flow in American life. Briefly, America has experienced four great waves of immigrants. The original European settlers were chiefly British and Scots-Irish. They were followed by a second wave, from Ireland and Germany. And then by a third wave, from northern Europe, chiefly Scandinavians. The final wave, before the closing of the gates in 1924, was from southern and eastern Europe—Poles, southern Slavs, Italians, Jews. Then for half a century, the melting pot and the war brought Americans to a common and new culture.

Americans are now entertaining entirely new ethnic migrations —chiefly from Caribbean and Asian states. Whether these new immigrants can, as did the earlier waves, bridge the gap between their own cultures and the European culture which in the past shaped American life is the great social experiment of our times. Certainly, hundreds of thousands can—but in what proportion, and what of those who cannot?

The change in origin and quality of the immigrant flow to America in the last few decades is profiled in figures. In 1965, before the passage of the Immigration Act of that year, legal immigrants into the United States still resembled those who had come before. Canadians led (with 38,327); next came Mexicans (with 37,969); then British (with 27,358); then Germans (with 24,045), out of a total of 296,697.

The Immigration Act of 1965 changed all previous patterns, and in so doing, probably changed the future of America. Immigration laws of the previous forty years had rested on the idea of "national origins": New immigrants should reflect the ethnic composition of the nation already here. The new act of 1965 was noble, revolutionary—and probably the most thoughtless of the many acts of the Great Society. It conceived of America as being open to all the world, its sources of fresh arrivals determined not by those already here, but by the push and pressures of those everywhere who hungered to enter. In wiping out statutory discrimination against Asian immigrants, a blow against racism, it was to reduce dramatically the traditional European sources of American heritage. No country, said the legislation, could send to the United States in any one year more than 20,000 people. Any nation, so denominated by the United Nations, could send the same number—20,000—including all the former colonies of European imperialism, large or small, from Asia, the West Indies, Africa. By 1978, interpretation of the law had so changed that the 20,000 legal limit had become a fiction, and the sources of legal immigration read as follows: (1) Mexico, with 92,000; (2) Vietnam, with 88,000; (3) the Philippines, with 37,000; (4) Cuba, with 30,000; (5) Korea, with 29,000; (6) China-Taiwan, with 21,000; (7) India, with 20,000; and so on down the line, for a legally admitted total of 601,-442. Well down the list came the chief source of America's original immigrants, the British (with 14,200); and of the fourth-wave immigrants, only the Italians placed in the first fifteen (as the fifteenth), with 7,400. From such figures came echoes of a distant past. In the seven years of the starvation (1847 through 1854), the Irish had sent 1,186,000 people to an America that then held a total population of only 26,561,000. They had averaged, in those sailing-ship days, 148,-250 immigrants a year. By 1980, only 982 Irish immigrated to the United States (plus 410 from troubled Ulster). The new immigration law was changing the texture of American life.

The change in the nation's texture brought by the Asian-Caribbean migration wave showed most in the cities. New York's shrinking population included, nonetheless, a rise in legally counted Asians from 94,500 to 231,500, a jump of 250 percent in the past decade. Korean greengrocers with their arrays of fresh fruits and vegetables, Chinese restaurants with their scarlet and black facades, Indian boutiques offering native handicrafts, had multiplied all across the city. Spanish, far more than Yiddish or Italian had ever been, was the second language in midtown Manhattan. In Chicago, the presence of Hispanics was more than ever evident, as was the presence of the newly arrived Arabs in Detroit. Los Angeles had, in effect, ceased to be a community of European culture, although no one could guess what would emerge from a city that now clustered Hindus and blacks, Koreans and Japanese, Mexicans and Filipinos, Vietnamese and Israelis. The city was still held together by the old culture expressed in its two dominant newspapers (the *Times* and the *Herald-Examiner*), the common law descended from England, the laws of the United States, and the roads of American engineering. A new Athens might emerge—or a new Calcutta. From their heights in Beverly Hills and Pasadena, people of the older culture might look down on the seething below, but could only wonder. They sped on their freeways to the new Civic Center or to work, and drove home at night to their safe hills or suburbs.

But the change in character of immigration to America could be only roughly defined by the 1980 Census. It could not measure the influx of illegal or "undocumented" aliens. Illegal aliens escaped the 1980 Census count although they were guaranteed every protection by the counters. Thus, at this point an observer must leave the uncertain realm of figures and move on to the total murk of guesswork.

Those "illegals" or "undocumenteds" who came to this country in the decade since 1970 are probably more numerous, more abused, and more law-evading than the number who came through legally. They may number as many as twelve million or as few as three million. No one knows. The general consensus of scholars is that somewhere between three million and eight million furtive and hopeful illegal residents now live in the United States.

The problem of the illegals is *de jure,* one of law enforcement —or of law definition. But the problem *de facto* torments the soul with a plea for understanding, mercy, and realism.

It is generally accepted that the southern border of our country has become porous almost to the condition of nonexistence. And the chief invasion comes from that two-thousand-mile stretch which separates Mexico from the United States. Since that pressure from Latin America *does* insist on change in American institutions rather than acceptance of them, we shall return to the Hispanic demand later.

But it should be noted that our porous southern border is not the only zone of illegal entry to American rights and privileges.

At any point on the perimeter of the United States, those who flee from hunger or danger find easy entry. A French-speaking Haitian can either venture the eight-hundred-mile crossing in a leaky boat to Miami, or purchase a five-hundred-dollar round-trip ticket (half of it recoverable) to Montreal. In Canada, he can get a visitor's visa and buy a clandestine bus ride south, drop off half a mile from the Vermont border, walk through the lovely New England woods, get picked up by his bus on the safe side of the border, and move on —to Boston, perhaps, or to that tolerant city, New York. Or if the illegal is a citizen of the British commonwealth, from Pakistan or India, he can buy an air ticket to Ontario, contact a smuggler, take the bus to Windsor, cross the Canadian border by taxi to Detroit, where he simply disappears. World shipping is dominated by the Japanese, but almost all ships that fly Third World flags are largely manned by Chinese. This world shipping congregates at the Port of New York. It is said that half the Chinese crews who enter New York do not leave with their ships. They go overside and disappear in New York's Chinatown—where they are, forever, undetectable. By law, the United States permits only six hundred Hong Kong Chinese to enter each year because Hong Kong is a British colony. (An estimated five thousand more from Hong Kong manage to obtain British or other passports.) And in any ten-block area of New York's Chinatown, one can find twice more than six hundred Hong Kong Chinese serving in Chinese restaurants, speaking the dialect of their origin.

The complications in coping with illegal penetration of the United States are infinite. There are 272 million legal crossings of the American borders every single year. Overwhelmingly these crossings are simply routine—by tourists from around the world come to see the sights; by Mexicans with shopping permits to buy in American stores; or by Canadians who go back and forth to work in their sister country. Or students. And of students much more might be said: of English students, of Nigerian students, of Asian students. They come on student visas and they stay. A single figure illuminates the story. Of the 16,000 Taiwanese students admitted to the United States between 1962 and 1969, only 3 percent ever returned to their Chinese homeland. The others chose to remain.

It is quite clear that the Mexican penetration of the American border is not the only problem—but it remains, as all know, the chief problem. It is a condition of shame to Americans—and to the migrants, of sorrow, squalor, brutality, growing worse with the passing of years.

There are 6,000 miles of unfortified United States border frequently penetrated by "illegals," plus of course other entry points, such as the Florida coasts. At any given moment, the number of border patrolmen along our Mexican border is only 350, approximately the same number of patrolmen who walk the limited perimeter of the United States Capitol in Washington. The total budget of the United States Border Patrol—$77 million a year—is less than the police budget of Baltimore; and the patrol has only three helicopters and twenty-eight light planes to watch the lines. Illegal migrants from Mexico pass unnoticed all along the border—but half come through three relatively safe points: El Paso, Texas; Yuma, Arizona; and San Diego, California. Others, who cross through the deserts of the Southwest, riding hobo trains or guided by smugglers called "coyotes," suffer humiliation and torment beyond the tolerance of American conscience. Thirteen Salvadorans were found dead of thirst in 1980 in the Arizona desert; they had made their way through Mexico, then lost the way on this side of the border. Others, imported by American farmers as "stoop labor," may be reduced to a peonage close to slavery. Still others are raped on the way, or beaten, or robbed. The wave from fecund Mexico to the United States is almost a force of nature. Try as it will, the Immigration and Naturalization Service of the United States can do little to protect a boat filling with water faster than it can be bailed out. In 1979, the INS apprehended 1,058,000 illegal entrants into the United States; of these, 976,000 were Mexicans.

The census was of little help in grappling with the problem of Hispanics. It showed only that between 1970 and 1980, people of "Spanish Origin" in the United States had grown from 9,072,000 to 14,605,000. But it made no pretense that it had counted the illegals; and made no definition of the phrase "Spanish Origin." What "Spanish" or "Hispanic" means, no one knows. And it is difficult to discuss the gap in cultures between the new Mexican-Caribbean immigration and the European-based culture of the United States without exposing oneself to the charge of racism. But since the first of the great movements of Mexican-American expression called itself *La Raza*, "The Race," one must accept that self-definition of the race, more generally known as the "brown people," as distinct from the "white people" and the "black people" of America. Latin-Americans (including Mexicans) may be of one or several racial origins—African, Aztec, Spanish, Caribbean Indian. But they are all lumped together for statistical purposes as "Hispanic," or "Hispanic Surnames."

All, by recent regulations, are entitled to special rights, because of previous discrimination against them; compensatory action is required to remedy past injustice. The "Hispanics" so entitled may be fresh out of Spain from Barcelona; or Argentines, whom we, as Americans, never wronged. They may be Sephardic Jews whose names end with "ez," as in Lopez, or a vowel, as in Cardozo—entitled to rights not extended to Jews of European heritage whose names end with a "sky" or an "ovitz."

Some Hispanics have, however, made a demand never voiced by immigrants before: that the United States, in effect, officially recognize itself as a bicultural, bilingual nation. Puerto Rico, a "commonwealth" within the Union, is Spanish-speaking. In every state, however, immigrants have had to learn to speak English. If they chose, as did the Germans and the Jews, to teach their children the mother tongue, such communities themselves supported private schools or evening schools, where children might learn the language and tradition of their heritage. Japanese-Americans and Chinese-Americans have recently begun to follow this honorable practice—sending their children to public schools and universities, but preserving by their own effort the language of heritage. The demand of the migrants from the Caribbean and Mexico is different. The Hispanics demand that the United States become a bilingual country, with all children entitled to be taught in the language of their heritage, at public expense. No better hymn to the American tradition has ever been written than *The Education of Hyman Kaplan,* by Leo Rosten, which describes with tears and laughter the efforts of the earlier immigrants—Italians, Jews, Lithuanians, Slavs—to learn the language of the country in which they wished to live. In New York today, forty years later, Hispanic entitlement has created a college, Hostos Community College—supported by public taxes—which is officially bilingual; half its students receive instruction primarily in Spanish, as they strive to escape from the subculture of the Spanish ghetto. Bilingualism is an awkward word—but it has torn apart communities from Canada to Brittany, from Belgium to India. It expresses not a sense of tolerance but a demand for divisions. There are no Hispanics in my little village of Bridgewater, Connecticut (population 1,600); but the law now requires the town to print its ballots in Spanish as well as English. In San Francisco, ballots must be printed in English, Chinese, Spanish, and Tagalog (for the Filipinos).

What was once a matter of tolerance becomes a demand from the newly arrived that America change its evolving culture to accommodate their heritage.

No presidential candidate I spoke with in the year 1980—except John Connally—gave any public utterance to the problems of the new immigration to the United States. All were aware of the problems. But none dared speak publicly about what was happening to the nation of immigrants as the new immigration swelled.

These new immigrants—a total of 5,171,500 in the decade, with perhaps as many more illegals—were for the moment, as were black Americans thirty years before, objects of a national debate, not participants. They would be participants in the debate in the 1990s, but that was far off. The main subjects of the campaign of 1980 were, of course, the inflation, the role of government, the national defense, and the humiliation. But under these grand themes, the technical planning of both campaigns addressed itself to the groups already here, particularly to those whose forebears had arrived in the immigration of 1880–1920. If this was indeed a nation of immigrants, the grandchildren of such immigrants had surfaced as communities demanding recognition, ready to present their demands as separate, yet thoroughly American, groups within the whole. No candidate could ignore them.

Electoral America, like ancient Gaul, can be divided into three parts—not geographically, but by constellations of communities.

There are the minorities, whom the census has had to record separately, because recording their numbers entitles entire groups to rights of compensation. Next come the ethnics. Last come the old-stock Americans, whom no one can define precisely.

The minorities are easiest to identify. In 1980, so said the census, there were approximately 46 million counted minorities entitled to special treatment—26.5 million blacks, 14.6 million Hispanics (an undercount), 1.4 million American Indians, Aleuts, and Eskimos, as well as 3.5 million Asians and Pacific Islanders. Altogether, such minorities, sometimes referred to officially as "protected classes," came to roughly one-fifth of America. That they were far more conspicuous than their number was easily explained; they gathered in America's big cities. Twelve states had black populations of one million or more, mostly the big-city states, led by New York (with 2,-401,000 blacks), followed by California, Texas, and Illinois. Blacks had risen fast in the previous twenty years. From two black congressmen in 1960, their number had grown to seventeen by 1980. I recall meeting one of the original two, Bill Dawson of Chicago, an unromantic but effective defender of his people. What do you want for your people, I asked him in 1955, and I remember his answer clearly: "All I can get—everything that ain't pinned down." Dawson's demand had been softened, civilized, mollified, but it perfectly expressed the sentiment of the 1980 black caucus. Their constituents were the poor, the hungry, the fatherless, the slum dwellers, as well as the aspiring black middle class trying to escape into the suburbs. Government was their only protector; they wanted jobs and dignities, jobs most of all—jobs for the roaming adolescents of summertime, freed in the streets from school but looking for work; jobs for the middle class (not just "nigger jobs," said one, but "real jobs"). Congressional seniority was moving such black big-city representatives, all with tenured seats, up through chairmanships of subcommittees; slowly and surely, the chairmanships would come to them when their seniorities forced out the Southern Democrats. And behind the blacks came the Hispanics, with their caucus; and behind came the other minorities.

The ethnics were a second category, more difficult to define. Although the Census of 1980, for the first time, tried to define all Americans by self-chosen heritage groups, the figures were late in coming and are not yet available. Ethnics were those who lived in that space between old-stock Americans and certified minorities. They were difficult to define because some families had now been here since the 1880s and 1890s, and their grandchildren were native-born of native-born parents. Or they had so intermarried that the grandchildren no longer knew how to define themselves.

"Ethnics" in American politics generally means four particular heritages: those of the Slavic East European people; those of the Jews, who had come here from throughout their diaspora; those of the Italians; and those of the Irish. They might number anywhere between forty and sixty million of the American population, and they were certainly *there.* No politician could ignore the Greek vote in Massachusetts, the Serbo-Croat vote in Cleveland, the Cajun vote in Louisiana, or the French-Canadian vote in New Hampshire. "Ethnics" had become so important that it had become a subject of American scholarship. In 1980, the Harvard University Press, leader in this field of study, published a magnificent encyclopedia that counted and told the stories of no less than 121 ethnic elements that made up the American population, from the Acadians and the Afghans to the Yankees and the Zoroastrians.* It is probably the best book ever published on the subject; its greatest virtue is that it does

---

Harvard Encyclopedia of American Ethnic Groups, Stephan Thernstrom, ed. (Cambridge, Mass., and London: Harvard University Press, Belknap Press, 1980).

not try to make the ethnic mix of America a matter of numerical analysis; it leaves the mysterious truth properly cloaked in uncertainty.

Politicians cannot deal with such scholarly uncertainties except by instinct or by public opinion surveys. The census is of little help, for people generally do not want to be tangled in yes-or-no questions about their ancestry, or wish to mark off a little black circle which leaves out their Indian great-grandmother, their Irish grandfather, their Norwegian great-aunt, their grandfather who had been a rabbi in Pinsk.

Among the ethnics, nonetheless, a number of critical groups should be signaled:

First, of course, the Irish, who were here from the beginning, alarming the Protestant colonists with their "papist" inclinations. There was a time when the Irish could be outlined as a distinct group. In some cities, like New York, Boston, or Jersey City, in 1860, one-quarter of all the population was Irish-born. But time then had its way with the Irish and their children, as they moved on and up, as did the Germans, to leave the label of "ethnic" behind. Sometime between the 1950s and the 1970s, Irish-Americans found themselves changing from a working-class to a middle-class community. Solid Irish voting districts still remain in Boston, in the outer boroughs of New York, in working-class enclaves of Pennsylvania and New Jersey. But their old control of the big-city vote, where they spoke for all immigrant groups, has vanished—vanished in Chicago with the passage of Daley; vanished in Boston, where once the Democratic party would present an "all-green" ticket against the Republicans; vanished in New York, Kansas City, Pittsburgh. Until Franklin Roosevelt's time, only three Irish-Americans had ever been appointed to the highest level of federal posts. With Roosevelt came the names of such people as Joseph P. Kennedy (chairman of the SEC, ambassador to England), Frank Murphy (Supreme Court), Thomas Corcoran and James Rowe of the White House, James Farley (Postmaster General) —and then other names too numerous to list. By 1980, Irish-Americans had spread through executive, intellectual, and literary leadership as a presence too broad to define. The large political figures of Irish origin, like Moynihan of New York or Brown of California, spoke not as Irish-Americans but as Americans. There is no current definition of the Irish presence; the last attempt to do so was made in the fifties, when the census drew up an unpublished survey of American origins. At that time, the Irish were estimated as the third-largest white stock in the United States, after the British-Americans and the German-Americans. It was guessed then that there might be fourteen million Americans of Irish descent. No one can make such a guess now. And it would be irrelevant, for the Irish now vote Republican as often as Democratic; two Irish-American Presidents have come since the old times, Kennedy (Democratic) and Reagan (Republican). The Irish are subject to appeal, culturally, but they no longer come in a package.

The Jews, the people of my own roots, should be signaled next. Numerically, they are a diminishing population group in the United States. Once estimated at more than six million, their numbers are now shrinking, reflecting a low birth rate and intermarriage. Their peak of political influence was probably reached by 1980, when no less than eight of the one hundred United States senators were of Jewish heritage. One dropped out, two were eliminated that year. Jewish influence remains strong because Jews vote ardently, particularly in primaries, trooping to the polls with an attendance unmatched by any other group. They are heavily influential in the cultural life of the nation—at universities, in television, in film, in science, in the news system. Politically, they are still Democratic property, but much less so than formerly. If Israel is threatened with extermination, they crystallize into a compact mass of votes against a repetition of the Holocaust. But on general issues, they, like the Irish, are ever less predictable.

The Polish-Americans, Bohemian-Americans, Baltic-Americans, Serbo-Croatian Americans, are again uncountable, but may number from ten to fifteen million Americans of common origin. These Slavic-Americans, just beginning to find their voice, vote heavily all through the industrial belt of the Great Lakes and in several New England states (notably Connecticut and Maine). They have most recently presented statesmen like Edmund Muskie, leverage congressmen like Dan Rostenkowski, scholars like Zbigniew Brzezinski and Michael Novak, to serious public attention. But they have only begun to move, and still do not mobilize their vote effectively.

The most important among the rising ethnic groups are the Italian-Americans. Of the 5.2 million Italian immigrants to the United States recorded since immigration records began, 80 percent came from southern Italy and Sicily (mostly to the East Coast), 20 percent from northern Italy, mostly to the West Coast. How many Americans now count themselves of Italian descent is guesswork. Twenty-one million, says the *Harvard Encyclopedia;* fifteen million, say other scholars; twenty-five million is the count of the Sons of Italy. But what is certain is that they have moved up from the pick-and-shovel jobs they once occupied. In the northeast arc of Atlantic states, Italians are the newest dynamic political force. Not only do they operate as technicians, but by public approval they increasingly win acceptance at the polls—as, for example, did John Volpe of Massachusetts, Ella Grasso of Connecticut, John Pastore of Rhode Island, Alfonse D'Amato of New York, Peter Rodino of New Jersey. In Congress today, there are at least twenty-nine Italian-American representatives.

It would be as unfair to Italian-Americans to list only the names of their political leaders as it would have been to list such Irish-American, or Jewish-American, names forty years ago. The Italian surge, coming late but strong, has in the past fifteen years cast up names of lateral entry into leadership won by talent alone: men like Joseph Califano or John Zucotti did not reach their eminence because of the vowels in their names; they entered leadership on quality. The Italian-Americans, at least in the East, have arrived at the center, and when they talk of moving on to the presidency, they talk of people like A. Bartlett Giamatti, the first ethnic stock president of Yale. "He could be our John F. Kennedy," said one.

There is a last and most intriguing ethnic group, not yet considered by politicians as a serious voting bloc. Asian-Americans, though their numbers have more than doubled since the Immigration Act of 1965, still numbered in 1980 only 3.5 million of the total population. But they were significant for their spectacular speed into American cultural life, science, and finance. They illustrated, as so many predecessors had, that "ethnics" move forward by internal dynamics of their own. California is where most Asian-Americans gather. Its state university has rigorous standards—only the top 12.5 percent of high school graduates may enter. In 1980, the old-stock "Anglos" qualified 16.5 percent of their high school graduates for the multi-university; the blacks 5 percent; the Hispanics 4.7 percent. But Asian families (chiefly Japanese- and Chinese-Americans) qualified 39 percent of their high school graduates for entry into California's university system! If Asian-Americans were not yet in 1980 a political voting power, certainly by 1990 they would become a large, imponderable force, impossible to disregard.

All these and many other groups, heritages, factions, went into the planning of the campaign of 1980. Such ethnics were critical in a country split into thirds—minorities, ethnics, and old stock. But the majority, and still the vital majority, remained the people who called themselves "plain Americans," and to these, in largest part, both campaigns of 1980 were addressed.

If it is difficult to define the second part of the American political constituency, the "ethnic Americans," it is even more difficult to define the third part, those old-stock Americans more commonly referred to as "plain Americans." Even the distinguished new *Harvard Encyclopedia* on ethnics has difficulty here. "Some scholars," it says, "estimate that a majority of the population of the United States belongs in this category ["plain Americans"]; others claim that it is a large minority."

Figures are of little help in this exploration of election weights; and the last thorough, though unpublished, census estimates (those of 1954) are almost three decades old. They are now useful only as clues to the past, and they run thus: of British descent, 52 million Americans; of German descent, 21 million; of Irish descent, 14 million; of Italian descent, 7 million; of Scandinavian descent, 6 million; of Polish descent, 5 million. But these old estimates are useless because so many Americans were listed as of "origin unknown" or "unreported" or "others." These "others" (not including blacks) could not state their origins because they were "plain Americans," whose roots were so tangled over centuries of intermarriage that they could not cut themselves into quarters, eighths, sixteenths, of English, Irish, Indian, or Scandinavian grandparents.* It is embarrassing to ask Americans of mixed origin to classify themselves, choosing among their forebears with whom they wish to identify. It is distasteful that a nation whose seal bears the inscription *E Pluribus Unum* (From the Many, One) should be asked to divide itself from the one nation into many tribes.

It is best to discuss the electoral weight of these "old-stock" or "plain" Americans by discarding the fashionable silliness of such labels as "WASP" (White Anglo-Saxon Protestant), or the more flattering label "colonial stock," and accept the term "old-stock Americans" as describing those whose grandparents were here before the

---

*The *Harvard Encyclopedia* offers a later census sampling of 1973, which lists English descent as only 25,993,000, German descent as 20,517,000, Irish descent as 12,240,-000. But "others" and "unreported" came to a total of 120,495,000, more than half the population of the country. "Others" and "unreported" included blacks, along with persons who did not state their origins or claimed two or more origins. The vast difference between the two census surveys in less than a generation may be resolved when the Census of 1980 finishes its final tabulations sometime in 1982.

Civil War. Colonial America had already absorbed into its English-Scots matrix millions of Irish, and would also accept the Protestant Scandinavians and Germans. Such old-stock Americans probably remain today the diminishing majority of all American peoples. These were the people whose ancestors fought the Civil War and, split among themselves, furnished both the Abolitionists of New England and the Ku Klux Klanners of the South. These were the descendants of the London convicts shipped off to the new world, of the God-seeking Pilgrims from Kent and Dorset, of the Germans fleeing from the tyranny of princelings, of the Irish driven over the waters by famine.

From these people have come the dominant culture of the United States, and its English tradition of government by law. From them came the tradition of public education, culminating in the Morrill Land Grant Act of 1862. From them, too, came the first flourishing of American science and medicine. Split though they were between those who came to dig for coal or farm the land, those who came to make fortunes or to worship God as they chose, derided as they have been as Babbitts or deified as the founding fathers—all these, nonetheless, were what can be called "mainstream Americans."

These people, then, were still the prime audience of the presidential condidates, divided, as were all the others, among mothers who did not want war, fathers who winced under the endless lash of inflation, patriots mortified by the humiliations abroad, the rich, the poor, the working people. Ethnic and minority peoples were specific targets of both the Democratic and the Republican campaigns. To speak to them, in their divisions, was vital; finding the way to their hearts, cardinal. But overriding every ethnic or minority appeal, there still remained the appeal to the central audience—the mainstream Americans.

Politics do not work this way anywhere else in the world. It is a miracle that American politics work at all; it would be an even greater miracle if this multiracial society, split and cross-hatched by so many groups of special demands and special pleadings, should survive into the twenty-first century as one nation.

Thus, then, as Ronald Reagan and Jimmy Carter went on to their final appeals to the vast and diverse American electorate, the country approached a self-examination.

CHAPTER THIRTEEN

THE CAMPAIGN:
BREAKUP OF
THE GRAND COALITION

It was not at all clear, as the conventions ended, that a landslide lay ahead.

Nor was it yet clear how the candidates would come to grips with each other. Before them, as always, lay the everlasting tactical problem: how to score the image of their personalities on American emotions, yet connect the image to the issues they were trying to score on the American mind.

What *was* clear was that the nature of campaigning had changed, and it was difficult to strip away nostalgia from memory of other campaigns. There were no banners in the streets, few posters in the windows, few buttons, no screamers or jumpers as the motorcades passed, little noise, no more torchlight parades. Demonstrations, violence, hecklings—mostly gone too. On the roofs of small towns, uniformed sharpshooters now scowled at the crowds below, while platoons of Secret Service men escorted the candidates—watching, always watching, for the assassin who might lurk in the throng. The press corps had swollen, sometimes two hundred following a single candidate, all festooned with blue passes, white passes, national Secret Service passes, pool passes. But this campaign was being conducted for television. Colored balloons danced down over rallies and halls to catch the television eye. On the candidate's lead plane rode the men and women of television, nine seats reserved for each network, the "pencil press" taking seats left over, each stopdown planned for tactical effect on the tube. No longer, as in 1960, could a John F. Kennedy grow instantly indignant on hearing of the arrest of a Martin Luther King, Jr., and march, on impulse, from his plane to a telephone booth to insist that King be protected. Now such a gesture would have to be planned by staff so that television might cover it, and the tactic fit to strategy.

Yet underlying all techniques, new and old, lay the historic conundrum which Franklin D. Roosevelt had refreshed half a century before: What was the proper role of government in a country of free people? In defining that role, Roosevelt had built his grand coalition based on the underprivileged and led by an administrative and scholarly elite drawn from the ever growing middle classes. That coalition had governed Congress and shaped the nation's policies ever since.

Could it be broken up? Could it be defended? How?

All would depend on how the candidates penetrated the thinking of the American voters in the eighty days between the Democratic convention and the November election. And in that perspective, campaign strategy would have to deal first of all with images.

The two candidates seemed evenly matched—two small-town boys, characters out of Mark Twain, Zane Grey, or Sinclair Lewis.

There was the one, Jimmy Carter, earnest, pious, a Sunday school teacher, whose eloquence at its best could twinge the inner chords of conscience. He was the preacher. There was the other, Ronald Reagan. His campaign poster showed him as he wanted to be seen, in broad-brimmed Western hat, stern yet smiling. He might be the sheriff, quick on the draw for the high-noon shoot-out.

Behind the one, Carter, stood all the formidable resources of the Democratic party, still, as it had been since Roosevelt, the majority party of the United States. Behind him, too, was the formidable authority of the presidency, with all its power to control events and make things happen. But what *was* it he was doing with this power?

Behind the other, Reagan, stood the Republican party, with its superior financing, and its renascent force in the West and South. Behind him, even more importantly, was the strange restlessness of the nation, humiliated by madmen abroad and, at home, apparently powerless to control either the terrifying inflation or the economy as a whole. What was the government doing with all its power? asked Reagan. What should it do?

The targets, for both, were the minds of the American people, and here, in defining these targets, political technology had progressed. Second in importance only to the candidates themselves were the men in both camps who managed the polls and probings of public opinion, for it was in the minds of the people that the election was to be won.

The polls had become, in twenty-five years, instruments of esoteric sophistication. The Gallup Poll's miscall of the Truman-Dewey election in 1948 had been the last major blunder of the polling men. They had since advanced from nose counters to analysts, senior strategists—experts in perception. In an election, it is not what is really happening that counts but how people perceive such happenings. Opinion is like a set of giant balloons tethered to the hull of a ship below the horizon. The winds of the media—of the press and of television—cause the balloons to blow now this way, now that. But the ship below the horizon continues on its course, until ultimately the balloons are tugged the way the ship goes. It may take years before people see that direction, as it took twelve years, from 1933 to 1945, for the Germans to recognize in Hitler the demon that he was. In an eighty-day American election campaign, however, the winds blow back and forth; and unless events intervene to alter the ship's course, the breezes and storms of opinion prevail over reality.

To measure perceptions and push them beyond impulse to reflection is the job of the polling technicians. And to begin the story of the final campaign of 1980, it is wise to examine the analyses of the two men who, second only to the candidates, mapped and shaped the contest.

These were Richard Wirthlin (then forty-nine) and Patrick Caddell (then thirty). And two more dissimilar characters would have been difficult to find.

Richard Wirthlin, chief analyst for Ronald Reagan, was almost an ascetic. His father had been presiding bishop of the Mormon Church. Wirthlin, at the age of nineteen, had served his Mormon duty with a tour as a missionary in Switzerland, before becoming an economist (Ph.D., Berkeley), then a professor at Brigham Young University. Fascinated by econometrics, he had then applied numbers to politics, dabbled in political polling. With his remarkable successes in political analyses, he had begun to poll for Reagan in 1974 and, by 1976, had moved into the Reagan inner circle. Ever cheerful and courteous, he remained a devout Mormon, who would not smoke or drink; coffee was his chief indulgence. He was a devoted husband and father (eight children), but was also a workaholic, in love with computers and the digits that encoded the rustlings of American opinion.

Patrick Caddell was of totally different heritage. He was born the year Wirthlin was off to Europe as a teenage missionary. A Southerner (he grew up in Jacksonville, Florida, where his father was a coast guard officer) and a Catholic, he was sensitive to the emotions of both minority groups. Approaching the campaign of 1980 he was a handsome young man, his sleek black beard streaked with a single lock of premature gray. He was young enough to enjoy the wine and the bourbon, and lived his bachelor life to the full. Wirthlin looked like the father he was. Caddell was the one you hoped would ask your daughter out but not go too far.

An intellectual, like Wirthlin, Caddell had much earlier become enchanted by the numbers game. While still in high school, he had been absorbed in local politics, recognized as a whiz kid who could predict elections. He had been admitted to Harvard (on scholarship), and before graduating was already, at the age of twenty-one, chief polling analyst for George McGovern in the campaign of 1972.

Caddell had been a major in history and government at Harvard; he had written his thesis on the changing politics of his native South. Caddell's papers sparkle with both military and historical metaphors. He had, moreover, been trained in the ways of the press during the 1972 campaign, at the direction of that man of gnomelike charm and political wisdom, Frank Mankiewicz, the inventor of the post-primary briefing. In 1972, primary after primary, Mankiewicz had invited correspondents, exhausted from writing the late-night stories of the race, to an explanatory briefing of why McGovern had won the night before. His star was young Caddell. On the morning after voting results are reported, all reporters still must write a "follow-up" story of analysis. Caddell provided that follow-up—with results from key precincts, ethnic breakdowns, blue-collar breakdowns—and discovered how easy and pleasant it was to deal with and manipulate the press. He had thus happened into a comradely relationship with the revolving club of political writers, and by the time of the Carter administration's gas crisis in 1979, had become that administration's chief unofficial spokesman to the press—far more so than Jody Powell, the nominal and administrative press secretary. It would be wrong to call Caddell the Carter administration's chief leak; but he was, nonetheless, its chief phrase-maker. The famous Carter "malaise" speech (in which Carter, as noted, never once used the word) is remembered because of the Caddell memorandum that provoked it, in which "malaise" appears fleetingly.

Caddell had to be recognized as the administration's most effective spokesman. But in his private memoranda to the President on the campaign problems of 1980, he could be accused of nothing but flabbergasting candor.

His first campaign memorandum on general election strategy is dated June 25, 1980. The primary campaign is over and won. Ted Kennedy has been defeated. Ronald Reagan will be the Republican nominee.

The memo is addressed to the White House, for Jimmy Carter's perusal. He starts:

"This memo is an attempt to give some early attention to the need for strategy/themes which we neglected to address until late in the 1976 campaign—much to our woe. . . . President Carter faces an extremely difficult re-election . . . we face a united Republican party with a challenger posed to our right attempting to crowd our center. . . . The issue structures could not be worse. After a long period of runaway inflation . . . we face what could be a worse *political* problem—unemployment. . . . The public is anxious, confused, hostile, and sour. . . . *More to the point, the American people do not want Jimmy Carter as their President. Not forced to choose a specific candidate, voters by almost 2 to 1 would reject Carter as President.*"

The introduction closes with a bleak overview: ". . . *by and large the American people do not like Jimmy Carter.* Indeed a large segment could be said to loathe the President."

This from the President's personal pollster to the President himself!

Then comes the Caddell analysis of the campaign. People in various states like Carter personally. But they think he is incompetent. In California, according to Caddell's polls, *hard-core* Democratic primary voters rate Carter's job performance as unfavorable by 71 to 28, in Ohio by 65 to 35, in New Jersey by 68 to 32. Other discouraging reports follow, and then Caddell gives his survey results. Pessimistically, he gives Carter only eight safe states—Massachusetts (14 electoral votes), Georgia (12), Minnesota (10), Maryland (10), West Virginia (6), Arkansas (6), Hawaii (4), Rhode Island (4), plus the District of Columbia (3)—for a total of only 69 electoral votes out of the 270 necessary to win. (Caddell, pessimistic as he was, was insufficiently so—Massachusetts and Arkansas ultimately went to Reagan.)

Carter, Caddell continued, "is having problems again with Catholics, Jews, liberals, the young, et al., particularly in the Northeast." The strategy is clear. "Our approach must be as follows:

"1. The South must be secured. We need a base and the home region must be it.

"2. Our major focus must be on the northern big states (Ohio, Pennsylvania, Illinois, Texas, Michigan, New Jersey, Missouri, Wisconsin). This should be our major thrust.

"3. We must take either New York or California." And then, after other points: "Texas and Florida become crucial. . . . We must work to solidify blue collar and middle class Catholics. We must solidify Blacks and Browns. We need to improve with Jews, liberals, upper educated young. . . . Except for a weakened South, Carter has no real base, particularly when it comes to Democratic constituencies. Little enthusiasm."

What Carter has going for him, says Caddell, is the presidency itself. "The passage from prospective candidate to possible President of the United States is invisible and perilous. In this judgment, unlike a primary, doubt is almost always resolved against a challenger. . . . The vote for President is rarely a frivolous one. It is consciously and subconsciously weighted, debated, and struggled with by almost every voter. . . .

"At the moment, the 1980 campaign is adrift—searching for a definition. In a vacuum, the public and events may move to construct a definition that may or may not be advantageous to our prospects."

The problem thus becomes, in this basic strategic memorandum, to construct a definition. "PEOPLE MUST BE GIVEN A POSITIVE REASON TO VOTE FOR JIMMY CARTER." The risk/safety factor is essential —people know Jimmy Carter is a man of peace. The campaign must stress the risk in Ronald Reagan. Only the office of the Presidency can make the positives and negatives come out clearly. Speeches will not do the job.

Commenting on the President's one-day primary foray into Ohio, Caddell remarks that after the jaunt, "our lead dropped from a solid fifteen points to barely six on primary day." Therefore, concludes Caddell, on the basis of his surveys, the first priority is for the President to act, using the presidency to define issues. Next is the "image" priority: Get Reagan! Turn the heat on him. The old Whitaker-Baxter maxim still held: Make the enemy the focus of discussion —Reagan is dangerous. "Thus we must make people not only concentrate on President Reagan, but we must help make that as uncomfortable a notion for them as possible." The memorandum goes on for some length, and is followed by others down until late October —all accompanied by Caddell's sputterings of exasperation in private at the failure of the White House command to use the White House to control events—until finally, by the time of the presidential debate in late October, Caddell had all but given up hope.

It is amusing to compare the basic Caddell memorandum with the planning of his rival duelist, Wirthlin, whose confidential black book, "Reagan for President Campaign Plan," is dated June 29, 1980, just four days after the Caddell memorandum. At this stage, Reagan is running 10 to 16 points ahead of Carter in the opinion polls, public and private. Caddell's purpose had been to cry: Alarm! Wirthlin's purpose is to warn: Caution! The campaign, according to Wirthlin, is not yet won; tight, hard planning is required. If it is to be won, it will be won in the last twenty days, for which all resources must be husbanded for a television blitz, which Wirthlin urges to counteract what he calls Carter's "October surprise."

The Wirthlin plan is an executive plan, which runs to 176 pages. What intrigues most are the passages on mood, on thrust, on history; it is as if Wirthlin and Caddell were surveying the same topography of American politics, yet choosing different passes through the mountains to suggest to their chiefs.

For Wirthlin, looking back over the record, the key condition of victory is to break up the old Roosevelt Democratic coalition. Because Democrats and Independents leaning Democratic represent 54 percent of the electorate, the Reagan campaign must move to center. Where Caddell says that the Southern home base must be held by Carter, Wirthlin agrees—but he sees it as the prime target of the Reagan campaign.

"The Reagan for President 1980 campaign," says Wirthlin, "must convert into Reagan votes the disappointment felt by:

- "Southern white Protestants,
- "blue collar workers in the industrial states,
- "urban ethnics, and
- "rural voters, especially in upstate New York, Pennsylvania and Ohio."

Wirthlin then turns to the historical mood of the country and its voters.

"Since the quiet, relatively passive years of the Eisenhower period, the American public has been severely battered by political events." He lists the well-known disturbances—the Great Society drive, the racial revolution, the Vietnam War, the Watergate scandal. From his polling, he reports: "From 1973 to 1980 fewer than 20 percent of the country felt the nation was on the 'right track.' 75 out of every 100 Americans thought the country was misdirected and in disarray. . . .

"The shattering of traditional confidence in America in the last twenty years stems from an erosion in the expectation that, given an abundant environment and an adequate amount of time, the individual—with sufficient diligence and ingenuity—would achieve a measure of economic security and a reasonably comfortable lifestyle. . . ." Wirthlin continues: "The lack of confidence in . . . American value structure relates directly to the American presidency. . . . The primal questions of 'who governs, and why should the governed obey the governors?' emerge demanding satisfactory answers."

From this, then, comes the Wirthlin conclusion: The candidate, Reagan, must affirm his image of leadership.

Wirthlin's memorandum is a mirror image of Caddell's. Caddell has said that the most vulnerable period for Reagan will come after the convention. Then, if ever, Caddell has said, a campaign for nomination transforms itself into a campaign for election, an entirely different affair. It is then that Carter must attack, attack, attack, to throw Reagan off balance. Wirthlin also knows this, and he offers his solutions to the problem. He describes the Carter campaign he thinks the Reagan team must face: "Carter and his administration will use fully the political power of the Presidency. . . . There will be no hesitancy to mount extremely personal attacks on Ronald Reagan. While Carter himself may remain above the fray of personal attacks early in the contest, his own 'positive' position will be carefully crafted to give added emphasis to the negative charges his surrogates and media will make against Ronald Reagan."

Wirthlin describes what he presumes correctly to be "The Elements of Jimmy's Carter's Attack Strategy." The "image" problem is uppermost. "We can," he says, "expect Ronald Reagan to be pictured as a simplistic and untried lightweight (dumb), a person who consciously misuses facts to overblow his own record (deceptive) and, if President, one who would be too anxious to engage our country in a nuclear holocaust (dangerous)."

Issue strategy lay elsewhere in the Reagan campaign. But Wirthlin (having noted that the economy and inflation were the overriding issues) goes on to numbers.

He focuses on the numbers furnished by the electoral college. Here, trying to puncture the overconfidence of the Reagan team and the euphoria induced by the public polls, he lists the Carter base states as against the Reagan base states. He gives Carter in June no less than fourteen states—eight of them in the Old South—plus Massachusetts, Minnesota, the District of Columbia, West Virginia, Hawaii, and Rhode Island. This is a base of 115 electoral votes of the 270 needed. Against this, Reagan has a base of only 86 electoral votes (seventeen small states, chiefly Western, plus New Hampshire, Vermont, Indiana, Nebraska, Iowa, and Kansas). Therefore, the election will be decided in two critical areas of effort: in the industrial Northeastern ethnic states, and in the South, where Reagan must, somehow, undermine the native support for one of their own. Five great states must be the prime target of Reagan's time and resources: California, Illinois, Texas, Ohio, and Pennsylvania, whose 149 electoral votes, plus the 86 base votes, would bring Reagan within kissing distance of the magic 270. New York and Michigan were critical states, thought Wirthlin in June, and must be targets of opportunity, deserving attention and money if later polling showed a real chance there. Wirthlin's political map was clear: Reagan must capture the ethnic, blue-collar vote of the Northeast, while trying to deny Carter his Southern base.

One must draw away from this close-up planning of the 1980 campaign to the larger view. The old electoral college, designed two hundred years ago, was now, in 1980, all but obsolete, though its central virtue still remained firm. It preserved the idea of a federal system, a union of states, that chose the national leader by states. And in the showdown, the election would go the way the states cast their votes as states, not individuals. Long ago, the electoral college had been a gathering in each state of its wise and senior citizens, who would meet to weigh the merits and choose the candidates. Now the college had become a collection of artificial containers, each container counted separately, although within the containers new kinds of people rocked and jostled each other. A speech by a candidate to the B'nai B'rith in Washington affected Jews in every other container where their numbers clustered; a visit by a candidate to the Italian market in Philadelphia, telecast nationally, influenced Italian-Americans throughout the critical Northeast. The trick was to capture the proper number of containers to win 270 electoral votes; yet to confirm that vote, if it was close, it would be necessary to sift the entire voting population for the popular majority that would give the President the political authority to govern.

All campaigns go through an evolutionary shakedown after the national conventions. The shift from the one-on-one campaigning of the early primaries, from the local Rotary Club luncheons in small towns to the sweep and breadth of a transcontinental campaign, is hard. The gap a campaign staff must jump from one form of politics to the other is immeasurable. In the final campaign—usually ten or twelve weeks—themes become vital; schedules must serve them. Themes and appearances must mesh—but always, the paramount consideration must be the personality of the candidate, the image of President he projects.

Always, in every campaign, has come this sag as a candidate and his staff try to change focus, perspective, organization, to reach an electorate where votes shift in the millions, not in the tens of thousands of the primaries. Eisenhower's veteran leadership had fumbled so badly in the first month after his nomination that the phrase remembered is that he was "running like a dry creek." The same sag had come in the Kennedy campaign of 1960, as campaign manager Bobby Kennedy, bursting out of his office in September, vented his exasperation on his old friends and staff. "You know what's happened to our 'smooth well-oiled machine'?" responded Pierre Salinger. "It's diffusing. This country is just too big." And the disastrous sag of the 1972 McGovern candidacy, as the Eagleton affair presented its first crisis, was never to be recovered.

Few such sags, however, were more apparent than the early sag of the Reagan campaign in August of 1980. The campaign strategy, based on Wirthlin's thinking, was that each week must have a new theme—to be hammered home successively in an exercise called "focus impact." One idea would follow another—the plight of the big cities first, national defense next, foreign affairs next, then inflation and the economy and so on, until Ronald Reagan came clear. All the literature, all the speakers of the Republican party would focus on the one theme each week and drive it home. But no one had coordinated theme with schedule; travel and appearance with ideas; or the personality of the candidate with his image.

Thus, then, came Reagan's weeks of near-disaster. Scheduled to hammer away at the plight of the cities, where the maps and the analysis told him that the campaign must be won or lost, he found himself previously scheduled into Neshoba County, Mississippi. There he told a cheering white Southern audience, deep in segregationist country, that he believed in "states' rights"; but that evening he must fly to New York City to address the National Urban League, one of the prime black leadership groups. ("We weren't expecting to pick up any black votes in New York," said one of the planners. "We just wanted to show moderates and liberals that Reagan wasn't anti-black.") The black audience listened courteously but unenthusiastically; and when Reagan went on for the ritual visit to Charlotte Street, epicenter of the south Bronx devastation, he was jeered and booed. It made good pictures; but the headlines provoked by the responses of the two audiences contradicted each other in the papers —"states' rights" versus "civil rights," two code words challenging each other.

Reagan was off next to a short rest in California while the Democratic convention made the headlines, and then, bruised by the beating he had taken from the three chief Democratic orators, he responded that the Democrats were trying to portray him "as a combination of Ebenezer Scrooge and the mad bomber." He followed by violating the oldest rule of politics—which is to make the other fellow the target, without responding as if he, himself, was the target. Kennedy had quoted Reagan as saying that trees cause 80 percent of air pollution. Reagan now insisted that it *was* so: "This is what causes the haze that gave the Big Smoky Mountains their name is [*sic*] oxides of nitrogen from decaying vegetation." He crowned a press conference by defending his assertion that fascism was the inspiration of the New Deal: ". . . anyone who wants to look at the writings of the members of the brain trust of the New Deal will find that President Roosevelt's advisers admired the fascist system. . . . They coined the expression that Mussolini made the trains run on time. They thought that private ownership with government management and control à la the Italian system was the way to go and that has been evident in all their writings."

The Democrats had been trying to give the nation the impression that Reagan was a clutter bag of odd quotations, clippings, and misinformation. Reagan's first few weeks bore them out. But on he went to the scheduled focus impact week on national defense and a speech before the Veterans of Foreign Wars in Chicago. His speech had been drafted very carefully by his staff to present him as a man of peace-through-strength; but on his way to the rendezvous, Reagan had carefully penciled in the phrase "a noble cause" to express his personal view of the Vietnam War. Reagan scheduled his vice-presidential running mate, George Bush, for a quick trip to China, to show he sought peace with all the world. Here now followed a five-day delight for the press, for Reagan proclaimed himself in favor of "official government relations" with Taiwan, while his running mate was trying to strengthen official relations with Peking's China. Which

China was Reagan for? Reagan's aides, trying to straighten out the confusion, only confused it more.

The China flap was followed by yet further blunders. Traditionally, the final phase of a presidential campaign starts on Labor Day. Reagan began Labor Day 1980 at an "ethnic picnic" in Liberty State Park in New Jersey—where he could be photographed for the evening television news, himself in shirtsleeves and the Statue of Liberty in the background. Here, he came out for Lech Walesa and the Polish insurgents, and then flew on to Detroit for a cookout with steel and auto workers before going on to the Michigan State Fair. There he proclaimed himself "happy to be" with the working people of that smitten automobile city (mostly black) while his opponent, Carter, was "opening his campaign" in Tuscumbia, Alabama, "the city that gave birth to and is the parent body of the Ku Klux Klan." Reagan said to Michael Deaver, his closest personal aide, as he drove away, "Oh, my God. I should have never said that."

The Democrats made the most of Reagan's totally inaccurate statement. The next day Reagan was forced to retract, but the impression of an erratic, uninformed, hip-shooting politician had been scored again.

The consternation in the Reagan command now forced them to face the awkward realities of transition. There would be two headquarters, the first of them, which we may call "Base Camp," in Arlington, Virginia. There Meese and Casey had recruited key veterans of other Republican campaigns. From the old Ford team, Jim Baker; from the old Nixon command, William Timmons; from the old Goldwater command, Clifton White, all veterans in attack, manipulation, planning. But on the plane with Reagan there would now be what might be called the "Damage Control Squad," or "Capsule Command"—Californians all, image experts. There would be Lyn Nofziger, in awe of neither the press nor the candidate; there would be Stuart Spencer, aboard the plane within a few days after the Ku Klux Klan gaffe, a consummate professional of the Whitaker-Baxter school; there would be Michael Deaver, a loyalist so devout that he had resigned his post as majordomo when he felt, wrongly, that John Sears was more important than he to Reagan's success; and finally, Reagan's house intellectual, Dr. Martin Anderson, an encyclopedia of history, ideas, and fact. Among them, they could restrain the candidate on the road, while Base Camp prepared the attack on Carter.

There is a time lag between event, press perception, and public seepage. In this time lag, the only measures of movement are the public opinion polls, which trace reaction after television has squeezed reporting into its two- or three-minute snatches. There are now four major public opinion polls in American politics, and most are combinations of resources, for the cost of polling has gone up even faster than the cost of postage stamps. These four are: an NBC News poll, joined with the resources of the Associated Press; a CBS News poll, joined with the New York *Times;* an ABC poll, conducted by Louis Harris of the Gannett newspaper chain; and the most august and traditional, the Gallup Poll, independent. In addition, polls were conducted by all independent media with resources large enough to pay the fee, chief among them Time Incorporated, relying on the Yankelovich polling; and regional polls conducted by all the great newspapers, from the Boston *Globe* to the Los Angeles *Times.*

All of these measures now, slowly but simultaneously, turned down on Ronald Reagan. The polls showed the results: by the last week in August, the Time/Yankelovich poll showed Reagan and Carter as even (with 39 points each). So, too, did the Washington *Post,* in its own independent survey (37 points each). Only the NBC and ABC polls showed Reagan as still holding a marginal lead. The CBS/New York *Times* poll actually showed Carter ahead on September 14—by a margin of 38 to 35.

At least a week before this, however, the Reagan campaign had come together, both Base and Capsule commands learning how to deal with each other; and both learning how to control a candidate who, when asked a question, would not fail to give the first answer that came to mind. The polls were behind the reality of reorganization.

It was at this point that the media's attention switched from Reagan to Carter.

It is a short period of three weeks that we are discussing. In years gone by, movements of public opinion rose and fell slowly, like wave swells. But the speed of reaction in American politics has now reached the speed of electronic transmission, which is the speed of light and entirely too fast. Now the instant response is required. The candidate comes down from the airplane, is greeted by reporters and cameramen, and is told that his rival, half a continent away, has just said thus and so. What is the candidate's response, *now,* in time for the evening news? The questions are forced on the reporters by the news system's code of fairness.

There must be two parallel columns in the newspapers the next day, giving each candidate his hearing; there will be only six, eight, or even ten minutes on the nightly news, meticulously measured by seconds to grant them equal time.

By mid-September, thus, the press, having portrayed Reagan as a muddlehead and dangerous to boot, was prepared to pay attention to Carter.

Carter had moved off briskly after his convention, trying to shore up the grand Democratic coalition. On the morning after the Democratic convention he had told a listless meeting of the Democratic National Committee of his visions, and of the battle they must face ("With the possible exception of Goldwater versus Johnson, there has never been a sharper distinction about what this election can mean"); he had gone on next to a cheering meeting of two hundred black delegates and told them: "I have a secret weapon, and that is the black people of this country, who know they have a friend in Jimmy Carter." A pause in the campaign—then the next step, to Boston, to appear for a front-page picture with Kennedy and address the American Legion there. On September 1, Labor Day, to the South, to TVA country in northern Alabama (at Tuscumbia), to shore up his Southern base, and extol the brave workers of insurgent Poland, whom Reagan was also championing that day. "The working men and women of Poland," says Carter, "have set an example for all those who cherish freedom and human dignity"; and on back to the White House for a Labor Day picnic on the lawn, with the chieftains of the AFL-CIO and their families present.

Still touching the bases of the old Democratic coalition, Carter was off the next day to the shrine of Harry Truman, in Independence, Missouri. The following day, he touched the ethnic bases further, going into the Italian market of Philadelphia before returning to Washington to champion Israel before the B'nai B'rith. In the game of ethnic catch-up, he and Reagan would leapfrog each other day by day. Somehow in the week's travels, Carter's first positive thematic step—another package of economic stimulation, with an immediate infusion of $4 billion—had been lost to public attention. And his next step in the campaign strategy, the attack on Ronald Reagan, was to backfire.

The Carter campaign was now to enter, according to the press, its "meanness" phase.

Reagan had exposed himself by his off-the-cuff remarks; his poll ratings were dropping; now, the Carter campaign felt, was the time to go on the assault. Carter began his counterattack in a speech before a black audience in Atlanta. "You've seen in this campaign the stirrings of hate and the rebirth of code words like 'states' rights.' . . . That is a message that creates a cloud on the political horizon. Hatred has no place in this country. Racism has no place in this country." "Racism" is a word that clings like slime; it sticks to the accused and stinks, and cannot ever be entirely wiped off. In Los Angeles almost a week later, on September 22, Carter capped his earlier accusation by painting Reagan as a man of war. "Six weeks from now you will determine what kind of life you and your families will have . . . whether we have peace or war."

The strategy was, of course, correct—make the other fellow stand accused. But the language was exaggerated, and the news system, patrolling the contest, landed on Carter. James Reston of the New York *Times*, the capital's senior witness, summed it up: ". . . many of his [Carter's] supporters—even many members of his own Administration—are deeply disappointed by the mean and cunning antics of his campaign. . . . He may very well win but not be able to command the respect of either his friends or his opponents and therefore not be able to govern effectively."

If the Washington press corps found Carter "mean," then television, the great transmission belt of impressions, would also find him "mean." The Washington press corps had been weighing Carter's performance for more than three years, and beyond a personal distaste for his style, had found little on which to hang their dislike beyond the unwieldy fact that Carter could manage neither the economy nor the humiliation in Iran. His style had offended the senior columnists whose syndicated wisdom crosses the nation—not only Reston, but McGrory, Kraft, Evans and Novak, Will, and Greenfield. Like almost all of the Washington press baronage, they winced at Carter's style and behavior. In vain, Caddell and others had pleaded with the President to do something, anything, to repair those relations with the press that his press office seemed unable to mend. On August 18, after the convention, Caddell had written the President: "The Press' attitude to date has been very negative on you. . . . We have three options, 1) dump on the Press in public, 2) do nothing, or 3) try some approaches at rapprochement. My feeling is that we must pursue the third. . . . To some extent you should plan to spend more time, unpleasant a task as it is, with key reporters and columnists trying to warm the chill of our frozen relations. . . . In any event, we should give some consideration to a press strategy." By the time Carter realized that his sharpening of the issues had divided him from the center, it was too late.

On October 8, the Washington *Post* front-paged a story: "Carter's Campaign Stalls"; that evening, Carter entertained Barbara Walters, the queen of ABC's constellation of stars, and declared that he wanted to get his campaign "back on track." He admitted that he had been "carried away on a couple of occasions" and had made comments that were probably "ill-advised." From now on, the White House would comment on issues. But it was too late.

Real issues, like those of 1980, or 1960, are always sensed by voters like the menace of far-off thunder. Voters are concerned, but they do not know which way to go. Thus, at any given moment they judge the rivals for leadership through the slit that television offers them as an eye piece. Through this slit they had observed Reagan as a cocky, genial man, strong in leadership qualities. But until early September they had also seen him as an ignorant, possibly a dangerous man, a wisecracker, too ready to outface Russians or Cubans or Iranians, with guns drawn across the table. They had viewed Carter as a decent, trustworthy man, one concerned for the poor—but now they were seeing him as nasty, mean, uncertain.

Refurbishing images had, therefore, become the priority in both camps, more important for the moment than issues. For Reagan's planners, the momentary need joined happily with momentary opportunity—an invitation to debate with both Jimmy Carter and John Anderson at once. Carter would not debate Anderson, whom he despised—"mean" Jimmy Carter again. But Reagan announced that he would share national attention generously with the hopeless Anderson. The debate in Baltimore, on September 21, went on as scheduled, Carter absent. Anderson is a formidable debater, an intense and concerned man, with a crackle of righteousness in every phrase. But Reagan was prepared, the model of a friendly man, cocking his head from side to side, enjoying himself, genially calling his rival by his first name. For a full hour and a half, Reagan let Anderson carry the attack on Carter while he showed himself not as a demon but rather as a quizzical, cheerful man.

Three days later, the polling apparatus of the nation began to report the results. Though Anderson had scored best, as one-on-one over Reagan, the big loser was not Reagan, but Carter. The image the Carter campaign had painted of Reagan the killer had, simply, not shown on the screen. From the near-even race during the three weeks of Reagan's diarrhea of words, the polling results had shifted.

CBS, which had had Reagan down by 36 to Carter's 40 before the debate with Anderson, found that another vast shift had taken place a week after the debate. Reagan was ahead, 40/35. ABC confirmed Carter as down, 42/36. NBC, whose polling constantly showed a wider margin for Reagan than any of the other polls, checked in with 42/33.

From that point on, the personality contest was over; Reagan was never again behind, except in the Washington *Post* poll of the climactic weekend.*

I would go out on jaunts with the two candidates, swinging back and forth between Washington and New York, and would fill my notebooks with facts. Yet, as I look back, the outdoor reporting seems to shrink in significance, and what remain most relevant are the quiet moments at my desk, tuning in on television, reading the newspapers, assembling bits and pieces as the news system spewed them out —bits and pieces of the larger, rumbling world that housed the stage on which the candidates contended. The southern flank of the country was blistering. Nicaragua had drifted into civil war; El Salvador seemed also to be slipping; refugees had been pouring in from Cuba and Haiti, and television showed their plight as well as the plight of those in Miami who were receiving them. In Poland, the workers of Gdansk had begun their uprising. If the Polish regime was unstable, so were all other regimes around the unstable world: a coup in Turkey to crush terrorists; a mysterious change of regime taking place in Peking. In the Middle East, events zigzagged. And there was always Iran, shackled about Carter's campaign. Now Iran and Iraq were at war, in an obscure fanaticism of rival Moslem sects; and the lineup was incomprehensible. Jordan was backing Iraq; but Syria, Libya, and Saudi Arabia were backing Iran. The prime rate was climbing again; after its summer restraint by the Federal Reserve, it was now back up to 12 percent and rising. Food prices were continuing up. I could sit at home and learn as much or more about the frame of the campaign as I could on the road. In no other campaign had distant events so swiftly intruded. I quote from my notes of the final weeks, as the campaign showed at home on pauses between rounds:

*It is noteworthy that the only private poll to show a dip in Reagan's popularity after the Anderson debate was his own. Wirthlin's running average showed Reagan down by two points (39/41) for the week ending October 11. Reagan still held a lead in electoral votes, however, and by October 30 he was five points ahead in the popularity ratings, and lengthened the margin insuperably after the debate with Carter.

September 22, 1980

. . . This campaign has been administered and managed—not fought and won. . . . If there's any novelty it is the open carpentering of the ethnics together. . . . Largely, this reflects the change as America comes apart, the fractioning of America. It happens because the dissection tools of the pollsters are sharper, can cut cleaner; and because the issues to be debated are so complex that no one, not even the candidates, understands them. We all ask for a clear call. There is none.

. . . I mumble what everyone else is mumbling. It's gone on too long. . . . First of the debates took place in Iowa, in January. How long can you stay interested in the problems of inflation and the tax cut? There were five national elections in Germany the year before Hitler came to power in 1933; the last, which Hitler won, showed a sharp dropoff in votes. We've had politics up to our ears, are gorged with it.

September 29, 1980

. . . I begin today with the New York *Times.* It occurs to me, reading in bed, this is an odd front page. I'm fascinated by the items one by one, distracted by all the fascinating information that Abe Rosenthal pumps in. Am looking for something. Not until the end of the third section do I realize what's missing: Nothing about the presidential campaign! Five weeks until voting day—and nothing?! So I go back frantically, and look, then give up. I read the finance section, and then on the very last inside page of the last section find two-thirds of a page on the campaign, with an excellent piece by Adam Clymer saying that nothing's happening.

That's it. Most of the news are blips traced on the radar of television, plotted in their course to reach the key media markets as defined by Wirthlin and Caddell. Whole thing a nuttiness, for the news is the *news of a game.* So with no big polls reporting over the weekend, and the candidates resting their weary bodies, there's nothing until the very last inner page.

. . . this is a game of quadridimensional chess. There is a flat board of polling and television ads; there is the tactical board of what-states-do-we-want-to-carry (Ohio, New York, Pennsylvania, Texas, Florida); there's the international chessboard of the Strait of Hormuz, the mountain passes between Afghanistan and Iran, the balance between China and Russia. Then there's the chessboard of futures—what kind of America and world do we want to have.

October 3, 1980
(Just back from an outing with Reagan)

I had a sneaking likeness for the Reagan plane, and wanted to go on with it. Maybe I should. There's no fun in the Carter entourage. Difficult to describe the plane, called *LeaderShip '80*. First of all, the correspondents are so much younger (is that because I'm the oldest correspondent aboard?) . . . a fun crowd, they have whistles and lip sirens. They enjoy horseplay. Atmosphere frolicsome, plenty of booze. . . . Attitude to Reagan is one of mixed affection and disdain. They've heard his speech too often. Nancy Reagan daintily passes out chocolates in the morning . . . characteristic, Reagan lets fling an orange when the plane takes off and tilts up, to see if it can roll all the way down aisle through the press on the uptilt. On one of the takeoffs, I caught the orange. . . .

Reagan works and works and works. I don't know what the hell he takes or does. He can go up the steep steps of a construction site faster than me; without gripping the rail. He looks good, especially since he's switched his suits to a dark cherry-brown. Sometimes his cheeks are flushed, I can't tell why. . . . Sense of cockiness on the plane. As for example, George Shultz (of Bechtel Corp.) and Reagan conferring up front about economic policy *after* election. . . .

Next morning . . . on to a clanking old steel mill (Cyclops) which looks like one of the rebuilt ruins of the Ruhr after the war. They make stainless steel. Just laid off 200 men. Men angry. Japanese make stainless cheaper because they pay lower wages than Pennsylvania. Japanese are screwing them. They listen to Reagan make a speech on reviving American steel industry. One of the workers says he hates "the fucking Japanese" as well as the "fucking buttercup-yellow politicians you can't trust." Carter, the same day, is in Detroit touting American automobiles, telling the American people that ours are the *best* cars in the world, better than any foreign model.

October 6, 1980
(Back in New York. Two weeks after Von Steuben Day for the Germans, a week after Pulaski Day for the Poles, a week before

Columbus Day for the Italians) . . . So the year ends as it began: each night the evening's news starts and ends with the turbulence in Iran. Last year it was the rioting, killing, then the hostages. Now it's flame, crimson and orange and black oil smoke, and the little patterns of skyfighters against the blue [I had obviously been watching the early sputterings of the Iran-Iraq war on television].

. . . The Carter campaign is aimless, a hit and dart campaign. Though he talks "vision," he really talks fear. So, too, does Reagan talk "visions." But no one knows what vision means any longer, for no one's eyes are fixed on reality.

. . . we worry about the Moral Majority here. But I think it's a worldwide phenomenon, a revolt against hedonism, which reaches all the way from Iran and Israel to the United States. . . .

October 11, 1980

. . . Reagan's sitting on his lead (à la Dewey); won't attack on foreign policy . . . is dangerously vulnerable, more so than he imagines in this Iran crisis.

. . . candidates say less and less because the chance remark, the meandering thought, the snap-back answers, are apt to explode.

. . . my opinion this week, Reagan ahead slightly in popular vote, and ahead decisively in electoral vote. Anderson fading fast.

. . . lunched with . . . today, who had seen Ted Kennedy this week. Kennedy had asked, "Hey, do you want to see some good news?" and then pulled out some private polls of Pennsylvania, *with Carter trailing.*

It was unlike previous campaigns. Fifty years of Democratic dominance of American opinion were being challenged—and challenged at every level. The opinion of the thinking classes was divided: Here one had the great civil libertarian, Democrat Morris Abram, coming out for Reagan; as did Edward Costikyan, the first of the original Democratic reformers of Manhattan. And then two of the country's most distinguished blacks, the Reverend Ralph Abernathy of Atlanta, successor to Martin Luther King, and Hosea Williams both came out in support of Reagan.

And over all, the pounding and pricking of television—the commercials of both parties flogging their messages over the networks.

The Rafshoon/Carter commercials emphasized that the presidency is the toughest job in the world, the problems immense, involving war and peace, and who do you want in the White House with his finger on the button of Holocaust? The Dailey/Reagan commercials were cold, hard, with graphics and charts and prices, prices five years ago, prices now. Judge for yourself. The Rafshoon commercials were far more artful, pinned on personality rather than issue. The Dailey commercials seemed awkward, technically cold—but far more effective. They reached at the pocketbook, and invited questions.

Yet, finally, there remained the elementary value of traveling with the candidates. The candidate, on the road, links his personality with the issues, and both with the tactics that make up the strategy.

By October, Reagan had clarified the issue strategy. "We're heavy on two things," said Lyn Nofziger. "We're running against Carter on the economy, and we're trying to make Reagan into a man of peace." His tours now were arranged in bloc chunks designed by Wirthlin's polling, and his stopovers were designed to fit into the large strategy—the dissolution and final breakup of the coalition which had governed America and controlled Congress since Franklin Roosevelt.

Reagan woke, for example, on Wednesday, October 1, at the Waldorf-Astoria, early enough to go over his clips (from the New York *Times* and the Washington *Post,* as well as the summary of the previous night's network newscasts), sort out his telephone calls, listen to and speak with a group of small businessmen, two blacks conspicuously present on the platform with him. He said he believed "small business creates neighborhoods, we ought to zone areas in the big cities for jobs," and added that the estate tax had to be adjusted to preserve "family-owned farms and family-owned businesses." He gave them a joke and closed by saying he needed their help.

He was off next to court the hard-hat vote at the construction site of New York's controversial Sixty-third Street subway tunnel. The subway, under construction for fifteen years, is a spectacular example of a project dependent on federal funds. Almost half a billion dollars (almost all federal money) has already been spent. By 1984, when the first section is scheduled to open, the total cost will be $800 million. Though the tunnel is an engineering marvel, the changing pattern of New York life will probably make it obsolete by the time it is completed to the original plan—if ever. Reagan was presumably unaware of its history, which symbolized all he stood against. But he was after the blue-collar vote, the Italian vote, and for television the pictures were gorgeous—a glistening yellow crane behind; the hard-hats in their enameled helmets of blue, yellow, red, green; an American flag over the super's wagon against which he spoke. The hard-hats hoisted banners: SANDHOGS FOR REAGAN; ITALIANS FOR REAGAN; BRING HOME OUR HOSTAGES. Wearing a red hard-hat himself, Reagan stood there, fielded a football someone had tossed ("Catch this one, Gipper"), and poured it on with patriotism, with his reminder that he was the only one running for President who had been a union president; he told them an Irish joke, raised a laugh, and closed in the vernacular: "If you guys stick around and give me a little help, I'll be cutting ribbons on projects like this next year."

Then he was off to Paterson, New Jersey, a decaying industrial city, a cocktail of ethnics—blacks, Hispanics, Italians, Slavs. Standing in front of its Renaissance-Gothic city hall, he talked of jobs and joblessness, of the budget ("There's enough fat in the budget so that, if you rendered it, you could make soap for the entire world"). This scene, too, was a natural for the cameras, and they stayed on Reagan, while on the fringes of the crowd a few hundred black and Hispanic members of the "Revolutionary Communist Party of the U.S.A." shouted, booed, jeered, waved their banners (GO HOME REAGAN; REAGAN FOR THE RICH, WHAT ABOUT THE POOR). When they began to yell, "You're a prick, Reagan," or "Bullshit, Bullshit, Bullshit," Reagan said, "I wish they'd shut up," and continued his denunciation of Carter's economics.

From Paterson, Reagan was off to Wilkes-Barre, Pennsylvania. With the sun slanting through the pin oaks over the green, and balloons floating down, he is greeted by three thousand people. The local newspaper has sent six reporters and two photographers to cover the rally, for in Wilkes-Barre, a visit by a presidential candidate is a Big Event. One of the reporters tells the visiting press of the permanent local unemployment since the anthracite mines ran out. On the local *Democratic* calling list, he says, in blue-collar precincts, Reagan is running ahead of Carter. The demonstrators on the outskirts of this crowd are prim and gallant ladies of suburbia carrying neatly hand-lettered signs: THE ONLY WOMAN IN AMERICA WHO GOT HER FREEDOM FROM REAGAN IS JANE WYMAN. One ERA lady carries another neat sign: NO SELF-RESPECTING WOMAN SHOULD WISH OR WORK FOR THE SUCCESS OF A PARTY THAT IGNORES HER SEX— SUSAN B. ANTHONY. This is a very sedate demonstration, with no yelling or profanity, so Reagan can ignore the protesting women and speak only to his primary audience of blue-collar unemployed. He is onto two of his favorite themes, inflation and joblessness. Carter tells us, says Reagan, that the average rate of unemployment is 8 percent.

That reminds him of the story of the fellow trying to cross a river. He was told that the average depth of crossing was three feet. But when he got to the middle, he drowned.

Then, at dusk, on to Pittsburgh, with no public appearances scheduled that night. Reagan has targeted the ethnics on this tour in New York, New Jersey, and Pennsylvania. Combined, the three states carry 89 electoral votes. And he has scored. The local 6:00 P.M. news in New York had carried three "bites" of the morning's work: a snatch of the small-business meeting at the Waldorf, a snatch of the hard-hats at the tunnel site, a snatch of the Paterson rally. And the 7:00 P.M. NBC *Nightly News* carries nationwide the colorful scene of many-hued helmeted sandhogs digging the never-to-be-finished tunnel. The Wilkes-Barre appearance is carried both locally and in Pittsburgh.

In Pittsburgh, I spend the evening talking with Mike Deaver and Stu Spencer, the senior strategists of Capsule Command ("I ran two campaigns for him," says Spencer, "and one campaign against him"). They are worried about the Iran-Iraq war, about oil, above all about the hostages. But Reagan must be silent. They will have to support the President on the hostages no matter what he does. "If the election were taken today," says Deaver, "we'd win." But what will Carter do, what surprise deal can he bring off? "We're between a rock and a hard place," Spencer says as we talk of the Strait of Hormuz, the oil throttle of the Western world. The team is bringing George Bush into this more and more, and Bush, ex-director of the CIA, will join Reagan next week in his CIA briefing. Breaking up the coalition here at home seems easy—but Iran? Iraq? Saudi Arabia? They are worried and claim that Reagan "insists on being very careful." It is much like the 1956 Suez crisis, and Ike made the wrong move on that one. Then, after dinner, Deaver and Spencer are off to the evening council with the Reagans—and Nofziger and Martin Anderson. They have to be up by six the next morning to read the papers flowing in from Base Camp, to brief Reagan when he gets up. ("We're being flooded with papers and speech texts," says Nofziger, who has contempt for everyone at Base Camp, all except Baker and Wirthlin. "If you looked at all their papers you wouldn't have time to think.")

Traveling with Carter, two and a half weeks later, is very different. It is gloomy.

Carter is still trying to shore up the coalition. But he is also burdened by the crushing weight of a presidency in action—the hostage situation in Iran, the war in Iraq, negotiations with the Russians, a stubborn Federal Reserve Board, which is steadily turning the screws higher on the prime rate. He has been up this Monday, October 20, since five o'clock, and then left the White House for the Midwest, to hammer away at the Great Lakes blue collars. In late afternoon, he arrives in New York to work other ethnics.

Carter's first stop in New York is at the Concord Baptist, a black church in Brooklyn's Bedford-Stuyvesant. It is a handsome building and a choir of magnificent voices is still practicing hymns as the President arrives. The Reverend V. Simpson Turner opens proceedings with an invocation and the demand "that the ills of this community be lifted." The entourage rises for introductions: Muhammad Ali, who says that we "are in the position to choose the right white"; Representative Shirley Chisholm, who speaks briefly; then Ted Kennedy, to tremendous applause. Finally, Carter, who promises 600,000 youth jobs and talks of his war on drugs—which, in this black community, so ravaged by drugs, brings tremendous applause. Carter speaks of his diplomacy in black Africa ("I turned to a great black leader, Andy Young"), in Nigeria, Zimbabwe, and other names that lift this audience.

From there he is off to a Chinatown restaurant to court the Chinese of New York: "I'm the first President ever to visit Chinatown . . . our first President, George Washington, lived just a few blocks from here. But that doesn't count. He was President, but this was not Chinatown, right?" Then to a meeting with a private gathering of Jewish community leaders; followed by a fund-raising dinner of regular Democrats. Then he is off, to be back in the White House by midnight, and be up at six the next morning for a swing through the South.

On the morning of October 21, the President is scheduled into Miami at nine. The waiting politicians at the airport tell us that Reagan is leading in Florida. They hope this Carter trip can give them a lift.

But it does not. Carter goes directly from the airport to a staged "town meeting," packed with Democratic loyalists. In the morning light he looks gaunt and gray, but slowly his spirits lift and, with this audience, eloquence comes to him. In his opening remarks, he mentions the refugee problem and is roundly booed. He responds: "I presume that your families didn't immigrate to this country. You must be native American Indians. The rest of us have all come here later. . . . Our laws were not designed to accommodate three or four thousand refugees coming here per day. Our laws were designed for people to be screened in a foreign country, carefully catalogued, and brought here a few at a time. This just didn't happen. . . . Once those boats were loaded, as President I had a choice to treat them as human beings with a precious life or see their lives lost at sea. And I did what was right." Questions surface, one after the other, all resentful. From a black: "Why doesn't the money get to us?" From a voice in the back: "I'm also wondering why there's not a greater force toward protecting the rights of Christians in our community?" Another question on Christians and their rights. He responds to that question with: "I've prayed more since I've been President than I ever did before in my life, because I feel the need for it more."

The President spends the entire morning in Miami. He talks to a meeting of Dade County Democrats, but saves his best for three privately scheduled interviews for local television stations, which will reach far more people.

North, then, to a picnic in Orlando, Florida. Only three hundred people have come, mostly oldsters. Carter is obviously depressed. He has put his all into the interviews for TV, the three in Miami and now three here. On the plane out of Orlando, he gives one more interview, to a Shreveport newspaper, for he is en route to Louisiana, also a shaky state in the eroding base. At a rally in New Orleans, he promises to make the city a great port once again. Then to bed (with the cables of crisis trickling in from abroad), and off in the morning to Texas.

Texas must be held. He is scheduled into Beaumont. Beaumont is a union town, a workingman's town in the new South, and Beaumont, with country music, lays it on for Carter. From the airport rally, a quick trip to the waterfront, where the stupendous offshore drilling effort becomes visible. The shipyards here stab the skyline with the drilling platforms they are building, $50 million to $100 million each. It is beautiful television scenery—the angle shots of gantries and cranes, of towers and turrets of gray steel.

Here, Carter is at his best. Standing on the platform, shirtsleeves rolled up, his biceps showing, he is speaking to his own kind—the Southern workingman. The workers have changed: They now sport beards and have let their hair grow long. But Carter is in tune with this audience. They are patriotic—he talks of arms. They are Democrats—and he runs through the roster of Democratic saints from Franklin Roosevelt on. They are kin: "My parents came here long ago, and I'm the only one in my family to go to college." It is the best speech of his jaunt.

From there to Waco, Texas, in a blistering-hot sun. On the platform is Lady Bird Johnson.

This is farm country, and Carter begins with: "I grew up on a farm and I know you need high-top boots for things besides stomping Republicans. As you well know . . . Republicans have a habit of spreading a lot of horse manure around right before an election. And lately, as you also know, it's getting pretty deep all over this country." But the purpose of this trip to patriotic Texas is to spread the idea that he stands firm on national defense, that the Republicans ran down defense for seven of the eight years they were in power. The thought is lost to posterity, unless he has privately managed to convey it in the three additional interviews he has given local TV stations here in Waco. The press is drowsy with the heat, exhausted by days of following this melancholy entourage, seeking a theme. A news agency has just reported that at a secret meeting in Iran, it was decided to release the hostages on Sunday. The press tries to find confirmation; that could be the lead story from the President today. Jody Powell quashes the rumor ("You fellows are a lot more excited about these stories than we are").

Off, then, to Texarkana. Here, the President is very good. He faces off in the square opposite the statue of a Confederate veteran. Green and white balloons float down. Pretty girls are here in orange skirts for the Texas band, red for the Arkansas band. Integration is very apparent, for the bands include both blacks and whites. Reagan people have organized a counterdemonstration: IF JIMMY CARTER WINS, WE LOSE. The unions, however, have turned out for Carter: UAW LOCAL 237; IBEW LOCAL 3 TEXARKANA. The crowd is far more friendly than hostile.

Carter starts out: "Hello, everybody from Arkansas. How are you doing? Hello, everybody from Texas. How are you doing?" Then: "I look across this square and I see a monument to the heroes of the Confederacy, and I think back in history. . . . I was a farmer. My family lived in this nation more than three hundred years. All of us have been farmers." Then on to what the Democratic party has done for working people, poor people, farmers. "I come from the part of the nation, as you do too, that believes in hard work, self-sacrifice, trust in our families, strong communities, a deep belief in God, and I pray that we never forget those values, which never change." He goes on with the litany of Democratic heroes, with Medicare, with the old populist message, with the jobs he has created in his administration. He leaves at dusk, with one more television interview to give on his plane (for a TV station in Illinois, also a shaky state). At the White House, he will have to pay attention to Iran, the Middle East, China, plus the campaign headquarters report. And above all, the negotiations on the forthcoming debate with Ronald Reagan.

The debate with Reagan is Carter's last chance to pull ahead, to make clear the message which two months of campaigning has failed to do. He has been mousetrapped into it; he has been taunting Reagan to debate, confident he could expose his rival as a political illiterate. And Reagan has closed the trap on him, snapping it shut after seeing Carter perform at the Alfred E. Smith Memorial dinner, New York's grand festival of successful ethnics.

The "great" debates have become as stylized a scene of action in American politics as the conventions—and perhaps more important.

The nationally televised debate is where, finally, the struggle over image and issue links. There, the two candidates not only must perform, but must explain. They bring together in one audience the majority vote of the plain Americans, and the critical votes of the ethnic and minority blocs. The debates shift votes more than any other single action of the final electoral campaign.

So important and so fixed in the public mind are these debates as "classic" encounters that it is interesting to recall their short history. They had begun in 1960, between Kennedy and Nixon, because Congress lifted, for that year only, an obscure clause in the Federal Communications Act, Section 315. Section 315 had insisted that all candidates for President be given equal access to air time; but there were no less than fourteen other candidates running that year, and a debate of sixteen men was impossible. Yielding to reality, Congress permitted television to limit the debates to the two major candidates; and in the image-issue junction of the debates, Kennedy won. He had been portrayed by the Republicans as a rich, callow, inexperienced youth. But from the moment Kennedy began, "In the election of 1860, Abraham Lincoln said the question was whether this nation could exist half slave or half free. In the election of 1960 . . . the question is whether the world will exist half slave or half free"—from that moment, he held his audience mesmerized. He was, on the platform, easily the equal in maturity, wisdom, and presence of Vice-President Nixon. Kennedy had won the debates, if not on issue points, on personality.

Sixteen years were to go by before the next debate, as Section

315 came back in force and the lead candidates, President Johnson, then President Nixon, ducked behind the legality and refused to debate.

Finally, a subterfuge was found. What if a debate was not a television show, but a news event which the television networks decided to cover? No law restrained any citizens group from inviting candidates of their choice to debate. The idea of the subterfuge originated in a small group in Chicago, the Benton Foundation. Though a foundation was forbidden to intervene in politics, it might, nonetheless, contribute to education and philanthropy; and it found cover in the Education Fund of the League of Women Voters. The Benton Foundation would put up the tiny seed money ($60,000); the League would invite candidates to debate—and the television nets might just "happen along" to report the proceedings. In two quadrennials since (1976 and 1980), the League of Women Voters has acquired an institutional importance, a commanding authority over presidential debates, and, perhaps, a permanent lock on all such future debates.

By 1980, the League's authority was already not to be challenged. It insisted it would make the rules, set the dates, choose the sites, invite or exclude candidates. Its arrogance annoyed the Carter staff. The League insisted on choosing the debaters, based on the public opinion polls—which meant that it would include John Anderson, the born-again liberal Republican, whose inroads into the traditional upper-middle-class liberal vote ("the wine and cheese set") were, in August and September, alarming to the Democrats. Carter had refused to appear with Anderson. ("He's never won a primary, even in his own home state. He's never won a caucus contest in any state in the nation. He ran as a Republican, and he still is a Republican. He hasn't had a convention. He doesn't have a party. He and his wife hand-picked his vice-presidential nominee.") Carter would accept only a one-on-one debate with Ronald Reagan. The "ladies" balked. They proceeded with a one-on-one Anderson-Reagan debate in Baltimore. The big loser, all agreed, was the absent man—Carter.

By October came movement again: a statement by Carter that he was still ready to debate Reagan, one-on-one, still convinced that, with his knowledge of the presidency and his command of facts, he could expose Reagan as a fraud and a risk. At Base Camp, the Reagan staff was now negative—Wirthlin, Casey, Timmons opposed; only James Baker in favor. They rested the case on the upturn in the private Reagan polls, with their candidate six points ahead. "I wasn't all that enthusiastic; debates are high-risk events. You're putting a lot of political capital on the table for an hour and a half," said Wirthlin.

But in Capsule Command, those closest to Reagan, the feeling was otherwise. They had awakened in Detroit on October 16, and slowly they realized they had come to a common decision: Reagan should debate. On the plane to New York, Reagan had listened to them perfunctorily and said he and Nancy had already decided: They wanted to debate. That night they had attended the Alfred E. Smith dinner at the Waldorf-Astoria Hotel. Carter's performance at this gathering of the elite of the ethnics astonished them. Carter had secluded himself in his room and had appeared neither at the reception line to shake hands with the guests, nor at the dinner itself, but had arrived, taut, just before speech-making was to begin. Reagan had spoken with grace and wit; Carter had let his partisan tension surface. Both Reagan commands, Base and Capsule, had gathered the next morning at the Waldorf to argue their differences. But Reagan had so clearly outdone Carter at the evening dinner, the differences had faded. Reagan would debate Carter. Wherever the "ladies" chose, and when.

Promptly, the League chose the date: October 28; the place: Cleveland, Ohio. On the flip of a coin, Carter won the choice positions—lead off and close. "And they came," said Reagan later, "and wanted to trade. They said if I would go first, they didn't care if I went last. And I jumped at it."

They met thus in Cleveland one week before election. Cleveland had decorated itself in buntings and banners and put its Convention Center at the League's disposal. There the candidates would debate for an hour and a half. Twenty years earlier, the first of the four Kennedy-Nixon debates had drawn an audience estimated at between 65 and 75 million people. In 1980, the audience for this debate would be, by the low estimate, 100 million; by the high estimate (NBC), 105 to 110 million. The listeners, thus, were almost half the population of the United States.

There are two ways now to reflect on this debate—by content, and by images.

First, the content. The participating panel of news people had been well chosen, and their questions went to the heart of the central issues. Of all presidential debates, it was, perhaps, the finest I have heard. The panel began its questions, properly, with War and Peace. Inflation followed; then the Decline of the Cities. The first round closed with the joined issues of Iran, the hostages, and terrorism. In the second round, the questions concerned other fundamentals: Arms Control and SALT; Oil and Energy; Social Security; Leadership Ability. The text, as it reads, is of extraordinary quality. Most important, the questions were completely different from those of the first debates, in 1960. Those questions had reflected a nation so confident of itself that all revolved around the problem of how American power should be used. The answers stumbled on trivia and irrelevancies, Kennedy insisting that America could be greater and must move again, Nixon insisting that America, under eight years of Eisenhower, stood in triumph, and progress was unlimited.

I made the mistake of listening to this 1980 debate with a group of friends, almost all of them upper-level Democrats, in the comfort of a New York parlor. I have listened to the debates in the past in the auditoriums, behind the scenes, and at home. It is best, I have decided, to watch presidential debates at home, alone or with family. Surrounded by people at a party, one listens not to what the candidates say, but to how they say it. Performances engage a party more than issues, and the chatter is one of applause or of groans, of smart comment overtaking smart comment.

Images, thus, not issues, dominate my notes on the debate. There was the hall, all blue carpeting and blue trimmings; there was Carter, somewhat puffy, his sandy hair turning gray. There was Reagan, hair dark; old, but still handsome. They were evenly matched, it seemed, until the second round, when arms control and SALT came up in a question from Marvin Stone of *U.S. News & World Report*. Carter responded with, "I had a discussion with my [thirteen-year-old] daughter Amy the other day before I came here to ask me [*sic*] what the most important issue was. She said she thought nuclear weaponry and the control of nuclear arms." (The group around me, devout Democrats, groaned.) The debate went on, but we were now scoring for personality. And then, as the debate grew more personal, Reagan responded to Carter's assault on his record on Medicare by drawing himself to his full height and, in a sorrowful, head-shaking putdown of the President, said ruefully, "There you go again." As if admonishing a poor student, he corrected the President on the facts. Months later, President Reagan chuckled, recalling the moment, and told me that the two things I must not omit from an account of his campaign were, first, his response to the moderator in the Nashua debate ("That's when I got mad," he said), and his response to Carter of "There you go again" ("That was certainly unpremeditated and off the top of my head").

On points, and in text, the two had come out even. But on image and personality, there could be no doubt that Reagan had won the edge. Just as Kennedy had erased the image of inexperience in his first debate with Nixon, so Reagan had erased the killer image in his appearance. He had opened the debate, on the first question of war and peace, by saying: "I'm only here to tell you that I believe with all my heart that first priority must be world peace, and that use of force is always, and only, a last resort when everything else has failed." Then, using the advantage the Carter choice of positions had given him, he had closed, an hour and a half later: "Are you better off than you were four years ago? Is it easier for you to go and buy things in the stores than it was four years ago? . . . Is America as respected throughout the world as it was? . . . That we're as strong as we were four years ago? . . . I would like to lead that crusade . . . to take government off the backs of the great people of this country and turn you loose again to do those things that I know you can do so well, because you did them and made this country great."

Both Caddell and Wirthlin had registered Reagan narrowly or substantially ahead of Carter as they entered the debate. Now came an overnight Reagan surge. In the image contest, Wirthlin had coached his man well. It was a genial but firm man the public saw on television—no bomb thrower, no button pusher. And with the final erasure of Reagan's haunting image of risk, the campaign would in the last week turn on issues: on the direction the country would take and which man could lead it there better. "The wolf," said Gerald Rafshoon, "was no longer at the door. He was inside, running through the house." "In the end," commented Caddell with melancholy, "good performances are rewarded, and so are bad performances. We had kept the focus on the opposition for months—but how long can you keep away the winter snow?"

It was now, in the final week, not an election between images but a referendum on directions.

The last week of the election campaign was without savor, as had been the last week of Johnson's contest with Goldwater, and Nixon's with McGovern.

For Reagan, it was happiness week. When did he sense the election was turning, I later asked him, when did he feel it was won? It had been growing on him for a while, he said, but "particularly after the debate I could feel what you could call a momentum or something, a tide rolling, and there was no way to go out and campaign as heavily as I was campaigning, meeting the people, without sensing it. You know, to wind up in San Diego with over thirty thousand people standing out in the night, in a night rally. In Peoria, they estimated there in the street, in the morning of a working day, fifteen thousand people standing out there in the street. . . . from the debate on, those polls also reflected what I was feeling, that something had just taken off. . . . but [Carter] being in the White House and with the hostage thing . . . could something like that happen and create a euphoria that would change these polls? That was on my mind."

For Reagan, the day after the debate, it was down to Texas, to nail down that crucial state. When he asked his rhetorical questions, back came the chant from the crowd: "Ask Amy! Ask Amy!" Across the country he would go all through the week, sprinkling jokes, anecdotes, and waiting for the "Amy" chant. From Arkansas (still considered shaky) and Louisiana, he hop-skipped the next day to the East, winding up in Lodi, New Jersey. The underlying message, the underlying theme, was still the same: inflation. Speaking to a group of old folks on Social Security, he punched it home like this: "If the present rate of food price inflation continues for the next four years, a pound of ground beef that now costs $2.00 would cost $4.92, chicken that costs 80 cents a pound now would cost $1.97, a dozen eggs that now cost $1.10 would cost $2.71, and a gallon of milk that now costs $1.75 would cost $4.31." On Friday, October 31, he was working the Midwest heartland again (still pursuing the blue-collar vote), in Pittsburgh, then to Chicago suburbs, thence to Milwaukee, and overnight in Michigan. Saturday he campaigned through the automobile state with Gerald Ford, Michigan's own favorite son, and then all day Sunday through Ohio, joined by television personality Bob Hope. Reagan's staff was now drenching the television waves with commercials—of his $19 million budget for commercial advertising, he was spending $10 million in the last ten days.

For the President of the United States it was not a happy time. What television traced on the screen showed Carter as he moved to patch together the dissolving elements of the old Democratic coalition. From Cleveland to Pittsburgh, preceding Reagan by two days, for a town meeting; to a rally in Rochester, to hold his upstate New York Protestant vote; to New Jersey, to speak to blacks and hold them in line. The next morning he was in Philadelphia to exhort Polish-Americans, and then to speak at a meeting of the Young Men's Hebrew Association; to New York to speak at the classic rally of the garment workers, Democratic even before the time of Franklin Roosevelt. From there to Michigan, to the unemployed automobile workers, then to Saint Louis. By Friday, Carter was back in the South (South Carolina, Tennessee, Florida) and Texas, following Reagan by two days, as both crisscrossed the country. And from Texas to Milwaukee and an overnight in Chicago, where Carter was scheduled to speak on Sunday morning to a black ministers' gathering.

But it was not to be. The blips of the candidates' travels across the targeted states were being faded out by history itself. The campaign was ending, as it had begun, with a bewilderment about America's place in the world, with—to be specific—the crisis in Iran, and the fifty-two Americans still imprisoned there.

One cannot but be sympathetic to Jimmy Carter in those last days of the campaign. However fumbling his frantic effort to retrieve his inherited coalition, however focused his effort to turn Americans to consider the risk of Ronald Reagan, he behaved admirably as a President. His campaign, as a candidate, might be stuttering; but as chief executive, he was firm.

Night after night, as the anniversary of the seizure of the hostages approached its one-year mark, to coincide with election day, the Iranians dominated the television screen. The cadence built. There, on Thursday, October 30, on the screens, was Carter denouncing the Japanese to Michigan automobile workers and offering visions to New York garment workers. But there the same night was the scene of the Iranian Majlis, in the blue-carpeted hall built by the deposed Shah, screaming, yelling, and shaking fists at each other. And the next night, with Carter fighting for his Southern base from Memphis to Houston, the dominating scene for viewers was Iran again: frenzied crowds in the streets of Teheran, yelling, "Death to the United States! Death to Carter!" and the Prime Minister threatening, "this arch-Satan, we will drag out his throat."

October 31, Friday, was Halloween, and television in its half-hour commercial frame jammed a great deal into its twenty-two minutes of comment. A rumored deal on the hostages, with a DC-8 standing by in London to fly them out; no, said another report, the plane was standing by in Sweden. But Halloween had to be celebrated. One network showed a Halloween celebration in New York —a group of gays dressed in skull-and-skeleton costumes. As I watched, it occurred to me: No one had rung my bell. Twenty-five years earlier, when I first moved into the house in New York, little children would ring the bell, shouting, "Trick or treat." Even black children would come down from Harlem, and jingle "Trick or Treat," and I would give them candy. No black children had rung my bell for ten years; they are afraid to come into this white district at night. Now even the white boys and girls are afraid to venture out after dark. So I had no need for the candies and fruits I had bought; the city had changed, the country had changed, and Halloween as shown on television was celebrated by the homosexuals. I noticed on the screen also that there was a shot of the Reagan plane, the correspondents obviously relaxed—and today, with unerring instinct, Reagan, at takeoff, was rolling a pumpkin, not an orange, down the aisle.

The weekend builds toward its Iranian climax. Each network must have, because the other networks certainly will, an anniversary retrospective on the seizure of the hostages one year ago. The weekend is drenched with the humiliation.

Although Carter is observing all political rituals as he tries to hold the coalition together, behind the scenes he is acting as a President must and should. Through diplomatic channels has come a report to Washington that the Iranians are offering terms. Hamilton Jordan flies on Saturday to discuss the terms with the campaigning President, who will alight in Chicago that night. They decide they must scratch the critical meeting with black ministers the next day; and at four o'clock in the morning, the President rouses his staff to fly to Washington, the national command post. A morning conference. As the leadership of America, they must reject the Iranian terms for timed, tortured release, first of some of the hostages, then others, then one by one. But then a political question: Is it wiser for the President to use this opportunity for an all-out patriotic, flag-waving repudiation of the Iranian terrorist terms? Or to pass, continuing silent negotiations, in order to get all the hostages out safely on better terms? The President makes the proper decision. He will not voice a call of belligerence. He makes a brief public appearance in the pressroom, and now must be off again, to politick across the country.

Ronald Reagan that Monday is in happy-land; even the most cynical reporters on his plane know they are with the winner. They wind up in San Diego. Reagan is relaxed—when he is heckled, he snaps out, "Aw, shut up!" then apologizes—and flies off, content, home to Los Angeles.

It is no day of relaxation at the President's White House base in Washington. All weekend, Caddell has been polling, but events have overtaken tactics. Caddell speaks to Jody Powell, traveling with the President, and finds Powell depressed by the previous night's television shows, and the remark of some unnamed Iranian that "we have brought America to its knees." Caddell's apparatus has been polling voters all across the nation over the weekend, and they have been shifting. The voters now feel that the President cannot get the hostages home in the next few days. The shift is sharp. In twenty-four hours, the percent of those expecting a quick release of the hostages has dropped from 40 to 36. The number of those with little expectation of quick release has risen sharply. The shift is most marked among union workers and Catholics, the coalition base. Somehow these voters have lost faith in this leadership.

At midnight on Monday, Caddell again visits his office, where the results of this last day's survey of 1,500–2,000 people are being coded. He recalls entering the office and seeing the silhouettes of his coders, bent over their charts and figures—all silent. At two o'clock in the morning, he calls Hamilton Jordan. They arrange to meet hastily, Jordan, Rafshoon, and Caddell at the White House office of the chief of staff. They decide they should call the President, who is closing his campaign in Seattle.

It is a conference call. Powell tells them that it's been an "up day," the President has done so well. Caddell then speaks to the President. "How's it going?" asks Carter, upbeat. "Not so good, Mr. President," answers Caddell. Carter's tone changes. "Tell Jody about it," he says curtly, as he goes forward to his compartment on *Air Force One*, en route back to Plains, Georgia, where his political career began.

And thus, on November 4, 1980, while the President was flying back to Plains, they had already begun to vote in the East—in New Hampshire, which had shriveled to a detail; in the border states like Kentucky; in the plains states, like Kansas. They were moving to a verdict on Carter, on Reagan, and on the grand old coalition.

CHAPTER FOURTEEN

ANSWERS AND QUESTIONS

Ⅰt was over before the polls opened; the people had made up their minds.

Everyone knew it.

Reagan knew it. Wirthlin had reported, on the last Monday of the campaign, that his three-day rolling-average poll showed an eleven-point Reagan lead. The Reagan plane, *LeaderShip 80,* had taken off from San Diego shortly after eleven in a ground fog, and Reagan was home in Pacific Palisades in time for a good night's rest, ready for whatever tomorrow or the festering Iranian crisis might bring.

Carter knew it. He had known it since he left Seattle after midnight. He had punished himself again that day, but with more brutality to his constitution than usual. He had studied the Iranian cables on Sunday night, had risen early to sky-skip from Akron, Ohio, to Springfield, Missouri, to Detroit, to Portland and Seattle on the West Coast, then left Seattle for the long flight back to Georgia, arriving just after dawn. He had then voted at Plains High School and gone to his signature platform, the dingy little railroad station in the center of Plains. There, exhausted, choking back tears, his voice strained, Carter explained how he had tried to do his best through all the difficult decisions. "I've tried to honor my commitment to you," he concluded. And then, still exhausted, he had flown off to the White House to await the returns.

All the networks knew it. Their exit pollings through the day had been reporting the developing landslide, a Reagan sweep. By four o'clock in the afternoon, the networks also learned the results of the

Caddell polling: that it would be a downer by ten points, with the outcome of the senatorial races gloomy to the point of disaster. For the networks, there was only one remaining dilemma. They knew the results, *now,* by midafternoon; but reportorial custom required them *not* to announce what was inescapable fact until it became actual fact. I arrived early at the NBC central studio with its giant map and its banks of computorial analysts sorting out all races—presidential, senatorial, congressional, gubernatorial. I was due to make my ninety-second snatch of analysis shortly after the report went on air at 7:00 P.M. A brief flurry of conversation gave me the tone to adopt: I must talk as if the results were in, yet not show the results were certain; I was to stick to the theme that this was, probably, the end of an era.

It was, thus, to be a night of media showmanship and competition. By eight o'clock Eastern Standard Time, with half a dozen states already recorded, and the results certain, NBC moved to its sampling projections, first on the calls. John Chancellor, in his last election as anchorman, did a rat-tat-tat in less than two minutes. At 8:01: "Connecticut goes to Reagan . . . New Jersey for Reagan . . . Pennsylvania for Reagan . . ." and west across the board: "Michigan for Reagan . . . Tennessee for Reagan . . . Oklahoma for Reagan . . . Texas for Reagan." And, finally, unable to resist the overbearing reality, Chancellor, at 8:15, announced: "NBC News now makes its projection for the presidency. Reagan is our projected winner. Ronald Wilson Reagan of California, a sports announcer, a film actor, a governor of California, is our projected winner at 8:15 Eastern Standard Time on this election night."

In California, Ronald Reagan was in his shower, Nancy Reagan had just stepped out of her bathtub, when the television set, turned up loud, blared out NBC's call. "I ran out, and I wrapped a towel around me," Nancy Reagan told Barbara Walters later, "and Ronnie got out of the shower, wrapped a towel around him, in time to hear that they were giving him the election. It was five-fifteen, five-thirty in the afternoon. And there we were, standing in the bedroom with towels wrapped around us, dripping wet, hearing that he'd been elected President of the United States. And I said to him, 'I don't think this is the way it's supposed to be. . . . I somehow saw it completely differently from this.' And with that, the phone rang and it was Jimmy Carter. President Carter conceding the election."

It had been gloomy all day in the White House, where Carter had known since morning that his presidency was ending. He telephoned his staff about eight in the evening to tell them he wanted to get it over with quickly, concede now. One of his aides telephoned House Speaker Tip O'Neill to inform him the President was about to concede. O'Neill protested, because the polls in California were still open. But NBC had already proclaimed the victor, and so, at 9:52 P.M., there was Jimmy Carter on air, saying: "I promised you four years ago that I would never lie to you, so I can't stand here tonight and say it doesn't hurt. . . . we have faced the tough issues. We've stood for and fought for and achieved some very important goals for our country. . . . I've wanted to serve as President because I love this country and because I love the people of this nation. . . . I have not lost either love. Thank you very much."

The results of the election of 1980 can be posted in neat figures. However the figures are sorted out, they show that Ronald Reagan won by a landslide. But whether that landslide was simply a repudiation of the past, or the new beginning he had promised, remained on election night, and remains still today, the central uncertainty of America's near future. Critical elections are not fixed in history by election night returns; they depend on what the victor does with his victory.

Ronald Reagan won 43,899,248 votes, or 50.75 percent of the 86,495,678 Americans who voted. Jimmy Carter won 35,481,435, or 41.02 percent of those who voted. John Anderson, the independent, won 5,719,437 voters, or 6.61 percent. Superficially, the percentage of those eligible to vote had dropped to its lowest point since the election of Harry Truman. Only 53.95 percent of those eligible to vote had turned out, a drop-off viewed with alarm by many but not particularly important.*

Reagan won the electoral vote by 489 to Carter's 49. He carried all but six states of the Union: Georgia and Minnesota (home states of the two Democratic candidates), plus Maryland, Rhode Island, West Virginia, and Hawaii, as well as the District of Columbia. The sweep was so large that the breakdown of Reagan's vote is paralyzingly complex. One can note only that the peak of his vote came in the Mountain West and the prairie states, with high support in the

---

*One must always distinguish between those "eligible" and those "registered" to vote. Everyone over the age of eighteen is "eligible" to vote, and in shifting America, with its population changes, many of those technically eligible fail to register. Among those who register to vote, the people who care, the percentage that casts a ballot is probably as high in America as in any other democratic state in the Western world. That figure has always been high, and it remains high; but scholarship has yet to examine the figure for its meaning.

South. Nine states gave him 60 percent or more of their votes: Utah delivered 73 percent for Reagan; Idaho, Nebraska, Nevada, North Dakota, Wyoming, Arizona, South Dakota, and Oklahoma following. Of the three great states, California delivered 53 percent to Reagan; Texas, 56 percent; New York, 47 percent (to Carter's 44 percent).

The Republican sweep takes on more manageable shape as we come to the lesser races. The Republicans gained 33 seats in the House, making the margin 243 Democratic congressmen to 192 Republicans. If any vague pattern can be drawn about the Republican resurgence, it would trace the demography of suburban development. The safe seats of the Democrats lay in the big cities; but as Americans had moved from city to suburb, they had unsettled the old suburban/urban structure, and it was in suburbia that the Republicans gained most.

An even clearer shape came out of the Republican reconquest of the Senate, the most startling and unanticipated development of the election of 1980. The Republicans emerged from the 1980 campaign with a gain of 12 Senate seats, the largest Senate shift since the midterm elections of 1958. Their gain was even more important than a shift. They sent to the Senate 53 senators against the Democrats' 47. The last sure grip the Republicans had had on the Senate was so long ago as to be almost forgotten: in 1928, the Republicans had elected 56 senators. Now, with 53, they had their largest majority in more than half a century. The map shows the structure of this shift. Three gains were made in the Northwest (Alaska, Idaho, Washington), four in the South (Georgia, Alabama, Florida, North Carolina), four in the Midwest (South Dakota, Iowa, Wisconsin, Indiana), one in New England (New Hampshire). In the carnage had fallen Democratic liberals of great reputation—Magnuson of Washington, Nelson of Wisconsin, McGovern of South Dakota, Church of Idaho, Bayh of Indiana, as well as others of large prestige. The conservatives had targeted such men for destruction and had prevailed. With this unanticipated conquest of the Senate, Reagan could conduct foreign policy almost as he wished, and hope that on his budget and economic programs, the Senate could be swayed to go along.

Beneath these official figures lay other figures, more flexible and perplexing. There analysis rested on the uncertain measurements of the pollsters. Jimmy Carter had held the black vote by margins of 90 percent and up. To rebuild its majority, the Democratic party would have to rely in the future, for as far ahead as one could see, on this black base. Reagan narrowly lost the organized union voters; but by 48 percent to Carter's 45 percent, he had carried the blue-collar voters. He had won the vote of those over twenty-five by close margins, but the margins rose with age until, among those over sixty-five, he had won by 55 percent to 39 percent. Among all those making over $8,000 a year, he carried a majority; and of those making more than $35,000 a year, he won by two to one. Among Protestants he had won 57/36; among Catholics, 47/43. Where he had made his greatest targeted gains was among ethnics. Here, I rely on the NBC exit polling results. It was no surprise that Reagan carried the Irish vote in every major state, but the results are astounding (California 64/28, New York 53/35, Texas 65/31). Among other ethnics—Jewish, Slavic, Italian—his tactics had also worked with spectacular results. More than one out of every four Jewish voters who had voted for Carter in 1976 left to vote for Reagan. The overwhelming Jewish Democratic majority of tradition had been reduced to a margin of 4 to 3. In Pennsylvania, Jews had actually given Reagan a majority (45/39). Reagan had also cut heavily into the Hispanic-American vote, pulling at least 25 percent to the Republican ticket. Of the other great ethnic groups in American political life, it may be said that the shift was even more significant. The other ethnics are generally working-class people, thus tugged to the Democrats; but more and more they are homeowners, thus tugged to the Republicans. They moved to the Republicans in 1980.

Two groups among these ethnics should be marked for the results of prime and precise planning. The Polish/Slavic voters remained loyal to the Democrats in only three states: Pennsylvania, Maryland, Ohio. In New Jersey, 60 percent voted for Reagan to 29 percent for Carter; in Connecticut, 44/41; in Michigan, 49/44; in Texas, 62/33; in Illinois, 49/39; and so across the board. The vote of Italian-Americans was even more revealing of the rustlings beneath the surface. The Italian-American vote has always been Democratic, except for 1972. This time, in 1980, it moved clear over the line. Only in one state—Ohio—did Italian-Americans support Carter against Reagan. In New Jersey, where Republicans had targeted them as the prime vulnerables, they voted for Reagan over Carter 60/33; in New York, 57/37; in California, 64/26.

It might be said of the election of 1980 that the ethnics had, at least for the moment, joined the majority of "plain Americans." The Italians, the Slavs, and the Irish had all shifted. For the Asian-Americans there is no polling breakdown. They are still too few to provide pollsters with a meaningful sample. Only in Hawaii are they a majority, and the gross final vote in that state gives the sole clue to their movement: Jimmy Carter carried Hawaii by only 45 to 43.

The final vote confirmed the Reagan-Wirthlin strategy of attack on the old Roosevelt coalition, ripping away blue-collars, Southerners, ethnics from their former moorings. But Democrats might take cold comfort from the possible formation, in embryo, of what may someday be called the Carter coalition. Most important in the results, though disturbing, was the cleavage of Americans by race. Though no less than 90 percent of all black voters voted for Jimmy Carter, white voters, by contrast, gave Reagan 56 percent and Carter only 35 percent of their votes, the balance going to Anderson. Quite as significant in the composition of the Democratic results was the way the women voted. No such split between men and women had been seen in a national election in the sixty years since women gained the right to vote. In 1980, men cast 56 percent of their votes for Reagan, 36 percent for Carter. But women split almost evenly: 45 percent for Carter, 47 percent for Reagan. Whether the underlying issues of the Equal Rights Amendment and Reagan's stand on abortion pushed so many of them to vote for Carter is not known. Yet the split was there. With women, blacks, and other minorities (Hispanics and Jews), the Democrats might, someday, build another coalition—but it would differ from the old Roosevelt coalition.

One can look at the election map and dissect the understructure of the suburban, blue-collar, ethnic vote, and then of the income-level vote or age vote or women's vote, and go blind peering for meaning within the figures. Good scholars have begun to sift the figures; so have the professionals of modern electioneering. Depth surveys and responsible analyses have already been published, trying to grasp reality through the figures. Harvard's Kennedy School of Government; Rutgers University's scholars in New Jersey; the American Enterprise Institute in Washington, and others have put their thinking in print. More studies are on the way, more data than any one man can read. All of these analyses try to tell us whether this election was really significant, or merely an eddy in the flow. But those of us who write about politics suffer from information overload. Data-base analysis helps very little when too many facts smother understanding.

So I must retreat to a personal view of what has been happening and what the election meant.

Of the five great landslides in American politics since World War II, four have been for Republican Presidents. The American people must have been seeking something in them. But of these four land-slides, only one—the election of 1980—can be called, starkly, a repudiation. Whether it was the repudiation of one man, Jimmy Carter, or the repudiation of a national experience, no one can yet say for certain. Nor can one do more than note the contending analyses of those psephologists who claim that this was a passing accident of voting as against rival psephologists who claim that it was a rejection of an entire system of ideas, those framed by the Great Society, perhaps even those rooted in the New Deal.

I weigh in with those who believe that, in 1980, Americans decisively repudiated a set of experiences and ideas that had brought them to a time of self-questioning. The evidence seems too overwhelming for me to think otherwise.

There is, first, the blanketing reality that surrounds us. By the millions, all through the past decade, white Americans have been fleeing the great cities for the suburbs; and there they voted for Reagan.

There are, next, the fuzzy measurements of the exit pollsters, trying to capture the moods of voters as they walked away from the polls. I rely here again on the scanning system of NBC/AP, which questioned no less than 37,606 voters in a cross-country sampling and reported the following: When asked to identify one or two issues that most stirred them, 47 percent of those who voted for Reagan said it was "controlling inflation," and 45 percent said it was "strengthening America's position in the world." Of those who voted for Carter, only 20 percent mentioned America's position in the world, and only 24 percent declared inflation stirred them most. By contrast, "insuring peace" weighed far more heavily on the minds of Carter's voters (36 percent) than on Reagan's voters (5 percent). If there was a mandate for Reagan, it was for budget control and rearmament.

More important than such post-polling surveys are the solid voting results, particularly the vote for the United States Senate. It was not just that the Republicans sent sixteen new senators to Washington and gained twelve seats; almost all these new Republicans, with the exception of Rudman of New Hampshire and Specter of Pennsylvania, were archconservatives, people of the Robert Taft–Barry Goldwater persuasion. Those Democrats who succeeded in holding on to their seats, such as Glenn of Ohio and Cranston of California, stood out as individuals because they had managed to resist the flowing tide.

Even more important were the events of the months following the election, highlighted by Reagan's tactical and political mastery over a split new Congress. Democrats and Republicans alike vied in a tax-cutting stampede, an irresistible majority of both houses swept along by the spirit of largesse Reagan seemed to invite.

All these fragments of evidence seem, to me, to weigh decisively on the side of those who feel that a running tide swept over Jimmy Carter that nothing could stay.

Yet the repudiation cannot be entirely divorced from the personality of the two candidates. It was Carter who lost, Carter who was rejected, the first President elected by the vote of the people since Herbert Hoover to be spurned by them only four years later.

One of the saddest meetings I have ever had with any President was a breakfast with Jimmy Carter six months after his defeat. It must have been painful for him too, for I had to probe what must have ached—why he had lost. His normal shyness and muttered replies accentuated that impression of withdrawal he had given to all too many people. Now, out of office, he was the same—proud, melancholy, slow-spoken, reflective. He was precise as he listed the reasons for his defeat. First, Ted Kennedy. Kennedy had, he said, undermined the natural Democratic base, used up the party's resources in the primaries, so that, when it came to the election, ". . . I didn't have time to devote to the wooing of the farmers in the Midwest or wooing the Southerners. I had to spend my time . . . to recover the support and confidence of the traditional, historical Democratic constituency." On Kennedy, Carter was quite bitter; and even more bitter about the congressmen who ran away from him, who did not want to come to the convention. ("The only reason a Southern congressman goes to a Democratic convention is so he can walk out on it.")

The second reason for his loss, Carter said, was of course the inflation. Mrs. Carter, who was with us, intervened, perhaps to clarify or perhaps to protect her husband from an unfriendly questioner. "All the economists," she said, "as far as inflation is concerned, give you different answers . . . but Jimmy thought he was on the right track, that he was getting to the root of the problem." Her pretty face of 1976 was now drawn and lined, as if she had suffered more than her husband from the ordeal of power.

The third reason, continued Carter, was the situation in Iran, and the way television had celebrated the anniversary on that last weekend, the screens showing "the burning of the American flag, carrying out garbage in the Stars and Stripes." Again and again as we spoke, Mrs. Carter would intervene to explain why they had done as they did—"because it was right." She was a woman deserving of respect; his defeat was hers. At one point, she broke in to offer me coffee and toast. When I protested that a First Lady should not serve a visiting reporter breakfast, Carter said, mildly and proudly, "She's not the First Lady any longer; she's just a Southern woman now."

Other bitternesses trickled out: the Moral Majority claiming he advocated homosexuality, the National Rifle Association boasting it had spent $12 million to defeat Carter: "I just couldn't believe it. . . . My friend Wayne Hofster, I grew up with him, we'd shot quail and pheasant together, fished trout . . . and he was almost convinced that I was going to take away his gun."

The conversation ran for almost an hour and a half, and as it wore on, we got into the nitty-gritty of American politics. That stirred Carter from his "ah . . . hmm" replies to my provocations. As he moved to national politics, he was masterly on the structure of the vote. But pressing this once-President, I realized again two things: that he was a conceptualizer, and that his concepts did not quite fit together. He was, as he proclaimed himself in public, deeply concerned by the inflation, but just as deeply upset by the cruelty any remedy against inflation might bring. He was unyieldingly proud of his crusade for human rights, but just as proud of his call for attention to the African states, where human rights do not exist. He was a good man, but a confused one; a shy, proud man, who could not be shaken from the conviction that he and Rosalynn had done "what was right."

Though the repudiation of Jimmy Carter was far less a factor in his defeat than the repudiation of his party, one could not escape the role of personality—and that came clear in a talk I had with President Reagan soon after I visited Carter.

Perhaps because I had seen them both within so short a time, the contrast between them was sharp. Carter was a moody, thoughtful person, whose mind dwelt more on the questions than on the answers—while Reagan was such a jolly man, with no doubt about the answers to any questions. The cheerful man appealed more to voters than the pensive one. I talked with Reagan about the tactics of his campaign, and he spoke with zest, brio, and quip. He was only shortly recovered from his wound and the desperately dangerous assassination attempt on his life. But now he could make light even of that, as he retold the story. "There were these shots . . . in 2.8 seconds . . . and I didn't feel a thing. The Secret Service threw me in a car, and they flopped on me. I yelled, 'Get off, you're hurting my ribs' . . . then I had difficulty breathing and I was gulping blood and I said, 'See, you've broken my ribs, you've punctured my lungs!' . . . When we got to the hospital I was still mad and they put me on a wagon immediately. . . . Next thing I knew, they were cutting my new suit off me. I just bought it. I was furious. . . . The surgical staff was holding a meeting at that time, just upstairs, so there was no trouble calling them, they came right down."*

My talk with Reagan touched none of the high purposes of American life, or his ideas. We had spoken of that during the campaign—and there is no difference between Reagan's public and private statements. His idea, voiced so often in public, is that the best way forward may be found by going back first to find out where we missed the proper turn at the crossroads—and then starting all over again. What he had to say, he had said over and over to the point of monotony in twelve years of national campaigning.

It is difficult for the thinking classes, or the Democratic party, to accept Ronald Reagan as an intellectual—chiefly because he is *not*. But he has ideas, and the ideas, simple and stubborn, are compulsive for him. He is the most thoroughly ideological President since Herbert Hoover. Thus, like all ideological Presidents, and unlike Franklin Roosevelt or John Kennedy or Dwight Eisenhower, Reagan is a captive to his court of thinkers, who may or may not mislead him, as Carter's thinkers misled him.

There is no escaping the stark fact of the repudiation, in the election of 1980, of a regime that had outlived its time, and though the personalities of the candidates played a vital role, ideas, and the programs that flow from these ideas, are more important.

My thinking is that by the time of the 1980 election, the pursuit of equality had created a system of interlocking dependencies, and the American people were persuaded that the cost of equality had come to crush the promise of opportunity. These ideas struggled with each other all through the campaign, and the one idea prevailed over the other. This could make the election of 1980 a watershed in history. Except that the first year of the Reagan administration gives us no way yet of judging whether his ideas will work, how much they will cost in rising tensions—or whether some entirely new system of ideas must replace both his and those of Jimmy Carter.

I write this now, as Reagan's second and critical year begins,

---

*Interviews with Reagan in the White House are generally taped, two little switches placed conspicuously on the table before the fireplace, so that the interviewer is in no doubt of the recording. Reagan's account of the assassination attempt was not, however, recorded, since we were walking to the door; the conversation here is from notes I made shortly afterward.

almost as a passenger on a ship, familiar with captain and crew on bridge, knowing them bold sailors. But whether their navigation is correct remains to be seen. They have set a course which may be the most perilous in modern American politics—a "riverboat gamble," Senate Majority Leader Howard Baker has called it. If Reagan's navigation is wrong, all of us may founder; if the course is correct, we may all come safely through the storm ahead to a new and different land. But there is still no way of telling whether we are on a true bearing or steaming with compass demagnetized.

For the first full year of the Reagan experiment, the debate on the national course has been buried in the mystifying budgets of the United States. This debate becomes exciting only when one realizes that in it are twined the roots of all the past promises that have endowed so many groups and causes with their expectations for the future. It concerns who gets what from whom and what the national purpose requires from both those who get and those who must pay. The issue of the budget is now the longest ongoing debate in recent American politics; the first Reagan budget has not yet been settled, the second is already public controversy; and the struggle will go on, until the President is either triumphant or dismissed in disaster.

Several radical turnabout ideas are buried in these Reagan budgets. The first is that the federal government must cut its tax burdens, as well as its benefits, and urge the states, the communities, and private goodwill to share the cost of providing for cause groups and unfortunates; what this implies is a new form of federalism, repudiating the full sweep of centralization of the past thirty years. The second is that somehow the engines of American abundance must be refueled, by making investment and production more tempting to the risk-takers. That means that the venturers are invited to get richer, but the television screens fill with visuals of children deprived of free or low-cost school lunches and old folks worried about Social Security. There follows next the idea that America must spend to the limit increasing its armed force to outface the Russians. All these ideas, taken together, are what is being tested as we enter the critical middle years of the Reagan administration—and if they succeed, what will have happened is a revolution.

The ever-changing figures of the budget do not show the drama clearly. Reagan's first cut-slash-trim budget of $704 billion *did* cut more than $30 billion from the Carter projection of fiscal 1982—but nonetheless, it was *larger* by $42 billion than the last full Carter budget of 1981. Reagan's first budget did not cut dollar expenditures

—it cut expectations. And to untangle these expectations is to disturb the dependencies on which almost half the American population relies. What is being tested is whether it is possible, politically, now or ever, to reorient these expectations, or turn them around.

Each slash in budget disturbs an idea that has shaped the perspectives of a generation. Therein comes the drama. To take just one among many slashes—in federal aid for college education: In the first Reagan budget of $704 billion, the slash in aid to college students was almost a trifle—a projected cut of something less than $400 million from the last Carter student aid budget of almost $4.2 billion. But the slash rips away at an idea. Ever since the G.I. Bill of Rights, thirty-eight years ago, the federal government has become, increasingly, the sponsor of college education for all. No less than five programs now endow this right, and by the fall of 1981, college enrollments had risen to an all-time high of 12.3 million students. Of these students, no less than 3.5 million were being assisted by some form of federal loans or grants. But the right to an education seemed to carry no obligation; their predecessors had defaulted on an estimated $3.2 billion of loans they had promised to repay. The Reagan cut thus ran directly contrary to an expectation that is built into the thinking of young Americans. The figures of such grants and cuts, ever changing, are far less important than the questions they raise, immeasurable in dollars. Are all students entitled to federal loans? Or only the best and the brightest? How many should qualify for government grants and loans? What standards of scholarship should be set to qualify a youngster as a national investment?

Most of the unexpected political problems that confronted the Reagan administration in its first year of office came from just such expectations clashing with the discipline that Reagan in his campaign promised to impose on the American government. But with the exception of his substantial achievement in squeezing inflation from 12.4 percent a year to 8.9 percent, the general economy responded negatively to his dedicated effort to turn things about—unemployment rose to match postwar highs, revenues fell short of anticipation, an erratic Federal Reserve Board pushed interest rates up and down bewilderingly. If one took only the first year of the Reagan experiment, it could be read that neither the old economics nor his new economics could prevent that permanent dismaying cycle which swings between unemployment and inflation. Or else one would have to accept as real the slow, seeping belief that while the Great Society provided no answers, the Reagan experiment might provide no answers either. Perhaps in a free society no free economic system could be a stable one. But without an ever-growing economy, none of the social or political problems could be managed, by anyone.

So one must examine the assumptions of the Reagan recovery program. The governing thought has been what is commonly known as the "supply-side theory" of economics. This theory, on paper, has much allure, for it holds that encouraging investment and productivity promises all Americans a share in an increasing national wealth. But translated into the budget figures that it shaped, it defied common sense—almost as much as the illusion that by sheer will alone, people can learn to slide uphill. The theory fostered a four-month tax-cutting carnival by special-interest lobbies. The results could slash an estimated $90 billion yearly in personal income taxes and another $15 billion for corporations, large and small. A tidbit here and a tidbit there—for oil drillers, truckers, equipment leasers, building contractors, and any other group that could insinuate itself into the tax cutting. "The hogs were really feeding," said David Stockman, director of OMB, watching his neat budget projections come undone.* Then, to the mothering theory of supply-side economics was added the need to confront Russian rearmament. And when, on top of all, came the political need to maintain "safety net" programs which could not be cut further without convulsion, the first Reagan budget became unhinged. The prospective deficit, the motor of inflation, soared, estimate by estimate, until by the turning of the first year into the second, it was foreseen as $100 billion, twice the size of the last Carter deficit; future deficits might be even larger, giving Reagan's four-year term the largest cumulative budget deficit in all American history. And these deficits, as candidate Reagan so often pointed out, were drafts against the future, bills which sometime, somehow, would have to be paid by a future generation, either in a sharply reduced standard of living or in paper money.

It was too early to pass judgment on the bleak scene at the end of the first Reagan year, for the experiment in turnaround was pointed toward the future; the years ahead would be the trial years. Possibly production might recover quickly enough to confirm the supply-side faith and the unproved assumptions cranked into budget computers. "We are caught in Catch-22," said one of the managers

---

*For a masterly story of the adventures in the first Reagan budget, one can do no better than to read the account by William Greider in the December 1981 issue of the *Atlantic*.

of the Reagan program. "Recovery can't begin until investment begins again. But investment won't begin until recovery begins."

A historic perspective had to lead one out from the first year of the Reagan management to what was really happening in America: a fundamental reexamination of the functions and responsibilities of the federal government. Beneath the figures of the budget rumbled the debate over the management of American life. What is government supposed to do? Is it manageable? How is it to fulfill the constitutional command that it "promote the general welfare"? What *is* the general welfare?

So this book must approach its end as it began—with questions. What are the real questions that confront the Reagan administration, and the administrations that succeed it? A reporter cannot prescribe answers, but it is his calling to ask the questions.

Like so many of the war generation, I know that the ideas I held at the time of victory and for years thereafter have outlived that time. What were once creative truths have become bars on a prison of dogmas. What was valid and true in 1945, or 1948, or 1960, or 1965, still remains true—but only for those years and those times. Events have dissolved those truths, and new questions replace them.

To begin to list the questions that trap our politics, one must start with those that rise from the outside. The American system was built after World War II on the conviction that American dominance was everlasting—its suburbs, its industries, its generosity all rested on the belief that it was ours to deploy and control the world's resources as we wished. How much of that belief remains reality? How much is now illusion? England—both her working people and her government—failed to adjust in time to their loss of empire after the war. Will we also fail to adjust?

For example, our times are seeing the most mindless clash of unions and management since the Depression. The foundry industries of the Midwest still command the same resources of coal, steel, energy; their workers have not lost their skills. But the old familiar adversaries can be seen only as quarreling within a siege ring. They resemble the confused weavers and spinners of Chinese villages a century and a half ago, wiped out by the distant cotton industries of England's Lancashire. They are all under attack from hostiles outside. Thus questions rise:

Question: How much of the old American abundance can be

shared with a world so long encouraged to carve its piece out of it?

For example, the most precise and coordinated trade war of all time is being waged against American industry under the direction of the government of Japan. What shall we do about it? Over the past ten years, the Japanese have targeted one American industry after another to undermine and wipe out. In the spring of 1981, the last American manufacturer of black-and-white television sets (General Electric) gave up. No more black-and-white sets are made in the United States. Only two American companies make color television sets. The Japanese have pushed our steel mills to the wall; the automobile industry staggers; the microprocessing industry is being punished. This onslaught involves American jobs and livelihoods. Against such an onslaught directed by a foreign power, no single American corporation, no matter how large, neither General Motors nor United States Steel, can stand. The Japanese Ministry of International Trade and Industry (MITI) confronts them with a devastating adversary—a foreign government-industry partnership.

From this situation rise questions that challenge American tradition.

Does American industry require counterpart direction? Is a new American Department of International Trade and Industry (a DITI) necessary? Is American antitrust legislation still useful? It is now almost a century since the passage of the Sherman Anti-Trust Act, which succeeded in its purpose in its time and for generations thereafter. But is it now time to review the traditional faith in free-for-all industrial competition? Is our concept of industrial management obsolete? Above all, how can government coordinate the vital dynamics of free private enterprise with federal guidance?

Nor, in the free-trading world, whose architecture America designed with the Marshall Plan, have the Japanese been alone in penetrating America.

The United States is the last open gaming table left in the world for those who play a high-stakes game. But the players have changed. It is not one private-enterprise giant against another, Shell Oil against Exxon, or Krupp Industries against Caterpillar Tractor. The players are now even larger giants, great governments, moving onto the American gaming board. The French government, for example, through its instrument Elf Aquitaine, has bought control of the largest resources of sulfur in the United States. The British government controls one of the largest oil companies of the United States (Standard of Ohio) and through that company controls the second-largest reserves of oil in the United States; it also controls Kennecott Copper, the largest copper producer of our land. More sinister is Arab penetration. The so-called government of Kuwait, which permits no foreign investment in its resources, has acquired control of a corporation called Santa Fe International, which pioneered not only underground drilling techniques but some of the highest-technology secrets of American defense. Another group, headed by the former chief of Saudi Arabian intelligence, has spent several years trying to acquire control of the third-largest bank in Washington, with all its potential influence in dispensing credit and loan favors to the American bureaucracy and members of Congress. On and on one could go, even to the crowning irony, where one finds a Japanese electronics giant, Fujitsu, using technology derived from American research, suing the American Telephone and Telegraph Company on home grounds. Fujitsu claims AT&T is a monopoly which deprives the Japanese of their rights to build a fiber-optics link, critically important for defense, between Washington and Boston.

So the question: What remains valid and useful to Americans of their recent history of free trade—and what must be changed to protect the jobs of American working people in the endangered sectors?

Another question: that of the North Atlantic Treaty Organization. NATO was not an American idea but one we accepted; it was advanced by Ernest Bevin, Britain's Foreign Secretary in the Labor government of Clement Attlee. Bevin insisted that Americans put their troops on the line in Europe to defend the West against the Russians. This was a reasonable demand at a time when Europe was too shattered to defend itself. Europe now has enormous resources of manpower and industry, as large as the Russians'. If Europeans ask America to leave, as so many do these days, or insist that they must determine with what weapons and tactics America's divisions fight there, then one asks: Is there any continuing reason to burden America with the maintenance of so large a corps of hostages to the whimsies of European politics?

Questions follow questions: The United Nations—is it a useful forum for peace, or a functionaries' palace? And the "Third World" —does it exist even as a meaningful geographical expression, and if so, what is it? Is it useful to persist in America's role as chief policeman in the world's quarrels? What is it we must defend—and what should be defended by others?

There follows, then, yet another set of questions, no less important than our role in the outer world—questions about how the

American political system should be managed in an age of special interests, professional mercenaries, and television.

American politics have moved for almost twenty years through a parade of Presidents almost as discouraging as the clowns' pageant that ran from Grant to McKinley. Since the death of John Kennedy in 1963, one short-term President after another has been pushed out by his successor. The instability this has brought to American government is the most unsettling since the forgotten Presidents who immediately preceded the Civil War. But whose fault is it? Ours, or the system's?

Small questions mount to larger ones: How long shall the primaries continue as a gauntlet for political athletes, wearing out the spirit of candidates and the attention of the public? How long shall the Twelfth Amendment be allowed to tick away as a time bomb in presidential choice, waiting to explode the next time the cycle swings from landslide to squeaker? How can national conventions be freed from hit-and-run activists and be refreshed with adequate representation for the men and women elected to govern their communities?

Answers are being offered for all such questions. But there, in the management of the political system, one comes to shapeless questions. And of these, two rise above all others:

The first: How far can law go in separating money from influence, or discipline money's use? In the election of 1980, after twenty years of reform, the dynamics of unintended consequences flouted all the intent of reformers. More money than ever before—approximately $400 million—was poured into the 1980 campaign. Individuals, as always, bought their way to access, with Republicans raising $108 million from individual contributors; Democrats raised only $19 million. But then came that new device, the political action committee, which, multiplied, added $136.7 million from corporations, lobbies, unions, and moralist groups of right and left. Noteworthy among these were the negative campaigns of killer groups, a new phenomenon, of which "Nick-Pac" (National Conservative Political Action Committee) was the exemplar, spending $7.5 million to destroy liberals of their choosing. No one knows how much loose money went into the campaign of 1980. But in 1980, for the first time, more money from political action groups than from individuals financed senatorial and congressional races.

Money buys attention. It buys, above all, television and radio time; it buys expertise, computers, organization, travel, visuals for the evening news. How shall it be restrained? Can television be denied to any political cause or group? Or is that a restraint on freedom of speech? Or can, or should, some policing of television require that system to devote equal time, at every level, to all candidates, whether paid for or free?

And the second question: What should be the powers of the presidency?

It has been fashionable ever since the departure of Richard Nixon to speak of the "imperial presidency." But does the presidency now require strengthening rather than weakening? How can a President be given the authority to pull the nation together for a national purpose, at the same time preserving the authority of Congress to propose and dispose?

For example: A President is held responsible by the people for whether they have jobs or not, whether they eat or not. But can any President accept that responsibility if he does not have greater authority over the Federal Reserve Board? The board springs from a seventy-year-old idea for controlling the credit system. But by controlling credit rates, the board now determines whether young people can afford to buy homes or buy anything else on credit. Should it be more responsible to the President's policy? Or to Congress's?

Another example: The war powers of the President. Such powers have been clipped dramatically since Lyndon Johnson threw young Americans into an undeclared war in Vietnam, thus erasing all his honor in history. What should be the President's response powers in a tactical engagement using the regular forces? What should be his limits in calling on the young to die without the consent of Congress?

Such questions tangle with the reality of Washington politics, and tangle in such detail that only technical scholars or working politicians can sort them out.

To take a most extreme example: No one who has spent any time in Washington while the House Ways and Means Committee debated tax matters is unaware of the limitless greed, the irresistible pressures on Congress, of the growing lobbies, from the worst to the best. Each tax bill requires a new and exhausting campaign by a President to make his vision of the national purpose prevail over the needs of special interests. How can Congress be sustained as the original taxing authority of the nation, yet the President be allowed to restrain the coalitions of special interests which push taxes and benefits out of all reasonable shape?

Congress is generally a shifting and unstable majority of representatives who speak for their own people back home. When they join in logrolling alliances of steel congressmen, city congressmen, farm congressmen, black congressmen, they can patch together thin and transitory majorities that deny the public interest of the whole nation. Congressmen must do as they do. But how can a President dissolve such coalitions and challenge Congress to override him in a vote that expresses the whole? Technicians of government phrase that conundrum in the clinical expression "line-budget veto" or "item veto." "Item veto" lets the President eliminate from taxes and appropriations, item by item, those goodies inserted by gatherings of special interest. Congress could still override an item veto if it could muster two-thirds of both its houses to say their programs serve the national interest better than does his veto. Is "line-budget veto" the best or the only way to restore presidential authority, so crippled in the past fifteen years?

And then there are sets of problems which rise to the ultimate, for which all the thinking in American life has failed even to approach questions, not even shapeless ones. It is a rule of life, as well as of politics, that unless one knows how to ask the questions, one cannot ever reach the answers. Philosophers call this "cutting at the joints," and in the most tormenting problems of American life no one has yet felt out the joints.

To take two of the ultimates, where a reporter can only fumble for questions:

The American cities are becoming a despair of our civilization. More money has been spent to save our great cities, and more paper covered with reports on those cities, than on any other concern in American life. Yet they are desperate, more unsafe and more frighteningly trapped than at any time in our history. These are the centers of American industry and trade, of its arts and culture. What can be done to make them livable for the white and the black, for the poor and the rich, for the workingman and the middle class? Can they survive on their own resources any longer? Should the great cities be set aside as wards of the national government? Or must they remain locked into the state governments? Is it wise or perilous to set them apart by constitutional amendment as dependent federal commonwealths?

An even more tormenting question is that of immigration, only now rising from the murmurings of fear to the level of political discussion. Can the nation formulate a new national policy on immigration? The old policy had been to open the doors to all—though "all" then meant Europe, to which the Statue of Liberty beckoned. It had been succeeded in the 1920s by a "national origins" policy, which hoped to maintain the mix of Americans as they had come together at the beginning of this century. The new policy of 1965 made America a place open equally to all the nations of the world, with new people forced on our acceptance by turbulence and hunger abroad rather than by the decision of those already here. The questions involved in thinking about immigration could, conceivably, tear all American politics apart in the next decade. Who is entitled to become an American? Should that be decided by culture? by origin? by race? by need? by numbers? How should the many who came here from so many strange lands of heritage decide what other heritages would best help keep this land a nation?

America has always been a questioning nation, always in search of itself, and of what it means, and of what it promises to do. There will always be, I hope, a cascade of questions on how one governs this unique nation. Some must be answered now; others can drift in the stream of politics for ten or twenty years more. But it strikes me that over the years of my reporting, the largest change in American politics has come not from the inescapable pressures of the world outside; nor from the new technologies of vote-getting; nor from the stretch of American television. Nor will tomorrow's greatest changes be shaped by the upheavals already swelling, whether in the surge of women, or the mysteries of microprocessing, or the menace and promise of cable television. The change I find fundamental has come, and will continue to come, in the nature of the questions Americans ask of themselves, of their purpose in their search to find again an old civility of life, and communities in which that civility can reign.

I had thought such questions were posed and answered best in the lines all of us once learned at school: "Four score and seven years ago, our fathers brought forth on this continent a new nation, conceived in liberty and dedicated to the proposition that all men are created equal. Now we are engaged in a great civil war, testing whether that nation, or any nation so conceived and so dedicated, can long endure. . . ." Lincoln answered that question on the battlefield, for he was faced with one of those clear crises of politics where only one answer is possible, and the leader gives the answer.

It was with very slow awareness that I came to recognize that the problems of a community so conceived and so dedicated had not been solved. From the Civil War to the 1960s, other enduring issues seemed to take precedence; all campaigns, all appeals to the people, revolved about three everlasting themes: bread and butter, black and white, war and peace. All campaign rhetoric was an embroidery on these themes, sometimes spirited, sometimes dull. But then, in the campaigns of the sixties, there was the old Lincolnian theme resurgent: how could politics bring all the peoples of the land to live up to their one dedication?

I can recall when that recognition came to me—during the campaign of 1968, when, for the first time, Americans of our generation realized their government had lied to them and, also for the first time, young Americans refused to fight at the call of their government. It was Edmund Muskie, then running for Vice-President and later to become a superlative Secretary of State, who sounded the theme of "trust." His campaign had brought him in that year of bloody divisions to a rally in the coal-and-steel town of Washington, Pennsylvania, a center of primitive George Wallace blue-collar workers, and also home of Washington and Jefferson College. The students and the rowdies joined to boo him and to prevent him from speaking. Muskie offered to give any of their spokesmen ten minutes on the platform if they would then give him a ten-minute hearing too. And so he spoke of trust: without trust there was no community, no civility. No headlines picked up the theme that day. But a few days later, at a run-of-the-mill New York press conference of Broadway stars supporting Humphrey and Muskie, Muskie let go once more with the theme that had come to him at the Pennsylvania rally: "I believe that the great issue in America is whether or not, as in the past, Americans can trust each other . . . between people of different races and national origins . . . whether the American people will decide to learn to trust each other. We will move toward a united country, or we will go into a divided country where people will fear each other." A headline on the story ran: "Entertainers Hear HHH; Muskie Steals Show."

The theme caught. It became Humphrey's final thrust against Richard Nixon. "Who can you trust?" he chanted, one windy night in Nevada. "Who can you trust to hold this wonderful country of ours together as one people and one nation?"

By the end of the campaign, it had become Nixon's theme. In Nixon's first statement the morning after his 1968 victory, he chose to recall a late afternoon as he campaigned through Deshler, Ohio, where a young girl had held up a sign outside the grain elevators, a sign that said: "Bring Us Together." So, "Bring Us Together" was to be the theme of Nixon's administration. He failed at that.

I could dismiss that theme in 1968 as a bloviation of campaign rhetoric, for every presidential year has its own catch phrases. But again and again since, in each succeeding campaign, I have heard the theme rising—so commonly as to vulgarize it. Yet no vulgarization can cheapen the theme of "trust," undermine its validity, or reduce it to blather.

I can hear all the candidates since voicing a variation on the theme, as if when pressed to the wall of their conscience they must express their own need of a common cause. By 1972, the theme was voiced by George McGovern in his echoing address to the Democratic convention. "Come home, America," he called, ". . . to the founding ideals that nourished us in the beginning. . . . from the prejudice of race and sex, come home, America. . . . Come home to the affirmation that we have a dream." By 1976, the call had become the anthem of Jimmy Carter, who promised that he would never lie to the American people. Then finally, in 1980, came Ronald Reagan, as far from Muskie, Humphrey, McGovern, and Carter as the political spectrum stretches. And his campaign adopted as its slogan: "Together . . . A New Beginning."

When I set out on the campaign trail of 1956, this theme and quest had not yet risen from the subliminal to recognition. At the time Eisenhower and Stevenson faced off, it was quite commonly accepted that all local politicians were crooks (as so many were), but that the national government was to be trusted; the political questions of those days were rooted in a difference of opinion on how governmental power should be used. That difference of opinion was deep and cut sharply. But when the national government called, men marched. Local government distributed spoils, jobs, variances, favors, contracts. National government conferred duties, responsibilities, honors. Not even in the romantic campaign of 1960 between Kennedy and Nixon was the honor and trust of the national government called in question, as the parties' various troops, blocs, ethnics, and special interests divided and gathered to control the national government.

It was in the 1960s, I believe, that a new chapter in the search began. The search had run back as far as the Constitution, which offered nothing more than such a search: "We, the people of the United States, in order to form a more perfect union . . ." And the search has gone on ever since—except that in our time the search is more complex than ever, and the reach for home or a new beginning more difficult.

The United States moves now in a time of self-questioning, when new groups, new heritages, new peoples, seek to make a home here; and those who are here cannot find home by going back.

Only one other great republic has ever experienced such a change in the texture of its people—the Roman Republic. Just before it collapsed, it heard the sermonizing of a discredited elder statesman, Marcus Tullius Cicero, then worn out and thoughtful as he approached his end. Cicero tried to explain what a republic was. "A commonwealth," he wrote, "is not any collection of human beings . . . but an assembly of people joined in an agreement on justice and partnership for the common good." He held that a republic—and Rome, as he wrote, stretched over the known Western world—is nonetheless a community where civility must reign and all must live peacefully together. But Cicero's Rome could not pass on the heritage of its past to the people of its future. Thus, Cicero failed, and a few years later his head was cut off as he tried to flee a Rome that could no longer govern itself.

American politicians fascinated me when I first began. They were so different from the politicians I had met abroad—the romantics, killers, or doctrinarians who later hardened into the world's bureaucrats. American politicians were more colorful by far, though less learned. They were such vivid characters and the mix among them was an entertainment to be enjoyed. They came out of school committees and slum clubhouses, from old families and high industries, from faculty staffs and county courthouses. By and large, most were grubby, shortsighted, or cause-gripped people as they entered politics, cutting deals and paying with favors and honors for the money that financed them. One common thrust moved all politicians, in America as abroad: the appetite for power. Some sought power to enlarge their egos, some to pad their purses. But as they moved from politics into government, the American process seemed to sort them out; government tested them. Most were flushed out by history or fossilized into pleaders of special interests and groups. A handful grew by experience to become larger people than when they entered. Only the tiniest few survived the process to become men of state, worth remembering. It was this sifting process that fascinated me then, and fascinates me even more now.

On such politicians, as the decade of the 1980s opened, rested the questions that no wise men or budget mechanics could answer. Neither scholars, nor spoilsmen, nor demagogues of any heritage, can govern America. Only politicians can do so, resisting thieves and scoundrels, saints and scholars alike. That is their job—to tack and shift with the winds of pressure; they become statesmen only when they know the stars by which to navigate to the goals that change in every generation.

The American Republic had been made by politicians willing to stake their lives, their fortunes, and their "sacred honor" on their instinct to create a new community; they are remembered now as the "founding fathers," all noble in memory. It was to a new generation of politicians that America in the 1980s would have to turn for its remaking. If they were brave enough and wise enough, they might employ their calling of power to make America a community once again.

I write and close this book in a clouded time, not knowing whether it is twilight or dawn, an era ending or an era beginning. It is twilight if new policy carries us back to the old America, before its transformation; it is dawn if new policy carries us forward to release us from civil fear and the web of federal control. Somewhere, in the decades of upheaval, came a wrong turning. Another wrong turning in this decade could take politics away from traditional politicians and bring us to convulsion in the streets. It would require both strong nerves and real wisdom on the part of politicians in the 1980s to avoid that convulsion. Future historians will find the Reagan experiment a fascinating study as it approaches its climax. But this drama is for the politicians of today to manage; and it will be up to them to prove, once more, that America remains, as Lincoln said, "the last, best hope of earth."

APPENDIX

1980 ELECTION RESULTS

The following table is the official vote in the 1980 presidential election as reported by state election boards and compiled by the Federal Election Commission.

State	Reagan	Carter	Anderson	Others	State Total
Alabama	654,192	636,730	16,481	34,526	1,341,929
Alaska	86,112	41,842	11,156	18,479	157,589
Arizona	529,688	246,843	76,952	20,462	873,945
Arkansas	403,164	398,041	22,468	13,909	837,582
California	4,524,835	3,083,652	739,832	237,470	8,585,789
Colorado	652,264	368,009	130,633	33,544	1,184,450
Connecticut	677,210	541,732	171,807	15,536	1,406,285
Delaware	111,252	105,754	16,288	2,429	235,723
District of Columbia	23,313	130,231	16,131	4,214	173,889
Florida	2,046,951	1,419,475	189,692	30,809	3,686,926
Georgia	654,168	890,733	36,055	15,627	1,596,582
Hawaii	130,112	135,879	32,021	5,275	303,287
Idaho	290,699	110,192	27,058	9,482	437,431
Illinois	2,358,094	1,981,413	346,754	63,505	4,749,766
Indiana	1,255,656	844,197	111,639	30,541	2,242,033
Iowa	676,026	508,672	115,633	17,330	1,317,661
Kansas	566,812	326,150	68,231	18,593	979,786
Kentucky	635,274	617,417	31,127	11,809	1,295,627
Louisiana	792,853	708,453	26,345	20,940	1,548,591
Maine	238,522	220,974	53,450	10,188	523,134
Maryland	680,606	726,164	119,537	14,192	1,540,496
Massachusetts	1,056,223	1,053,802	382,539	32,066	2,524,630
Michigan	1,915,225	1,661,532	275,223	57,745	3,909,725
Minnesota	873,268	954,173	174,997	43,342	2,045,780
Mississippi	441,089	429,281	12,036	10,214	892,620
Missouri	1,074,181	931,182	77,920	16,541	2,099,824
Montana	206,814	118,032	29,281	9,825	363,952
Nebraska	419,214	166,424	44,854	9,041	639,533
Nevada	155,017	66,666	17,651	4,358	243,692
New Hampshire	221,705	108,864	49,693	3,737	383,999

State	Reagan	Carter	Anderson	Others	State Total
New Jersey	1,546,557	1,147,364	234,632	47,131	2,975,684
New Mexico	250,779	167,832	29,459	8,173	456,237
New York	2,893,831	2,728,372	467,801	111,955	6,201,959
North Carolina	915,018	875,635	52,800	12,380	1,855,833
North Dakota	193,695	79,189	23,640	5,021	301,545
Ohio	2,206,545	1,752,414	254,472	70,172	4,283,603
Oklahoma	695,570	402,026	38,284	13,828	1,149,708
Oregon	571,044	456,890	112,389	41,193	1,181,516
Pennsylvania	2,261,872	1,937,540	292,921	69,168	4,561,501
Rhode Island	154,793	198,342	59,819	3,013	415,967
South Carolina	441,841	430,385	14,071	6,893	893,190
South Dakota	198,343	103,855	21,431	4,074	327,703
Tennessee	787,761	783,051	35,991	10,813	1,617,616
Texas	2,510,705	1,881,147	111,613	38,171	4,541,636
Utah	439,687	124,266	30,284	9,915	604,152
Vermont	94,628	81,952	31,761	4,958	213,299
Virginia	989,609	752,174	95,418	28,831	1,866,032
Washington	865,244	650,193	185,073	41,884	1,742,394
West Virginia	334,206	367,462	31,691	4,356	737,715
Wisconsin	1,088,845	981,584	160,657	42,135	2,273,221
Wyoming	110,700	49,427	12,072	4,514	176,713
Totals	43,899,248	35,481,435	5,719,437	1,395,558	86,495,678

Totals for other candidates who were on the ballot in one or more states and for various write-in candidates: Ed Clark, Libertarian, 920,859; Barry Commoner, Citizens, 230,-377; Gus Hall, Communist, 43,871; John Rarick, American Independent, 41,172; Clifton DeBerry, Socialist Workers', 40,105; Ellen McCormack, Respect for Life, 32,319; Margaret Smith, Peace and Freedom, 18,117; Deirdre Griswold; Workers' World, 13,211; Benjamin Bubar, National Statesman, 7,100; David McReynolds, Socialist, 6,720; Percy Greaves, American, 6,539; Andrew Pulley, Socialist Workers', 6,032; Richard Congress, Socialist Workers', 4,029; Kurt Lynen, "Middle Class Candidate," 3,694; Bill Gahres, Down With Lawyers, 1,718; Frank Shelton, American, 1,555; Martin Wendelken, independent, 923; Harley McLain, National People's League, 296; write-ins, 16,921.

ACKNOWLEDGMENTS

The happiest moment in writing any book is to come to its end, when the writer can pause and acknowledge his debts to those who have helped.

I want to thank, first of all, four people unstinting in their devotion to our common effort:

Hedva Hadas Glickenhaus. She has been more than friend, though that comes first. She has been the supervising editor, chief researcher, stern disciplinarian, and devoted partner in this story from page one to page last.

Timothy Clark of the *National Journal*. One of the outstanding political reporters of Washington, Clark joined me, with inspired effort, at the toughest moments of reporting. He has enriched this book with contributions of great significance.

Beatrice Hofstadter. I owe her not only the thanks of a writer to his wife for her support in the dark moments. I owe to her as a historian the benefit of her professional knowledge and perspective. Her persuasive conviction that present politics are only a link between the American past and the American future shaped this entire work.

Simon Michael Bessie. To my editor for over twenty years, and the best publisher I know, I owe not only thanks for friendship but an intellectual debt. It was he who insisted constantly, sometimes over my vehement objection, that the dimension of this book be enlarged beyond detail and anecdote, to an essay on the history of our time. I hope I have pleased him.

There are others to thank, conspicuously: Lisa Morrill, who bull-dozed this book through the mysteries of the word processor to its deadline; and Marjorie Horvitz, who struggled with the copyediting until the sentences made sense.

None of those who have worked with me are responsible in any way for my errors or misjudgments. This book says what I want to say; any shortfalls are my own.

Two other companies of friends must also be thanked:

First, the corps of national political reporters. The quality of American political reporting has improved almost unbelievably in the past twenty-five years. A writer like myself must acknowledge that he is the prime beneficiary of the new insights and special knowledge his companions of the road and the capital have brought to our understanding of our system.

Lastly, the men and women of the National Broadcasting Company with whom I worked through the campaign of 1980, notably: John Chancellor, William Small, Lester Crystal, Ken Bode, Roy Wetzel, Richard Scammon, William Turque, Paul Greenberg, Gordon Manning, and the scholars of NBC's superlative analysis staff.

INDEX

Population *(cont.)*
1890, 344; of 1980, 347; shifts among states, 59–60, 64, 66, 347–348; urban composition, 313, 314, 349–350; world, increase, 139, 361

Portillo, López, 225

Poverty. *See* Anti-poverty programs

Powell, Jody, 257–258, 261, 378, 400, 409; at "crisis of confidence" meetings, 258–259, 265–267

Precincts, key, in election night reporting, 170, 176–177, 184–185

Presidency, 426, 427–428; "co-presidency" discussions, 323–324, 325; effect of changes in party nominating process on, 290; "Imperial," 211, 213, 214, 427; incumbency, 291, 380, 382; one-term trend, 187, 260; Republican vs. Democratic tenure of, 231; restriction of powers, 211, 427

Presidential elections: campaign themes, 430–431; electoral college vs. popular vote, 70, 383; image politics in, 69–71; intrusion of foreign affairs issues on, 16, 21, 86–95, 96, 298–299, 392, 397, 403–404; "landslides" vs. "squeakers," 229–230, 415–416, 426; *see also* Campaign financing; Election night projections; National conventions; Primaries

—of 1952, 168, 229; Democratic National Convention, 52, 338; primaries, 74, 76, 284; Republican National Convention, 34, 167–168; in South, 230

—of 1956, 71, 72–96, 431; Democratic National Convention, 76, 79–85; primaries, 73–79, 85, 284; result, 95, 229; in South, 230; Suez Crisis as issue in, 73, 85, 86–95, 96

—of 1960, 229, 431; CBS vs. NBC coverage of election night, 169; Kennedy campaign, 52, 169–170, 248, 278, 384; Kennedy-Nixon debates, 401, 403, 404, 405; in South, 230

—of 1964, 124, 175–178, 320, 388, 405; adversary TV commercials by Bernbach, 175–176; California primary, 176–178; Democratic National Convention, 106–107, 113, 285; landslide result, 121, 229, 230, 233; Republican National Convention, 175, 338, 339; in South, 230

—of 1968, 186, 229, 430–431; delegate analysis, 185; Democratic contenders, 112, 113, 180, 270; Democratic National Convention, 111, 112–114, 175, 178–181, 186, 286, 338; Republican National Convention, 185, 248; in South, 230

—of 1972, 229, 405, 414, 431; Democratic National Convention, 117–118, 175, 232, 331, 336, 431; Democratic platform, 118; McGovern candidacy, 117, 118, 190, 232, 255, 276, 320, 331, 378, 384, 431; Nixon candidacy, 6, 58, 118, 230, 402; number of primaries, 78; primaries, 117, 150, 287–288, 378; in South, 230; Wallace candidacy, 288

—of 1976, 187–194, 229–230, 233, 431; Brown's candidacy, 191, 280; Carter candidacy, 187, 188, 189–194, 232, 240, 280, 292, 303, 431; debates, 190, 193, 402; Democratic National Convention, 191–192, 223, 314, 332; Ford candidacy, 192, 193, 231, 233, 234, 244–245, 292, 386; primaries, 187–188, 190–191, 196, 200, 244, 280, 287; Reagan campaign, 162, 244, 248, 292, 309; in South, 230

—of 1980, 7, 71, 95–96, 115, 135, 136, 164, 375–409, 426; Anderson's Independent candidacy, 235, 390–391 and *n.*, 394, 402; announcements of candidacies, 13–14, 234, 235; assessment of meaning, 416, 419; California primary, 287, 301, 302; campaign commercials, 394–395, 406; cities' plight as issue in, 384–385, 403; debates, 390–391 and *n.*, 401–405; defense as issue in, 161, 307, 308, 384, 385, 400, 416; Democratic contenders, 13–14, 256, 269–283 (*see also* Brown, Edmund G., Jr.; Carter, James Earl "Jimmy"; Kennedy, Edward M.); Democratic National Convention, 81, 278, 301, 312, 315, 328–342; effect of hostage crisis on, 16, 21, 277, 296, 301, 403, 407, 408–409, 417; ethnic issues, 217–219; financing and spending, 166, 277–278, 316, 426; image politics in, 380, 382, 384–386, 390, 401, 404–405; inflation issue, 21, 33, 136, 138, 155, 161, 162–163, 257, 260, 280, 290, 298, 303, 307, 379, 384, 395, 403, 406, 416, 417; Iowa caucuses, 235, 240, 241, 250, 276–277, 278, 281, 282, 293, 296, 303, 304–305; Kennedy-Carter rivalry, 14, 23, 25, 276, 277–278, 279–281, 284, 301–302, 306, 329–332; Massachusetts primary, 22, 235, 304; Michigan primary, 288, 304; Mondale on problems and issues of, 290–291; Nashua debate of Republicans, 27, 30–32, 303, 304, 404; number of primaries, 78, 285; peace or war issue in, 380, 382, 389, 390, 395, 403, 404, 405, 416; Pennsylvania pri-

About the Author

Theodore H. White was born in Boston in 1915. He attended the Boston Public Latin School, then went on to Harvard College, where he studied history. He first won wide attention as a war correspondent in China and, after the war, as coauthor of *Thunder Out of China.* He spent the postwar years reporting the recovery of Europe, where he wrote *Fire in the Ashes.* He returned to America in 1953.

Since the mid-1950s, Theodore White has reported American politics, chiefly in his *The Making of the President* series, the first volume of which won a Pulitzer Prize in 1962. *America in Search of Itself* is the climax of that series, the story of the revolutionary transformation of contemporary American politics. He has also written *Breach of Faith: The Fall of Richard Nixon* and *In Search of History: A Personal Adventure,* two novels, one play, and several prize-winning television documentaries.

Mr. White lives in Connecticut with his wife, Beatrice Hofstadter. He has two children, Heyden, who teaches English, and David, a novelist and journalist.

1956

WASH. 9
ORE. 6
IDAHO 4
MONT. 4
N.D. 4
MINN. 11
WIS. 12
MICH. 20
N.Y. 45
ME. 5
VT. 3
N.H. 4
MASS. 16
NEV. 3
UTAH 4
WYO. 3
S.D. 4
IOWA 10
PA. 32
R.I. 4
CONN. 8
N.J. 16
DEL. 3
MD. 9
CALIF. 32
ARIZ. 4
COLO. 6
NEB. 6
ILL. 27
IND. 13
OHIO 25
W.VA. 8
VA. 12
N.M. 4
KANSAS 8
MO. 13
KY. 10
N.C. 14
OKLA. 8
ARK. 8
TENN. 11
S.C. 8
TEXAS 24
LA. 10
MISS. 8
ALA. 11
GA. 12
FLA. 10

TOTAL ELECTORAL VOTES
⭐ EISENHOWER 457
☆ STEVENSON ...73
☆ JONES (ALA.) ... 1

1960

WASH. 9
ORE. 6
IDAHO 4
MONT. 4
N.D. 4
MINN. 11
WIS. 12
MICH. 20
N.Y. 45
ME. 5
VT. 3
N.H. 4
MASS. 16
NEV. 3
UTAH 4
WYO. 3
S.D. 4
IOWA 10
PA. 32
CONN. 8
N.J. 16
DEL. 3
MD. 9
CALIF. 32
ARIZ. 4
COLO. 6
NEB. 6
ILL. 27
IND. 13
OHIO 25
W.VA. 8
VA. 12
N.M. 4
KANSAS 8
MO. 13
KY. 10
N.C. 14
OKLA. 8
ARK. 8
TENN. 11
S.C. 8
TEXAS 24
LA. 10
MISS. 8
ALA. 11
GA. 12
FLA. 10
ALASKA 3
HAWAII 3

TOTAL ELECTORAL VOTES
☆ KENNEDY 303
⭐ NIXON 219
☆ BYRD 15

1964

WASH. 9
ORE. 6
IDAHO 4
MONT. 4
N.D. 4
MINN. 10
WIS. 12
MICH. 21
N.Y. 43
ME. 4
VT. 3
N.H. 4
MASS. 14
NEV. 3
UTAH 4
WYO. 3
S.D. 4
IOWA 9
PA. 29
R.I. 4
CONN. 8
N.J. 17
DEL. 3
MD. 10
D.C. 3
CALIF. 40
ARIZ. 5
COLO. 6
NEB. 5
ILL. 26
IND. 13
OHIO 26
W.VA. 7
VA. 12
N.M. 4
KANSAS 7
MO. 12
KY. 9
N.C. 13
OKLA. 8
ARK. 6
TENN. 11
S.C. 8
TEXAS 25
LA. 10
MISS. 7
ALA. 10
GA. 12
FLA. 14
ALASKA 3
HAWAII 4

TOTAL ELECTORAL VOTE
☆ JOHNSON 48
⭐ GOLDWATER ..5

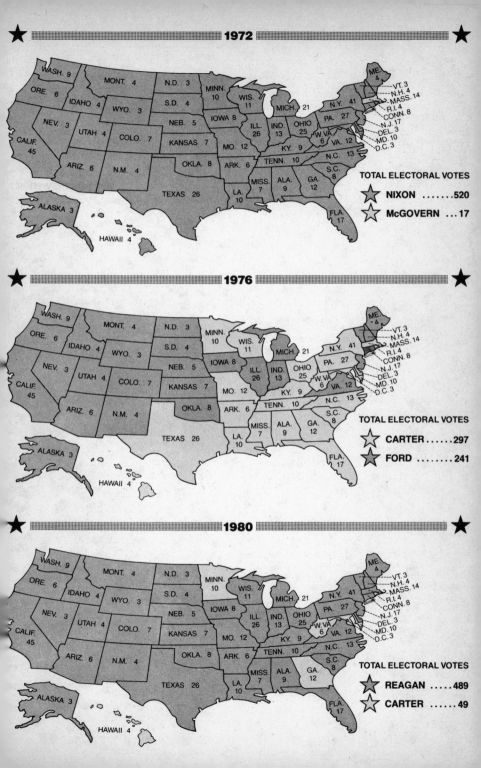